Maker Innovations Series

Jump start your path to discovery with the Apress Maker Innovations series! From the basics of electricity and components through to the most advanced options in robotics, Machine Learning, and even the metaverse, you'll forge a path to building ingenious hardware and controlling it with cutting-edge software. All while gaining new skills and experience with common toolsets you can take to new projects or even into a whole new career.

The Apress Maker Innovations series offers project-based learning with a strong foundation in theory and best practices. So you get hands-on experience while also learning the key concepts, terminology, and creative processes that professionals such as entrepreneurs, inventors, and engineers, use when developing and executing hardware projects. You can learn to design circuits, program AI, create IoT systems for your home or even city, or build immersive environments for the Metaverse. Each book provides the building blocks to bring your ideas to life, and so much more!

Whether you're a beginning hobbyist or a seasoned entrepreneur working out of your basement or garage, you'll scale up your skillset to become a hardware design and engineering pro. And often using low-cost and open-source software such as Raspberry Pi, Arduino, PIC microcontroller, and Robot Operating System (ROS). Programmers and software engineers will also find opportunities to expand their skills, as many projects use popular languages and operating systems like Python and Linux.

If you want to build a robot, set up a smart home, assemble a weather-ready meteorology system, create a brand-new circuit using breadboards and design software, or even build anything with LEGO, this series has all that and more! Written by creative and seasoned Makers, every book tackles both tested and leading-edge approaches and technologies, for bringing your visions and projects to life.

More information about this series at https://link.springer.com/bookseries/17311.

Mastering Verilog for FPGA Design

From Fundamentals to Advanced Digital Systems

Majid Pakdel

Apress®

Mastering Verilog for FPGA Design: From Fundamentals to Advanced Digital Systems

Majid Pakdel
Mianeh, Iran

ISBN-13 (pbk): 979-8-8688-2310-7   ISBN-13 (electronic): 979-8-8688-2311-4
https://doi.org/10.1007/979-8-8688-2311-4

Managing Director, Apress Media LLC: Welmoed Spahr
Acquisitions Editor: Miriam Haidara
Editorial Assistant: Jessica Vakili

Cover designed by eStudioCalamar

Distributed to the book trade worldwide by Springer Science+Business Media New York, 1 New York Plaza, New York, NY 10004. Phone 1-800-SPRINGER, fax (201) 348-4505, e-mail orders-ny@springer-sbm.com, or visit www.springeronline.com. Apress Media, LLC is a Delaware LLC and the sole member (owner) is Springer Science + Business Media Finance Inc (SSBM Finance Inc). SSBM Finance Inc is a **Delaware** corporation.

For information on translations, please e-mail booktranslations@springernature.com; for reprint, paperback, or audio rights, please e-mail bookpermissions@springernature.com.

Apress titles may be purchased in bulk for academic, corporate, or promotional use. eBook versions and licenses are also available for most titles. For more information, reference our Print and eBook Bulk Sales web page at http://www.apress.com/bulk-sales.

Any source code or other supplementary material referenced by the author in this book is available to readers on GitHub. For more detailed information, please visit https://www.apress.com/gp/services/source-code.

If disposing of this product, please recycle the paper

To the curious minds dedicated to mastering the art of digital design—may this book light your path.

And to my mother, Rahimeh Ghorbani, whose love and strength are the foundation for everything I do. Though she is no longer with us, her inspiration is on every page.

Table of Contents

About the Author

 **Majid Pakdel** is passionate about advancing the fields of electrical engineering and computer science. With a bachelor's degree in Electrical-Telecommunications Engineering, a master's in Electrical Power Engineering, and a PhD in the same field, along with a recent master's in Computer Engineering with a focus on Artificial Intelligence and Robotics, he has cultivated a diverse and comprehensive understanding of technology. Over the years, he has published over 20 papers and authored 8 books, driven by his commitment to sharing knowledge and fostering innovation.

About the Technical Reviewer

 **Massimo Nardone** has more than 30 years of experience in information and cybersecurity for IT/OT/IoT/IIoT, web/mobile development, cloud, and IT architecture. His true IT passions are security and Android. He holds an MSc degree in Computing Science from the University of Salerno, Italy. Throughout his working career, he has held various positions starting as a programming developer and then security teacher, PCI QSA, auditor, assessor, lead IT/OT/SCADA/ cloud architect, CISO, BISO, executive, program director, OT/IoT/IIoT security competence leader, etc. In his last working engagement, he worked as a seasoned cyber- and information security executive, CISO, and OT, IoT, and IIoT security competence leader, helping many clients to develop and implement cyber-, information, OT, and IoT security activities. He is currently working as Vice President of OT Security for SSH Communications Security. He is a co-author of numerous Apress books, including *Spring Security 6 Recipes*, *Secure RESTful APIs*, *Cybersecurity Threats and Attacks in the Gaming Industry*, *Pro Spring Security*, *Beginning EJB in Java EE 8*, *Pro JPA 2 in Java EE 8*, and *Pro Android Games*, and has reviewed more than 100 titles.

Acknowledgments

The creation of a technical book is a significant endeavor, one that relies on the expertise, support, and dedication of a great many people. It is with profound gratitude that I acknowledge those who were instrumental in bringing *Mastering Verilog for FPGA Design* to life.

My first and deepest thanks are reserved for the outstanding team at Apress. I would like to extend my appreciation to Welmoed Spahr, Managing Director of Apress Media LLC, for her leadership in fostering a publisher that truly serves the global technology community. I am immensely grateful to my acquisitions editor, Miriam Haidara, whose initial belief in this project and steadfast guidance throughout the process have been invaluable. A special thank you to Jessica Vakili, the editorial assistant, for seamlessly managing the countless logistical details that kept this project on track.

I am also deeply indebted to Krishnan Sathyamurthy, the production editor, and his entire team. Their meticulous work in copyediting, typesetting, and finalizing the layout has transformed the manuscript into the polished book you see today.

The technical integrity of this work owes a great deal to the rigorous efforts of Massimo Nardone, the technical reviewer. His insightful feedback and expert scrutiny were essential in ensuring the accuracy and clarity of the content.

Finally, to you, the reader. Thank you for choosing this book. I hope it serves as a trusted guide and a valuable resource on your path to mastering FPGA design.

Majid Pakdel

Introduction

Welcome to *Mastering Verilog for FPGA Design: From Fundamentals to Advanced Digital Systems*. This book is a practical journey through the world of digital design, using Verilog HDL (hardware description language) and Xilinx Vivado to transform theoretical concepts into functional hardware on a Field-Programmable Gate Array (FPGA). Digital design is more than just writing code; it is the art of architecting efficient, reliable, and high-performance electronic systems. While many resources teach the syntax of Verilog, this book focuses on the crucial link between that code and the physical logic gates it describes. Our goal is to equip you not only with the "how" but also with the "why," enabling you to tackle real-world design challenges with confidence.

This book is written for a broad audience of hardware enthusiasts, including university students in electrical engineering and computer science, hardware engineers and FPGA practitioners looking to solidify their fundamentals, embedded systems engineers seeking to understand hardware acceleration, and self-taught hobbyists ready to dive into the world of custom digital design. Readers are expected to have a basic familiarity with digital logic concepts like Boolean algebra, flip-flops, and registers, but no prior experience with Verilog or Vivado is required, as we build from the ground up.

The book is structured to take you on a logical progression from foundational skills to the implementation of complex systems. We begin by introducing the Xilinx Vivado design suite, your primary tool for the entire workflow. You will then dive into behavioral modeling in Verilog, learning how to describe digital circuits at a high level, with a strong emphasis on creating effective test benches, which are critical for verifying your designs before they are implemented in hardware. The journey continues by exploring the implementation of memory structures, from simple arrays to Block RAM (BRAM), and moves into lower-level abstractions with gate, switch, and structural modeling. These chapters are essential for understanding how your Verilog code translates into actual hardware and for designing reusable, parameterized modules.

The next part tackles the core of complex digital design. You will master designing Finite State Machines (FSMs) using robust methodologies before a dedicated chapter on block design and Intellectual Properties (IPs), which teaches you to build modular systems and create your own reusable Intellectual Property cores. We then apply these skills to practical communication interfaces like UART, SPI, and I2C, culminating in the ultimate digital system: the implementation of a RISC-V processor.

Theory is nothing without practice. Throughout this book, you will find numerous projects, code examples, and step-by-step guides. I strongly encourage you to open Vivado and work through these examples yourself. Experiment, modify the code, and observe the results in simulation. This hands-on interaction is the fastest path to true mastery. The field of digital design is vast and endlessly fascinating. It is my sincere hope that this book serves as both a trusted guide for your current projects and a springboard for your future innovations. Let's begin.

Majid Pakdel

CHAPTER 1

Introduction to Vivado

Modern digital design relies heavily on powerful and efficient tools to bring complex hardware concepts to life. Xilinx Vivado is one such industry-standard integrated design environment (IDE) that enables engineers to design, simulate, synthesize, and implement FPGA (Field-Programmable Gate Array) and SoC (System-on-Chip) solutions. Whether you are a beginner learning the fundamentals or an experienced developer optimizing high-performance systems, Vivado provides a comprehensive suite of features to streamline the entire design workflow.

This chapter serves as your starting point for mastering Vivado, guiding you through the essential steps of project creation, I/O planning, and full project execution. In the "Creating a New Project" section, you will learn how to set up a Vivado project from scratch, configure design sources, and establish target device settings. "The I/O Planning" section explores how to define pin assignments and optimize signal routing for your hardware design. Finally, "A Complete Project in Vivado" section walks you through a hands-on example, integrating all the concepts into a functional FPGA implementation.

By the end of this chapter, you will have a solid foundation in Vivado's core functionalities, preparing you for more advanced topics in subsequent chapters. Let's begin your journey into FPGA design with Vivado!

© Majid Pakdel 2026
M. Pakdel, *Mastering Verilog for FPGA Design*, Maker Innovations Series,
https://doi.org/10.1007/979-8-8688-2311-4_1

Creating a New Project

To start, we want to create a new project titled "AND_gate" in Vivado as shown in Figure 1-1.

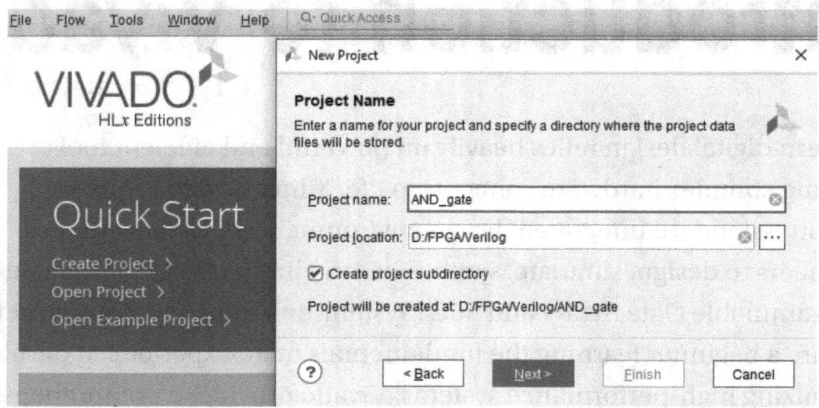

Figure 1-1. *Creating a new project*

Then we click the Next button until we get to the Default Part window, and we choose a default Xilinx part or board as depicted in Figure 1-2.

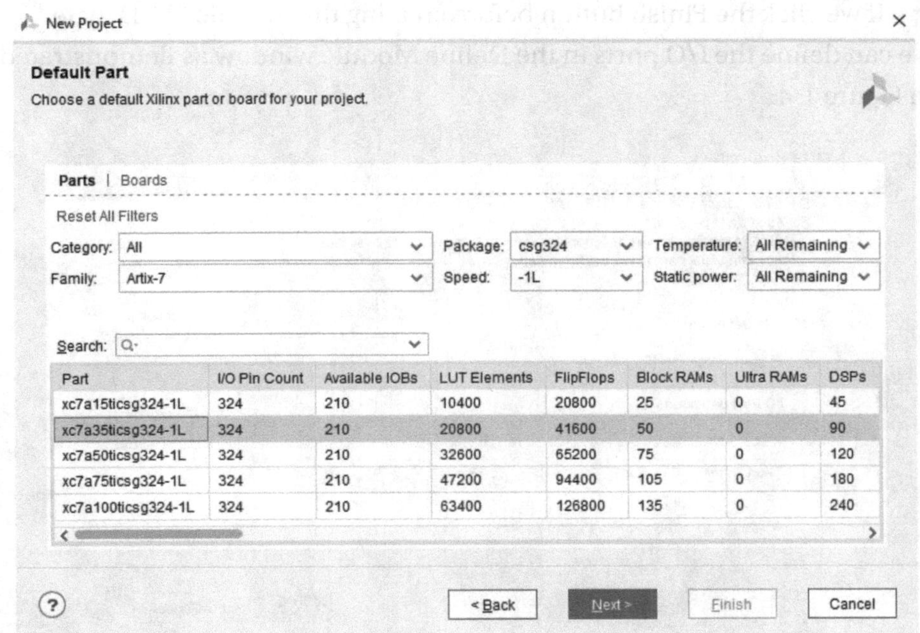

Figure 1-2. *Selecting a default Xilinx part or board*

Now, we right-click the Design Sources folder and select the Add Sources... option to create a new Verilog source file titled "AND_gate" as illustrated in Figure 1-3.

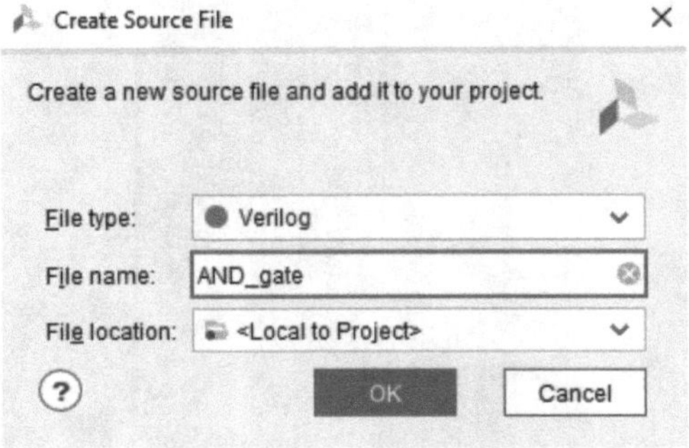

Figure 1-3. *Creating a new Verilog source file*

If we click the Finish button before creating the module "AND_gate," we can define the I/O ports in the Define Module window as demonstrated in Figure 1-4.

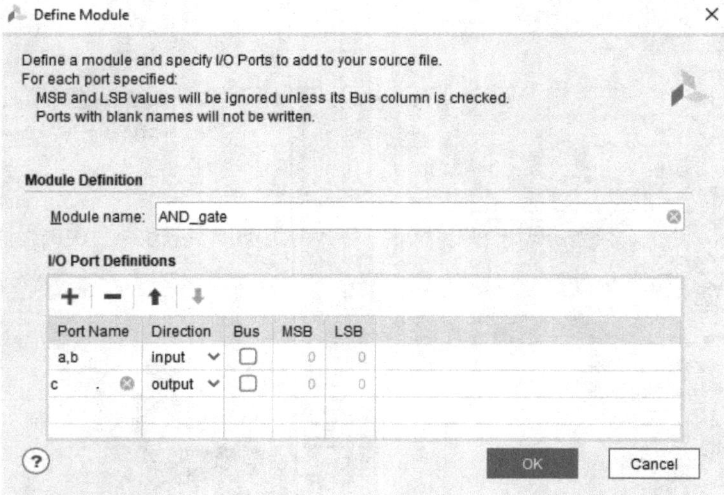

Figure 1-4. *Defining the I/O ports*

We write a simple Verilog code for our AND gate and run the synthesis analysis by clicking the "Run Synthesis" option, and we can see that the synthesis is successfully completed as shown in Figure 1-5.

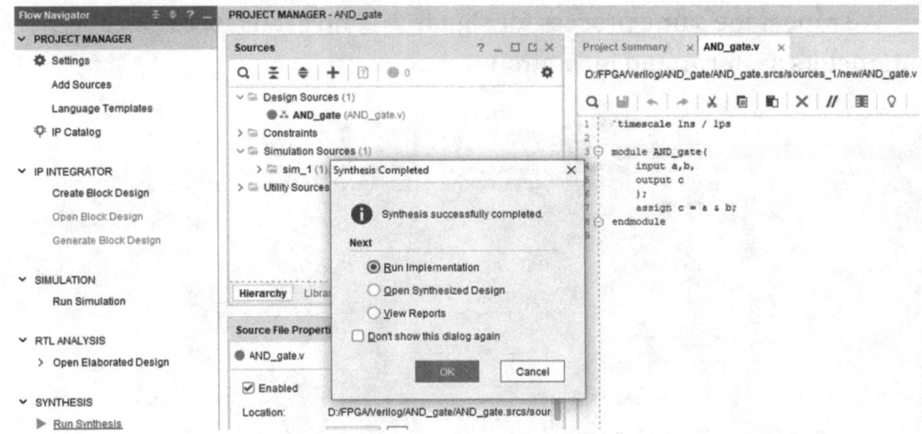

Figure 1-5. *Running the synthesis analysis for module "AND_gate"*

Now, we choose SIMULATION ➤ Run Simulation ➤ Run Behavioral Simulation to simulate our Verilog code. In the opened simulation window, we click the Restart button to clear the wave window. Then we right-click the signal "a" and select the Force clock... option and set its parameters as depicted in Figure 1-6.

Figure 1-6. *Setting the force clock parameters for signal "a"*

We repeat the same process for signal "b" and set its force clock parameters as illustrated in Figure 1-7.

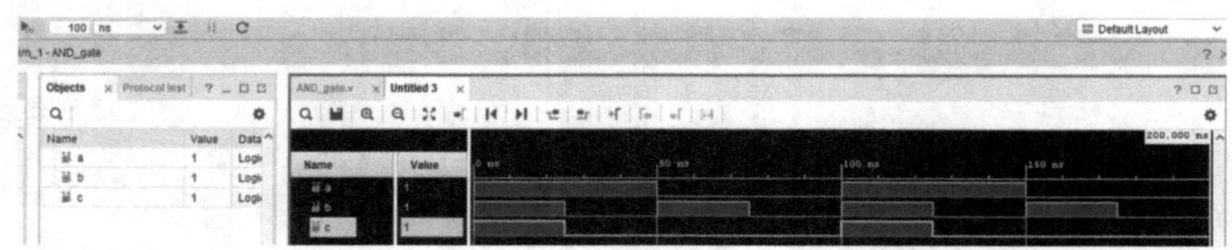

Figure 1-7. *Setting the force clock parameters for signal "b"*

We click the Run for 100µs button twice to simulate the signals on the wave window for 200µs as shown in Figure 1-8.

Figure 1-8. *Simulating the signals on the wave window for 200µs*

Now, if we click the schematic in the RTL ANALYSIS section, we can view the RTL analysis schematic as depicted in Figure 1-9.

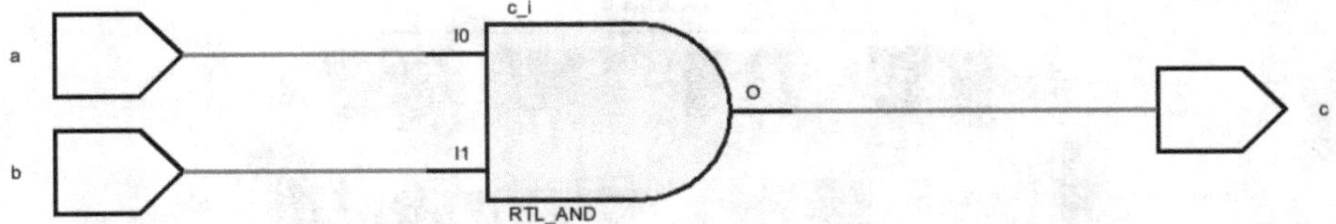

Figure 1-9. *The RTL analysis schematic*

If we click the schematic in the "Open Synthesized Design" section, we can see the synthesized design schematic as illustrated in Figure 1-10.

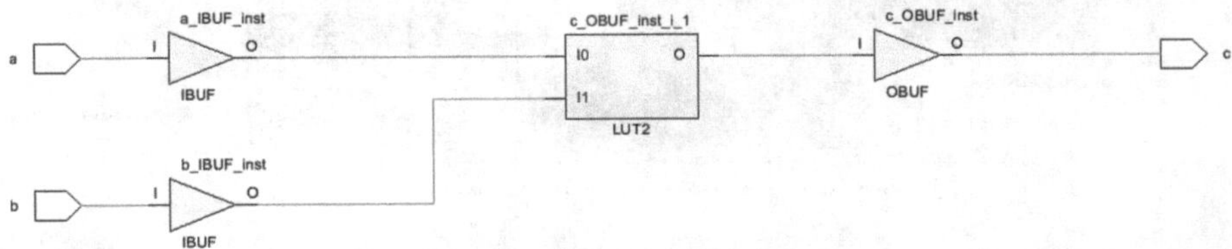

Figure 1-10. *The synthesized design schematic*

From the "Layout" menu we select the I/O Planning option as demonstrated in Figure 1-11.

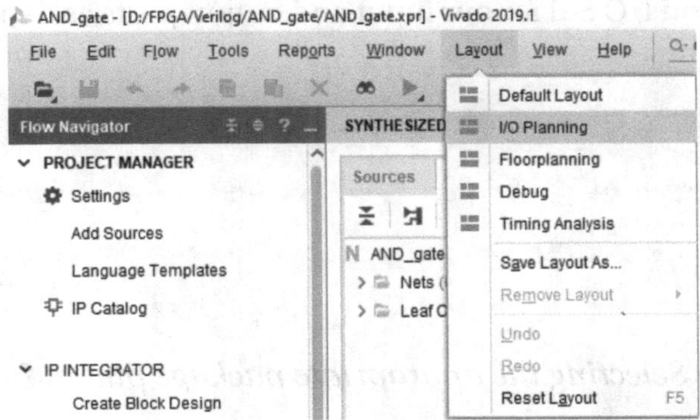

Figure 1-11. *Selecting the I/O Planning option*

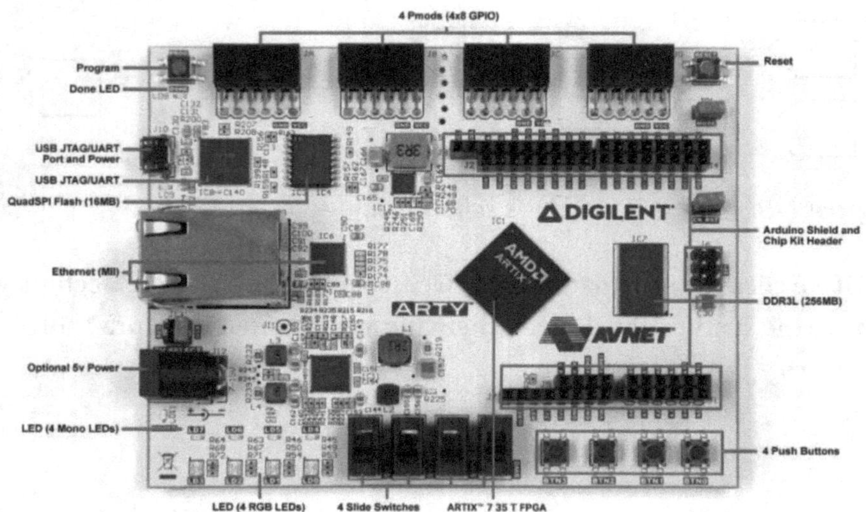

Figure 1-12. *The Arty A7 development board*

In the projects of this book, we use the Arty A7 development board as shown in Figure 1-12; however, we can use other Xilinx development boards as well. In the I/O planning window, we can select the appropriate package pin and I/O Std for our input and output ports as depicted in Figure 1-13.

Name	Direction	Neg Diff Pair	Package Pin	Fixed	Bank	I/O Std	Vcco	Vref	Drive Strength	Slew Type	Pull Type	Off-Chip Termination	IN_TERM
∨ ⌂ All ports (3)													
∨ ⌂ Scalar ports (3)													
IN			A8	✓	16	LVCMOS33*	3.300				NONE	NONE	
IN			C11	✓	16	LVCMOS33*	3.300				NONE	NONE	
OUT			H5	✓	35	LVCMOS33*	3.300		12	SLOW	NONE	FP_VTT_50	

Figure 1-13. *Selecting the appropriate package pin and I/O Std for scalar ports*

Now, we press "Ctrl + S" on the keyboard to save the constraints file (.xdc) and choose a file name for it and finally click the OK button as illustrated in Figure 1-14.

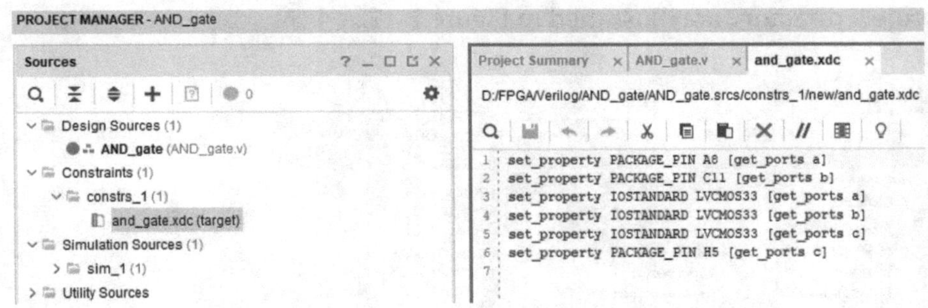

Figure 1-14. *Saving the constraints file (.xdc)*

Figure 1-15. *The constraints file contents*

The contents of the constraints file are shown in Figure 1-15. Now,
we click the "Generate Bitstream" option, and the bitstream generation is
successfully completed as depicted in Figure 1-16.

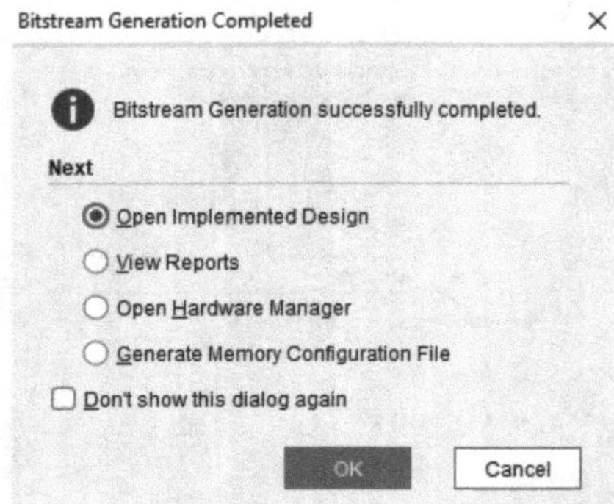

Figure 1-16. *The successful bitstream generation*

The generated bitstream file (AND_gate.bit) and its folder in the project directory are illustrated in Figure 1-17.

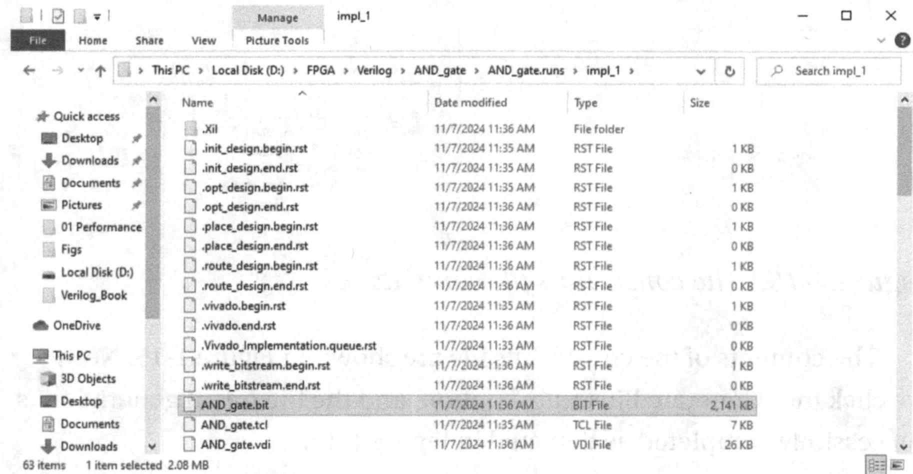

Figure 1-17. *The generated bitstream file*

The I/O Planning

Now, we create a new project titled "IO_planning" as shown in Figure 1-18.

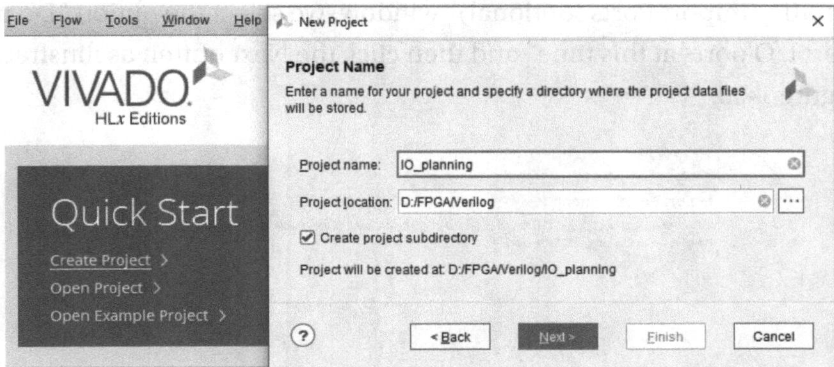

Figure 1-18. *Creating a new project*

We click the Next button. We choose "I/O Planning Project" as the project type and then click the Next button as depicted in Figure 1-19.

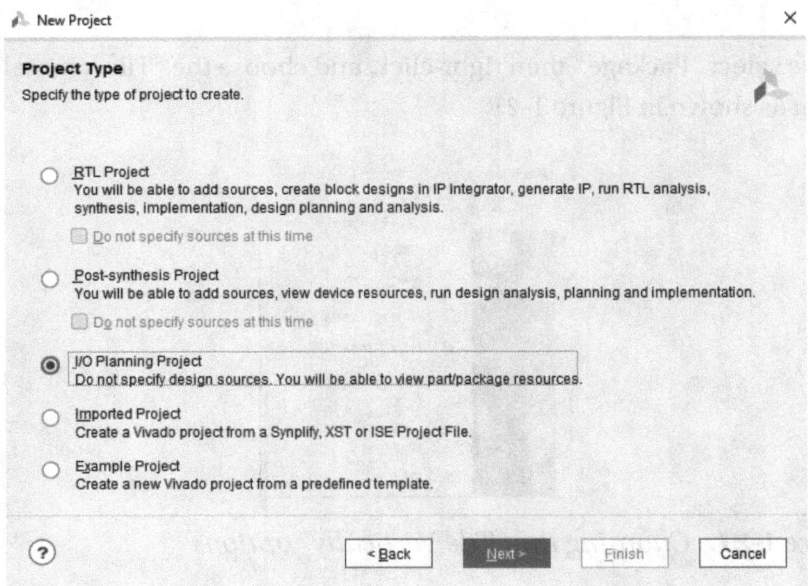

Figure 1-19. *Choosing "I/O Planning Project" as the project type*

In the "Import Ports (optional)" window, we select the option "Do not import I/O ports at this time" and then click the Next button as illustrated in Figure 1-20.

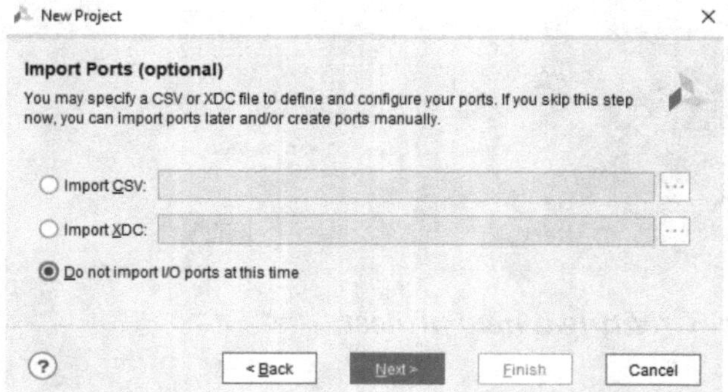

Figure 1-20. *Selecting the option "Do not import I/O ports at this time"*

We select "Package," then right-click, and choose the "Tile Vertically" option as shown in Figure 1-21.

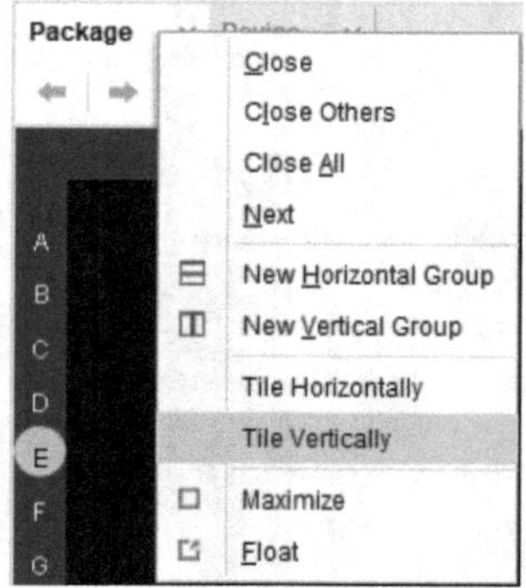

Figure 1-21. *Choosing the "Tile Vertically" option*

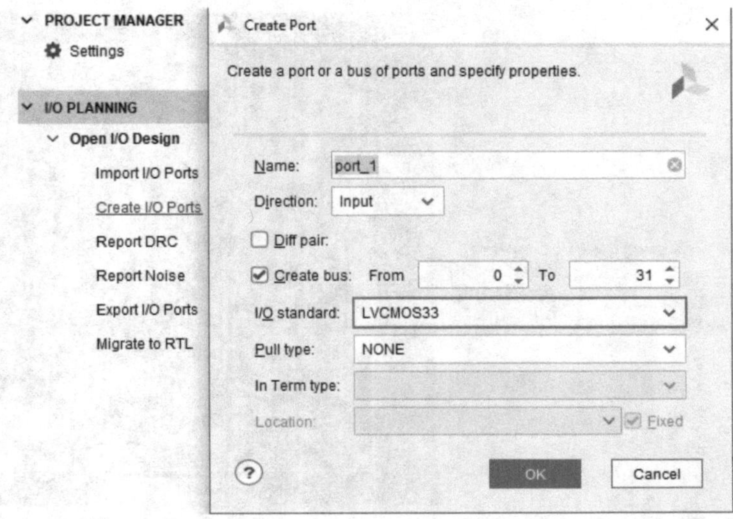

Figure 1-22. *Creating a port*

Now, in the I/O PLANNING section, we select the Create I/O
Ports option to create a port as depicted in Figure 1-22. We select the
created port and then drag and drop it to the pins layout as illustrated in
Figures 1-23 and 1-24, respectively.

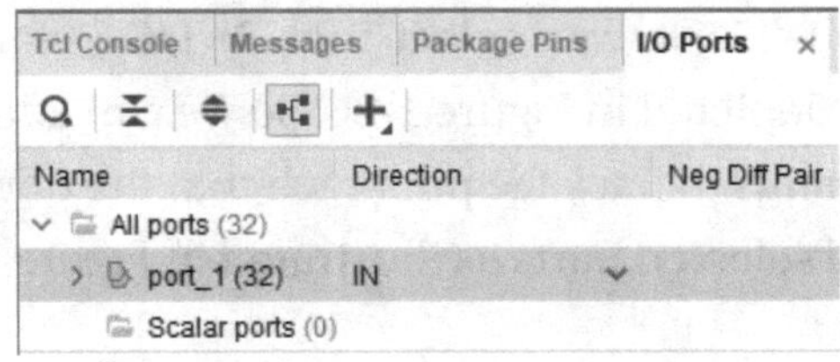

Figure 1-23. *Selecting the created port*

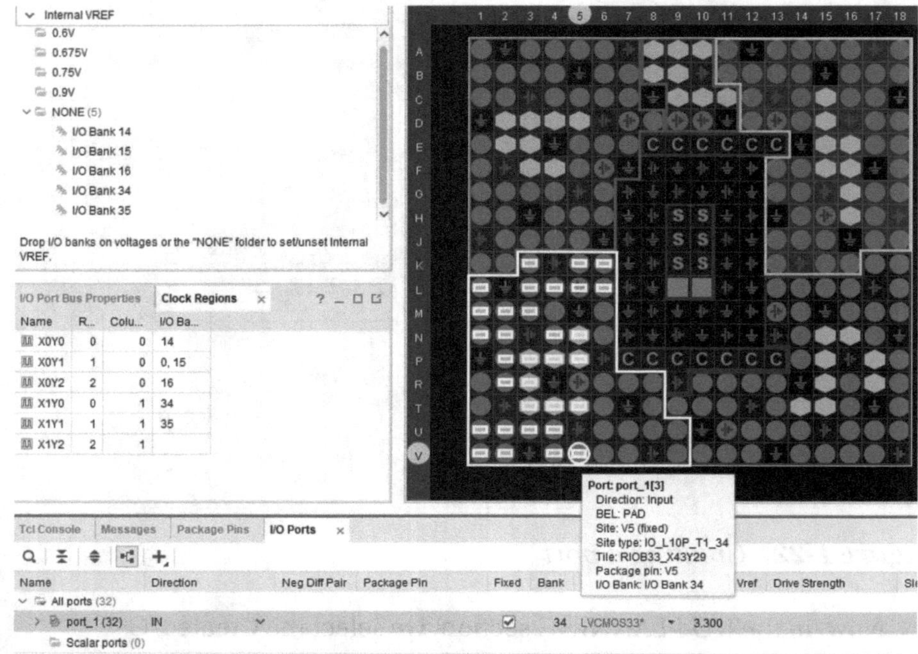

Figure 1-24. *Drag and drop the created port to the pins layout*

We can also see the created port as a white ribbon in the X1Y0 section
as shown in Figure 1-25. Now we select Tools ➤ I/O Planning ➤ Set Part
Compatibility… as depicted in Figure 1-26. So we can add or remove
the prohibit constraints to package pins such that the device will be
compatible with all selected parts as illustrated in Figure 1-27.

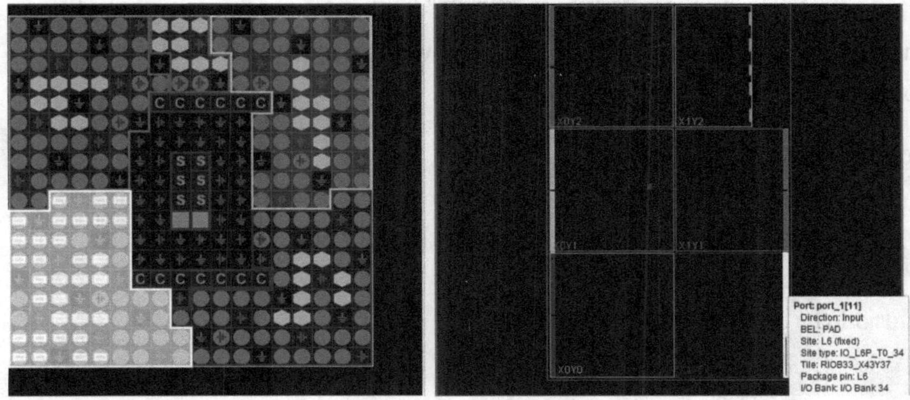

Figure 1-25. *The created port as a white ribbon in the X1Y0 section*

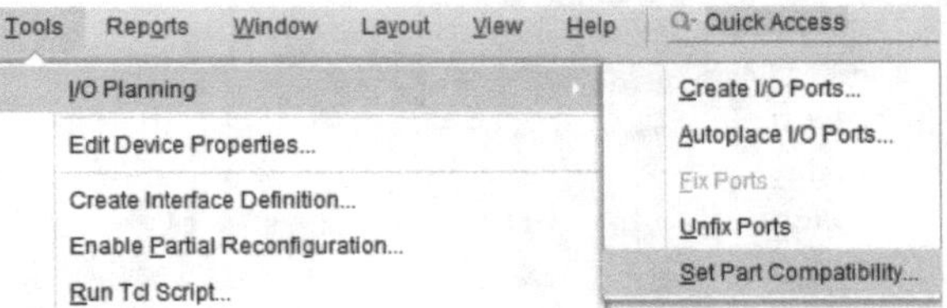

Figure 1-26. *Selecting "Set Part Compatibility…"*

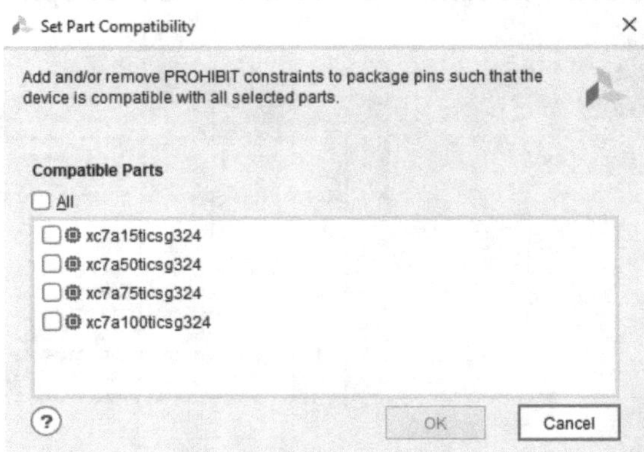

Figure 1-27. *Making the device compatible with all selected parts*

Now, if we click the "Migrate to RTL" option, we can create a Verilog module with generated I/O ports as shown in Figure 1-28 and the following generated Verilog codes:

```verilog
module ios(port_1);
  input [31:0] port_1;
  // internal wires associated with differential buffers
  // differential buffers
endmodule
```

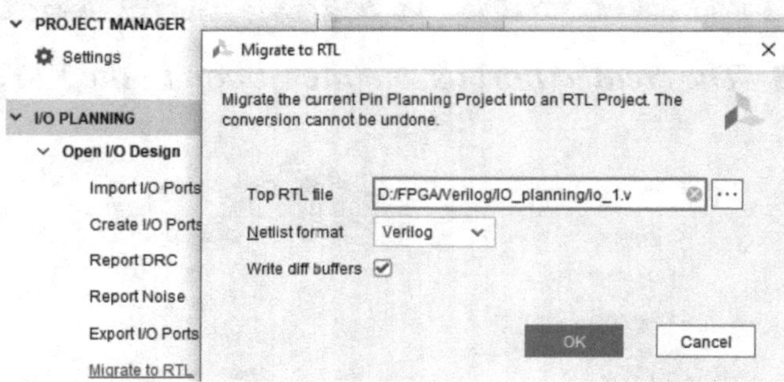

Figure 1-28. *Creating a Verilog module with generated I/O ports*

The contents of the generated constraints file are depicted in Figure 1-29.

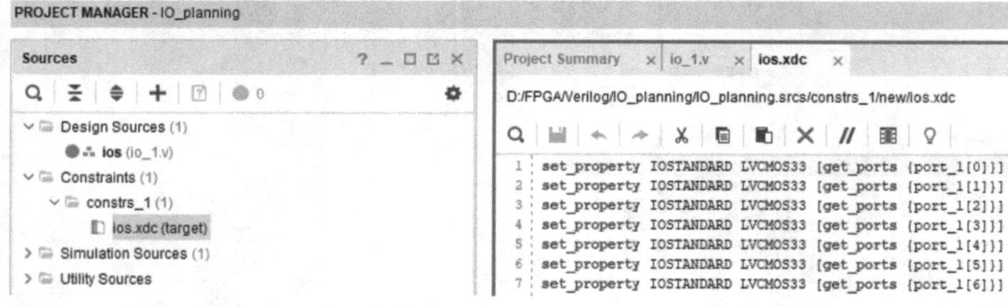

Figure 1-29. *The contents of the generated constraints file*

Then, in the Settings window, we select Synthesis from the Project Settings section, and we choose Options ➤ Strategy ➤ Vivado Synthesis Defaults, as illustrated in Figure 1-30.

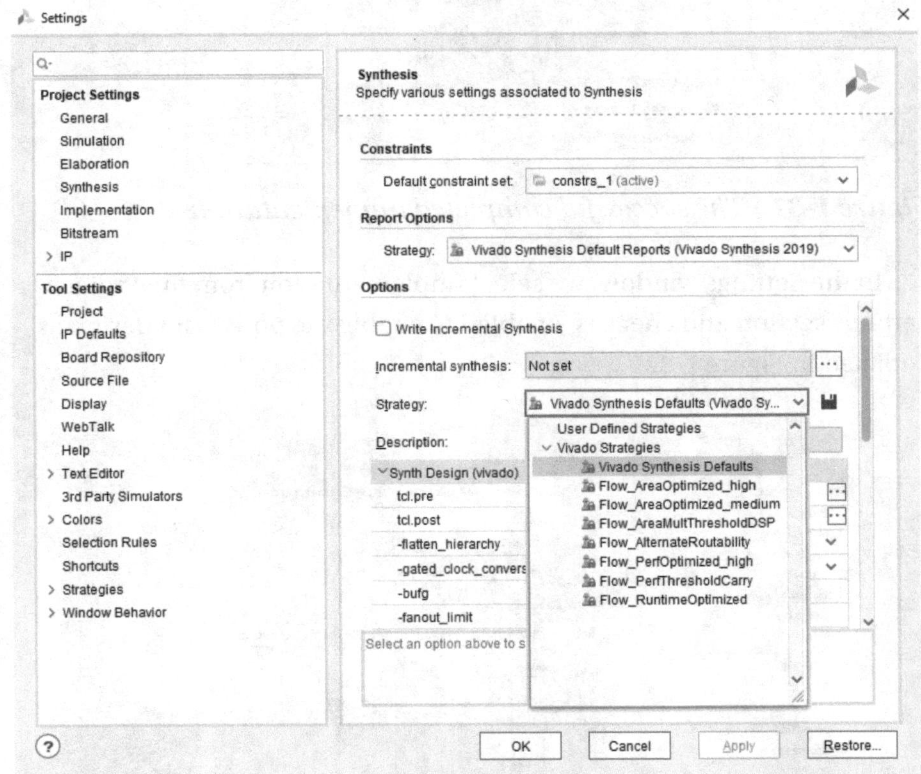

Figure 1-30. *Selecting Vivado Synthesis Defaults as the strategy*

Now, we click the "Run Implementation" option and see the implementation is successfully completed as shown in Figure 1-31.

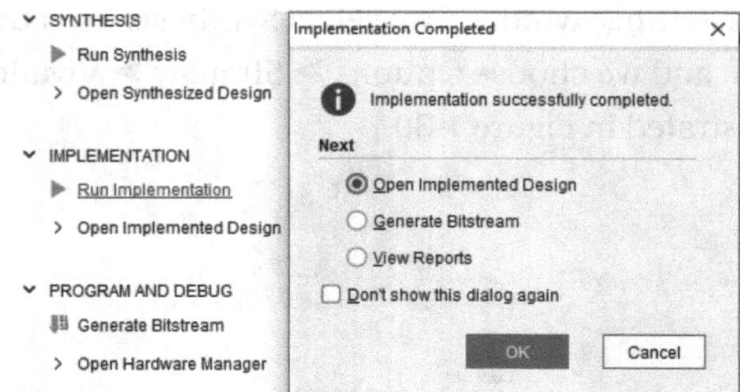

Figure 1-31. *The successful completed implementation*

In the Settings window, we select Implementation from the Project Settings section and check is_enabled to enable the power opt design as depicted in Figure 1-32.

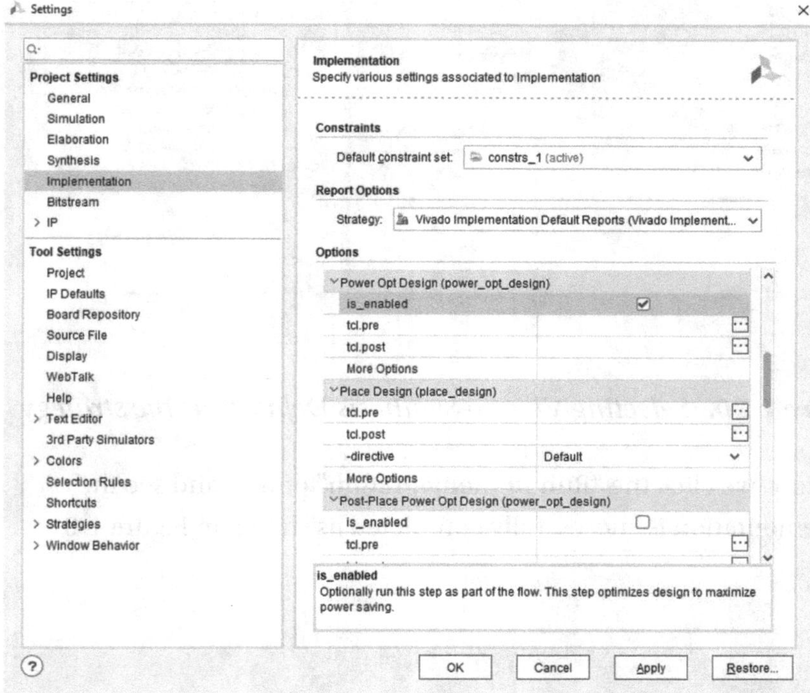

Figure 1-32. *Enabling the power opt design*

A Complete Project in Vivado

Now, we create a new project titled "top" and then click the Next button as illustrated in Figure 1-33.

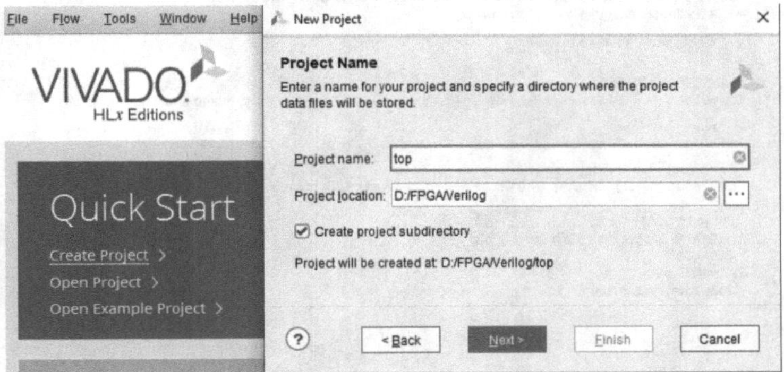

Figure 1-33. *Creating a new project*

We select RTL Project as the project type and click the Next button as shown in Figure 1-34. In the Add Sources window, we click the Create File button to create a source file titled "top" and then click the Next button as depicted in Figure 1-35.

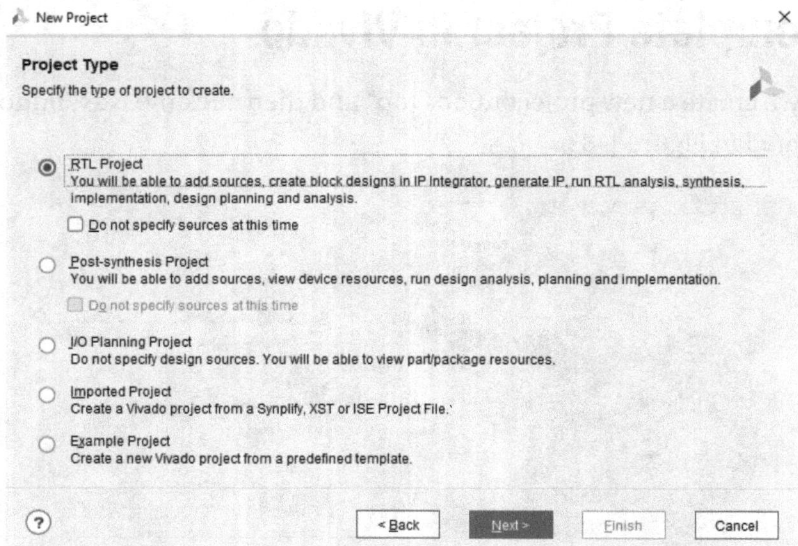

Figure 1-34. *Choosing RTL Project as the project type*

Figure 1-35. *Creating a source file titled "top"*

In the Add Constraints (optional) window, we click the Create File button to create a constraints file named "top" and then click the Next button as depicted in Figure 1-36.

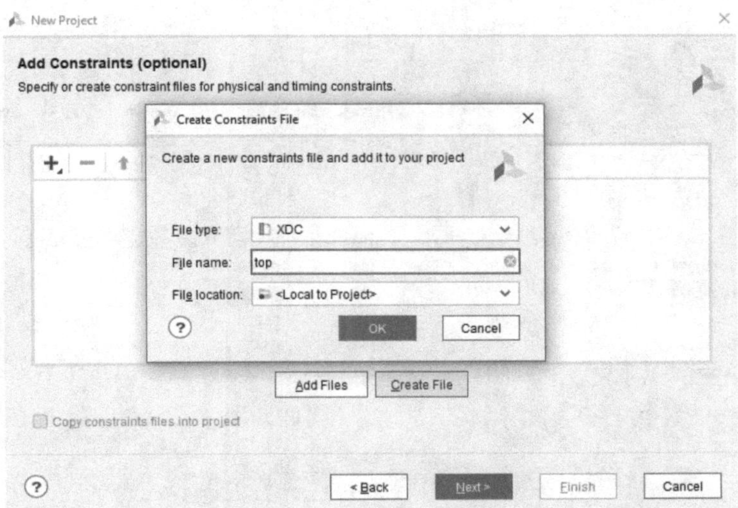

Figure 1-36. *Creating a constraints file named "top"*

In the Default Part window, we choose our Xilinx Arty A7 development board and click the Next button as illustrated in Figure 1-37.

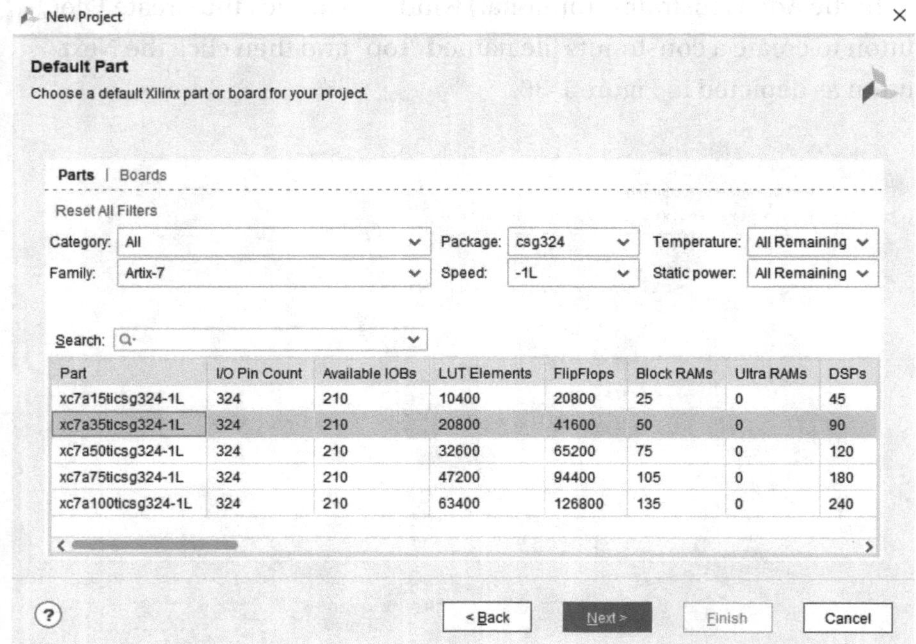

Figure 1-37. *Choosing our Xilinx Arty A7 development board*

In the New Project Summary window, we click the Finish button as shown in Figure 1-38.

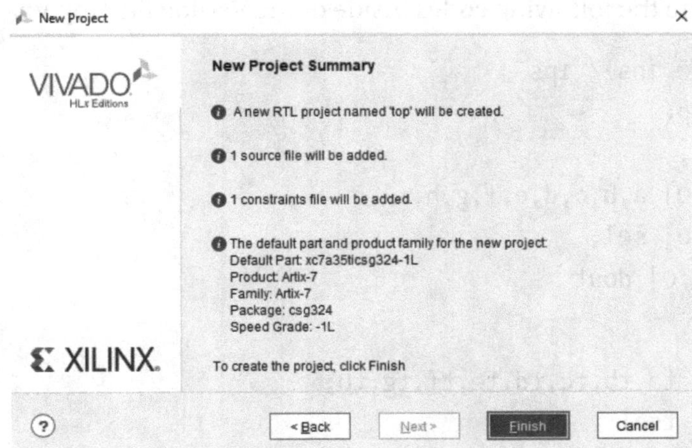

Figure 1-38. *Clicking the Finish button*

In the opened Define Module window, we just click the OK button as depicted in Figure 1-39.

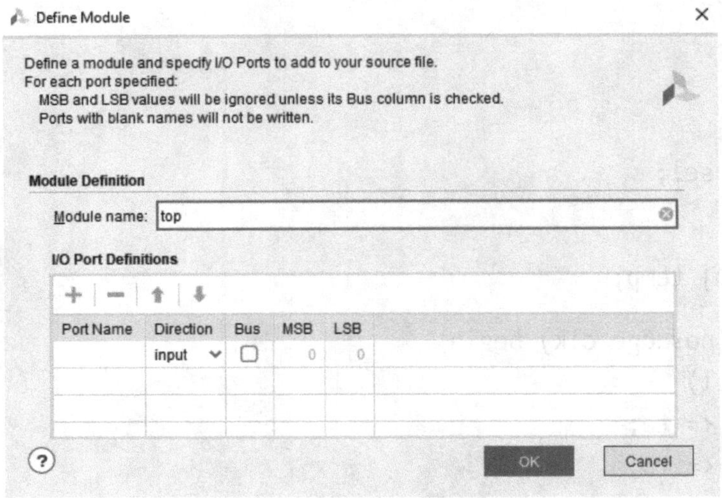

Figure 1-39. *Clicking the OK button*

We write the following codes inside of the Verilog file (top.v):

```verilog
`timescale 1ns / 1ps
module top(
input clk,
input [7:0] a,b,c,d,e,f,g,h,
input [2:0] sel,
output [7:0] dout
    );

reg [7:0] ta,tb,tc,td,te,tf,tg,th;
reg [2:0] tsel;
always@(posedge clk) begin
ta <= a;
tb <= b;
tc <= c;
td <= d;
te <= e;
tf <= f;
tg <= g;
th <= h;
tsel <= sel;
end

reg [7:0] temp;

always@(posedge clk) begin
case(tsel)
0: temp <= ta;
1: temp <= tb;
2: temp <= tc;
3: temp <= td;
4: temp <= te;
5: temp <= tf;
```

```
6: temp <= tg;
7: temp <= th;
default: temp <= 8'hzz;
endcase
end

assign dout = temp;
endmodule
```

Then, we right-click the Simulation sources folder and select the Add Sources... option. Now, in the Add or Create Simulation Sources window, we click the Create File button to create a test bench source file named "tb" and click the OK and Finish buttons, respectively, as illustrated in Figure 1-40.

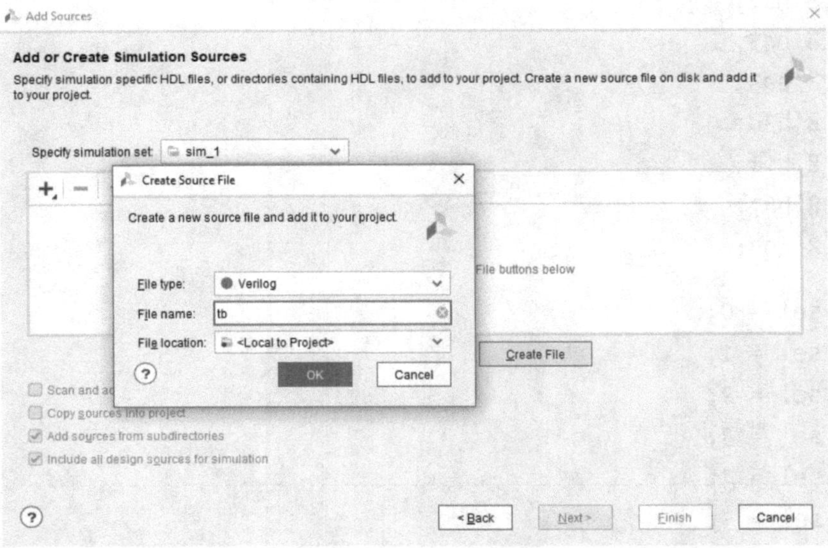

Figure 1-40. *Creating a test bench source file named "tb"*

We write the following codes inside of the test bench file (tb.v):

```verilog
`timescale 1ns / 1ps
module tb();
reg clk = 0;
reg [7:0] a,b,c,d,e,f,g,h;
reg [2:0] sel;
wire [7:0] dout;

top t1(clk,a,b,c,d,e,f,g,h,sel,dout);

always #5 clk = ~clk;

initial begin
a = 8'h34;
b = 8'h12;
c = 8'h45;
d = 8'ha3;
e = 8'h3d;
f = 8'hff;
g = 8'h67;
h = 8'h93;

#20 sel = 0;
#20 sel = 1;
#20 sel = 2;
#20 sel = 3;
#20 sel = 4;
#20 sel = 5;
#20 sel = 6;
#20 sel = 7;
#20 $stop;

end
endmodule
```

We select SIMULATION ➤ Run Simulation ➤ Run Behavioral
Simulation to view the signals on the wave window as shown in
Figure 1-41.

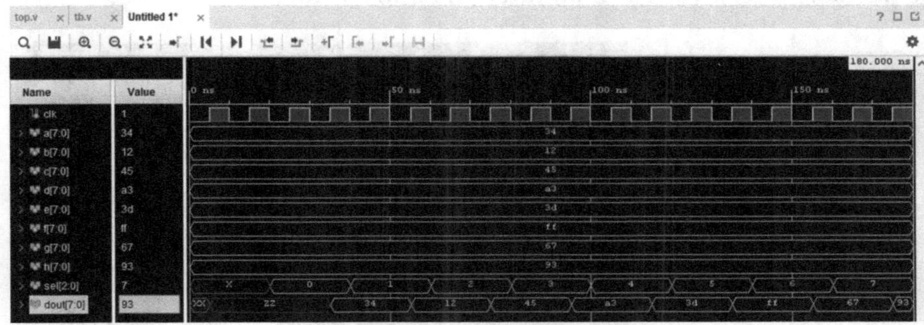

Figure 1-41. *The signals displayed on the wave window*

Now, we double-click the "Run Synthesis" option to begin the
synthesis analysis, and it is successfully completed as depicted in
Figure 1-42.

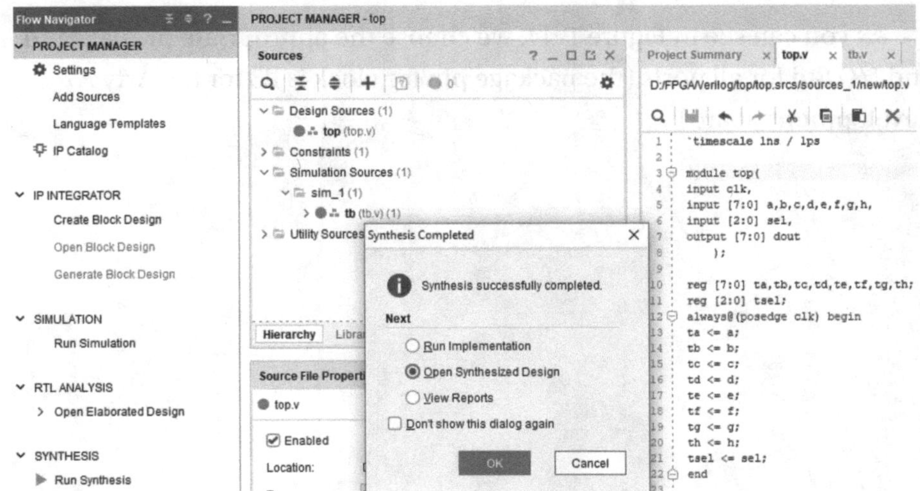

Figure 1-42. *The successful completed synthesis analysis*

Then, we select the Open Synthesized Design option and click the OK button as demonstrated in Figure 1-42. In the opened synthesized design, we select all ports in the I/O Ports section and then drag and drop them to the package pins layout as illustrated in Figure 1-43.

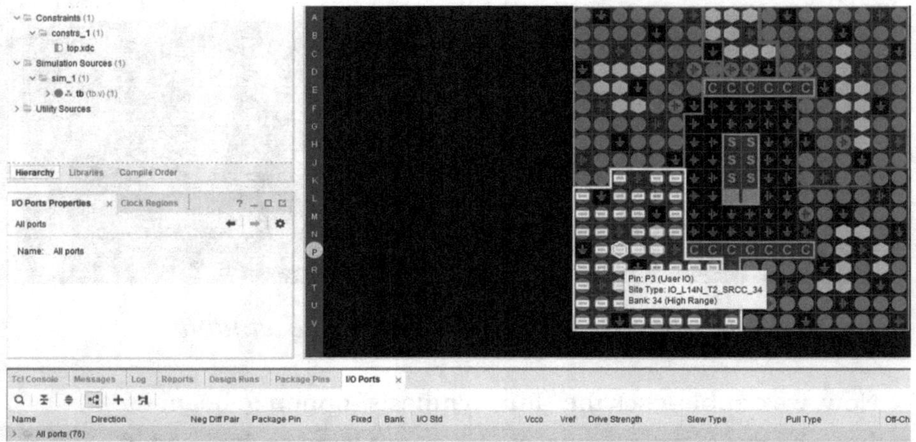

Figure 1-43. *Drag and drop all ports to the package pins layout*

As you can see in Figure 1-44, we choose the appropriate package pin and I/O Std for all ports (the package pin for clock is E3 for the Arty A7 development board).

Name	Direction	Neg Diff Pair	Package Pin	Fixed	Bank	I/O Std	Vcco
⌄ h (8)	IN			☑	35	LVCMOS33* ▾	3.300
h[7]	IN		H5 ⌄	☑	35	LVCMOS33* ▾	3.300
h[6]	IN		K2 ⌄	☑	35	LVCMOS33* ▾	3.300
h[5]	IN		K1 ⌄	☑	35	LVCMOS33* ▾	3.300
h[4]	IN		J3 ⌄	☑	35	LVCMOS33* ▾	3.300
h[3]	IN		J2 ⌄	☑	35	LVCMOS33* ▾	3.300
h[2]	IN		J4 ⌄	☑	35	LVCMOS33* ▾	3.300
h[1]	IN		H4 ⌄	☑	35	LVCMOS33* ▾	3.300
h[0]	IN		G4 ⌄	☑	35	LVCMOS33* ▾	3.300
⌄ sel (3)	IN			☑	35	LVCMOS33* ▾	3.300
sel[2]	IN		G2 ⌄	☑	35	LVCMOS33* ▾	3.300
sel[1]	IN		E2 ⌄	☑	35	LVCMOS33* ▾	3.300
sel[0]	IN		D2 ⌄	☑	35	LVCMOS33* ▾	3.300
⌄ Scalar ports (1)							
clk	IN		E3 ⌄	☑	35	LVCMOS33* ▾	3.300

Figure 1-44. *Choosing the appropriate package pin and I/O Std for all ports*

Now, we press "Ctrl + S" on the keyboard to save the constraints file (top.xdc) as shown in Figure 1-45.

Figure 1-45. *Saving the constraints file (top.xdc)*

We can view the contents of the saved constraints file as depicted in Figure 1-46.

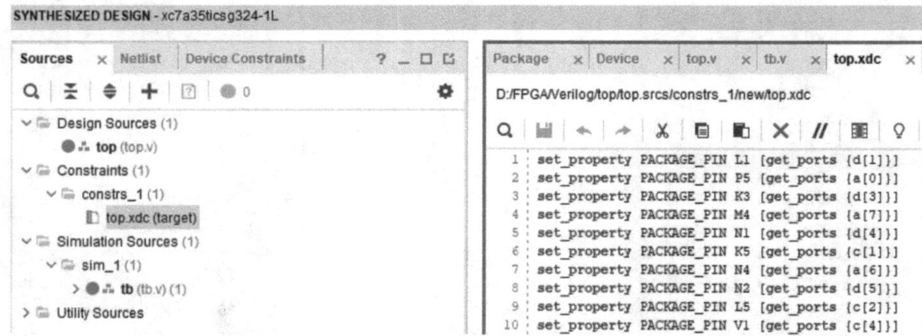

Figure 1-46. *The contents of the saved constraints file*

We double-click the schematic in the synthesized design, and as you can see in Figure 1-47, the clock enable (CE) pin is connected to a fixed power supply. So it is better to enable the optimized power supply design. Before doing that, we want to view the "Report Power" option by double-clicking it and then click the OK button as illustrated in Figure 1-48.

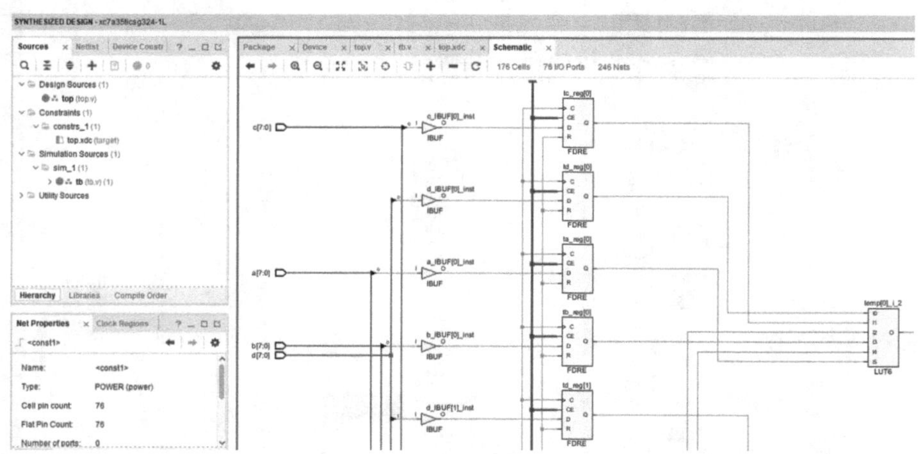

Figure 1-47. *The schematic in the synthesized design*

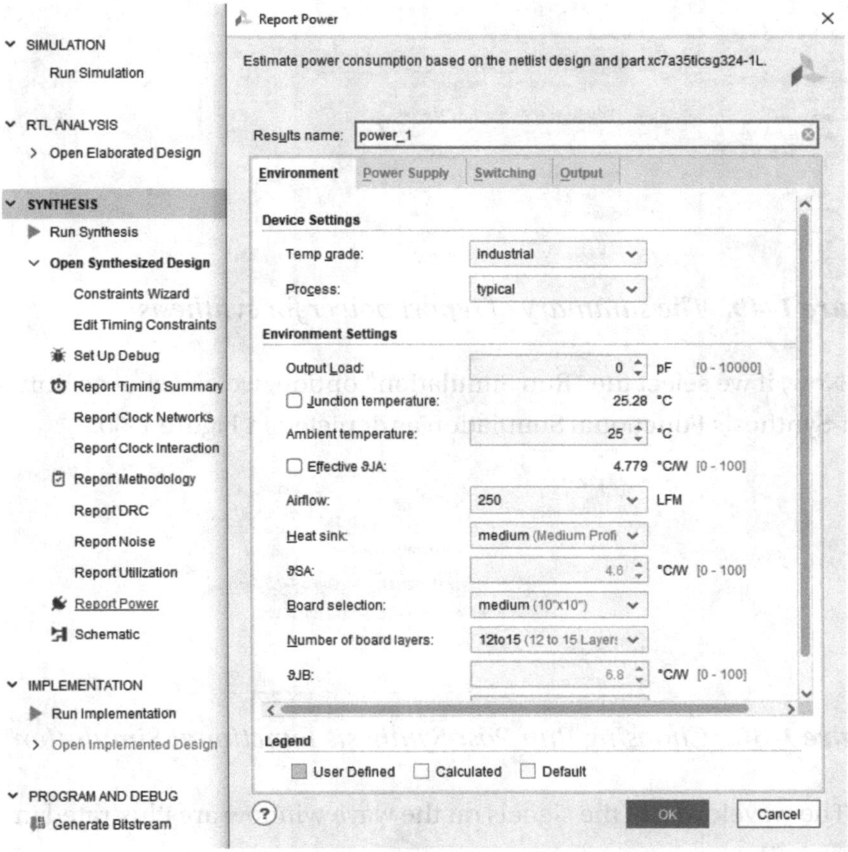

Figure 1-48. *The Report Power window*

We can view that the total on-chip power is 12.305W as shown in Figure 1-49.

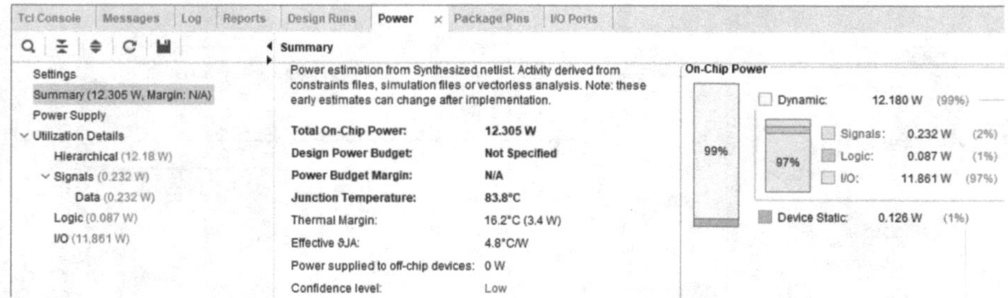

Figure 1-49. *The summary of report power for synthesis*

Now, if we select the "Run Simulation" option, we can choose Run Post-Synthesis Functional Simulation as depicted in Figure 1-50.

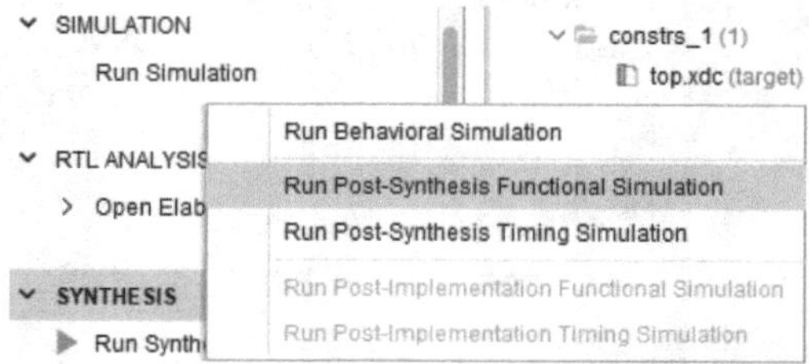

Figure 1-50. *Choosing Run Post-Synthesis Functional Simulation*

The waveforms of the signals on the wave window are illustrated in Figure 1-51.

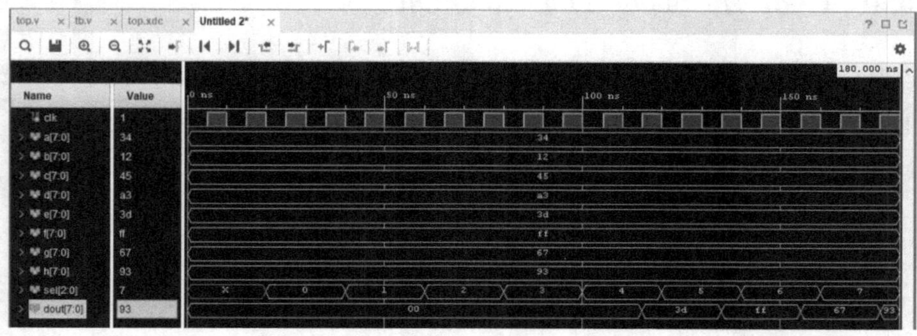

Figure 1-51. *The waveforms of the signals on the wave window*

To get appropriate simulation waveforms, we should use the modified test bench codes as shown in Figure 1-52.

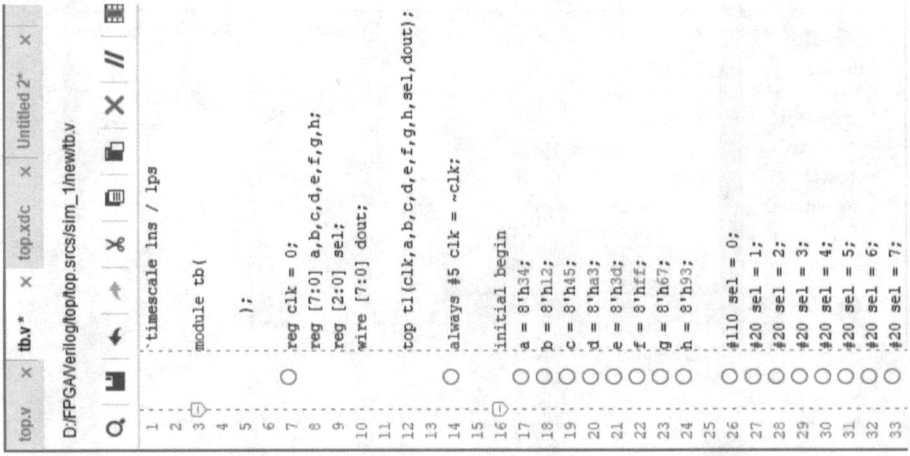

Figure 1-52. *The modified test bench codes*

As you can see, we have only changed the delay from 20ns to 110ns in code line 26. The modified waveforms on the wave window are depicted in Figure 1-53.

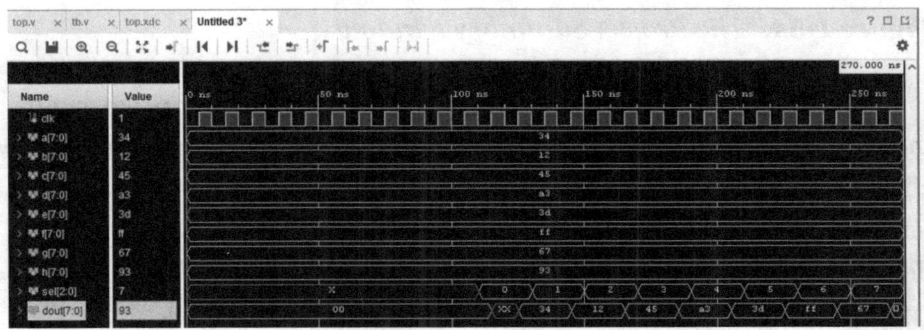

Figure 1-53. *The modified waveforms on the wave window*

In the Project Summary window, we can view the estimated utilization graph for post-synthesis as illustrated in Figure 1-54.

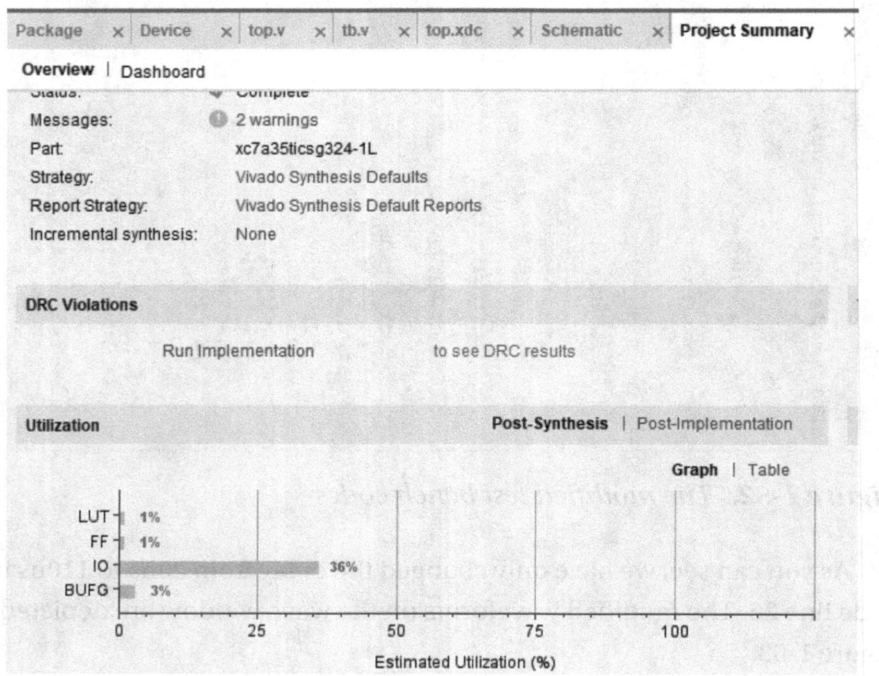

Figure 1-54. *The Project Summary window*

In the Settings window and in the Implementation section, we enable the power optimization design as shown in Figure 1-55. We double-click the Run Implementation option, and after a successful completed implementation, we select the Open Implemented Design option as depicted in Figure 1-56.

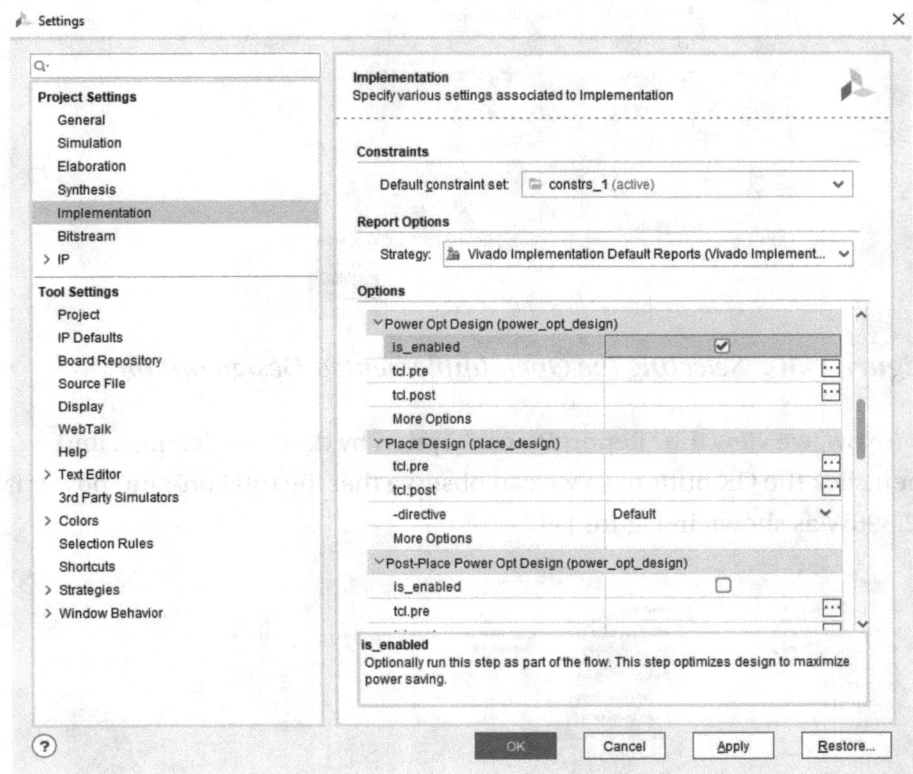

Figure 1-55. *Enabling the power optimization design for implementation*

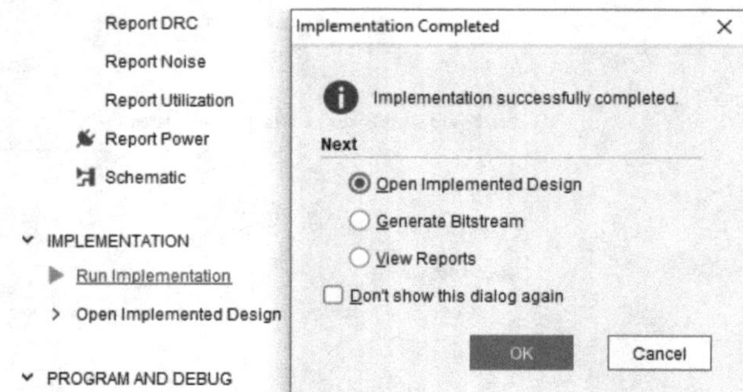

Figure 1-56. *Selecting the Open Implemented Design option*

Now, we view the "Report Power" option by double-clicking it and then click the OK button, so we can observe that the total on-chip power is 12.596W as shown in Figure 1-57.

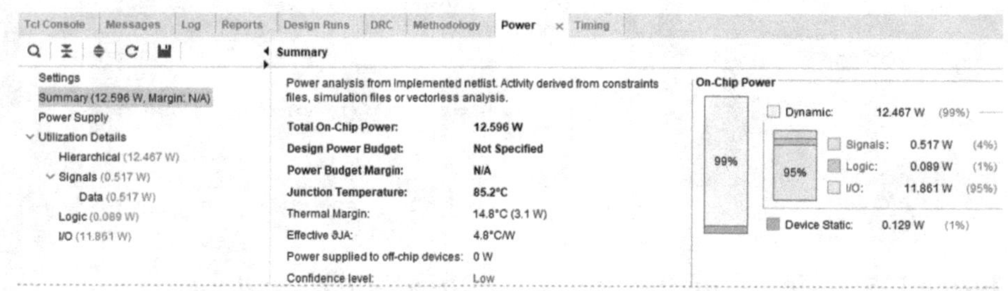

Figure 1-57. *The summary of report power for implementation*

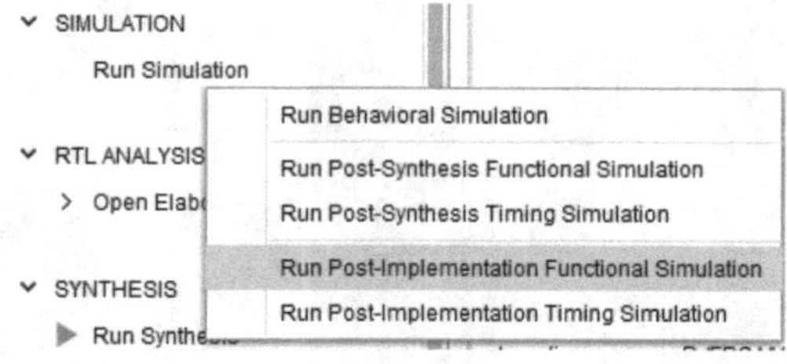

Figure 1-58. *Selecting the Run Post-Implementation Functional Simulation option*

After a successful implementation, we can go ahead to Run Simulation and select the Run Post-Implementation Functional Simulation option as depicted in Figure 1-58. The simulated waveforms on the wave window are illustrated in Figure 1-59, which are exactly the same as the waveforms of post-synthesis functional simulation in Figure 1-53.

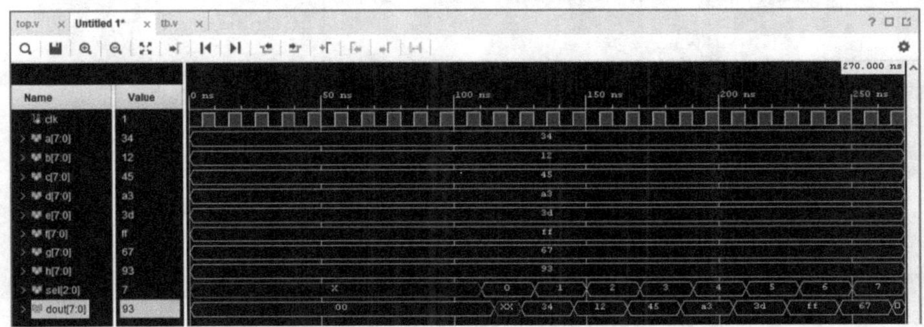

Figure 1-59. *The waveforms on the wave window*

Finally, we double click the Generate Bitstream option, and as you can see in Figure 1-60, the bitstream generation is successfully completed.

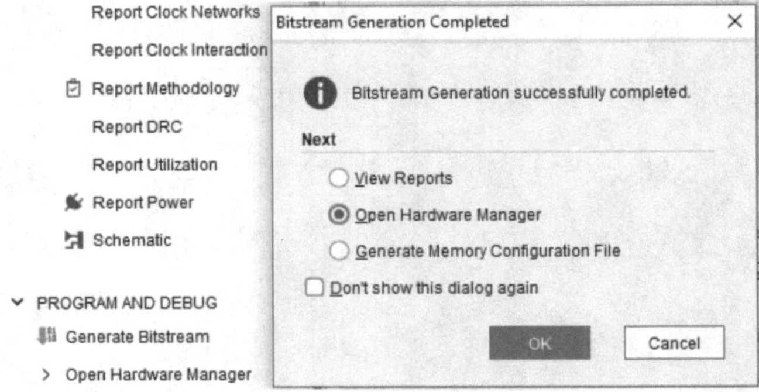

Figure 1-60. *The successful generated bitstream*

Now, we can select the Open Hardware Manager option and click the OK button as demonstrated in Figure 1-60. In the Hardware Manager window, we click Open target and choose the Auto Connect option to connect to the hardware as shown in Figure 1-61.

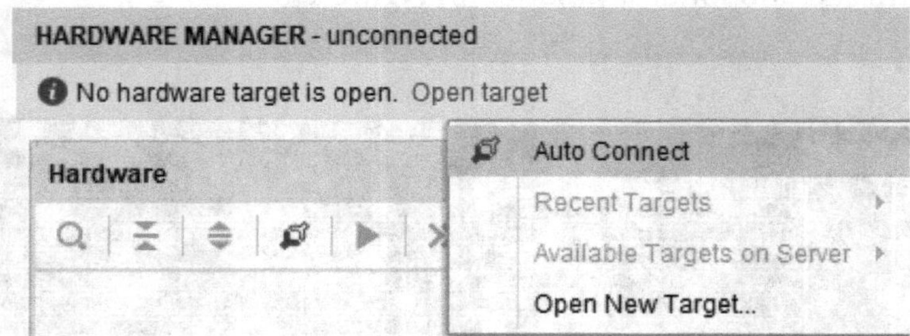

Figure 1-61. *Choosing the Auto Connect option*

CHAPTER 2

Behavioral Modeling in Verilog

After setting up your first FPGA project in Vivado (Chapter 1), the next crucial step is learning how to describe hardware behavior efficiently. Verilog, a leading hardware description language (HDL), enables designers to model digital circuits at different levels of abstraction. This chapter focuses on behavioral modeling, a high-level approach that emphasizes functionality over structural implementation, making it ideal for simulation, verification, and rapid prototyping.

In the Creating a Test Bench" section, you will learn how to develop simulation environments to verify your Verilog designs before deploying them on hardware. The "Blocking and Non-blocking Assignments" section clarifies a fundamental—yet often misunderstood—concept in Verilog, critical for writing correct sequential and combinational logic. "The Combinational Logic in Verilog" and "The Sequential Logic in Verilog" sections explore how to model basic digital circuits, from gates to flip-flops, while "The 4-Bit Up/Down Counter in Verilog" section ties these concepts together in a practical design example. Finally, The Verilog Case Statement" section demonstrates how to efficiently implement complex control logic using conditional branching.

© Majid Pakdel 2026

M. Pakdel, *Mastering Verilog for FPGA Design*, Maker Innovations Series, https://doi.org/10.1007/979-8-8688-2311-4_2

By the end of this chapter, you will be able to write, simulate, and analyze behavioral Verilog code, bridging the gap between theoretical concepts and real-world FPGA implementation. Let's dive into the power of behavioral modeling!

Creating a Test Bench

To start, we want to create a test bench. So we right-click the Simulation sources folder and select the Add Sources... option and then go ahead to create a simulation source file named "tb" as shown in Figure 2-1.

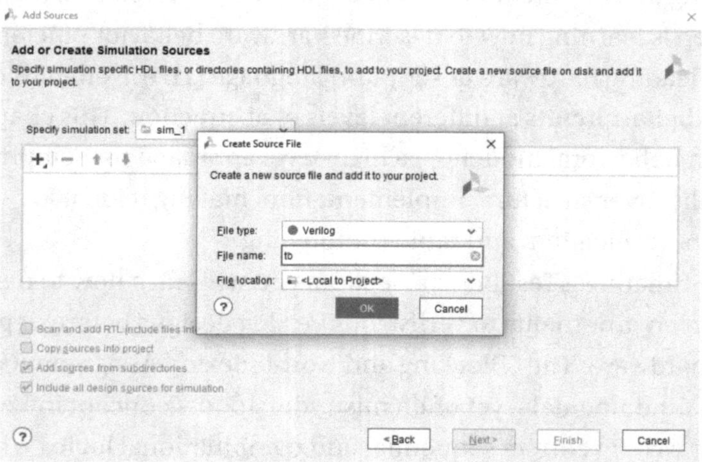

Figure 2-1. *Creating a simulation source file named "tb"*

Now, we write the following codes inside the "tb.v" file:

```verilog
`timescale 1ns / 1ps
module tb();
reg a;
reg clk;
wire b;
```

```verilog
/////////////Procedural Assignments//////////
initial begin
a = 0;
clk = 0;
end
always #5 clk = ~clk;
always@(posedge clk)
begin
a <= ~a;
end
/////////////Continuous Assignments//////////
assign b = clk;
endmodule
```

Then we select Flow ➤ Run Simulation ➤ Run Behavioral Simulation from the menu toolbar. The simulated waveforms on the wave window are depicted in Figure 2-2.

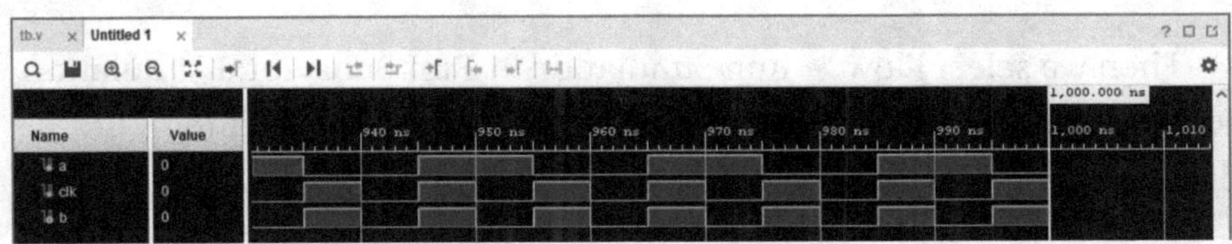

Figure 2-2. *The simulated waveforms on the wave window*

Blocking and Non-blocking Assignments

We right-click the Simulation sources folder and select the Add Sources... option to create another simulation source file named "tb_2" and write the codes below inside of it:

```verilog
`timescale 1ns / 1ps
//Blocking assignment and non-blocking assignment
```

```verilog
module tb_2();
reg a;
reg b;
reg c;
initial begin
//Blocking assignment
/*
a = 1;
#1 b = 1; //after 1ns
#2 c = 1; //after 2ns
*/
//Non-blocking assignment
a <= 1;
b <= #1 1;
c <= #2 1;
end
endmodule
```

Then we select Flow ➤ Run Simulation ➤ Run Behavioral Simulation from the menu toolbar. The simulated signals on the wave window are illustrated in Figure 2-3.

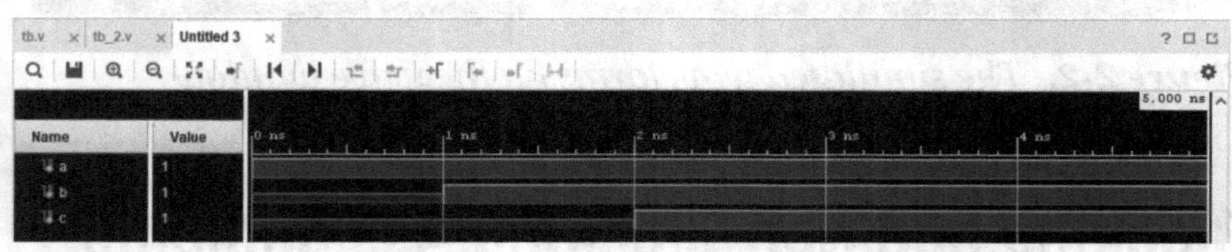

Figure 2-3. *The simulated signals on the wave window*

We right-click the Simulation sources folder and select the Add Sources… option to create another simulation source file named "tb_3" and write the following codes inside of it:

```
`timescale 1ns / 1ps
module tb_3();
reg [3:0] a,b,c;
initial begin
// Blocking assignments
a = 12;
$display("----------------------");
$display("Value of a, b, and c is %b, %b and %b",a,b,c);
$display("----------------------");
b = 10;
$display("----------------------");
$display("Value of a, b, and c is %b, %b and %b",a,b,c);
$display("----------------------");
c = 3;
$display("----------------------");
$display("Value of a, b, and c is %b, %b and %b",a,b,c);
$display("----------------------");
```

Now, we select Flow ➤ Run Simulation ➤ Run Behavioral Simulation from the menu toolbar. We click the Restart button in the simulation window and then click the Run for 100ns button, so the results are displayed on the Tcl Console as shown in Figure 2-4 (a). In this case, we have used the blocking assignments. Now, we want to use the non-blocking assignments as the codes below:

```
`timescale 1ns / 1ps
module tb_3();
reg [3:0] a,b,c;
initial begin
// Non-blocking assignments
a <= 12;
$display("----------------------");
```

```
$display("Value of a, b, and c is %b, %b and %b",a,b,c);
$display("--------------------");
b <= 10;
$display("--------------------");
$display("Value of a, b, and c is %b, %b and %b",a,b,c);
$display("--------------------");
c <= 3;
$display("--------------------");
$display("Value of a, b, and c is %b, %b and %b",a,b,c);
$display("--------------------");
end
endmodule
```

We choose Flow ➤ Run Simulation ➤ Run Behavioral Simulation from the menu toolbar, click the Restart button in the simulation window, and then click the Run for 100ns button, so the results are displayed on the Tcl Console as shown in Figure 2-4 (b). So, firstly, $display is executed, and then non-blocking assignment is applied, so we get x (do not care) values on the Tcl Console. However, if we use some delay before $display (e.g., 5ns delay—#5 $display(…)), we can achieve to the same results of blocking assignments.

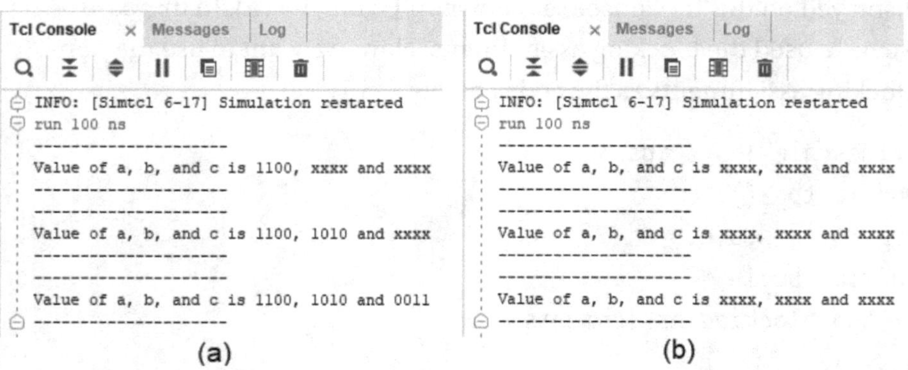

(a)   (b)

Figure 2-4. *The Tcl Console results for blocking and non-blocking assignments*

44

The Combinational Logic in Verilog

We create a 2 × 1 multiplexer project named "mux2_1" and then click the
Next button. We also select RTL Project as the project type, and in the Add
Sources window, we click the Create File button to create a source file
titled "mux2_1." Now, we use the following codes inside of it:

```verilog
`timescale 1ns / 1ps
module mux2_1(
    input a,b,sel,  // sel = 0 -> y = a, sel = 1 -> y = b
    output y
    );
reg yt;
initial begin
yt = 0;
end
always@(*) begin
   if (sel == 1'b0)
       yt = a;
   else
       yt = b;
end
 assign y = yt;
endmodule
```

We select Flow ➤ Run Simulation ➤ Run Behavioral Simulation from
the menu toolbar as depicted in Figure 2-5.

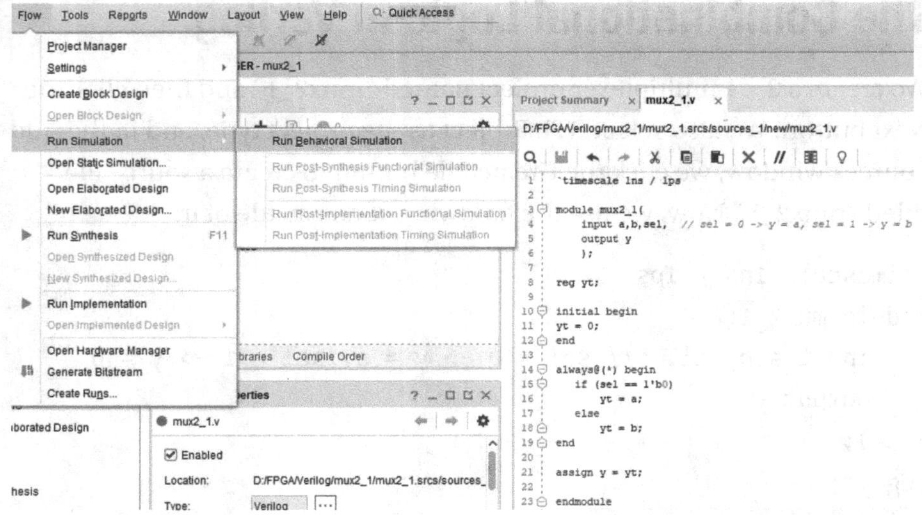

Figure 2-5. *Choosing Run Behavioral Simulation*

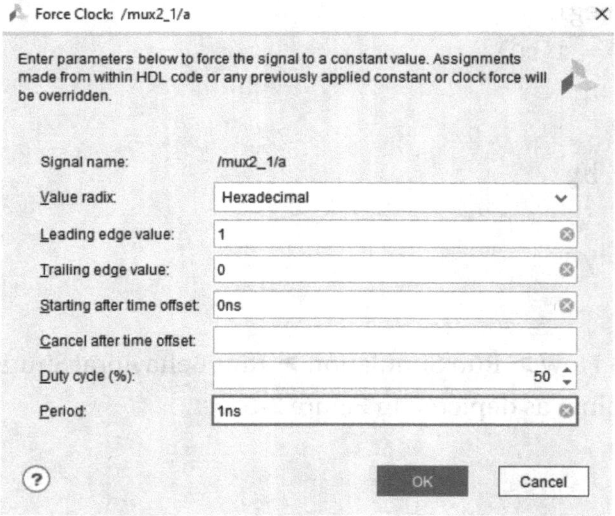

Figure 2-6. *Setting the force clock parameters for signal "a"*

In the opened simulation window, we click the Restart button, and we then right-click the signal "a" and select the Force clock... option to open the Force Clock window and set its parameters as illustrated in Figure 2-6. We also right-click the signal "b" and select the Force clock... option to open the Force Clock window and set its parameters as demonstrated in Figure 2-7.

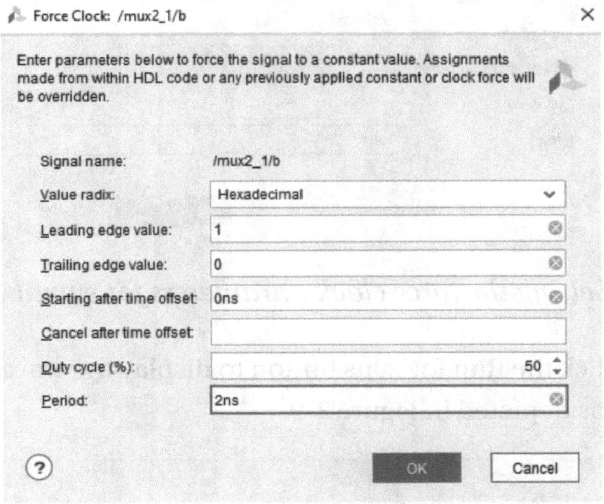

Figure 2-7. *Setting the force clock parameters for signal "b"*

Similarly, we right-click the signal "sel" and select the Force clock... option to open the Force Clock window and set its parameters as shown in Figure 2-8.

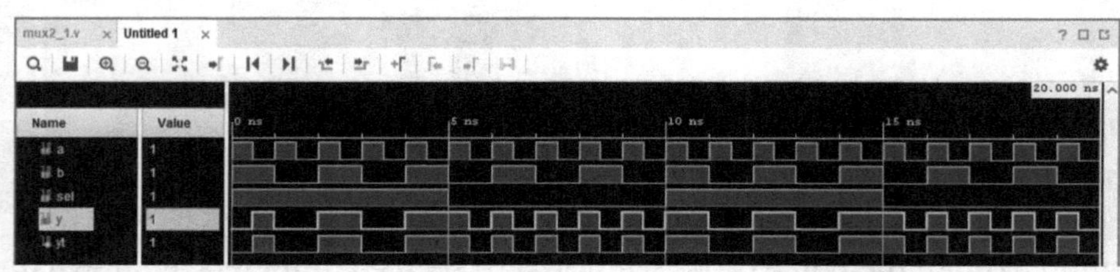

Figure 2-8. *Setting the force clock parameters for signal "sel"*

Now, we click the Run for 20ns button to display the waveforms on the wave window as depicted in Figure 2-9.

Figure 2-9. *The waveforms on the wave window*

Now, we want to create a 4 × 1 multiplexer Verilog file, so we right-click the Design Sources folder and select the Add Sources… option and create a source file named "mux4_1" and then click the Finish button as illustrated in Figure 2-10.

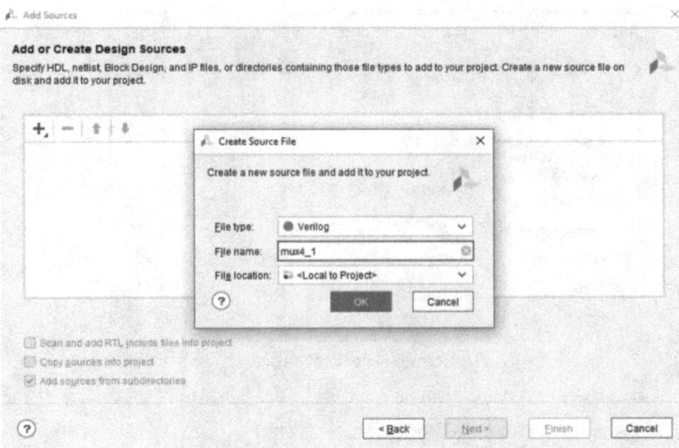

Figure 2-10. *Creating a source file named "mux4_1"*

In the Define Module window, we add the port names and directions as shown in Figure 2-11.

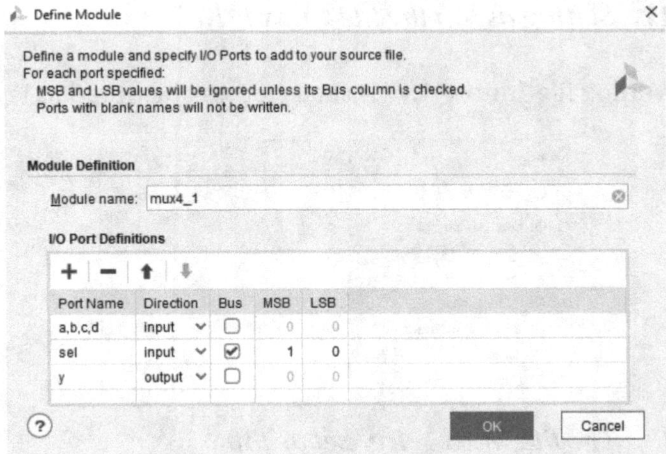

Figure 2-11. *Settings of the Define Module window*

First of all, we right-click the file "mux4_1.v" and choose the "Set as Top" option as depicted in Figure 2-12.

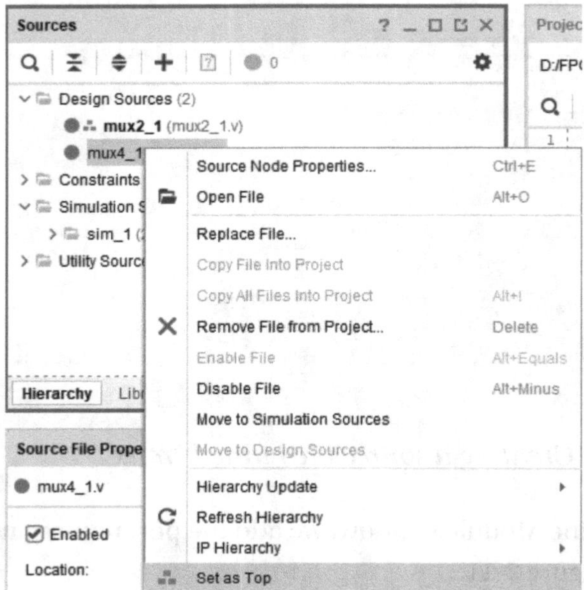

Figure 2-12. *Setting as top the file "mux4_1.v"*

So the Verilog file "mux4_1.v" is set as top as illustrated in Figure 2-13.

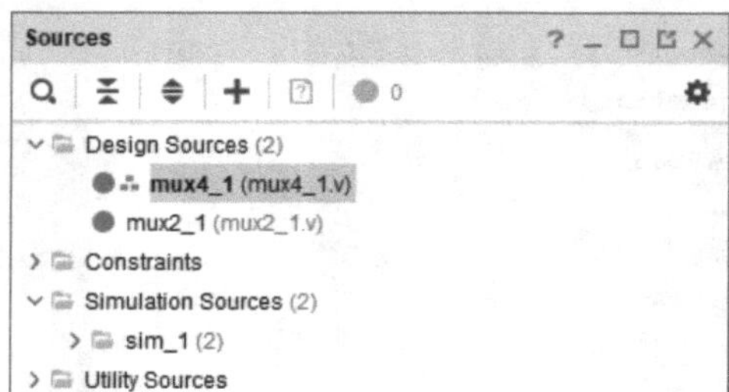

Figure 2-13. *The file "mux4_1.v" set as top*

We click the Settings button, and in the Simulation tab of Project Settings, we select the simulation top module name as "mux4_1" as shown in Figure 2-14.

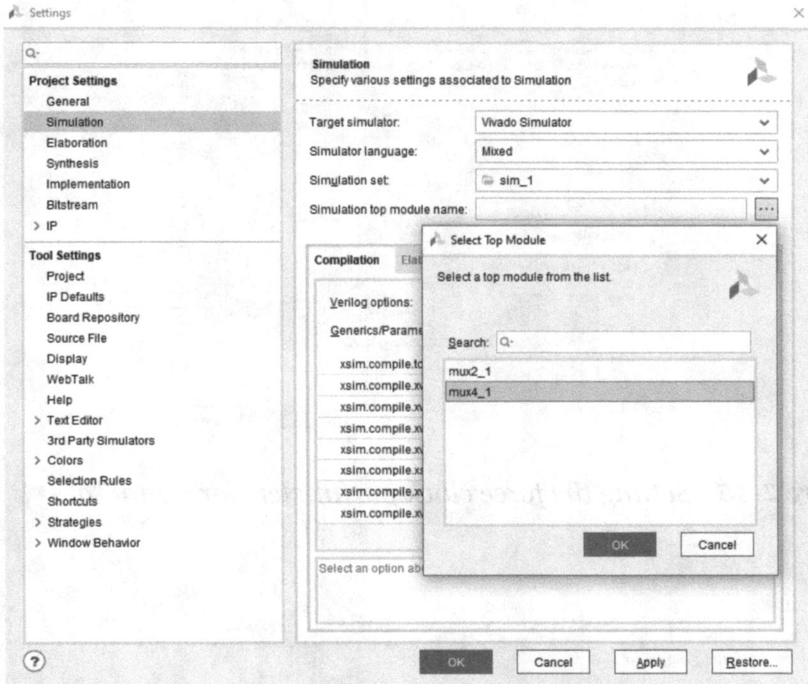

Figure 2-14. *Selecting the simulation top module name as "mux4_1"*

We select Flow ➤ Run Simulation ➤ Run Behavioral Simulation from the menu toolbar, and in the opened simulation window, we click the Restart button and then right-click the signal "a" and select the Force clock... option to open the Force Clock window and set its parameters as depicted in Figure 2-15. We also right-click the signal "b" and select the Force clock... option to open the Force Clock window and set its parameters as demonstrated in Figure 2-16.

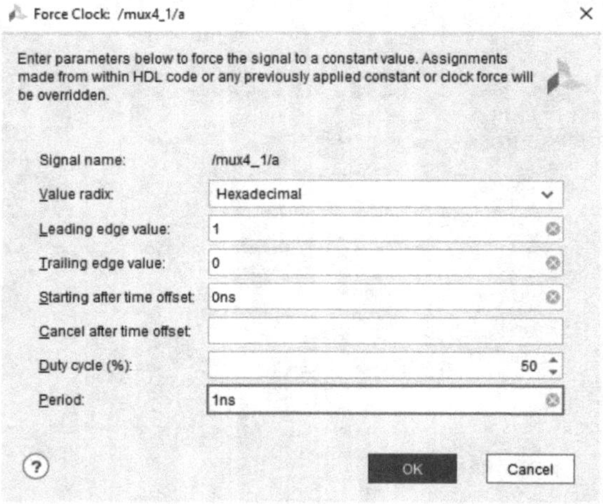

Figure 2-15. *Setting the force clock parameters for signal "a"*

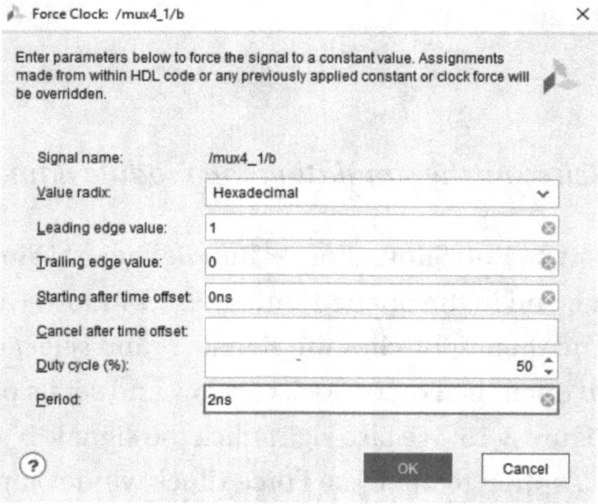

Figure 2-16. *Setting the force clock parameters for signal "b"*

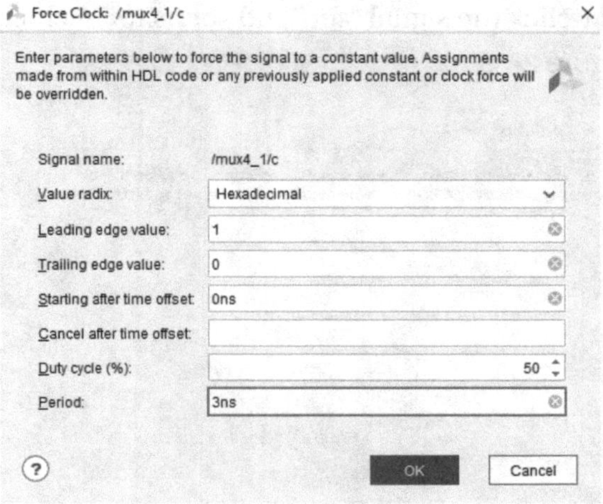

Force Clock: /mux4_1/c

Enter parameters below to force the signal to a constant value. Assignments made from within HDL code or any previously applied constant or clock force will be overridden.

Signal name: /mux4_1/c
Value radix: Hexadecimal
Leading edge value: 1
Trailing edge value: 0
Starting after time offset: 0ns
Cancel after time offset:
Duty cycle (%):   50
Period: 3ns

OK   Cancel

Figure 2-17. Setting the force clock parameters for signal "c"

Similarly, we right-click the signals "c" and "d" and select the Force clock... option to open the Force Clock window and set their parameters as shown in Figures 2-17 and 2-18, respectively.

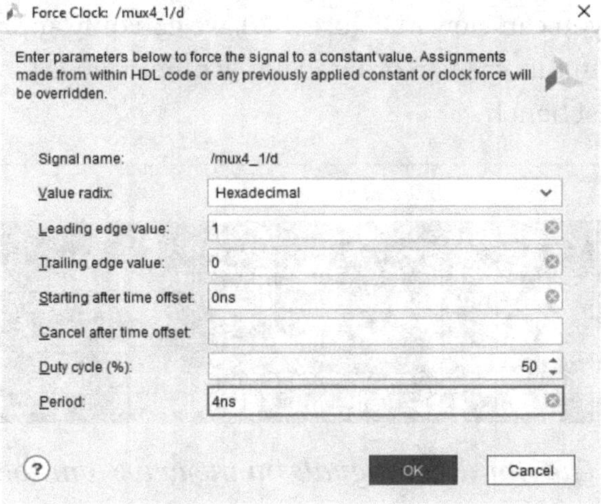

Force Clock: /mux4_1/d

Enter parameters below to force the signal to a constant value. Assignments made from within HDL code or any previously applied constant or clock force will be overridden.

Signal name: /mux4_1/d
Value radix: Hexadecimal
Leading edge value: 1
Trailing edge value: 0
Starting after time offset: 0ns
Cancel after time offset:
Duty cycle (%):   50
Period: 4ns

OK   Cancel

Figure 2-18. Setting the force clock parameters for signal "d"

We also right-click the signal "sel" and set its force clock parameters as illustrated in Figure 2-19.

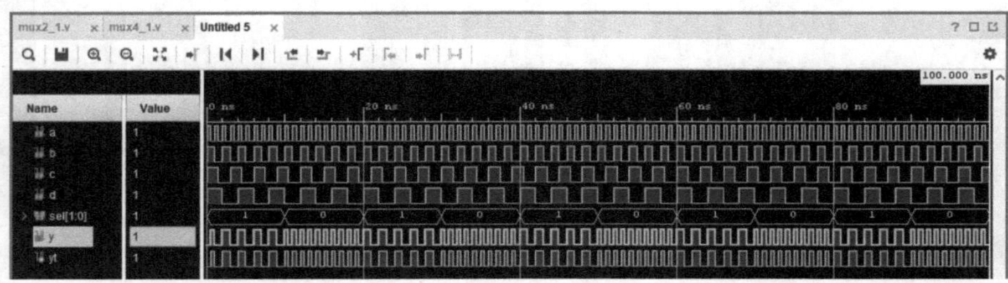

Figure 2-19. *Setting the force clock parameters for signal "sel"*

Now, we click the Run for 100ns button and click Zoom Fit in the wave window, so as you can view in Figure 2-20, we can only apply 1 or 0 values for signal "sel" in this case. In order to apply other values for signal "sel," we should use a test bench.

Figure 2-20. *The simulated signals on the wave window*

We right-click the Simulation sources folder and select the Add Sources… option and then create a simulation source file named "mux4_1tb" as shown in Figure 2-21.

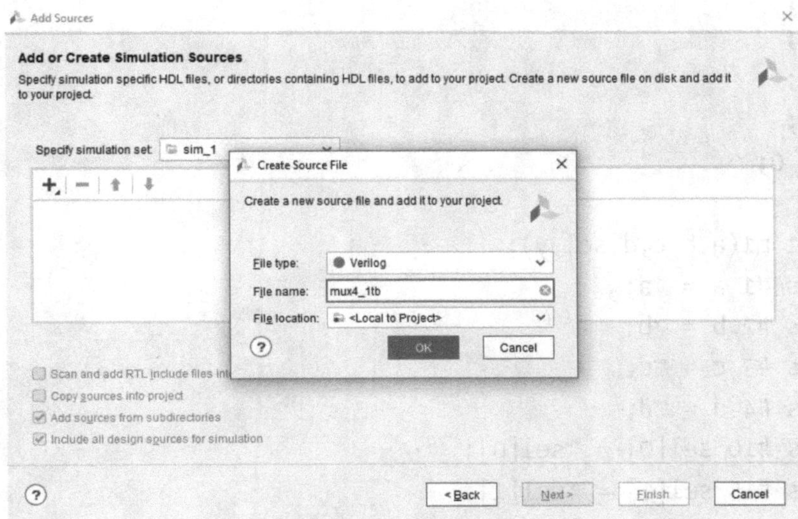

Figure 2-21. *Creating a simulation source file named "mux4_1tb"*

Now, we write the following codes inside the test bench file "mux4_1tb.v":

```verilog
`timescale 1ns / 1ps
/*
module mux4_1(
    input a,b,c,d,
    input [1:0] sel,
    output y
    );
*/
module mux4_1tb();
reg a,b,c,d;
```

```
reg [1:0] sel;
wire y;
initial begin
a = 0;
b = 0;
c = 0;
d = 0;
sel = 0;
end
mux4_1 m1(a,b,c,d,sel,y);
always #1 a = ~a;
always #2 b = ~b;
always #3 c = ~c;
always #4 d = ~d;
always #10 sel[0] = ~sel[0];
always #15 sel[1] = ~sel[1];
endmodule
```

We select Flow ➤ Run Simulation ➤ Run Behavioral Simulation from the menu toolbar to view the waveforms on the wave window as depicted in Figure 2-22.

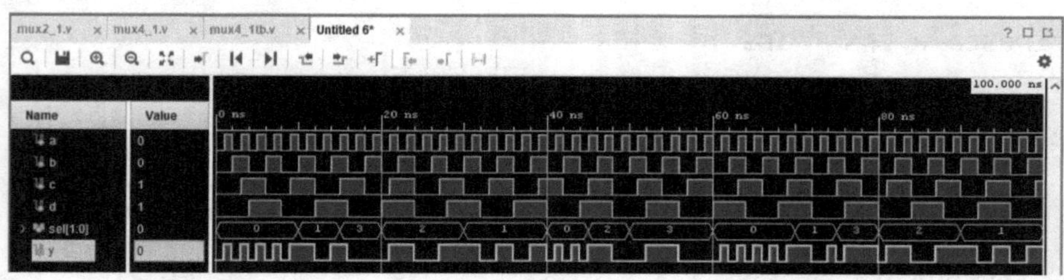

Figure 2-22. *The waveforms on the wave window*

The Sequential Logic in Verilog

We create a D-flip-flop project named "Flip_Flop" and then click the Next button. In the Add Sources window, we create a new source file named "FF" and then click the Finish button as illustrated in Figure 2-23.

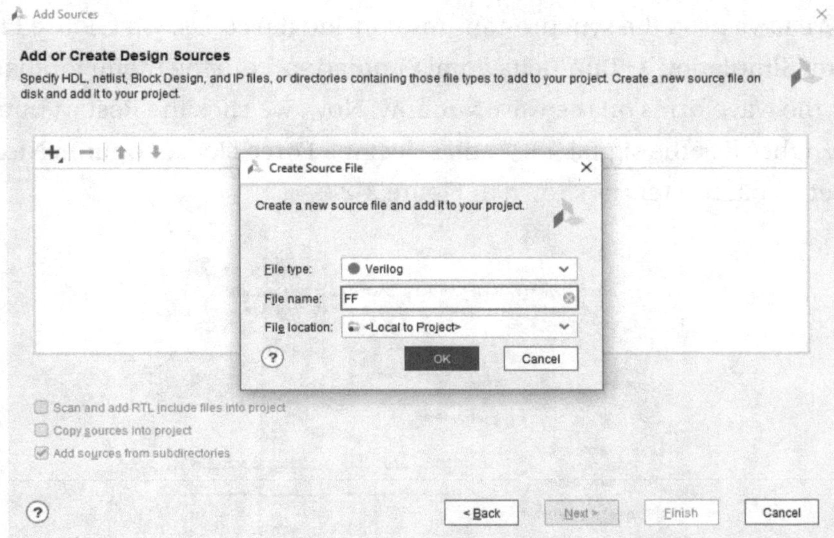

Figure 2-23. *Creating a new source file named "FF"*

We add the following codes inside the Verilog "FF.v" file:

```verilog
`timescale 1ns / 1ps
module FF(
input rst, clk, din,
output y
    );
reg yt = 0;
// Synchronous reset
always@(posedge clk)
begin
```

```
if (rst == 1'b1)
  yt <= 0;
else
  yt <= din;
end
```

We have used the synchronous reset inside the codes. We choose Flow ➤ Run Simulation ➤ Run Behavioral Simulation from the menu toolbar to view the waveforms on the wave window. Now, we click the Restart button, then right-click the signal "clk," and select the Force clock… option. Next, we set its parameters as shown in Figure 2-24.

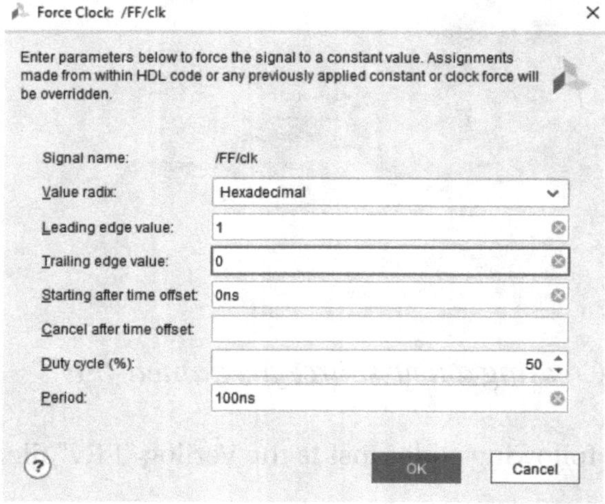

Figure 2-24. *Setting the force clock parameters of signal "clk"*

Then, we right-click the signal "rst" and force its constant value to 1 as depicted in Figure 2-25.

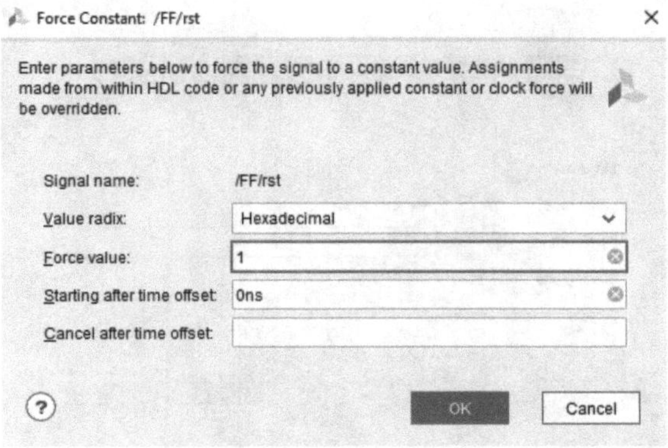

Figure 2-25. *Forcing the signal "rst" constant value to 1*

Similarly, we right-click the signal "din" and select the Force clock... option and then set its parameters as illustrated in Figure 2-26.

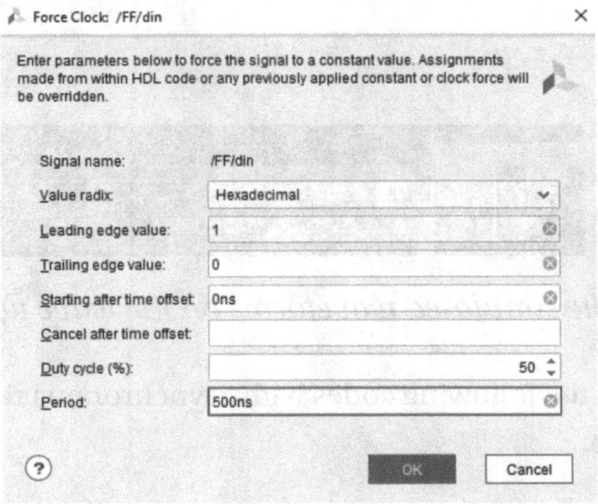

Figure 2-26. *Setting the force clock parameters of signal "din"*

We click the Run for 1µs button once and then force the constant value of signal "rst" to 0 as shown in Figure 2-27.

Figure 2-27. *Forcing the signal "rst" constant value to 0*

We click the Run for 1µs button twice and then click the Zoom Fit button in the wave window to view the simulated waveforms as depicted in Figure 2-28.

Figure 2-28. *The simulated waveforms on the wave window*

Now, we add the following codes with asynchronous reset inside the Verilog "FF.v" file:

```verilog
`timescale 1ns / 1ps
module FF(
input rst, clk, din,
output y
    );
reg yt = 0;
// Asynchronous reset
```

```
always@(posedge clk or posedge rst)
begin
if (rst == 1'b1)
   yt <= 0;
else
   yt <= din;
end
assign y = yt;
endmodule
```

If we choose Flow ➤ Run Simulation ➤ Run Behavioral Simulation from the menu toolbar and do the same settings as demonstrated in Figures 2-24, 2-25, 2-26, and 2-27, we will get the same simulation waveforms on the wave window as displayed in Figure 2-28.

The 4-Bit Up/Down Counter in Verilog

We create a 4-bit up/down counter project named "Up_Dn_Cnt" and then create a new source file titled "up_dn_cnt" as illustrated in Figure 2-29. We use the codes below inside of the file "up_dn_cnt.v":

```
`timescale 1ns / 1ps
module up_dn_cnt(
input clk,mode,clken,
output [3:0] dout
    );
reg [3:0] temp = 0;
always@(posedge clk) begin
if(clken == 1'b1) begin
    if(mode == 1'b1)
        temp <= temp + 1;
    else
```

```
        temp <= temp - 1;
    end
else
    temp <= 4'bxxxx; //do not care situation (z for high
                    impedance)
end
assign dout = temp;
endmodule
```

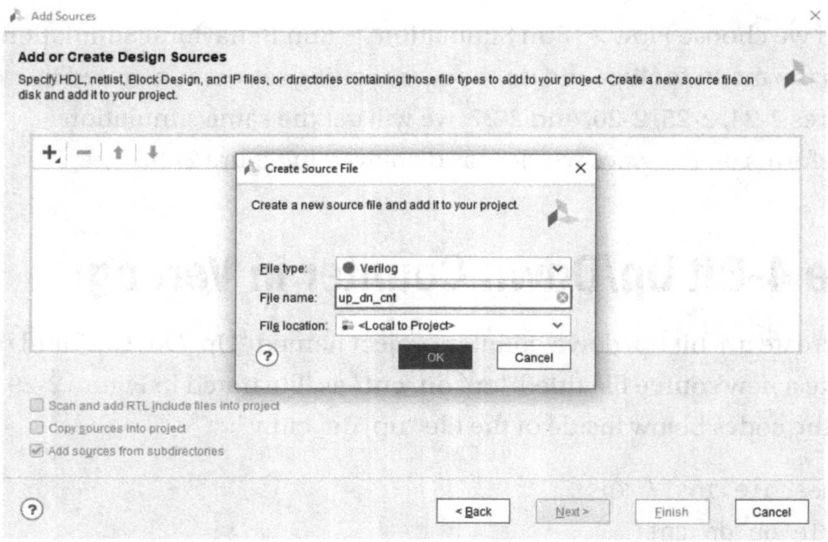

Figure 2-29. *Creating a new source file titled "up_dn_cnt"*

We choose Flow ➤ Run Simulation ➤ Run Behavioral Simulation from the menu toolbar to view the waveforms on the wave window. Now, we click the Restart button. Then we right-click the signal "clk" and select the Force clock... option so we can set its parameters as shown in Figure 2-30.

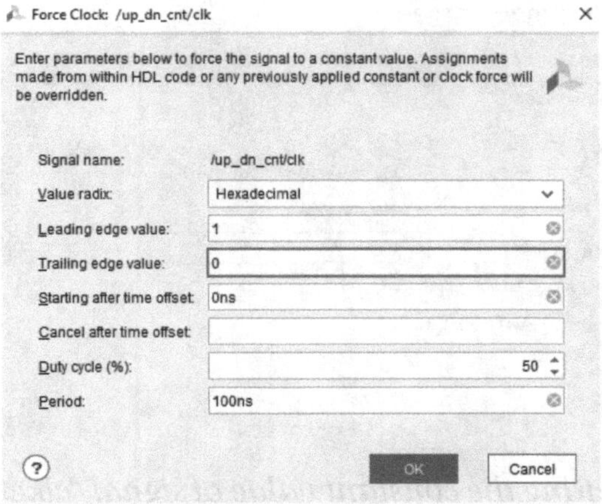

Figure 2-30. *Setting the force clock parameters of signal "clk"*

We also right-click the signal "mode" and select the Force constant... option so we set its constant value to 1 as depicted in Figure 2-31.

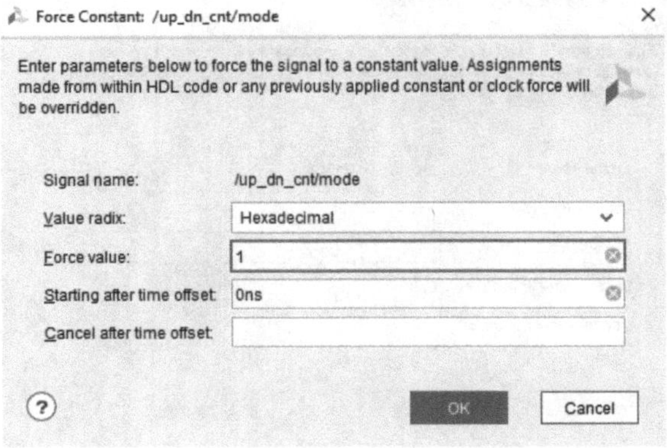

Figure 2-31. *Setting the constant value of signal "mode" to 1*

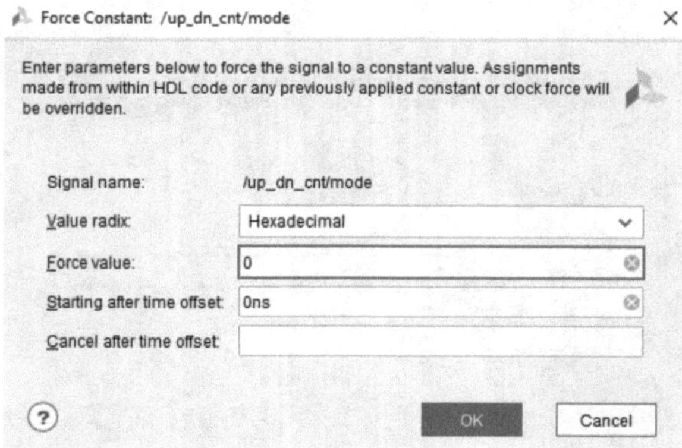

Figure 2-32. *Setting the constant value of signal "clken" to 1*

Similarly, we force the constant value of signal "clken" to the value of 1 as illustrated in Figure 2-32. Then we click the Run for 1µs button twice and force the constant value of signal "mode" to 0 as illustrated in Figure 2-33.

Figure 2-33. *Setting the constant value of signal "mode" to 0*

Now, we click the Run for 1µs button again and also click the Zoom Fit button in the wave window to view the simulated waveforms as shown in Figure 2-34.

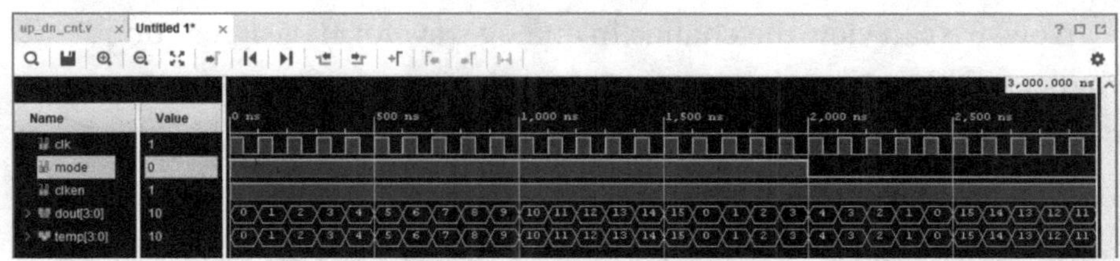

Figure 2-34. *The simulated waveforms on the wave window*

We right-click the signal "dout" and select the Radix option as Unsigned Decimal. Also, we right-click the signal "dout" and select the Waveform Style option as Analog as depicted in Figure 2-35.

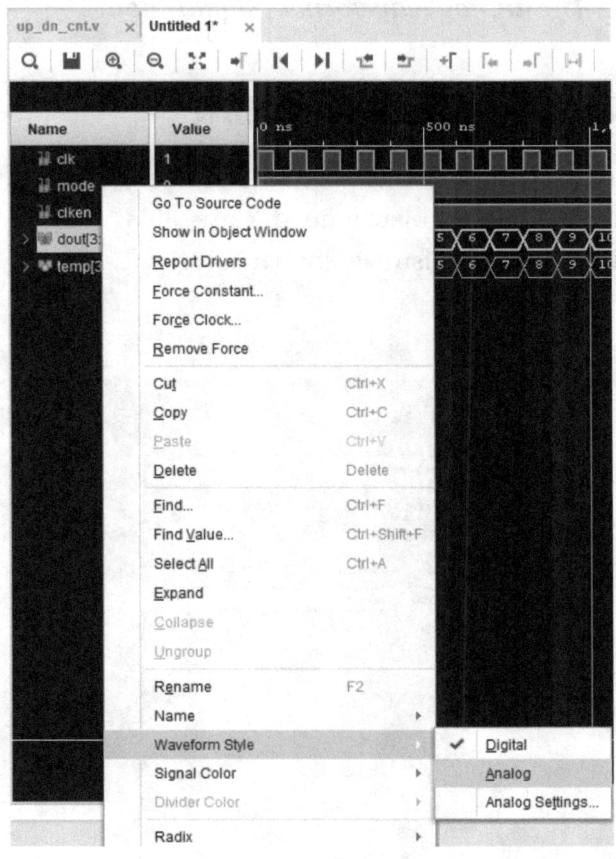

Figure 2-35. *Choosing the Waveform Style option as Analog*

Now, we can view the change in analog waveform of signal "dout" when it switches from down counting to up counting (from mode = 0 to mode = 1) as illustrated in Figure 2-36.

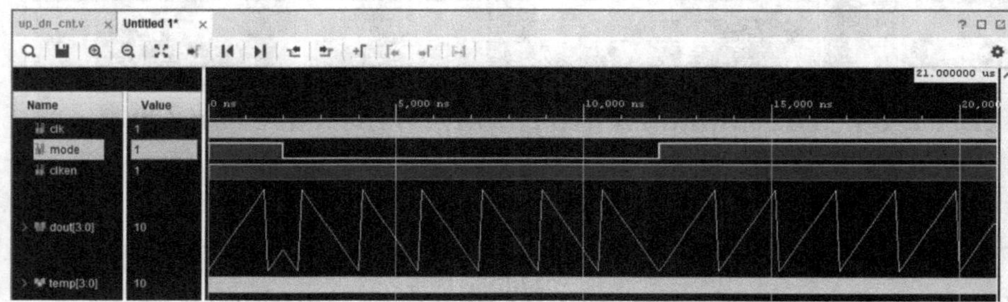

Figure 2-36. *The analog waveform of signal "dout"*

The Verilog Case Statement

We want to create a simple Finite State Machine project using the case statement. So we create a project named "Case_FSM" and then create a new source file titled "case_fsm" as shown in Figure 2-37.

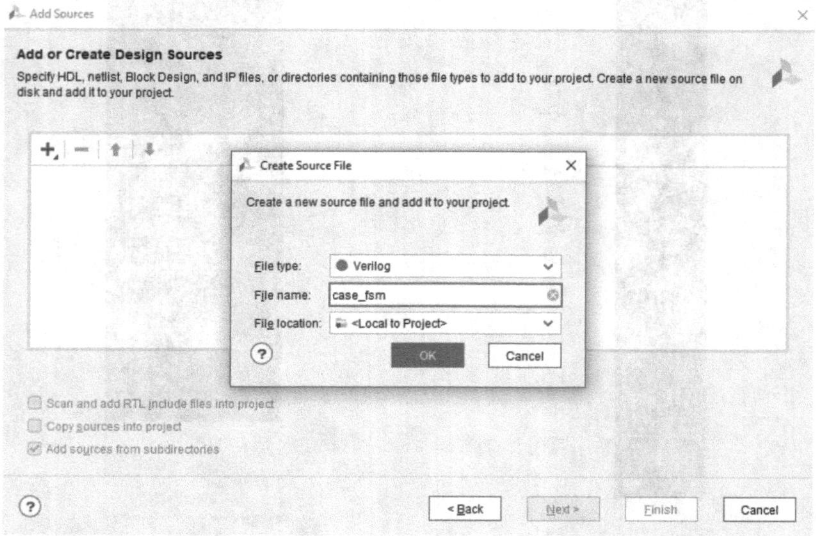

Figure 2-37. *Creating a new source file titled "case_fsm"*

We use the following codes inside of the file "case_fsm.v":

```verilog
`timescale 1ns / 1ps
module case_fsm(
input clk,
output led0, led1
    );
reg temp0,temp1;
reg state = 0;
always@(posedge clk) begin
case(state)
0: begin
temp0 <= 1'b1;
temp1 <= 1'b0;
end
1: begin
temp0 <= 1'b0;
temp1 <= 1'b1;
end
default: begin
temp0 <= 1'bx; //do not care situation
temp1 <= 1'bx; //do not care situation
end
endcase
end
assign led0 = temp0;
assign led1 = temp1;
endmodule
```

We select Flow ➤ Run Simulation ➤ Run Behavioral Simulation from
the menu toolbar to view the waveforms on the wave window. Now, we click
the Restart button, and then we right-click the signal "clk" and select the
Force clock... option so we can set its parameters as shown in Figure 2-38.

Force Clock: /case_fsm/clk

Enter parameters below to force the signal to a constant value. Assignments made from within HDL code or any previously applied constant or clock force will be overridden.

Signal name:	/case_fsm/clk
Value radix:	Hexadecimal
Leading edge value:	1
Trailing edge value:	0
Starting after time offset:	0ns
Cancel after time offset:	
Duty cycle (%):	50
Period:	100ns

OK   Cancel

Figure 2-38. *Setting the force clock parameters for signal "clk"*

Then, we run the simulation by clicking the Run for 1μs button once. We also right-click the signal "state" and select the Force constant... option so we can set its parameters as shown in Figure 2-39.

Force Constant: /case_fsm/state

Enter parameters below to force the signal to a constant value. Assignments made from within HDL code or any previously applied constant or clock force will be overridden.

Signal name:	/case_fsm/state
Value radix:	Hexadecimal
Force value:	1
Starting after time offset:	0ns
Cancel after time offset:	

OK   Cancel

Figure 2-39. *Setting the force constant parameters for signal "state"*

Now, we click the Zoom Fit button to view the overall simulation waveforms on the wave window as depicted in Figure 2-40.

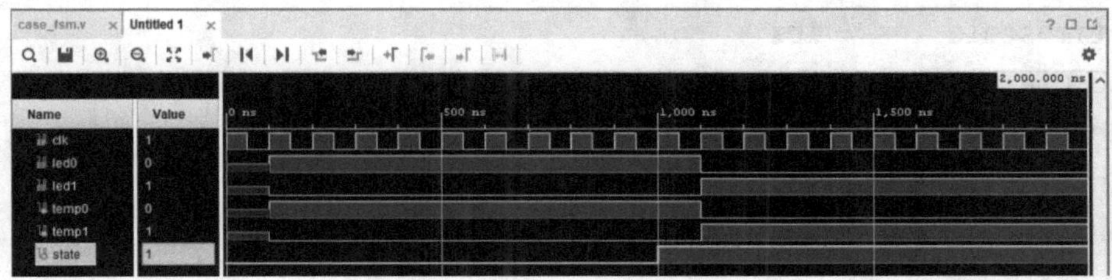

Figure 2-40. *The simulation waveforms on the wave window*

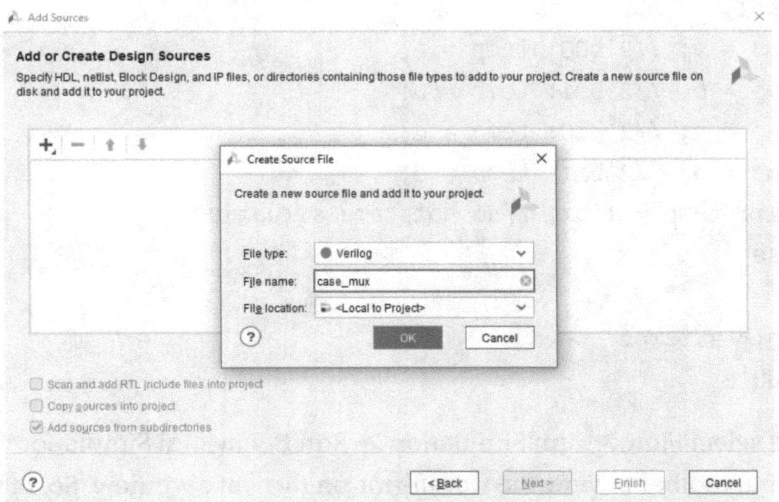

Figure 2-41. *Creating a Verilog source file "case_mux"*

We want to implement a 4 × 1 multiplexer using the case statement. So we create a new project named "Case_MUX" and then create a source file titled "case_mux" the same as the previous procedures as illustrated in Figure 2-41. Now, we add the following codes inside of the created file "case_mux.v":

```verilog
`timescale 1ns / 1ps
module case_mux(
input a,b,c,d,
input [1:0] sel,
output y
    );
reg temp = 0;
always@(*) begin
case(sel)
0: temp = a; //2'b00: temp = a;
1: temp = b; //2'b01: temp = b;
2: temp = c; //2'b10: temp = c;
3: temp = d; //2'b11: temp = d;
default: temp = 1'bx; //do not care situation
endcase
end
assign y = temp;
endmodule
```

We select Flow ➤ Run Simulation ➤ Run Behavioral Simulation from the menu toolbar to view the waveforms on the wave window. So, in the opened simulation window, we click the Restart button. Then we right-click the signals "a," "b," "c," and "d" and then select the Force clock... option so we can set their parameters as shown in Figures 2-42, 2-43, 2-44, and 2-45, respectively.

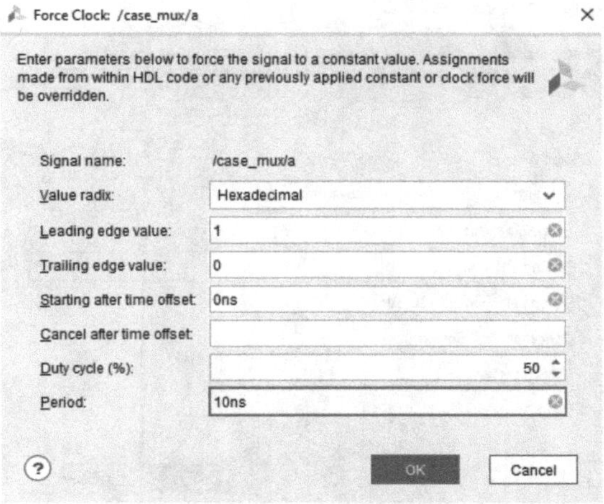

Figure 2-42. *Setting the force clock parameters for signal "a"*

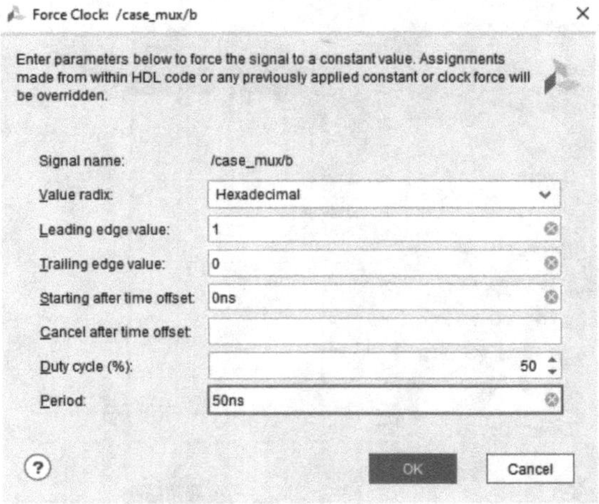

Figure 2-43. *Setting the force clock parameters for signal "b"*

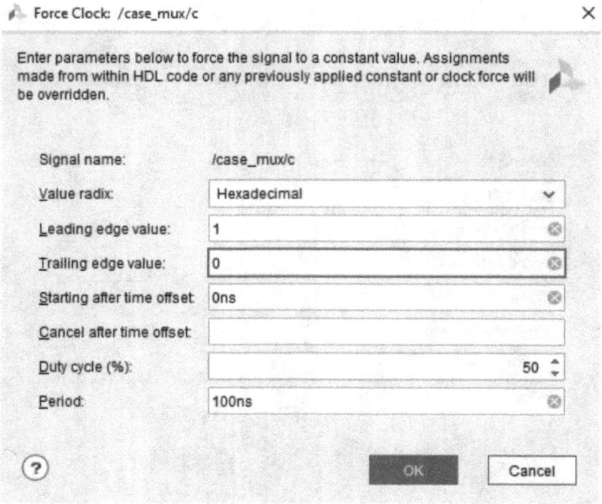

Figure 2-44. *Setting the force clock parameters for signal "c"*

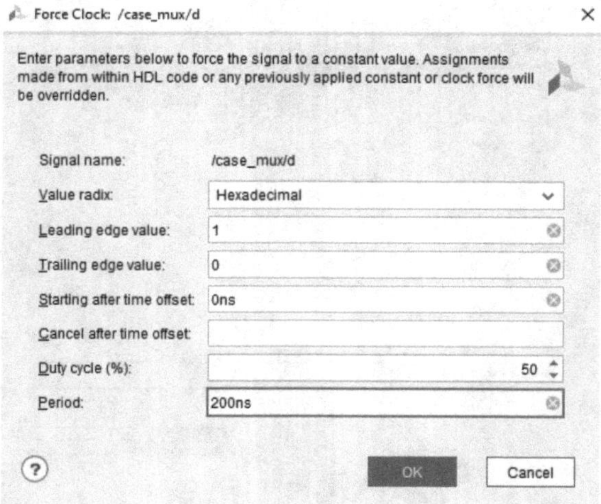

Figure 2-45. *Setting the force clock parameters for signal "d"*

Now, we right-click the signal "sel" and force its constant value to 0 as depicted in Figure 2-46.

Force Constant: /case_mux/sel

Enter parameters below to force the signal to a constant value. Assignments made from within HDL code or any previously applied constant or clock force will be overridden.

Signal name: /case_mux/sel
Value radix: Unsigned Decimal
Force value: 0
Starting after time offset: 0ns
Cancel after time offset:

OK   Cancel

Figure 2-46. *Setting the force constant parameters for signal "sel"*

We click the Run for 1μs button once and then force the constant value of signal "sel" to 1 as illustrated in Figure 2-47. Finally, we click the Run for 1μs button again and then click the Zoom Fit button to view the overall simulation waveforms on the wave window as shown in Figure 2-48.

Force Constant: /case_mux/sel

Enter parameters below to force the signal to a constant value. Assignments made from within HDL code or any previously applied constant or clock force will be overridden.

Signal name: /case_mux/sel
Value radix: Unsigned Decimal
Force value: 1
Starting after time offset: 0ns
Cancel after time offset:

OK   Cancel

Figure 2-47. *Forcing the constant value of signal "sel" to 1*

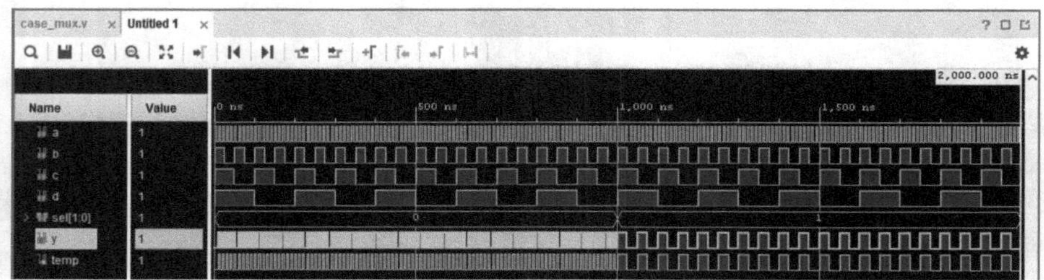

Figure 2-48. *The simulation waveforms on the wave window*

Test Bench Projects in Verilog

In Chapter 2, we explored behavioral modeling in Verilog, focusing on how to describe digital circuits using high-level constructs such as always and initial blocks. Now, in Chapter 3, we shift our attention to test bench development, a crucial aspect of digital design verification. A well-constructed test bench ensures that our designs function correctly under various input conditions by automating stimulus generation and response monitoring.

This chapter begins with the fundamentals of test bench simulation, followed by key Verilog constructs for test benches, including tasks, time monitoring, and random stimulus generation. We then examine loop constructs like repeat, for, and while for efficient test pattern generation. Finally, we apply these concepts to practical test benches for a 2 × 1 multiplexer, a 4-bit up counter, and Johnson and ring counters.

By the end of this chapter, you will be equipped to develop robust test benches that validate the functionality and timing of your Verilog designs.

© Majid Pakdel 2026
M. Pakdel, *Mastering Verilog for FPGA Design*, Maker Innovations Series,
https://doi.org/10.1007/979-8-8688-2311-4_3

Simulating a Test Bench

To start, we want to create a simple test bench and simulate it in Vivado. So we create a new project named "test_bench1" and a simulation source file titled "tb" as depicted in Figure 3-1.

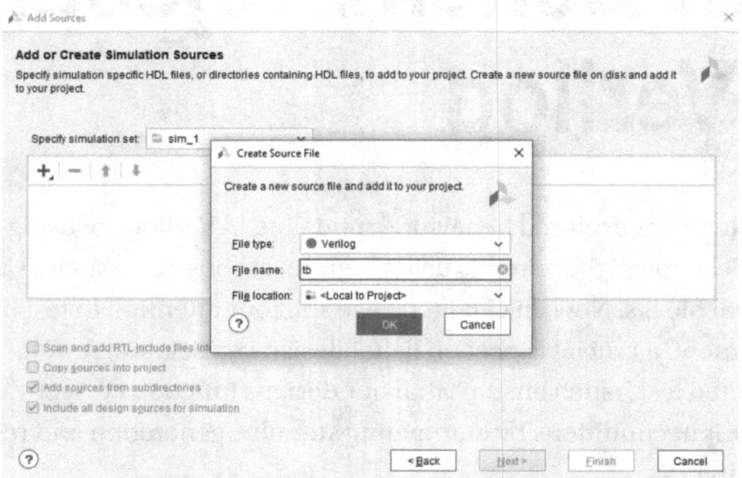

Figure 3-1. *Creating a Verilog source file titled "tb"*

Now, we add the following codes inside of the created source file "tb.v":

```verilog
`timescale 1ns / 1ps
module tb();
reg clk = 0;
always #5 clk = ~clk; //Clock period = 10ns
endmodule
```

We select Flow ➤ Run Simulation ➤ Run Behavioral Simulation from the menu toolbar to view the waveforms on the wave window. So, in the opened simulation window, we click the Restart button, then click the Run for 50ns button, and finally click the Zoom Fit button to view the signal "clk" waveform as illustrated in Figure 3-2.

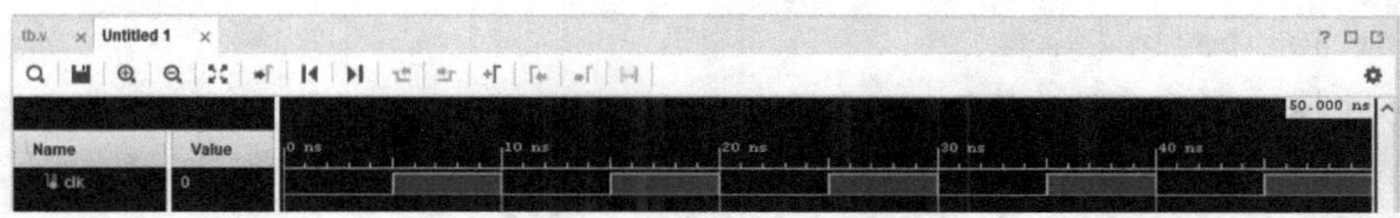

Figure 3-2. *The simulated signal "clk" on the wave window*

Now, we write the following codes inside of the Verilog file "tb.v":

```verilog
`timescale 1ns / 1ps
module tb();
reg clk = 0;
initial begin
#5 clk = ~clk;
#5 clk = ~clk;
#5 clk = ~clk;
#5 clk = ~clk;
end
endmodule
```

If we run the simulation for 40ns the same as the previous procedure, the simulated waveform is displayed on the wave window as shown in Figure 3-3.

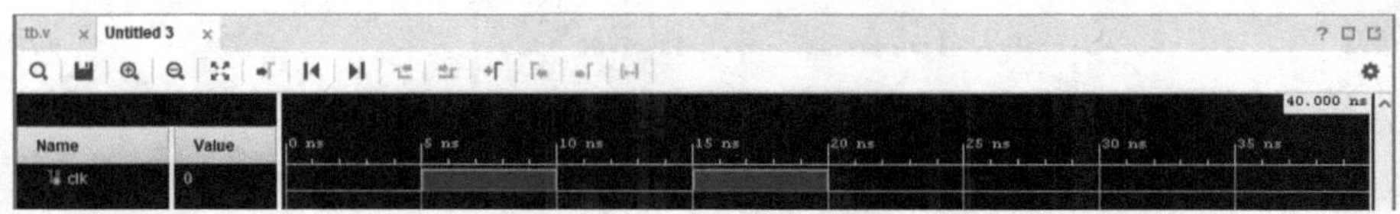

Figure 3-3. *The simulated signal "clk" on the wave window*

Then, we write the following codes inside of the Verilog file "tb.v":

```verilog
`timescale 1ns / 1ps
module tb();
reg clk = 0;
```

```
initial begin
#5 clk = 1;
   $display("CLK with display : %0b",clk);
   $monitor("CLK with monitor : %0b",clk);
#5 clk = 0;
#5 clk = 1;
end
endmodule
```

We choose Flow ➤ Run Simulation ➤ Run Behavioral Simulation from the menu toolbar to view the waveforms on the wave window. So, in the opened simulation window, we click the Restart button, then click the Run for 40ns button, and finally click the Zoom Fit button to view the waveform of signal "clk" as depicted in Figure 3-4. Also, we can see the results on the Tcl Console as illustrated in Figure 3-5.

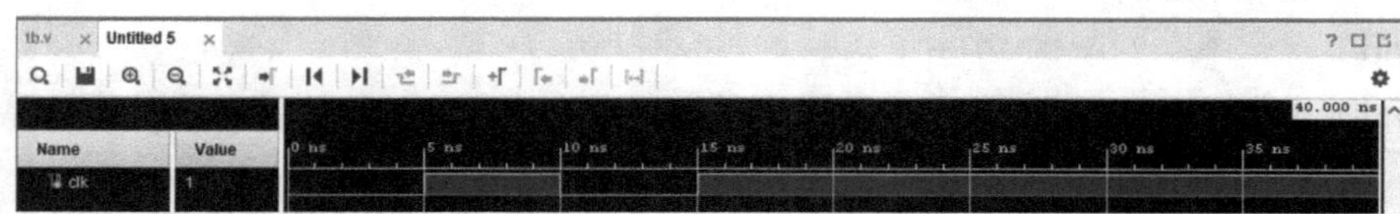

Figure 3-4. *The simulated waveform on the wave window*

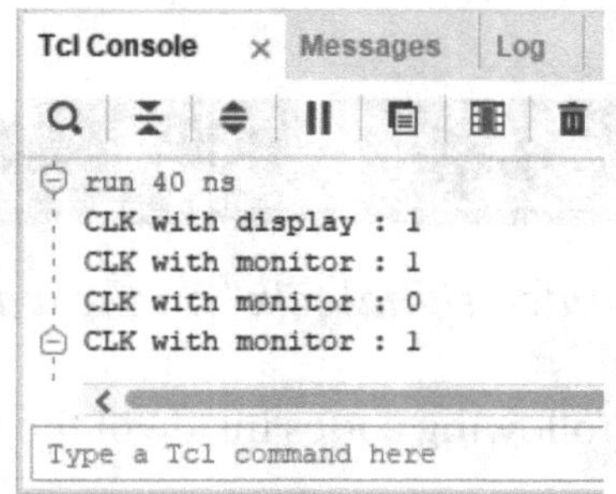

Figure 3-5. *The results of simulation on the Tcl Console*

The Task Statement

We want to create another test bench including the task statement and simulate it in Vivado. So we create a new project named "test_bench2" and a simulation source file titled "tb.v" then use the following codes inside of it:

```verilog
`timescale 1ns / 1ps
module tb();
reg clk = 0;
reg cs;
reg we;
reg [7:0] data1;
reg [7:0] data2;
always #5 clk = ~clk;
task read(input [7:0] d);
begin
  cs = 1'b1;
  we = 1'b0;
  data1 = d;
  data2 = $random;
end
endtask
initial begin
#5 read(8'b1001);
#5 read(8'b0001);
#5 read(8'b0011);
end
endmodule
```

We select Flow ➤ Run Simulation ➤ Run Behavioral Simulation from the menu toolbar to view the waveforms on the wave window. So, in the opened simulation window, we click the Restart button, then click the Run for 40ns button, and finally click the Zoom Fit button to view the waveforms as shown in Figure 3-6.

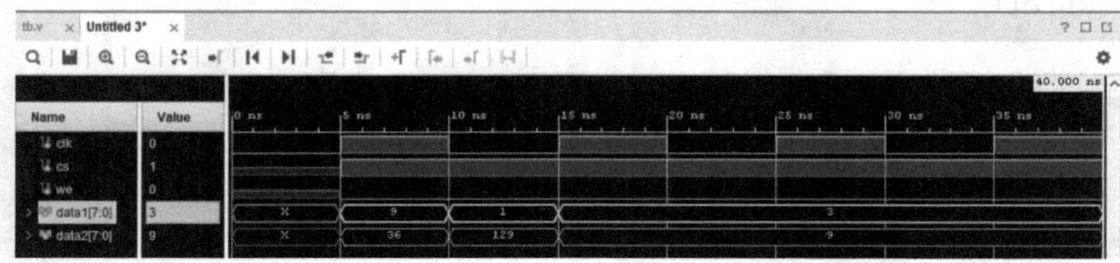

Figure 3-6. *The simulated waveforms on the wave window*

The Time Monitoring

We want to create another test bench to monitor the time and simulate it in Vivado. So we create a new project named "test_bench3" and a simulation source file titled "tb.v" and then use the following codes inside of it:

```verilog
`timescale 1ns / 1ns
module tb();
integer i;
initial begin
$monitor("The value of i = %0d and time = %0t",i,$time);
#1 i = 1;
#1 i = 2;
#0.7 i = 3;
end
endmodule
```

We choose Flow ➤ Run Simulation ➤ Run Behavioral Simulation from the menu toolbar to view the waveforms on the wave window. So, in the opened simulation window, we click the Restart button, then click the Run for 5ns button, and finally click the Zoom Fit button to view the waveform of signal "i" as depicted in Figure 3-7. Also, we can see the results on the Tcl Console as illustrated in Figure 3-8 (since the timescale is 1ns/1ns, the time delays greater than and lower than 0.5ns are considered as 1ns and 0ns, respectively).

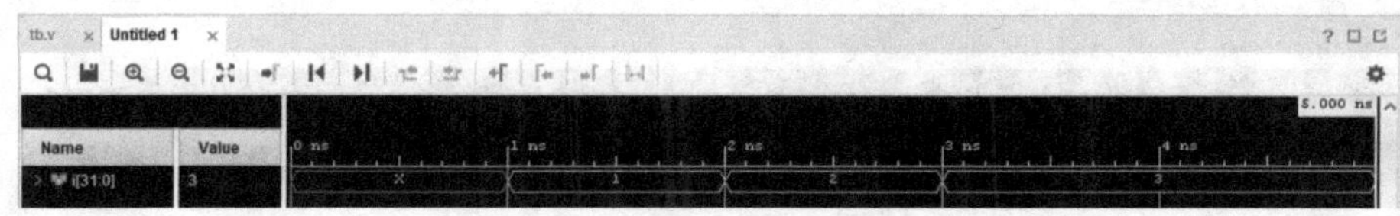

Figure 3-7. *The simulated waveform on the wave window*

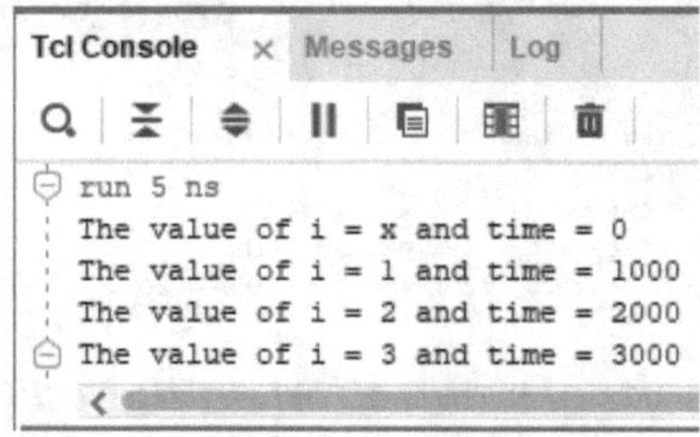

Figure 3-8. *The results of simulation on the Tcl Console*

Now, we use the following codes inside of the file "tb.v":

```verilog
`timescale 1ns / 1ns
module tb();
integer i;
initial begin
$monitor("The value of i = %0d and time = %0t",i,$time);
#1 i = 1;
```

```
#1 i = 2;
#0.4 i = 3;
end
endmodule
```

If we run the simulation the same as the previous procedures, we can view the simulated waveform on the wave window and Tcl Console as shown in Figures 3-9 and 3-10, respectively.

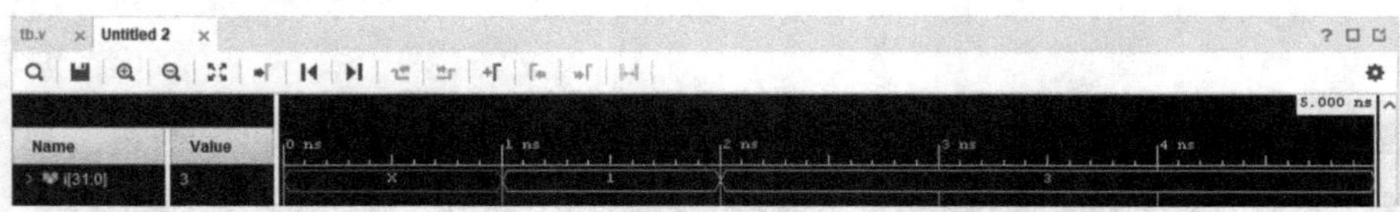

Figure 3-9. *The simulated waveform on the wave window*

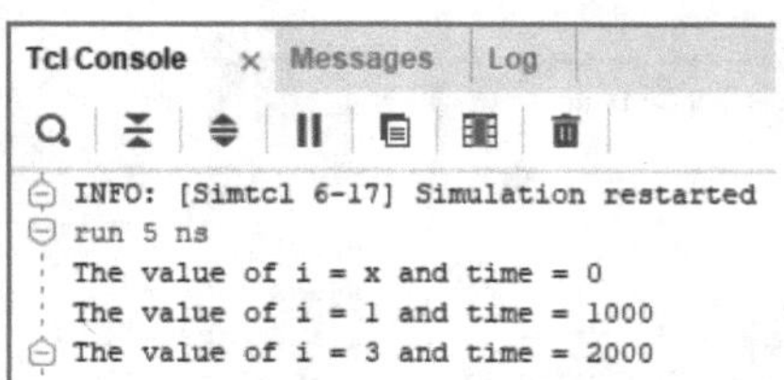

Figure 3-10. *The results of simulation on the Tcl Console*

Now, we create a new simulation source file named "tb2.v" and use the following codes inside of the file "tb2.v":

```
`timescale 1ns / 1ps
module tb2();
integer i;
initial begin
$monitor("The value of i = %0d and time = %0t",i,$time);
#1 i = 1;
#0.4 i = 2;
```

```
#1.5 i = 3;
#0.04 i = 4;
end
endmodule
```

If we run the simulation the same as the previous procedures, we can view the simulated waveform on the wave window and Tcl Console as depicted in Figures 3-11 and 3-12, respectively.

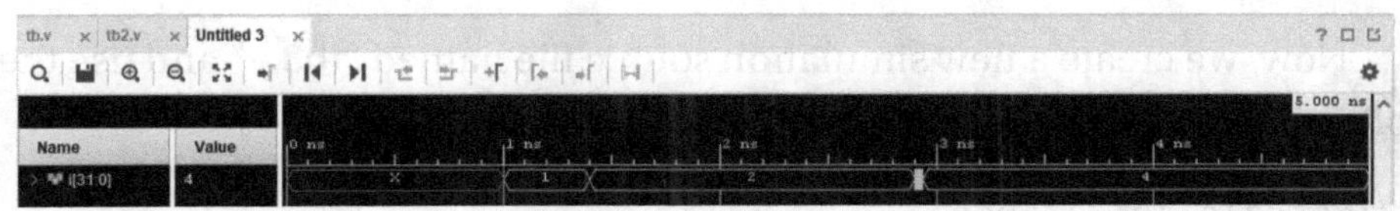

Figure 3-11. *The simulated waveform on the wave window*

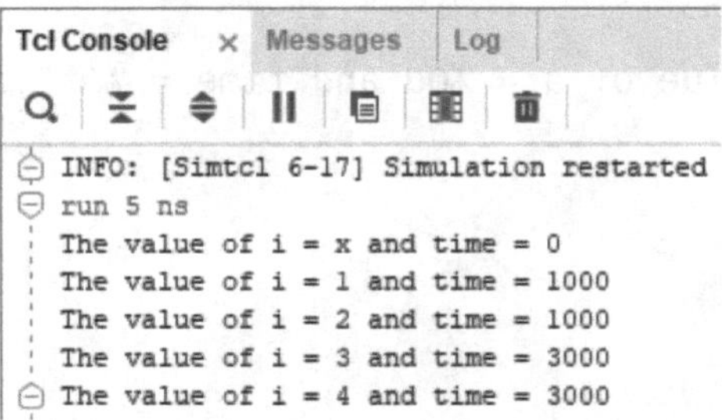

Figure 3-12. *The results of simulation on the Tcl Console*

Now, we use the following code line instead of the similar code line in the previous code:

```
$monitor("The value of i = %0d and time = %0t",i,$realtime);
```

If we run the simulation the same as the previous procedures, we can view the simulated waveform on the Tcl Console as illustrated in Figure 3-13.

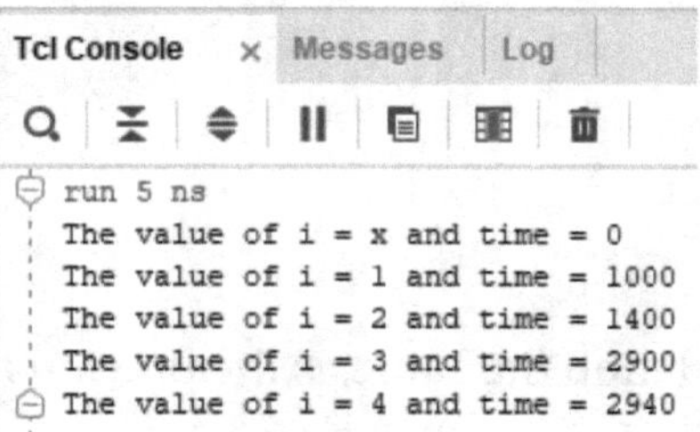

Figure 3-13. *The results of simulation on the Tcl Console*

Now, we create a new simulation source file named "tb3.v" and use the following codes inside of the file "tb3.v":

```verilog
`timescale 1ns / 1ps
module tb3();
reg [3:0] a;
initial begin
$monitor("The value of a = %0d and time = %0t",a,$time);
$display("----------------------------------------------------");
#1 a = 1;
#5 a = 5;
#15 a = 3;
#30 a = 15;
$display("----------------------------------------------------");
end
endmodule
```

If we run the simulation the same as the previous procedures, we can view the simulated waveform on the wave window and Tcl Console as depicted in Figures 3-14 and 3-15, respectively.

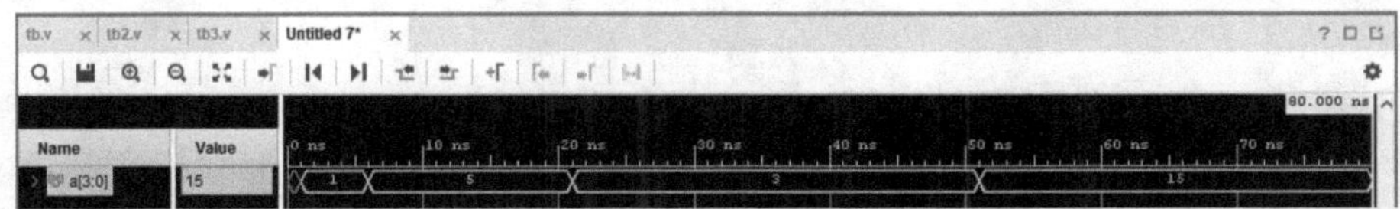

Figure 3-14. *The simulated waveform on the wave window*

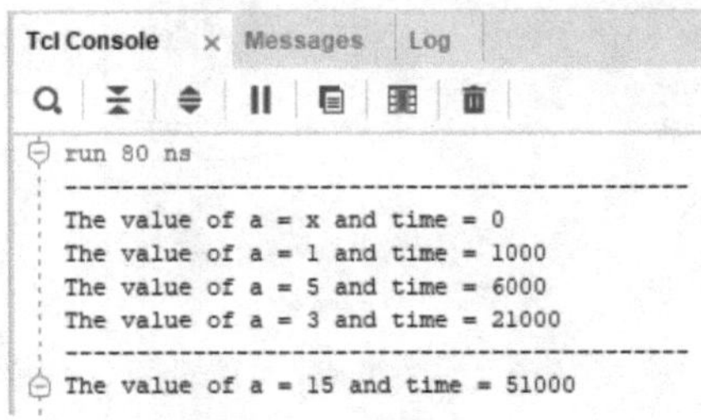

Figure 3-15. *The results of simulation on the Tcl Console*

As demonstrated in Figure 3-15, the time unit is picoseconds, and in order to change the display into nanoseconds, we enter the following command in the Elaboration tab of the Simulation section of the Settings window as shown in Figure 3-16:

```
xsim.elaborate.xelab.more_options: -timescale 1ns/1ns
-override_timeunit -override_timeprecision
```

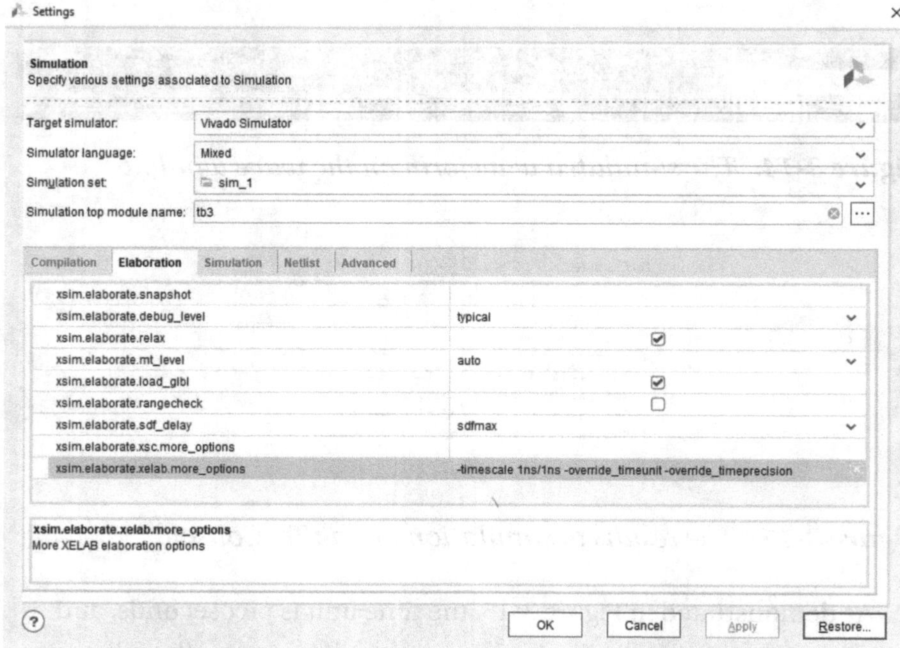

Figure 3-16. *The command used in the Elaboration tab of the Simulation section of the Settings window*

Now, if we run the simulation again, we can view the time results in nanoseconds on the Tcl Console as depicted in Figure 3-17.

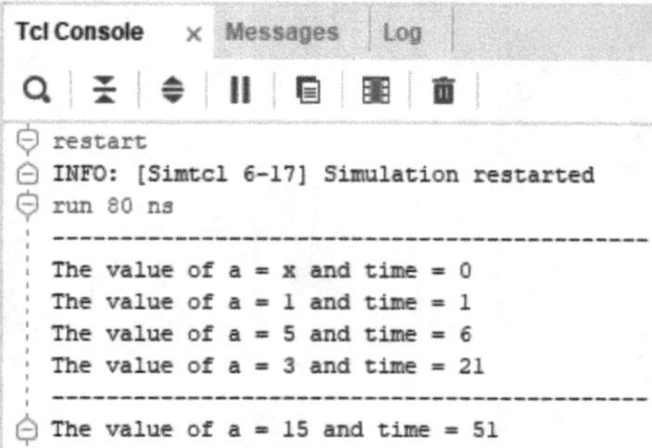

Figure 3-17. *The results of simulation on the Tcl Console*

To bring down the last dash lines in Figure 3-17, we use a 1ns delay before the last $display code as below:

```
#1 $display("---------------------------------------------");
```

Now, if we run the simulation again, we can get the desired results as illustrated in Figure 3-18.

```
Tcl Console   ×   Messages   Log

Q   ⤒   ⇕   ❙❙   ▤   ▦   🗑

INFO: [Simtcl 6-17] Simulation restarted
run 80 ns

------------------------------------------------
The value of a = x and time = 0
The value of a = 1 and time = 1
The value of a = 5 and time = 6
The value of a = 3 and time = 21
The value of a = 15 and time = 51
------------------------------------------------
```

Figure 3-18. *The desired results of simulation on the Tcl Console*

The Random Statement

We create a new project named "test_bench4" and also a design source file titled "top.v" and then add the following codes inside of it:

```
`timescale 1ns / 1ps
module top(
input [3:0] a,b,
output [4:0] y
    );
assign y = a + b;
endmodule
```

Now, we create a test bench file titled "tb.v" and use the following codes inside of it:

```verilog
`timescale 1ns / 1ps
module tb();
reg [3:0] a = 0, b = 0;
wire [4:0] y;
top t1(a,b,y);
integer i = 0;
//$random, $urandom, $urandom_range
initial begin
a = $random;
#1 b = $random;
#1 $display("The value of addition of a = %0d and b = %0d is
y = %0d",a,b,y);
end
endmodule
```

If we run the simulation the same as the previous procedures, we can view the simulated waveforms on the wave window and Tcl Console as shown in Figures 3-19 and 3-20, respectively.

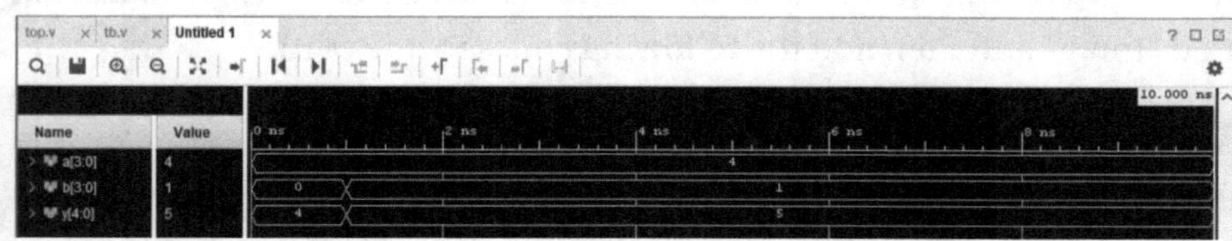

Figure 3-19. *The simulated waveforms on the wave window*

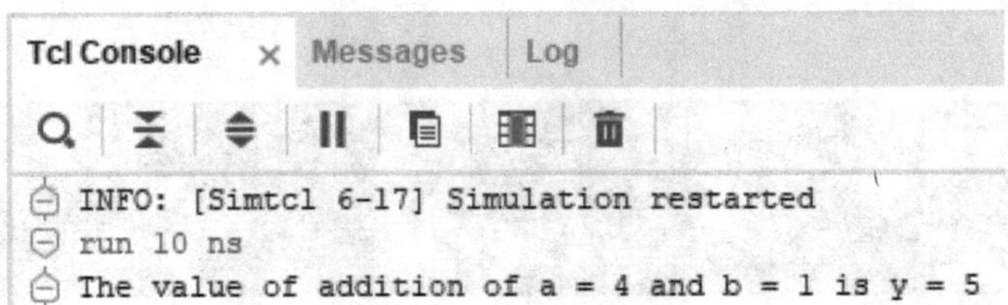

Figure 3-20. *The results of simulation on the Tcl Console*

Then, we use the following codes inside of the test bench file "tb.v":

```verilog
`timescale 1ns / 1ps
module tb();
reg [3:0] a = 0, b = 0;
wire [4:0] y;
top t1(a,b,y);
integer i = 0;
//$random, $urandom, $urandom_range
initial begin
for(i=0;i<5;i=i+1) begin
a = $random;
#1 b = $random;
#1 $display("The value of addition of a = %0d and b = %0d is
y = %0d",a,b,y);
end
end
endmodule
```

If we run the simulation the same as the previous procedures, we can view the simulated waveforms on the wave window and Tcl Console as depicted in Figures 3-21 and 3-22, respectively.

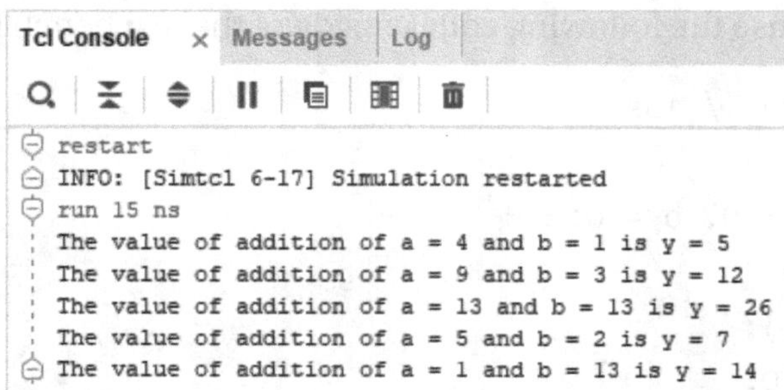

Figure 3-21. *The simulated waveforms on the wave window*

```
restart
INFO: [Simtcl 6-17] Simulation restarted
run 15 ns
The value of addition of a = 4 and b = 1 is y = 5
The value of addition of a = 9 and b = 3 is y = 12
The value of addition of a = 13 and b = 13 is y = 26
The value of addition of a = 5 and b = 2 is y = 7
The value of addition of a = 1 and b = 13 is y = 14
```

Figure 3-22. *The results of simulation on the Tcl Console*

Now, we use the following codes inside of the test bench file "tb.v":

```verilog
`timescale 1ns / 1ps
module tb();
reg [3:0] a = 0, b = 0;
wire [4:0] y;
top t1(a,b,y);
integer i = 0;
//$random, $urandom, $urandom_range
initial begin
for(i=0;i<5;i=i+1) begin
a = $urandom(2);
#1 b = $urandom();
```

```
#1 $display("The value of addition of a = %0d and b = %0d is
y = %0d",a,b,y);
end
end
endmodule
```

If we run the simulation the same as the previous procedures, we can view the simulated waveforms on the wave window and Tcl Console as illustrated in Figures 3-23 and 3-24, respectively.

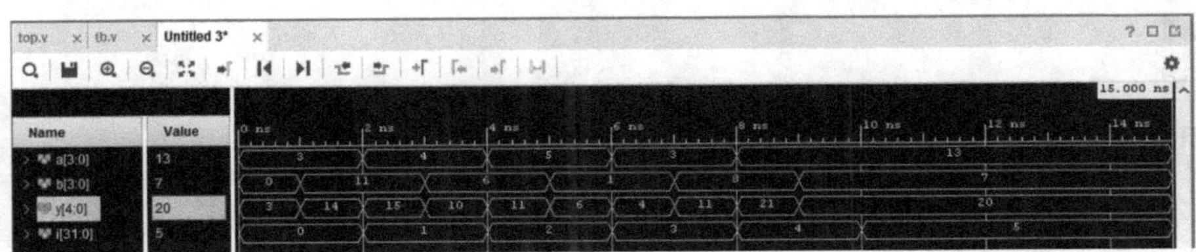

Figure 3-23. *The simulated waveforms on the wave window*

```
Tcl Console    Messages    Log
run 15 ns
The value of addition of a = 3 and b = 11 is y = 14
The value of addition of a = 4 and b = 6 is y = 10
The value of addition of a = 5 and b = 1 is y = 6
The value of addition of a = 3 and b = 8 is y = 11
The value of addition of a = 13 and b = 7 is y = 20
```

Figure 3-24. *The results of simulation on the Tcl Console*

Then, we use the following codes inside of the test bench file "tb.v":

```
`timescale 1ns / 1ps
module tb();
reg [3:0] a = 0, b = 0;
wire [4:0] y;
```

```
top t1(a,b,y);
integer i = 0;
//$random, $urandom, $urandom_range
initial begin
for(i=0;i<5;i=i+1) begin
a = $urandom_range(5,1);
b = $urandom_range(15,1);
$display("The value of addition of a = %0d and b = %0d is
y = %0d",a,b,y);
end
end
endmodule
```

If we run the simulation the same as the previous procedures, we can view the simulated waveforms on the wave window and Tcl Console as shown in Figures 3-25 and 3-26, respectively.

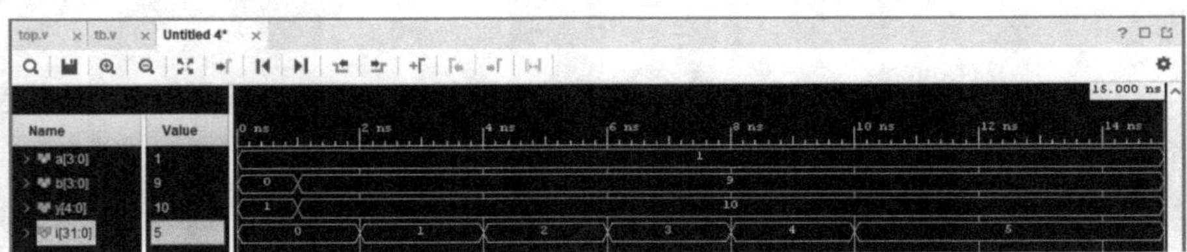

Figure 3-25. *The simulated waveforms on the wave window*

```
run 15 ns
The value of addition of a = 1 and b = 9 is y = 10
The value of addition of a = 1 and b = 9 is y = 10
The value of addition of a = 1 and b = 9 is y = 10
The value of addition of a = 1 and b = 9 is y = 10
The value of addition of a = 1 and b = 9 is y = 10
```

Figure 3-26. *The results of simulation on the Tcl Console*

As you can see in Figures 3-25 and 3-26, the random values for "a" and "b" are the same for five repeats. However, if we use the following codes instead of the previous similar code lines and run the simulation again, we can get the simulated waveforms on the wave window and Tcl Console as depicted in Figures 3-27 and 3-28, respectively:

```
#1 b = $urandom_range(15,1);
#1 $display("The value of addition of a = %0d and b = %0d is
y = %0d",a,b,y);
```

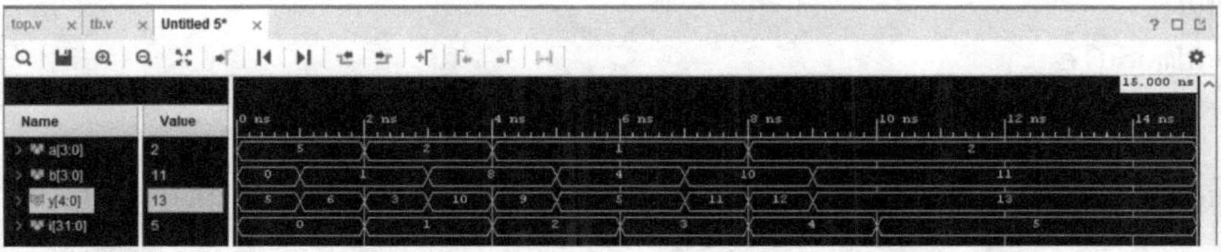

Figure 3-27. *The simulated waveforms on the wave window*

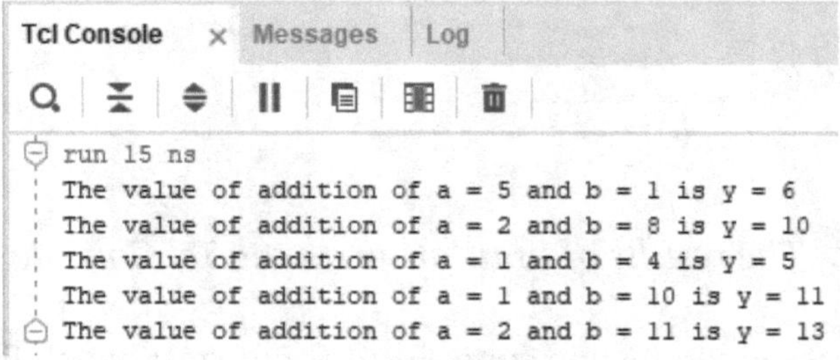

Figure 3-28. *The results of simulation on the Tcl Console*

The Repeat, For, and While Statements

We create a new project named "test_bench5" and also a simulation source file titled "tb.v" and then add the following codes inside of it:

```verilog
`timescale 1ns / 1ps
module tb();
reg [3:0] temp;
integer i = 0;
initial begin
repeat(4) begin
temp = $random;
#5 $display("Value of temp: %d",temp);
end
end
endmodule
```

If we run the simulation the same as the previous procedures, we can view the results on the Tcl Console as illustrated in Figure 3-29.

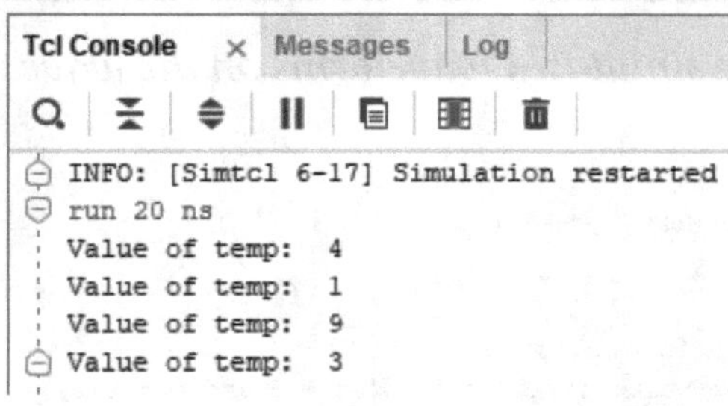

Figure 3-29. *The results of simulation on the Tcl Console*

Now, we use the following codes inside of the test bench file "tb.v":

```verilog
`timescale 1ns / 1ps
module tb();
reg [3:0] temp;
integer i = 0;
initial begin
for(i=0;i<4;i=i+1) begin
temp = $random;
```

```
#5 $display("Value of temp at index %0d: %0d",i,temp);
end
end
endmodule
```

If we run the simulation the same as the previous procedures, we can view the results on the Tcl Console as shown in Figure 3-30.

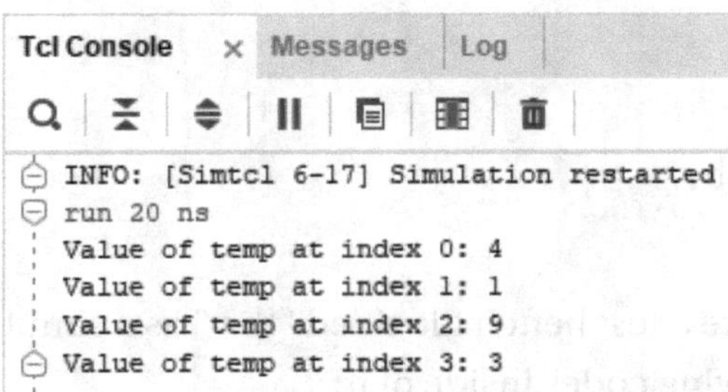

Figure 3-30. *The results of simulation on the Tcl Console*

Finally, we use the following codes inside of the test bench file "tb.v":

```
`timescale 1ns / 1ps
module tb();
reg [3:0] temp;
integer i = 0;
initial begin
while(i<4) begin
temp = $random;
#5 $display("Value of temp at index %0d: %0d",i,temp);
i = i + 1;
end
end
endmodule
```

If we run the simulation the same as the previous procedures, we can view the same results on the Tcl Console as demonstrated in Figure 3-30. Then, we create a new project named "test_bench6" and also a design source file titled "and2_1.v" and then add the following codes inside of it:

```verilog
`timescale 1ns / 1ps
module and2_1(
    input a,b,
    output c
    );
assign c = a & b;
endmodule
```

Now, we create a test bench file titled "tb.v" as a simulation source file and use the following codes inside of it:

```verilog
`timescale 1ns / 1ps
module tb();
reg a, b;
wire c;
//and2_1 a1(a,b,c);
and2_1 a1(.c(c),.b(b),.a(a));
initial begin
a = 0;
b = 0;
repeat(4) begin
a = $random;
b = $random;
#2 $display("a = %b, b = %b will result into c = %b",a,b,c);
end
end
endmodule
```

If we run the simulation the same as the previous procedures, we can view the results on the Tcl Console as depicted in Figure 3-31.

```
Tcl Console    ×   Messages    Log

restart
INFO: [Simtcl 6-17] Simulation restarted
run 20 ns
a = 0, b = 1 will result into c = 0
a = 1, b = 1 will result into c = 1
a = 1, b = 1 will result into c = 1
a = 1, b = 0 will result into c = 0
```

Figure 3-31. *The results of simulation on the Tcl Console*

A Test Bench for a 2 × 1 Multiplexer

We create a new project named "test_bench7" and also a design source file titled "mux_21.v" and then add the following codes inside of it:

```verilog
`timescale 1ns / 1ps
module mux_21(
input a,b,sel,
output y
    );
assign y = (sel == 1'b1) ? b: a;
endmodule
```

Now, we create a test bench file titled "tb.v" as a simulation source file and use the following codes inside of it:

```verilog
`timescale 1ns / 1ps
module tb();
reg a = 0, b = 0, sel = 0;
wire y;
mux_21 m1(a,b,sel,y);
```

```
always #5 a = ~a; //period = 10ns
always #10 b = ~b; //period = 20ns
always #20 sel = ~sel; //period = 40ns
endmodule
```

If we run the simulation the same as the previous procedures, we can view the simulated waveforms on the wave window as illustrated in Figure 3-32.

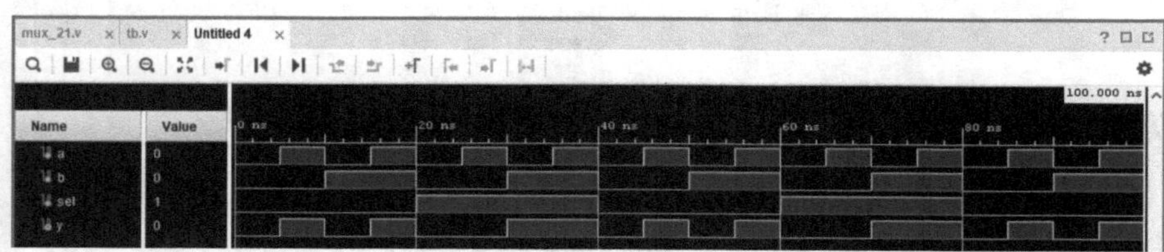

Figure 3-32. *The simulated waveforms on the wave window*

A 4-Bit Up Counter

We create a new project named "test_bench8" and also a design source file titled "counter.v" and then add the following codes inside of it:

```
`timescale 1ns / 1ps
module counter(
input clk, ld, ce,
input [3:0] loadin,
output [3:0] dout
    );
reg [3:0] temp = 0;
always@(posedge clk) begin
if (ld == 1'b1)
    temp <= loadin;
else
```

```verilog
    temp <= temp + 1;
end
assign dout = (ce == 1'b1) ? temp : 4'bzzzz;
endmodule
```

Now, we create a test bench file titled "tb.v" as a simulation source file and use the following codes inside of it:

```verilog
`timescale 1ns / 1ps
module tb();
reg clk = 0, ld = 0, ce = 0;
reg [3:0] loadin = 0;
wire [3:0] dout;
always #5 clk = ~clk;
counter c1(clk,ld,ce,loadin,dout);
initial begin
#1 ld = 1'b1;
loadin = 4'b0011;
#20 ld = 1'b0;
ce = 1'b1;
#100 ld = 1'b1;
loadin = 4'b0100;
ce = 1'b0;
#20 ld = 1'b0;
ce = 1'b1;
end
endmodule
```

If we run the simulation the same as the previous procedures, we can view the simulated waveforms on the wave window as illustrated in Figure 3-33.

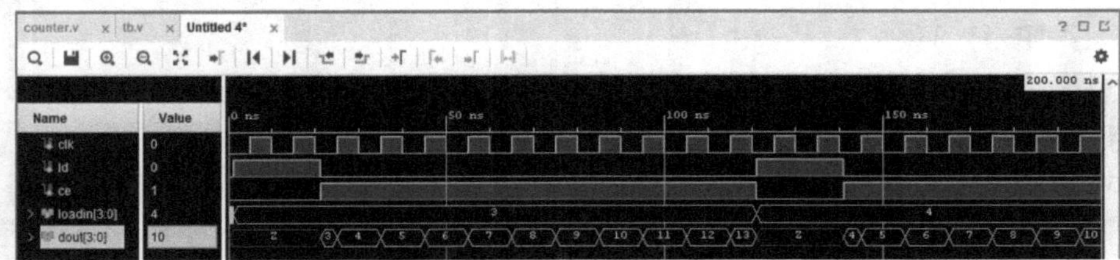

Figure 3-33. *The simulated waveforms on the wave window*

The Johnson and Ring Counters

We create a new project named "test_bench9" and also a design source
file for implementing the Johnson counter titled "jc.v" and then add the
following codes inside of it:

```verilog
`timescale 1ns / 1ps
module jc(
input clk,reset,
output [3:0] dout
    );
reg [3:0] temp;
integer i;
always@(posedge clk) begin
if (reset)
   temp = 4'b0000;
else begin
   temp[0] <= ~temp[3];
   for(i=0;i<3;i=i+1) begin
      temp[i+1] <= temp[i];
   end
end
end
assign dout = temp;
endmodule
```

Now, we create a test bench file titled "tb.v" as a simulation source file and use the following codes inside of it:

```verilog
`timescale 1ns / 1ps
module tb();
reg clk = 0 ,reset = 0;
wire [3:0] dout;
jc j1(clk,reset,dout);
always #5 clk = ~clk;
initial begin
reset = 1'b1;
#20 reset = 1'b0;
$monitor("The value of dout is : %b",dout);
    // we want to see every value and we do not want to truncate
        it to %0b
end
endmodule
```

If we run the simulation the same as the previous procedures, we can view the simulated waveforms on the wave window and Tcl Console as shown in Figures 3-34 and 3-35, respectively.

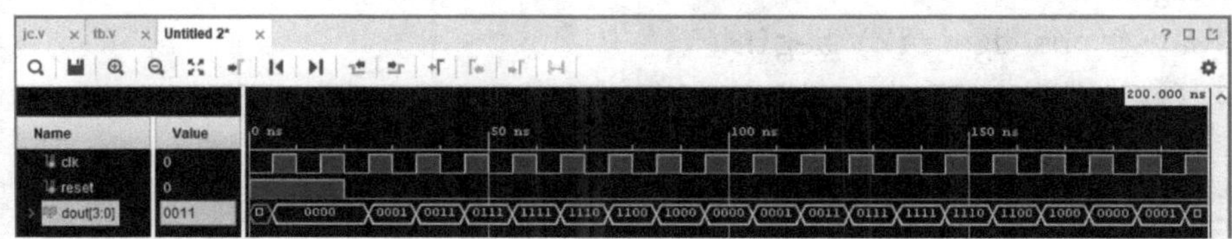

Figure 3-34. *The simulated waveforms on the wave window*

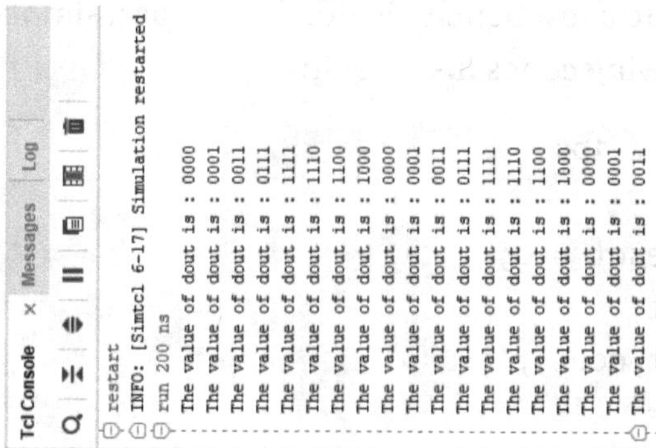

Figure 3-35. *The results of simulation on the Tcl Console*

Now, we create a design source file for implementing the ring counter titled "rc.v" and then add the following codes inside of it:

```verilog
`timescale 1ns / 1ps
module rc(
input clk,reset,
output [3:0] dout
    );
reg [3:0] temp;
integer i;
always@(posedge clk) begin
if (reset)
   temp = 4'b0001;
else begin
   temp[0] <= temp[3];
   for(i=0;i<3;i=i+1) begin
      temp[i+1] <= temp[i];
   end
end
end
assign dout = temp;
endmodule
```

Then, we create a test bench file titled "tb_rc.v" as a simulation source file and use the following codes inside of it:

```verilog
`timescale 1ns / 1ps
module tb_rc();
reg clk = 0 ,reset = 0;
wire [3:0] dout;
rc r1(clk,reset,dout);
always #5 clk = ~clk;
initial begin
reset = 1'b1;
#20 reset = 1'b0;
$monitor("The value of dout is : %b",dout);
    // we want to see every value and we do not want to truncate
        it to %0b
end
endmodule
```

If we run the simulation the same as the previous procedures, we can view the simulated waveforms on the wave window and Tcl Console as depicted in Figures 3-36 and 3-37, respectively.

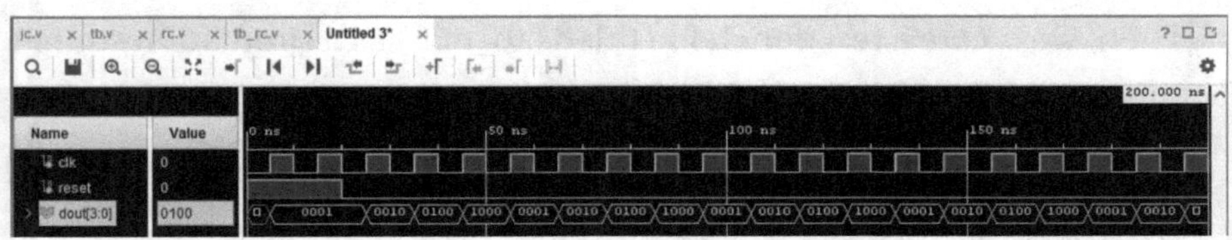

Figure 3-36. *The simulated waveforms on the wave window*

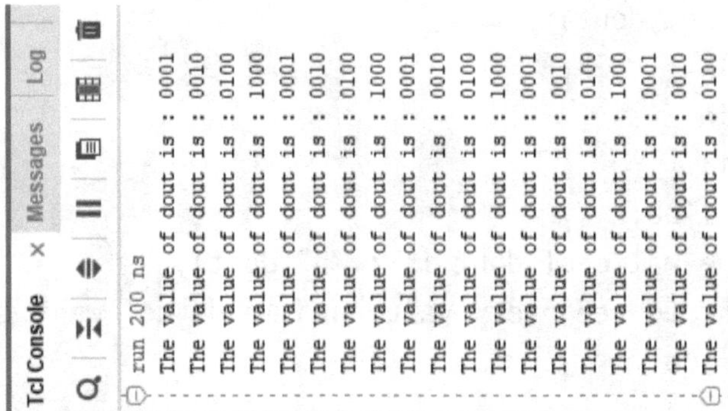

Figure 3-37. *The results of simulation on the Tcl Console*

CHAPTER 4

Implementations of Memory

In Chapter 3, we explored test bench development in Verilog, learning how to verify digital designs through simulation, automated stimulus generation, and response analysis. Building on these concepts, this chapter delves into memory implementation, a fundamental component in digital systems for data storage and retrieval.

This chapter begins with the design of a simple 16-byte memory, introducing basic memory addressing and read/write operations. We then examine Block RAM, a high-performance memory structure often used in FPGA designs for efficient storage. Finally, we apply memory concepts to practical signal generation by creating a sine wave using a ROM (Read-Only Memory), demonstrating how pre-stored data can produce analog-like waveforms in digital systems.

By the end of this chapter, you will understand key memory architectures in Verilog and how to integrate them into real-world applications, from data buffering to signal synthesis.

© Majid Pakdel 2026
M. Pakdel, *Mastering Verilog for FPGA Design*, Maker Innovations Series,
https://doi.org/10.1007/979-8-8688-2311-4_4

A Simple 16-Byte Memory

To start, we want to create a simple 16-byte memory and simulate it in
Vivado. So we create a new project named "memory" and also a design
source file titled "top.v" and then add the following codes inside of it:

```verilog
`timescale 1ns / 1ps
module top(
input wire clk,cs,
input wire [3:0] addr,
input wire we,
input wire [7:0] datain,
output reg [7:0] dataout
);
reg [7:0] mem [0:15];
always@(posedge clk) begin
if(cs) begin
   if(we)
      mem[addr] <= datain;
   else
      dataout <= mem[addr];
end
end
endmodule
```

Now, we create a test bench file titled "tb.v" as a simulation source file
and use the following codes inside of it:

```verilog
`timescale 1ns / 1ps
module tb();
reg clk, cs, we;
reg [5:0] addr;
reg [7:0] datain;
```

```verilog
wire [7:0] dataout;
integer i;
initial begin
clk = 0;
forever #5 clk = ~clk;
end
//tbram //t1(.clk(clk),.cs(cs),.we(we),.addr(addr),.
datain(datain),.dataout(dataout))//;
top t1(.clk(clk),.cs(cs),.we(we),.addr(addr),.datain(datain),.
dataout(dataout));
initial begin
cs = 0;
we = 0;
addr = 0;
datain = 0;
//initial step
#10 cs = 1'b1;
for(i=0;i<6;i=i+1) begin
@(posedge clk);
write();
end
for(i=0;i<6;i=i+1) begin
@(posedge clk);
read();
end
end
task read;
begin
we = 1'b0;
addr = addr - 1;
end
```

```
endtask
task write;
begin
we = 1'b1;
addr = addr + 1;
datain = $random;
end
endtask
endmodule
```

Now, we click the Run Synthesis option, and the synthesis is completed successfully as shown in Figure 4-1.

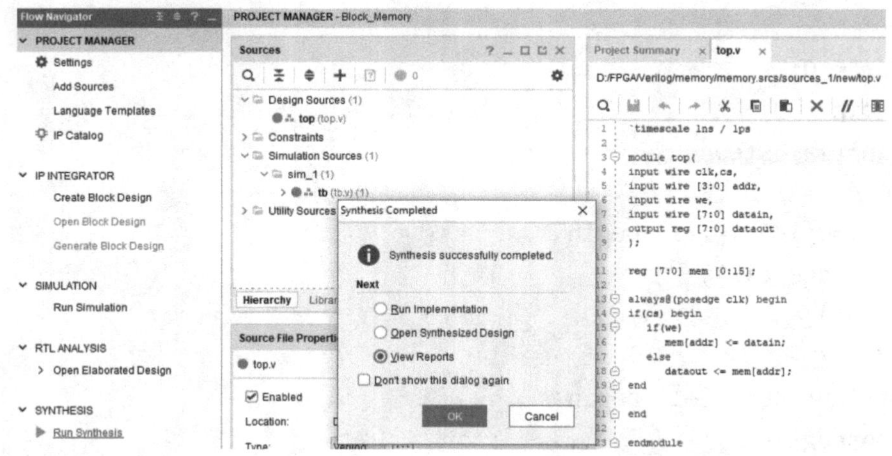

Figure 4-1. *The successful completed synthesis*

In the reports of synthesis analysis, we select the synth_1_synth_report_utilization_0 option, and as you can see in Figure 4-2, LUT as Distributed RAM has been used in this program.

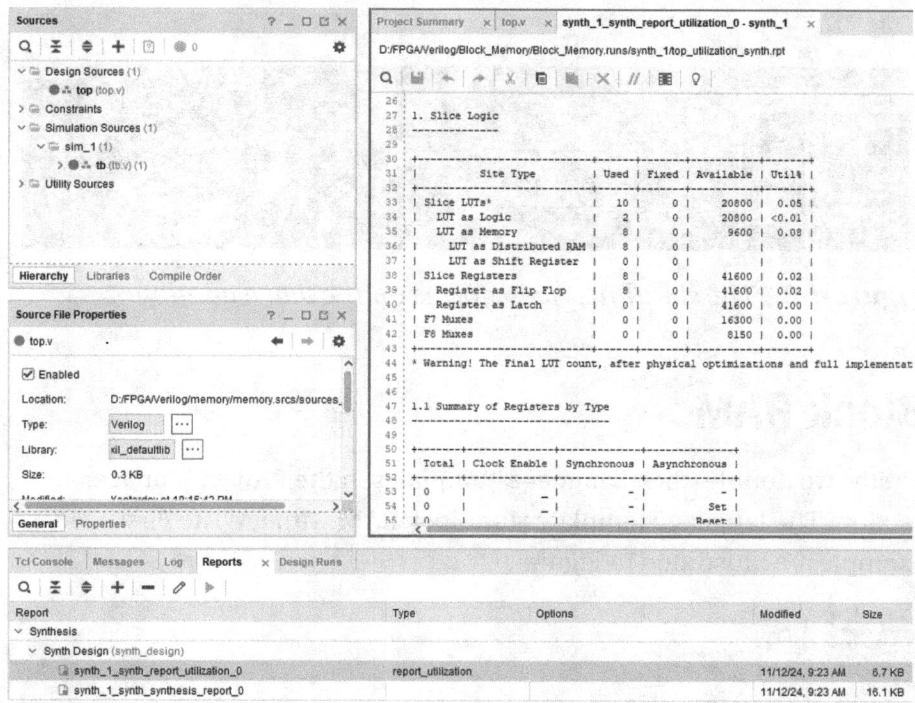

Figure 4-2. *The synthesis report utilization*

We choose Flow ➤ Run Simulation ➤ Run Behavioral Simulation from the menu toolbar to view the waveforms on the wave window. So, in the opened simulation window, we click the Restart button, then click the Run for 150ns button, and finally click the Zoom Fit button. Also we right-click the datain[7:0] and dataout[7:0] and select the Radix option as Unsigned Decimal, so we can view the waveforms as depicted in Figure 4-3.

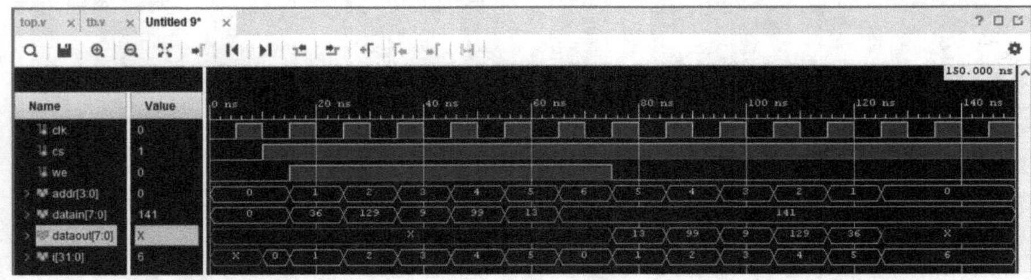

Figure 4-3. *The simulated waveforms on the wave window*

Block RAM

Firstly, we double-click Language Templates in the Project Manager section. The language templates for Block RAM with a Write First Mode example are illustrated in Figure 4-4.

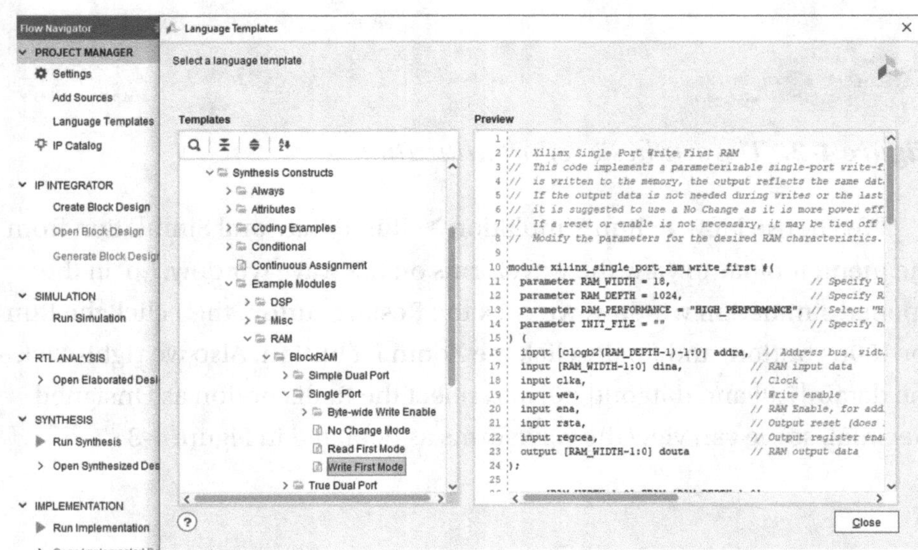

Figure 4-4. *The language templates for Block RAM (Write First Mode)*

Now, in the Project Manager section, we double-click the IP Catalog option and enter "bram" in the search area and choose the Block Memory Generator option as shown in Figure 4-5.

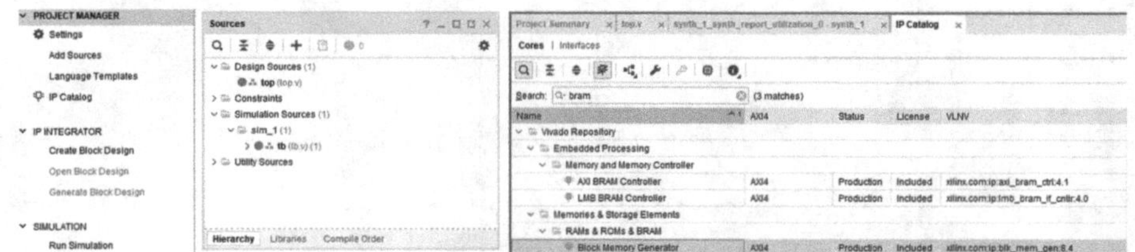

Figure 4-5. *Choosing the Block Memory Generator option*

In the Basic tab of the Customize IP window, we set the parameters as depicted in Figure 4-6.

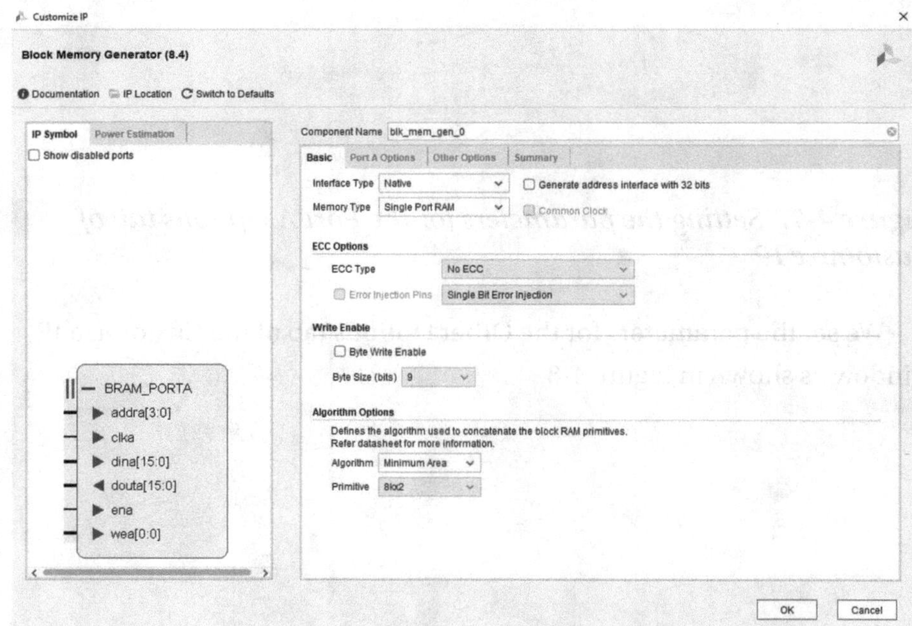

Figure 4-6. *Setting the parameters for the Basic tab of the Customize IP window*

We also set the parameters for the Port A Options tab of the Customize IP window as illustrated in Figure 4-7.

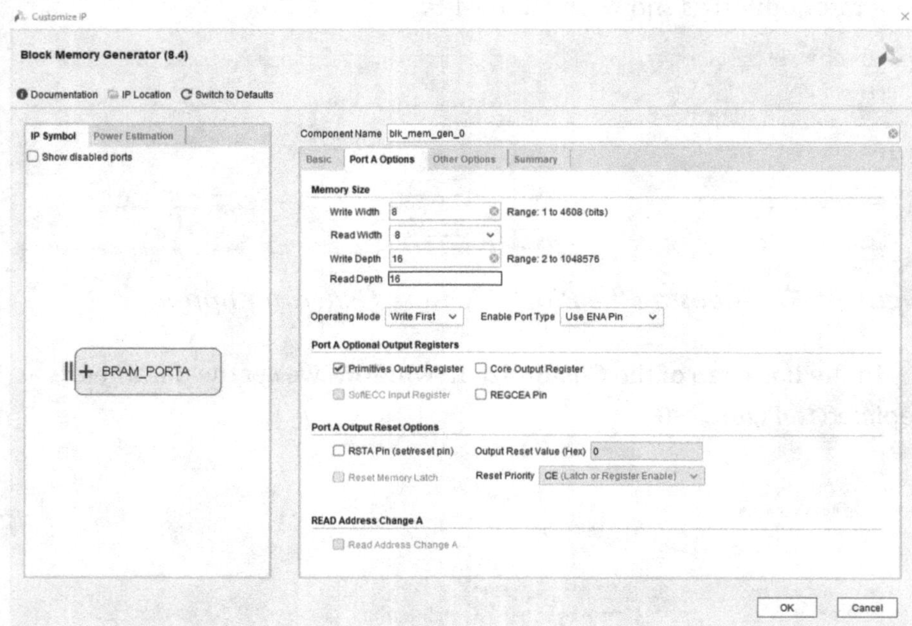

Figure 4-7. *Setting the parameters for the Port A Options tab of Customize IP*

We set the parameters for the Other Options tab of the Customize IP window as shown in Figure 4-8.

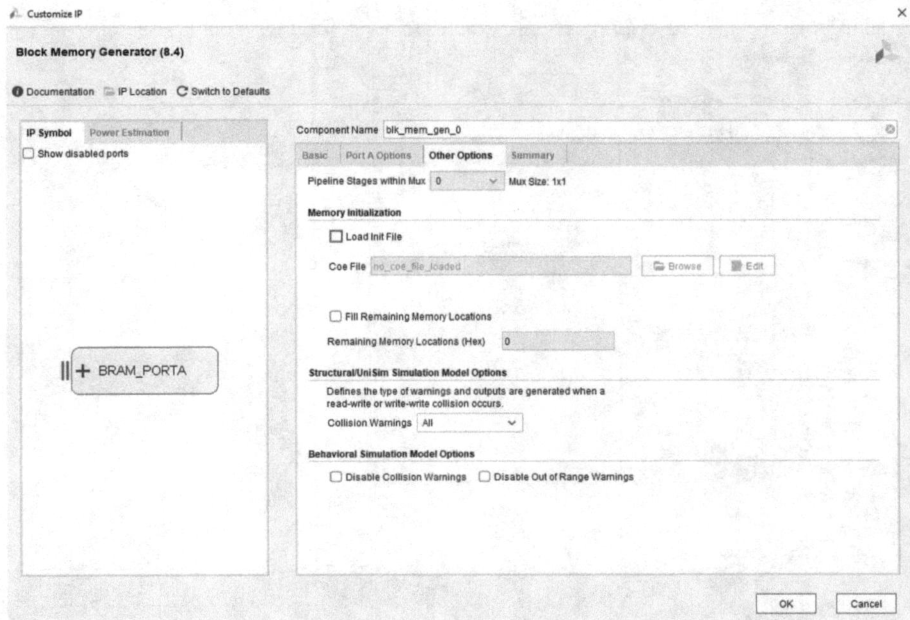

Figure 4-8. *Setting the parameters for the Other Options tab of the Customize IP window*

We also set the parameters for the Summary tab of the Customize IP window as depicted in Figure 4-9.

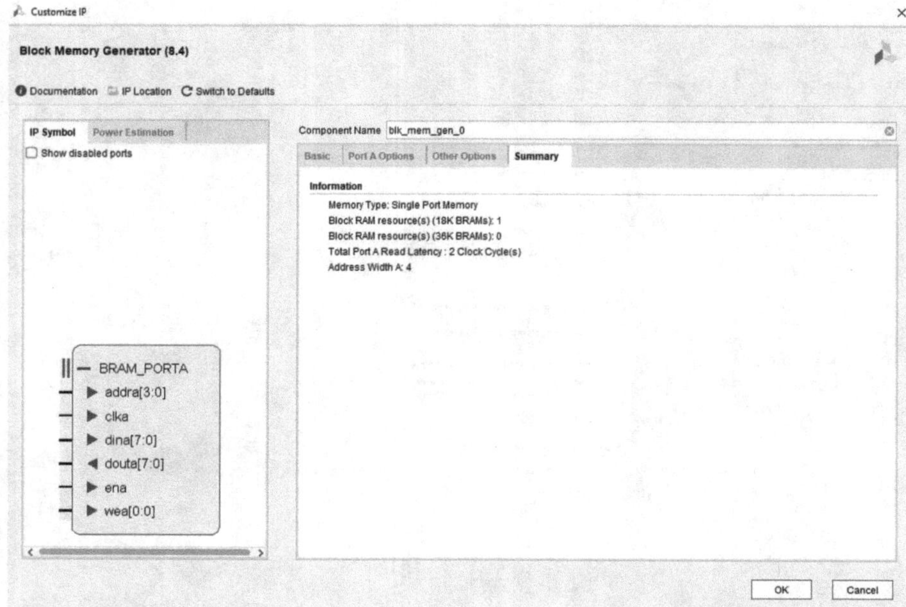

Figure 4-9. *Setting the parameters for the Summary tab of the Customize IP window*

After clicking the OK button, the Generate Output Products window pops up, and then we click the Generate button as illustrated in Figure 4-10.

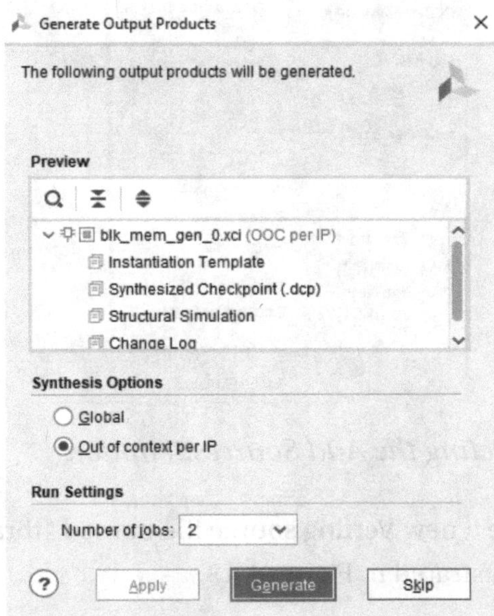

Figure 4-10. *Clicking the Generate button*

The generated block memory VHDL file (blk_mem_gen_0.vhd) is shown in Figure 4-11.

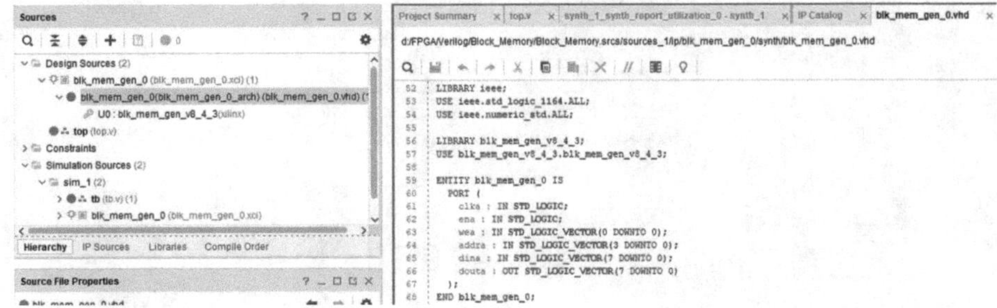

Figure 4-11. *The generated block memory VHDL file*

Now, we right-click the Design Sources folder and select the Add Sources... option as depicted in Figure 4-12.

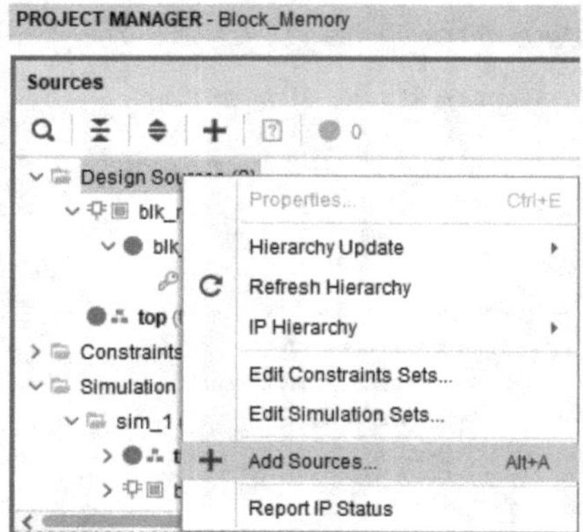

Figure 4-12. *Selecting the Add Sources... option*

Then, we create a new Verilog source file named "tbram" and click the Finish button as illustrated in Figure 4-13.

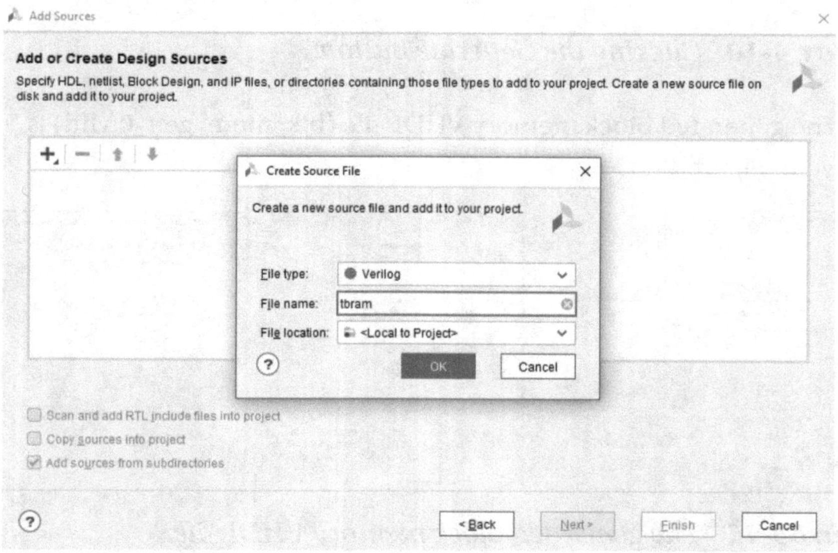

Figure 4-13. *Creating a new Verilog source file named "tbram"*

Now, we add the following codes inside of the Verilog file "tbram":

```verilog
`timescale 1ns / 1ps
module tbram(
input clk,cs,
input [3:0] addr,
input we,
input [7:0] datain,
output [7:0] dataout
    );
blk_mem_gen_0 b1(.clka(clk),.ena(cs),.wea(we),.addra(addr),.
dina(datain),.douta(dataout));
/*
ENTITY blk_mem_gen_0 IS
  PORT (
    clka : IN STD_LOGIC;
    ena : IN STD_LOGIC;
    wea : IN STD_LOGIC_VECTOR(0 DOWNTO 0);
    addra : IN STD_LOGIC_VECTOR(3 DOWNTO 0);
    dina : IN STD_LOGIC_VECTOR(7 DOWNTO 0);
    douta : OUT STD_LOGIC_VECTOR(7 DOWNTO 0)
  );
END blk_mem_gen_0;
*/
Endmodule
```

We double-click the Run Synthesis option, and the synthesis is successfully completed. Then we choose the View Reports option as shown in Figure 4-14.

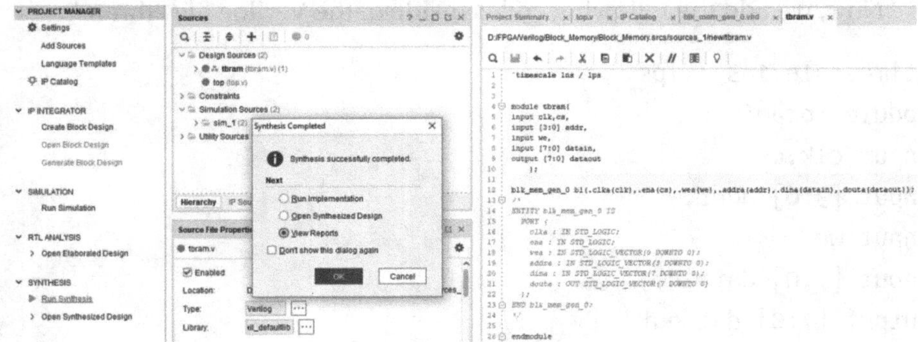

Figure 4-14. *The successful completed synthesis*

By clicking the synth_1_synth_report_utilization_0 option in the Reports tab, we can view the block memory utilization report as shown in Figure 4-15.

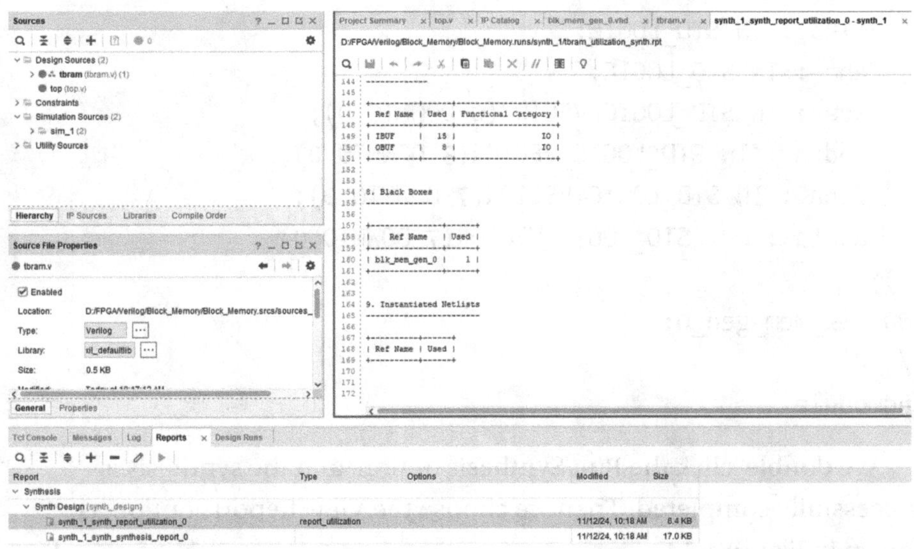

Figure 4-15. *The block memory utilization report*

Finally, we select Flow ➤ Run Simulation ➤ Run Behavioral Simulation from the menu toolbar to view the waveforms on the wave window. So, in the opened simulation window, we click the Restart button, then click the Run for 150ns button, and finally click the Zoom Fit button. Also we right-click the datain[7:0] and dataout[7:0] and select the Radix option as Unsigned Decimal, so we can view the waveforms as depicted in Figure 4-16, which are similar to the waveforms in Figure 4-3.

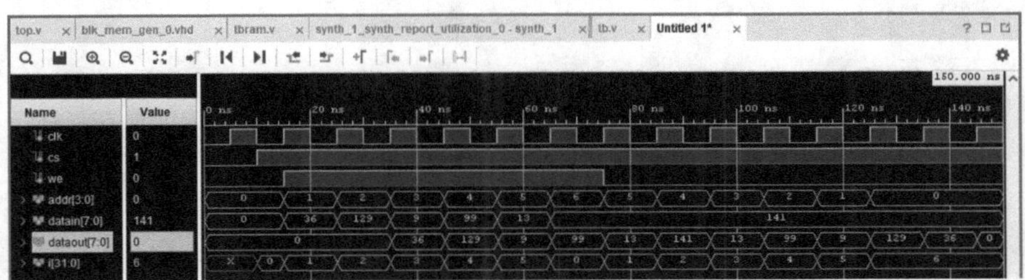

Figure 4-16. *The simulated waveforms on the wave window*

Creating a Sine Wave with a ROM

We create a new project named "ROM_Sine" and then double-click the Create Block Design option to create a block design titled "design_1" as illustrated in Figure 4-17.

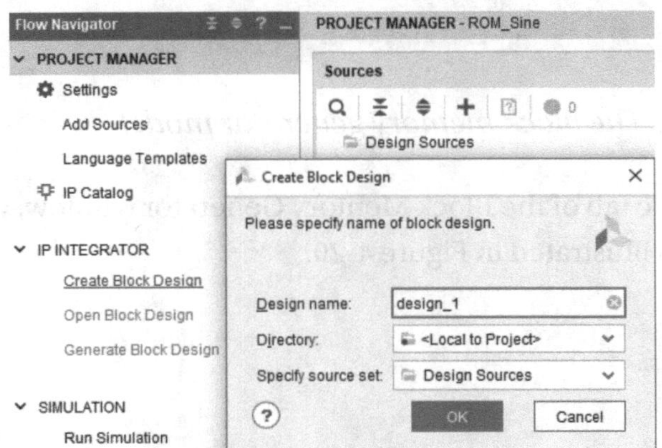

Figure 4-17. *Creating a block design titled "design_1"*

In the Diagram window, we click the add (+) button and enter "block" in the search area to select the Block Memory Generator option as shown in Figure 4-18. The block memory generator model is depicted in Figure 4-19.

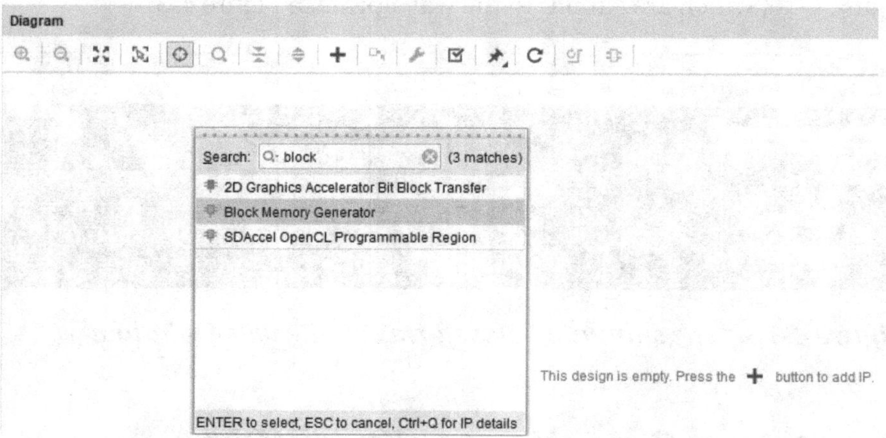

Figure 4-18. *Selecting the Block Memory Generator option*

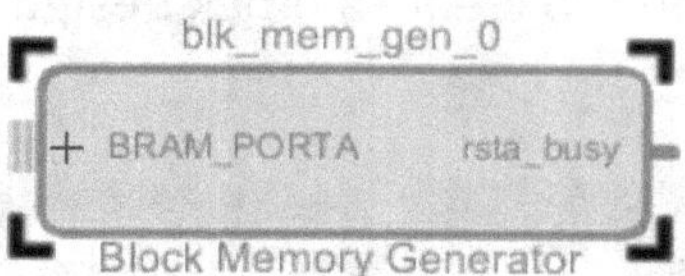

Figure 4-19. *The block memory generator model*

In the Basic tab of the Block Memory Generator window, we set the parameters as illustrated in Figure 4-20.

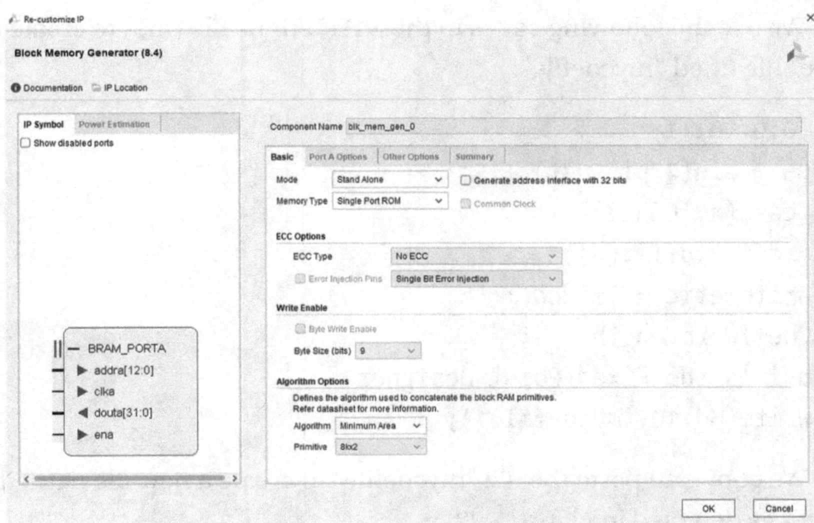

Figure 4-20. *The Basic tab of Block Memory Generator*

Also, in the Port A Options tab, we set the parameters as shown in Figure 4-21.

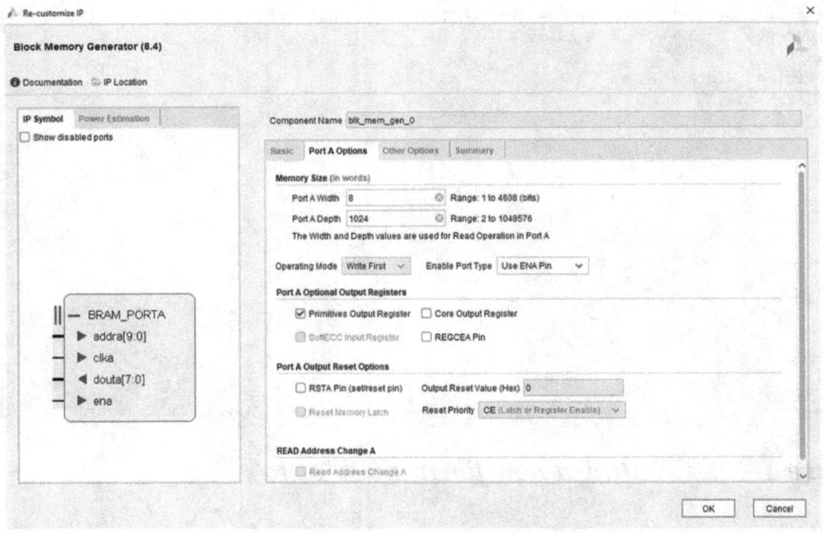

Figure 4-21. *Setting the parameters in the Port A Options tab*

We use the following codes in the MATLAB m-file (m1) to create the "coe" file titled "mycoefile":

```
t = 0:0.001:1;
x = 5 * sin(2*pi*50*t) + 5;
y = cast(x,'uint8');
Hd = dfilt.dffir(y);
Hd.arithmetic = 'fixed';
Hd.CoeffWordLength = 8;
%Requires the Fixed-Point Designer
coewrite(Hd,10,'mycoefile');
```

We copy and paste the file "mycoefile" to create a new file named "data" as depicted in Figure 4-22.

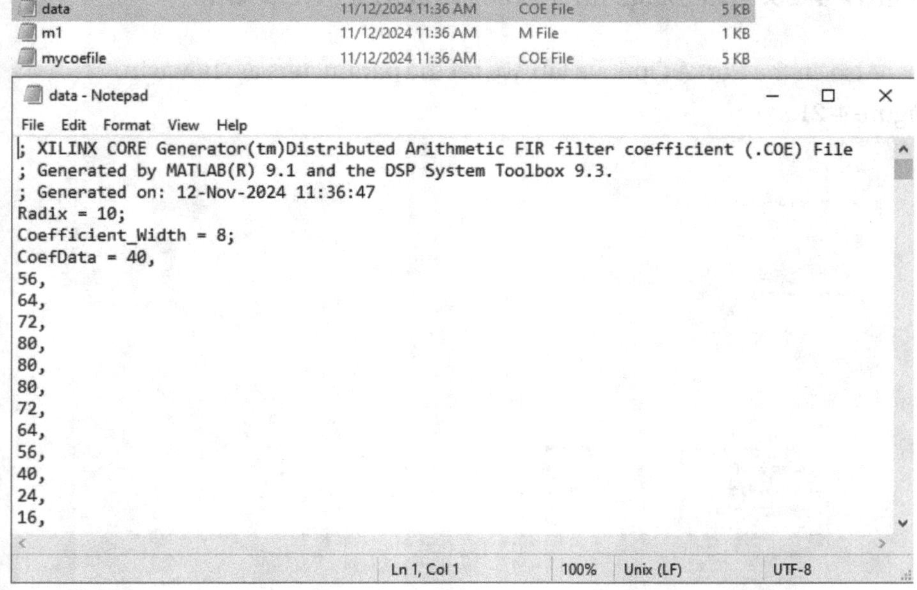

Figure 4-22. Creating a new file named "data"

In the Other Options tab of the Block Memory Generator window, we check Load Init File and click the Browse button to select the generated file "mycoefile.coe" as illustrated in Figure 4-23.

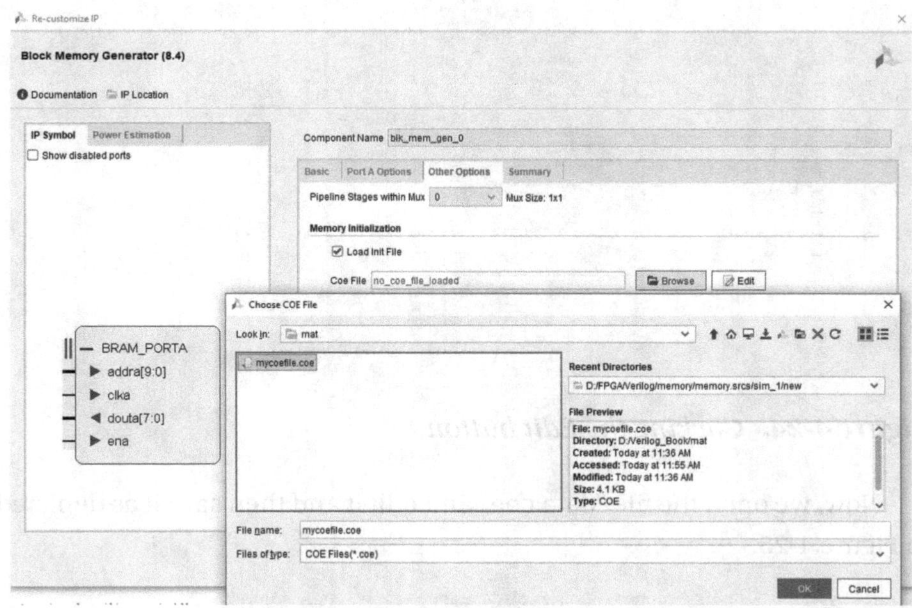

Figure 4-23. *Selecting the generated file "mycoefile.coe"*

In the "Coe File" section of the Other Options tab, we click the Edit button to see the keys as shown in Figure 4-24.

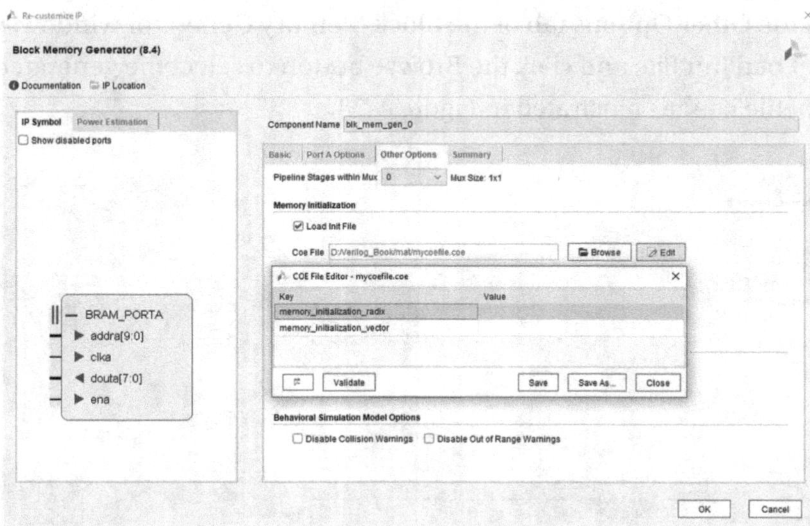

Figure 4-24. *Clicking the Edit button*

Now, we open the file "data.coe" and edit it and then save it as depicted in Figure 4-25.

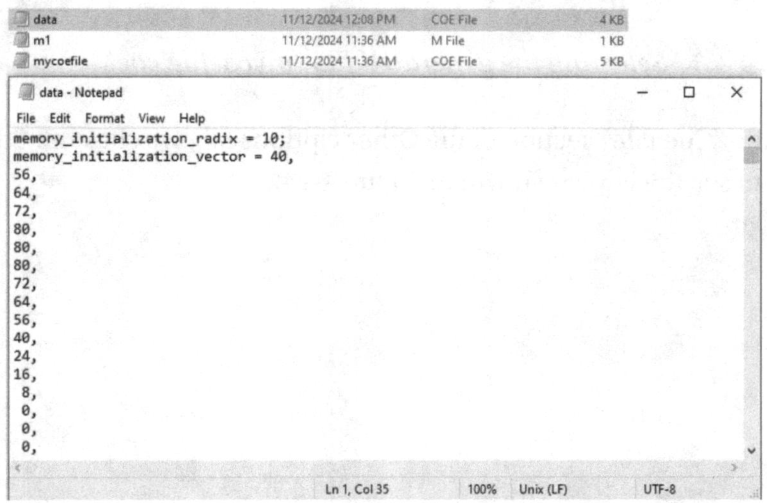

Figure 4-25. *Editing the file "data.coe"*

Now, we browse it as the "Coe File" and then click the Edit button and click the Validate button in the opened COE File Editor window, and the validation is successful as illustrated in Figure 4-26.

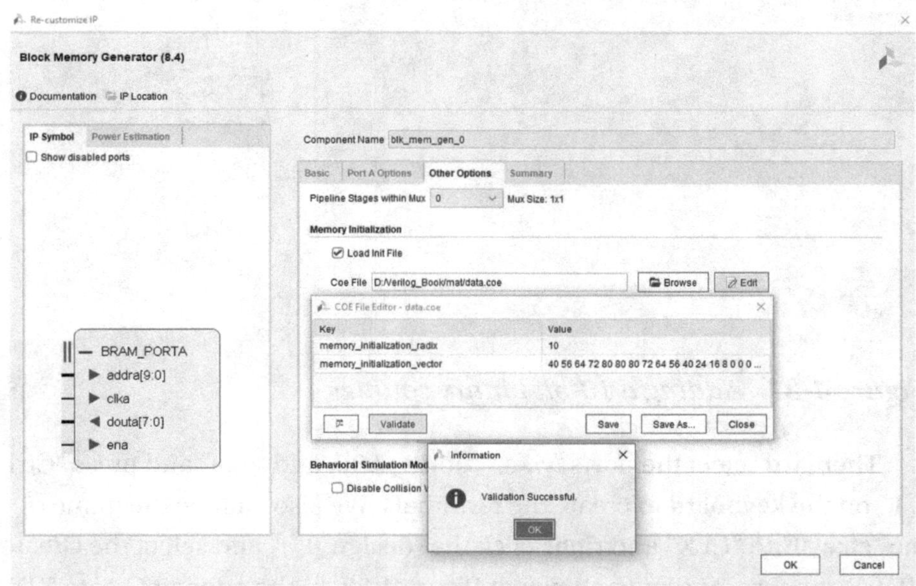

Figure 4-26. *The successful validation of COE file "data.coe"*

We also add a 10-bit binary up counter (with output width of 10) as shown in Figure 4-27.

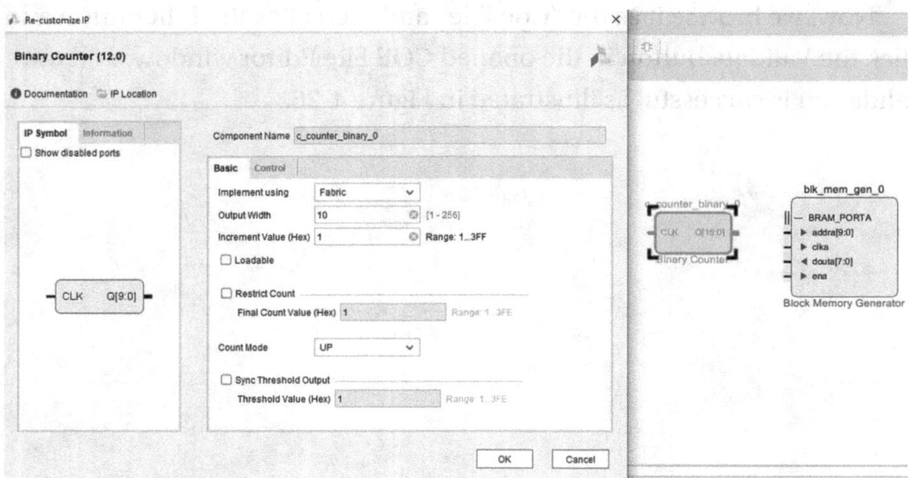

Figure 4-27. *Adding a 10-bit binary counter*

Then, we select the ports "clka," "douta[7:0]," and "ena" and press "Ctrl
+ T" on the keyboard to create the terminals. We also change the name of
the "clka_0" to "CLK" and right-click the "design_1_i" and select the Create
HDL Wrapper... option as shown in Figure 4-28. In the opened Create HDL
Wrapper window, we select the "Let Vivado manage wrapper and auto-
update" option as depicted in Figure 4-29.

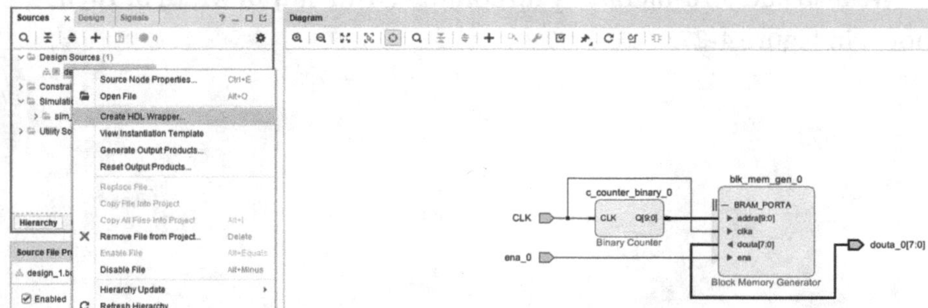

Figure 4-28. *The created block diagram*

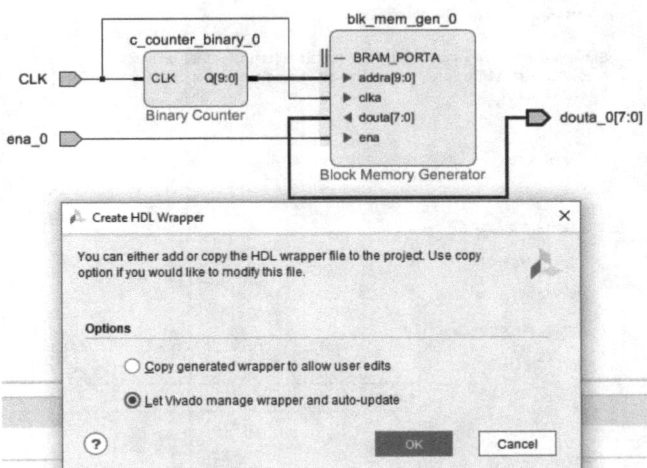

Figure 4-29. *Selecting the "Let Vivado manage wrapper and auto-update" option*

So the Verilog file "design_1_wrapper.v" is now created. Finally, we select Flow ➤ Run Simulation ➤ Run Behavioral Simulation from the menu toolbar to view the waveforms on the wave window. So, in the opened simulation window, we click the Restart button and then right-click the signal "CLK" and set the force clock parameters as illustrated in Figure 4-30.

Figure 4-30. *Setting the force clock parameters for signal "CLK"*

We also right-click the signal "ena_0" and set its force constant value to 1 as shown in Figure 4-31.

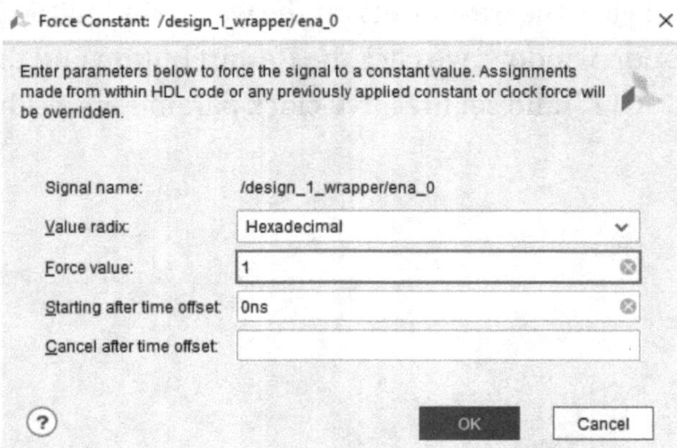

Figure 4-31. *Setting the force constant value of signal "ena_0" to 1*

Now, we click the Run for 300ns button and then click the Zoom Fit button on the wave window. Then, we right-click the signal "douta_0[7:0]" and set Waveform Style as Analog as depicted in Figure 4-32. The analog waveform of sine signal "dout_0[7:0]" is illustrated in Figure 4-33.

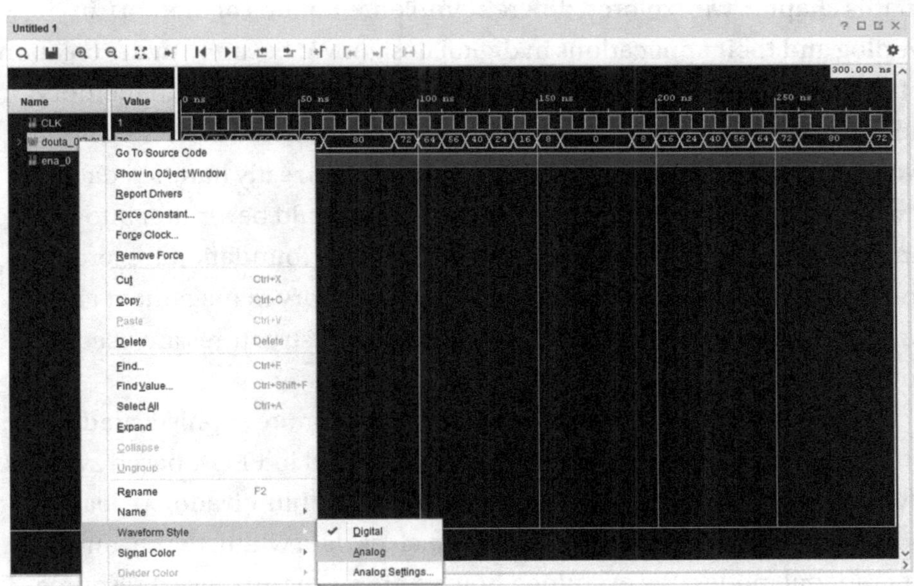

Figure 4-32. *Setting Waveform Style of signal "douta_0" as Analog*

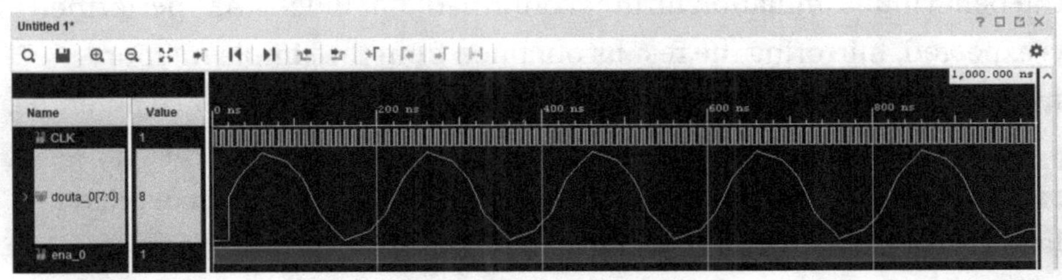

Figure 4-33. *The simulated waveforms on the wave window*

Summary and Key Takeaways

In this chapter, we explored different implementations of memory in Verilog and their applications in digital design. We began with the creation of a simple 16-byte memory, gaining practical experience with memory addressing, read and write operations, and simulation in Vivado. Through waveform analysis, we verified that our design correctly handled data storage and retrieval, demonstrating how data could be written into and read from memory locations effectively. This foundational exercise introduced the essential concepts of digital memory management and provided a basis for understanding how memory structures are used in more advanced designs.

Next, we moved on to Block RAM (BRAM), a more sophisticated and efficient memory structure that is commonly used in FPGA-based systems. By employing the Block Memory Generator IP within Vivado, we learned how to configure memory parameters such as data width, depth, and operational modes. We examined how synthesis reports reveal resource utilization, including LUTs and dedicated memory blocks, highlighting the optimization advantages of using BRAM over distributed memory. The behavioral simulation further confirmed that Block RAM performed as expected, mirroring the results obtained from the simple memory implementation but with improved scalability and performance potential.

Finally, we applied these memory concepts to a practical design example by creating a sine wave using a ROM. By generating coefficient data with MATLAB and exporting it as a COE file, we were able to initialize the ROM with precomputed sine values. Integrating a binary counter as an address generator allowed the ROM to sequentially output the sine wave data, effectively producing an analog-like waveform in a digital simulation environment. This exercise demonstrated how ROM-based data storage can be used for signal synthesis, waveform generation, and other applications in digital signal processing.

By now you have gained a clear understanding of memory architectures in Verilog, from simple register arrays to IP-based block memory and ROM applications. You have also developed the skills to integrate these memory components into complete digital systems, verify their functionality, and interpret synthesis reports to evaluate hardware utilization.

In the next chapter, we will move beyond memory design to explore gate, switch, and structural modeling in Verilog. You will learn how to describe circuits using logic gates, transistor-level modeling, and hierarchical structural representations—essential techniques for understanding how complex digital systems are built from fundamental hardware components.

CHAPTER 5

Gate, Switch, and Structural Modeling

In Chapter 4, we explored memory implementations, focusing on storage elements like RAM and ROM, which form the backbone of data retention in digital systems. Now, in this chapter, we shift our focus to low-level hardware modeling in Verilog, examining how digital circuits can be described at different abstraction levels—gate, switch, and structural—for finer control over design implementation.

This chapter begins with gate-level modeling, where we construct circuits using predefined logic gates (AND, OR, NOT, etc.), closely resembling physical hardware interconnections. Next, we delve into switch-level modeling, an even lower-level abstraction that models transistors as switches, useful for custom cell design and analog–digital mixed simulations. We then explore structural modeling, which emphasizes hierarchical design by interconnecting modules, promoting reusability and modularity. Finally, we introduce two powerful Verilog constructs—parameterized designs for configurable modules and functions for reusable procedural blocks—to enhance design flexibility and efficiency.

By the end of this chapter, you will be able to model digital circuits at multiple abstraction levels, from high-level behavioral descriptions down to gate and transistor representations while leveraging structural techniques for scalable and maintainable designs.

© Majid Pakdel 2026

M. Pakdel, *Mastering Verilog for FPGA Design*, Maker Innovations Series, https://doi.org/10.1007/979-8-8688-2311-4_5

The Gate-Level Modeling

To start, we want to create a new project named "Half_Adder" and also a design source file titled "halfadder.v" and then add the following codes inside of it:

```verilog
`timescale 1ns / 1ps
module halfadder(
input a,b,
output sum, carry
    );
xor x1(sum,a,b);
and a1(carry,a,b);
endmodule
```

We select Flow ➤ Run Simulation ➤ Run Behavioral Simulation from the menu toolbar to view the waveforms on the wave window. So, in the opened simulation window, we click the Restart button and then right-click the signal "a" and set the force clock parameters as shown in Figure 5-1.

Figure 5-1. *Setting the force clock parameters for signal "a"*

We also right-click the signal "b" and set the force clock parameters as depicted in Figure 5-2.

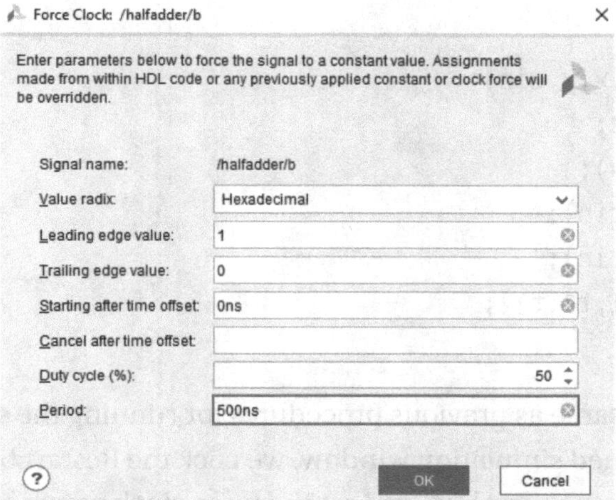

Figure 5-2. *Setting the force clock parameters for signal "b"*

Now, we click the Run for 1μs button and then the Zoom Fit button to view the simulated waveforms on the wave window as illustrated in Figure 5-3.

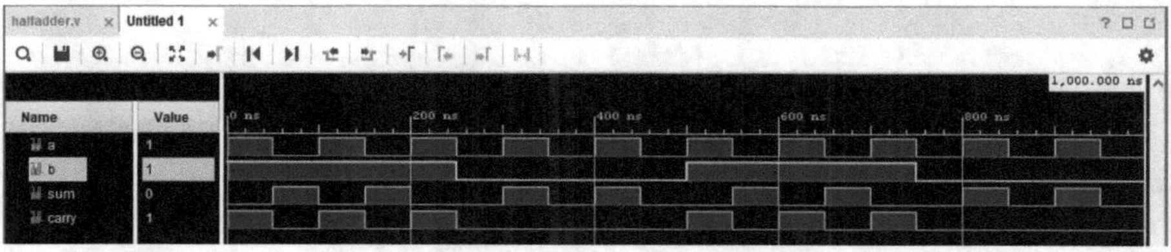

Figure 5-3. *The simulated waveforms on the wave window*

We want to create another project named "Full_Adder" and also a design source file titled "fulladder.v" and then add the following codes inside of it:

```
`timescale 1ns / 1ps
```

```
module fulladder(
input x,y,cin,
output s,cout
    );
    xor x1(s,x,y,cin);
wire t1,t2,t3;
and a1(t1,x,y);
and a2(t2,x,cin);
and a3(t3,y,cin);
or o1(cout,t1,t2,t3);
endmodule
```

We do the same as previous procedures for running the simulation, and in the opened simulation window, we click the Restart button and then right-click the signal "x" and set the force clock parameters as shown in Figure 5-4. We also right-click the signal "y" and set the force clock parameters as depicted in Figure 5-5.

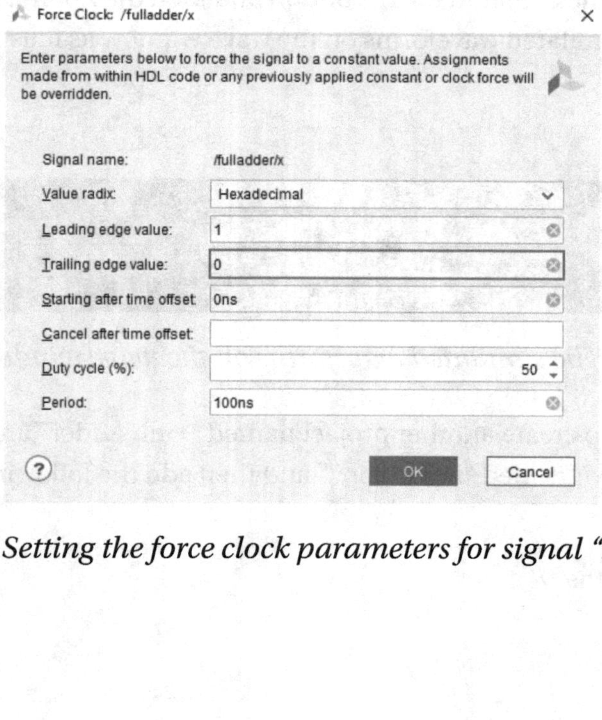

Figure 5-4. *Setting the force clock parameters for signal "x"*

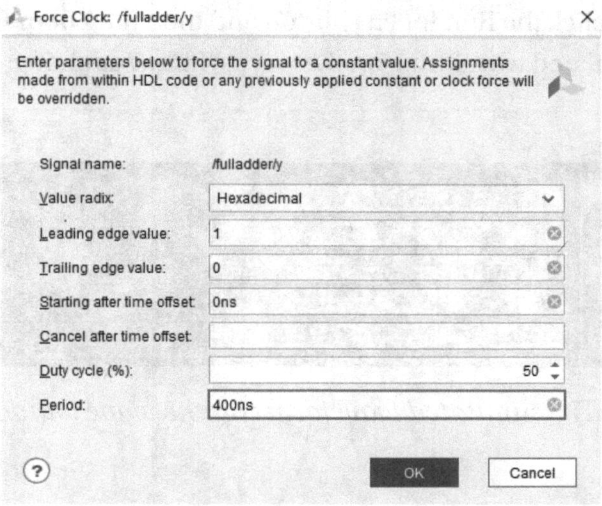

Figure 5-5. *Setting the force clock parameters for signal "y"*

Then, we right-click the signal "cin" and set the force clock parameters as illustrated in Figure 5-6.

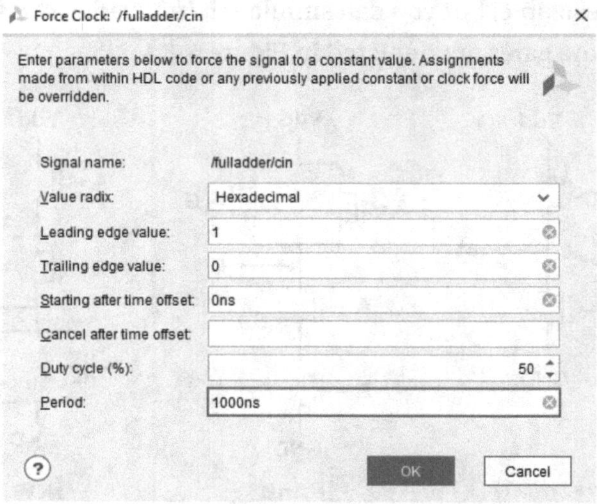

Figure 5-6. *Setting the force clock parameters for signal "cin"*

Now, we click the Run for 2µs button and then the Zoom Fit button to view the simulated waveforms on the wave window as shown in Figure 5-7.

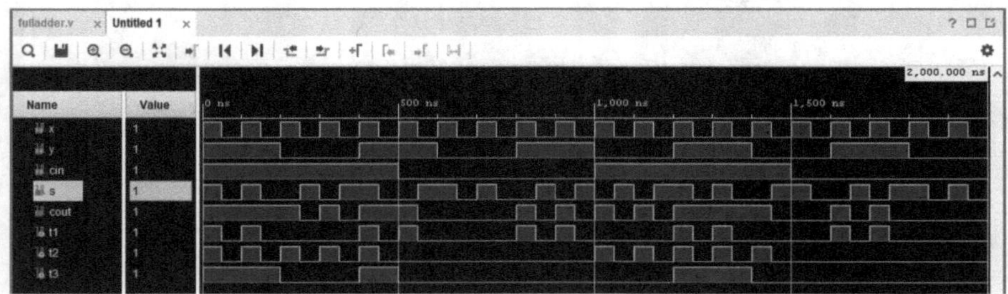

Figure 5-7. *The simulated waveforms on the wave window*

The Switch-Level Modeling

We use switch-level modeling when we can replace the system with switches. It is rarely used with Vivado since we usually prefer backend VLSI software like Cadence if we really wish to design at the switch level. Also, it is not synthesizable, but you can simulate it in Vivado. The switch-level models for some gates are depicted in Figure 5-8.

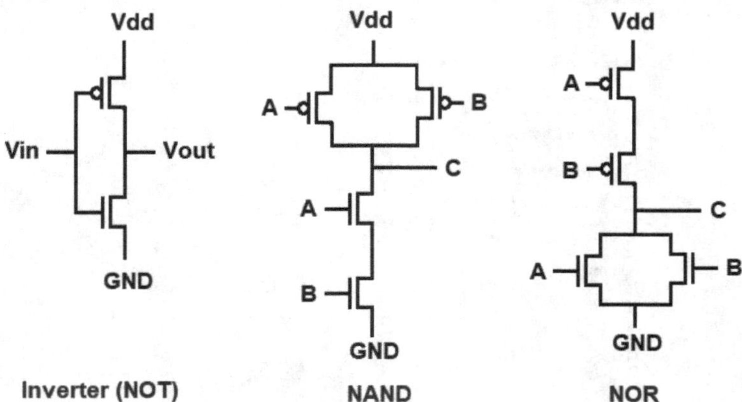

Figure 5-8. *The switch-level models for some gates*

The implementation commands for switch-level modeling are illustrated in Figure 5-9.

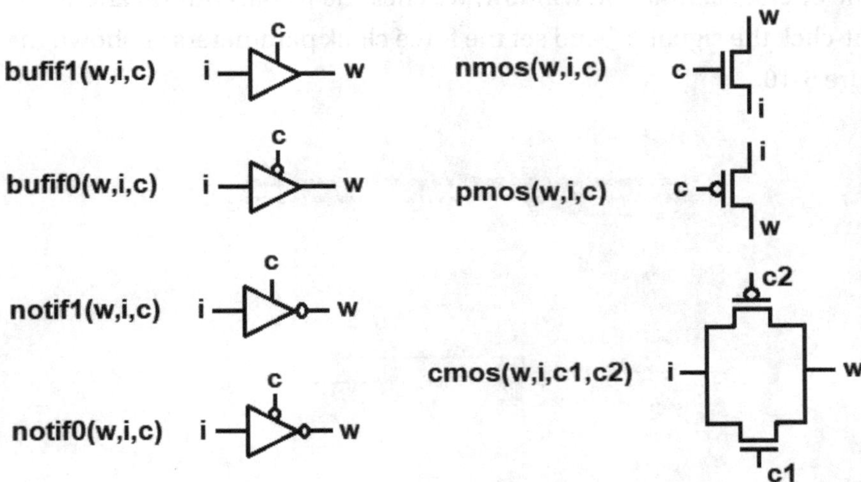

Figure 5-9. *The implementation commands for switch-level modeling*

We create a new project named "Inverter_Switch" and also a design source file titled "inv.v" and then add the following codes inside of it:

```
`timescale 1ns / 1ps
module inv(
input a,
output y
    );
supply1 vdd;
supply0 gnd;
pmos p1(y,vdd,a);
nmos n1(y,gnd,a);
endmodule
```

We choose Flow ➤ Run Simulation ➤ Run Behavioral Simulation from the menu toolbar to view the waveforms on the wave window. So, in the opened simulation window, we click the Restart button and then right-click the signal "a" and set the force clock parameters as shown in Figure 5-10.

Figure 5-10. *Setting the force clock parameters for signal "a"*

Now, we click the Run for 1µs button and then the Zoom Fit button to view the simulated waveforms on the wave window as shown in Figure 5-11.

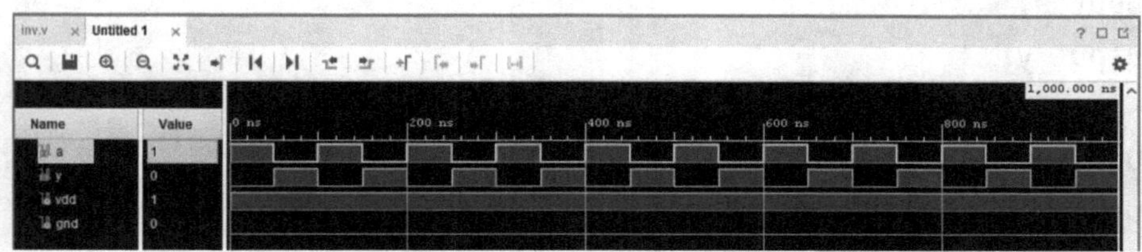

Figure 5-11. *The simulated waveforms on the wave window*

If we double-click the Run Synthesis option to run the synthesis, we can view that the synthesis failed since the command "pmos" is not supported as depicted in Figures 5-12 and 5-13, respectively.

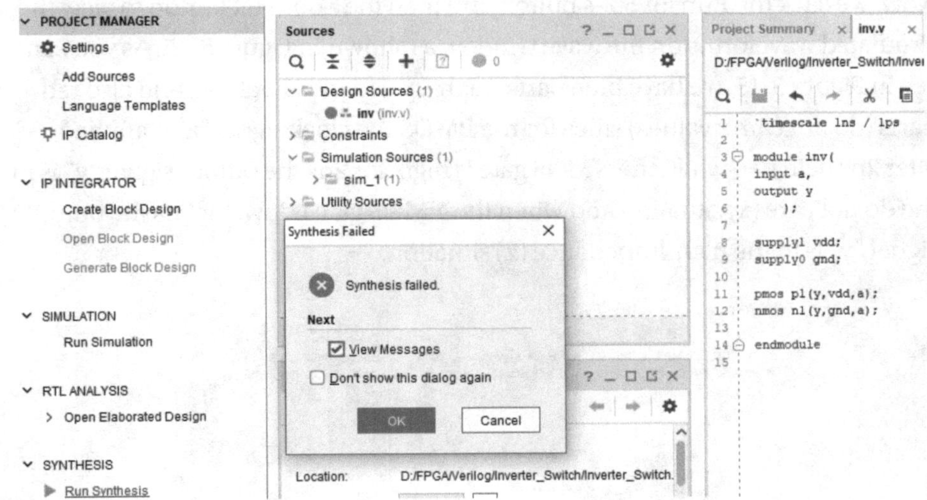

Figure 5-12. *The failed synthesis*

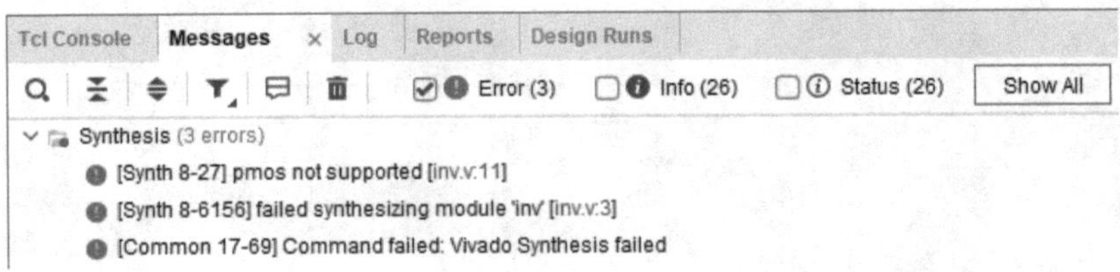

Figure 5-13. *The failed synthesis messages*

Now, we add a delay of 2ns in the command "pmos" line, and the code is changed as below:

```
pmos #2 p1(y,vdd,a);
```

We do the same as previous procedures for running the simulation, and in the opened simulation window, we click the Restart button and then right-click the signal "a" and set the force clock parameters as illustrated in Figure 5-14. Now, we click the Run for 50ns button and then the Zoom Fit button to view the simulated waveforms on the wave window as shown in Figure 5-15. As you can see in Figure 5-15, we have blue parts (high-impedance z values) and also red parts (do not care x values) since for the PMOS the clock signal "a" is applied after 2ns delay, so when the NMOS gate is high, for 2ns the output signal "y" is in the do not care (x) situation and when the NMOS gate is low, for 2ns the output signal "y" is in the high-impedance (z) situation.

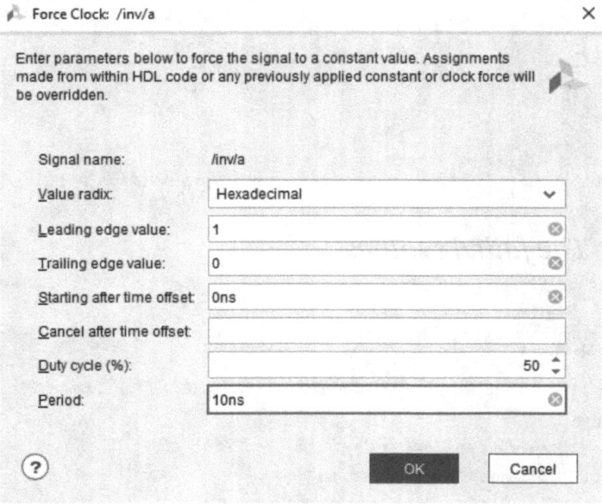

Figure 5-14. *Setting the force clock parameters for signal "a"*

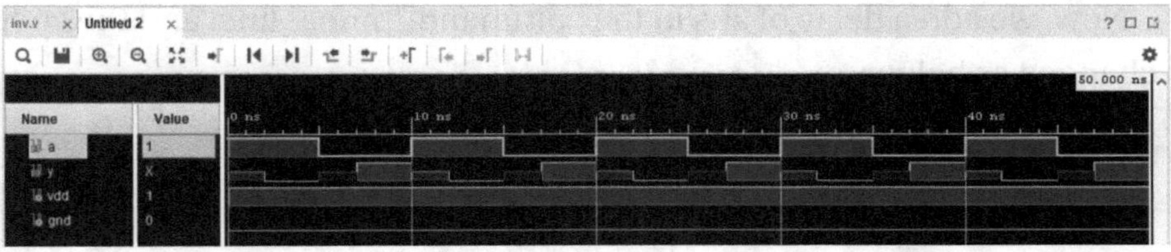

Figure 5-15. *The simulated waveforms on the wave window*

Now, we want to implement a 4-bit array of inverters. So we use the following codes inside of the file "inv.v":

```verilog
`timescale 1ns / 1ps
module inv(
input [3:0] a,
output [3:0] y
    );
supply1 vdd;
supply0 gnd;
pmos p1 [3:0] (y,vdd,a);
nmos n1 [3:0] (y,gnd,a);
endmodule
```

We do the same as previous procedures for running the simulation, and in the opened simulation window, we click the Restart button and then right-click the signal "a" and set the force constant parameters as illustrated in Figure 5-16.

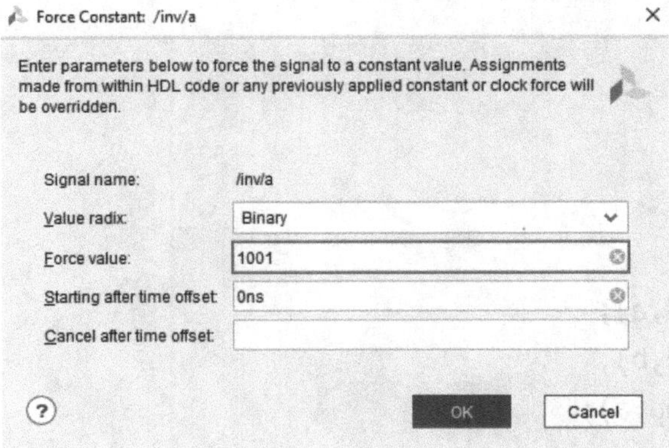

Figure 5-16. *Setting the force constant parameters for signal "a"*

Now, we click the Run for 50ns button and then the Zoom Fit button to view the simulated waveforms on the wave window, and also we right-click signals "a[3:0]" and "y[3:0]" and choose the Radix option as Binary as shown in Figure 5-17.

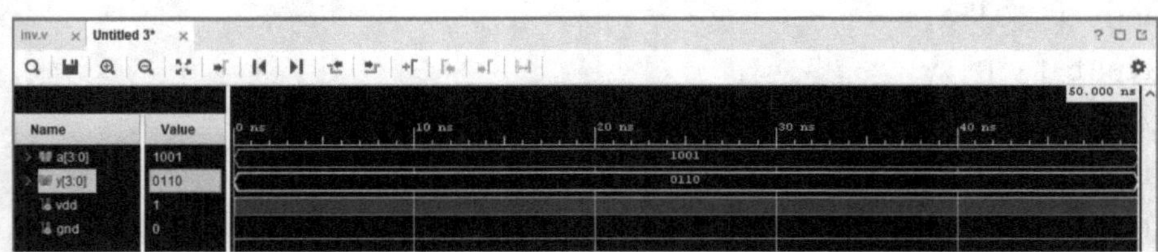

Figure 5-17. *The simulated waveforms on the wave window*

We create a new project named "NAND_switch" and also a design source file titled "nand2.v" and then add the following codes inside of it. The switch-level model for the NAND gate is demonstrated in Figure 5-8:

```verilog
`timescale 1ns / 1ps
module nand2(
input a,b,
output y
    );
supply1 vdd;
supply0 vss;
wire temp;
pmos p1(y,vdd,a);
pmos p2(y,vdd,b);
nmos n1(y,temp,a);
nmos n2(temp,vss,b);
endmodule
```

We do the same as previous procedures for running the simulation, and in the opened simulation window, we click the Restart button and then right-click the signals "a" and "b" and set their force clock parameters as depicted in Figures 5-18 and 5-19, respectively.

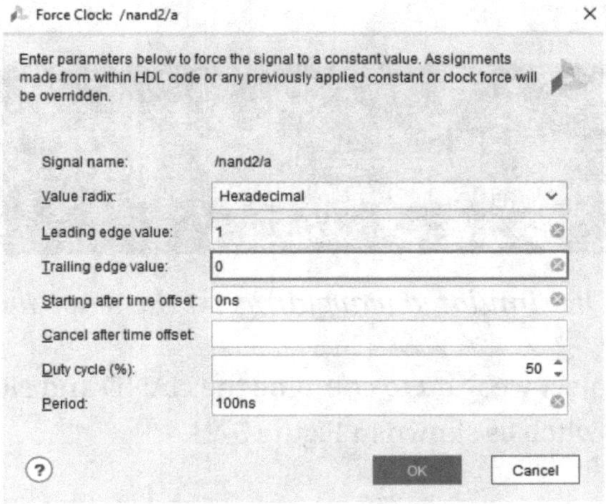

Figure 5-18. *Setting the force clock parameters for signal "a"*

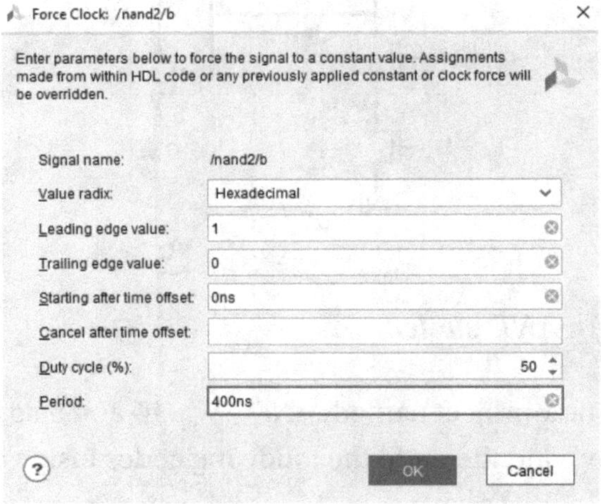

Figure 5-19. *Setting the force clock parameters for signal "b"*

Now, we click the Run for 1μs button and then the Zoom Fit button
to view the simulated waveforms on the wave window as illustrated in
Figure 5-20.

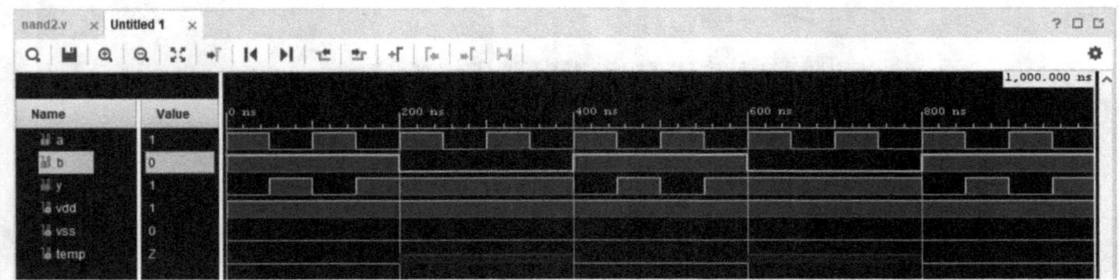

Figure 5-20. *The simulated waveforms on the wave window*

As a next project we want to combine the NAND and NOT switches to create an AND switch as shown in Figure 5-21.

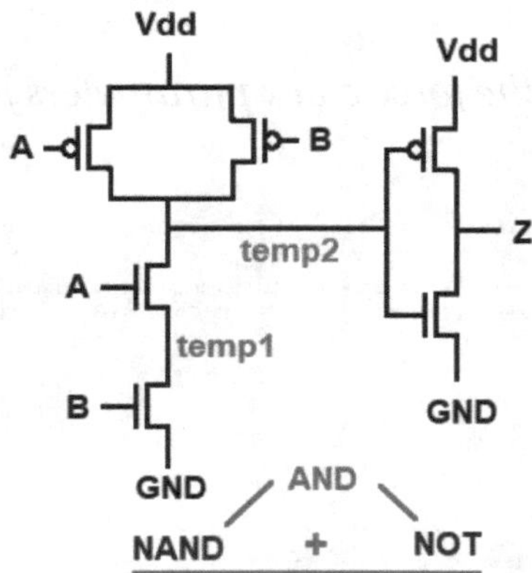

Figure 5-21. *An AND switch*

We create a new project named "AND_switch" and also a design source file titled "and2.v" and then add the following codes inside of it:

```
`timescale 1ns / 1ps
module and2(
input a,b,
output y
    );
supply1 vdd;
```

```
supply0 gnd;
wire temp1,temp2;
pmos p1(temp2,vdd,a);
pmos p2(temp2,vdd,b);
pmos p3(y,vdd,temp2);
nmos n1(temp2,temp1,a);
nmos n2(temp1,gnd,b);
nmos n3(y,gnd,temp2);
endmodule
```

We do the same as previous procedures for running the simulation, and in the opened simulation window, we click the Restart button and then right-click the signals "a" and "b" and set their force clock parameters as depicted in Figures 5-22 and 5-23, respectively.

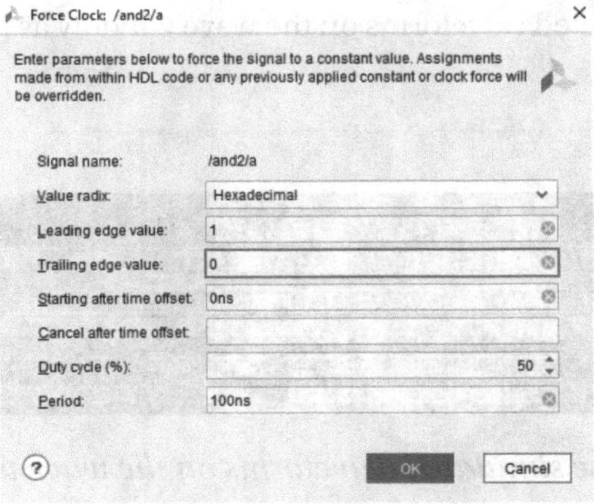

Figure 5-22. Setting the force clock parameters for signal "a"

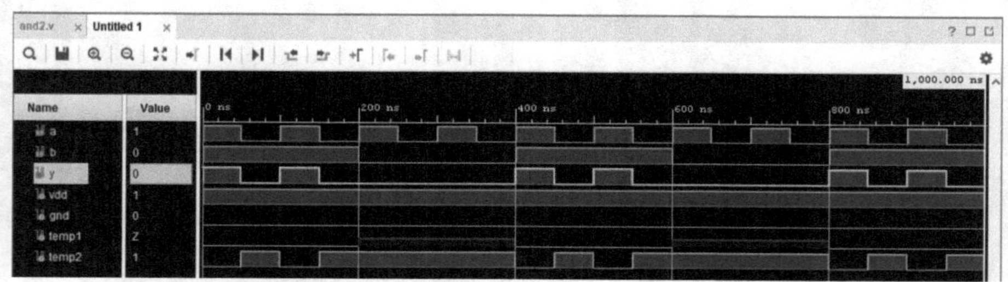

Figure 5-23. *Setting the force clock parameters for signal "b"*

Now, we click the Run for 1μs button and then the Zoom Fit button to view the simulated waveforms on the wave window as illustrated in Figure 5-24.

Figure 5-24. *The simulated waveforms on the wave window*

The Structural Modeling

In this section we want to use the structural modeling style in Verilog programming. To start, we want to implement a 4 × 1 multiplexer using three 2 × 1 multiplexers as shown in Figure 5-25.

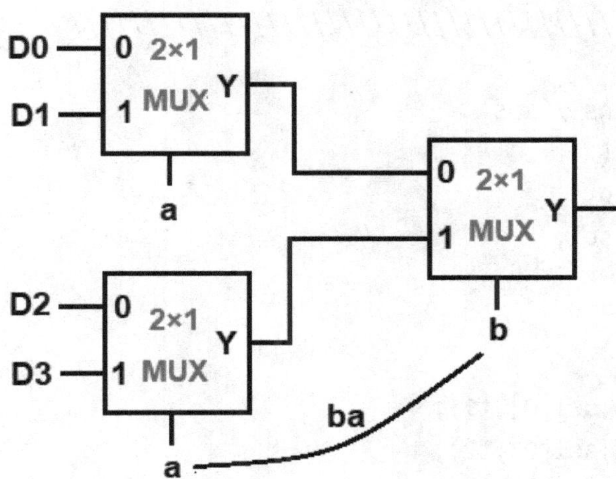

Figure 5-25. *A 4 × 1 multiplexer using three 2 × 1 multiplexers*

So we create a new project named "MUX_structure" and also two design source files titled "mux21.v" and "mux41.v" and then add the following codes inside of them:

```verilog
//mux21.v
`timescale 1ns / 1ps
module mux21(
input a,b,sel,
output y
    );
reg temp = 0;
always@(*) begin
if (sel == 1'b0)
    temp = a;
else
    temp = b;
end
assign y = temp;
endmodule
```

```verilog
/////////////////////////////////////////////////
//mux41.v
`timescale 1ns / 1ps
module mux41(
input a,b,c,d,
input [1:0] sel,
output y
    );
wire t1,t2;
mux21 m1(a,b,sel[0],t1);
mux21 m2(c,d,sel[0],t2);
mux21 m3(t1,t2,sel[1],y);
endmodule
```

We do the same as previous procedures for running the simulation, and in the opened simulation window, we click the Restart button and then right-click the signals "a," "b," "c," and "d" and set their force clock parameters as depicted in Figures 5-26, 5-27, 5-28, and 5-29, respectively.

Figure 5-26. *Setting the force clock parameters for signal "a"*

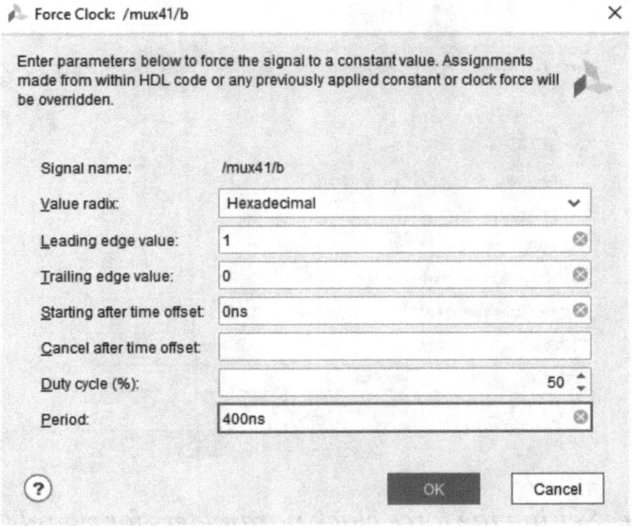

Figure 5-27. *Setting the force clock parameters for signal "b"*

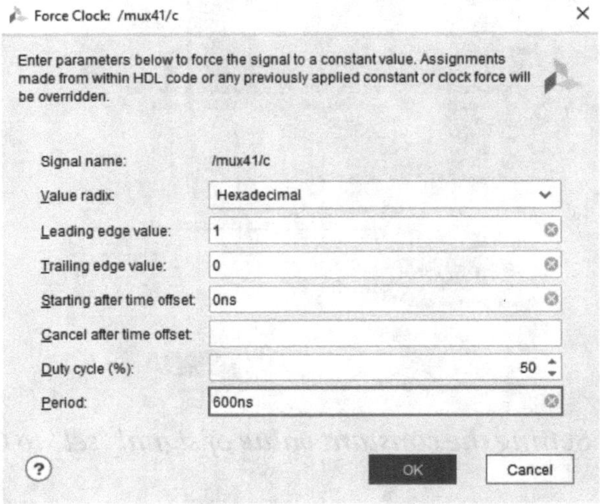

Figure 5-28. *Setting the force clock parameters for signal "c"*

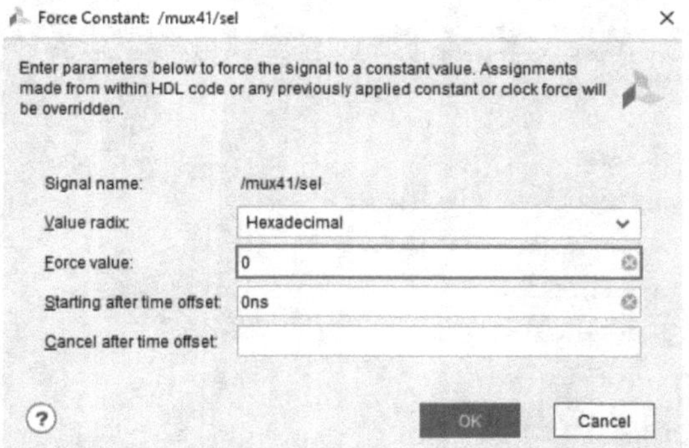

Figure 5-29. *Setting the force clock parameters for signal "d"*

Also, we right-click the signal "sel" and set its constant value to 0 as illustrated in Figure 5-30.

Figure 5-30. *Setting the constant value of signal "sel" to 0*

Now, we click the Run for 1µs button once, and then we right-click the signal "sel" and set its constant value to 1 as shown in Figure 5-31.

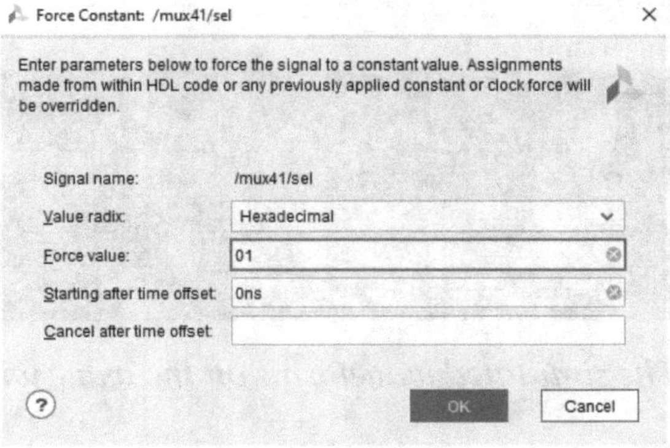

Figure 5-31. *Setting the constant value of signal "sel" to 1*

Now, we click the Run for 2µs button once, and then we right-click the signal "sel" and set its binary constant value to 11 as depicted in Figure 5-32.

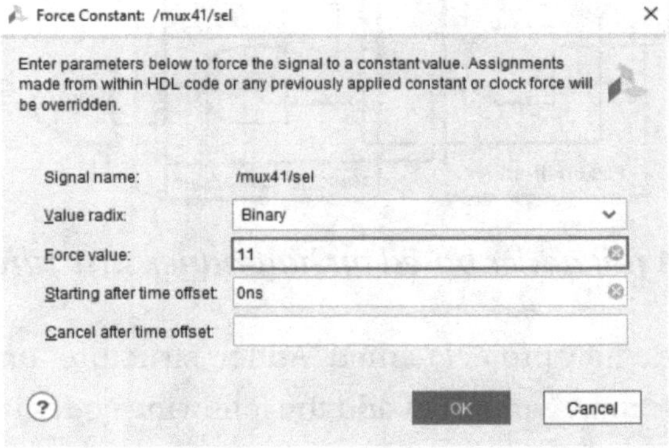

Figure 5-32. *Setting the binary constant value of signal "sel" to 11*

Now, we click the Run for 3µs button once and then click the Zoom Fit button in the wave window to view the simulated waveforms as illustrated in Figure 5-33.

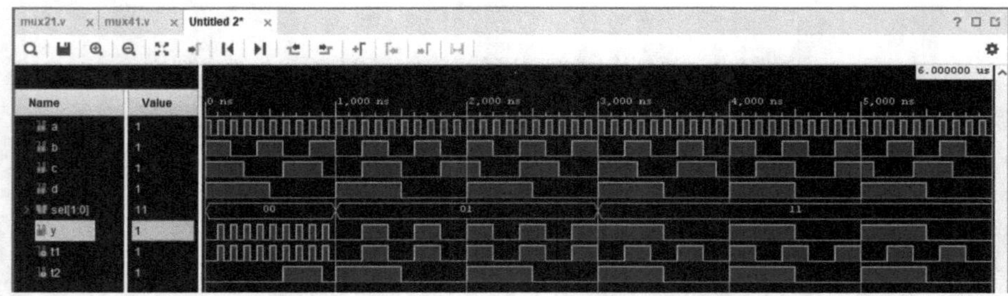

Figure 5-33. *The simulated waveforms on the wave window*

Now, we want to create another project that is a full adder based on half-adder structures as shown in Figure 5-34.

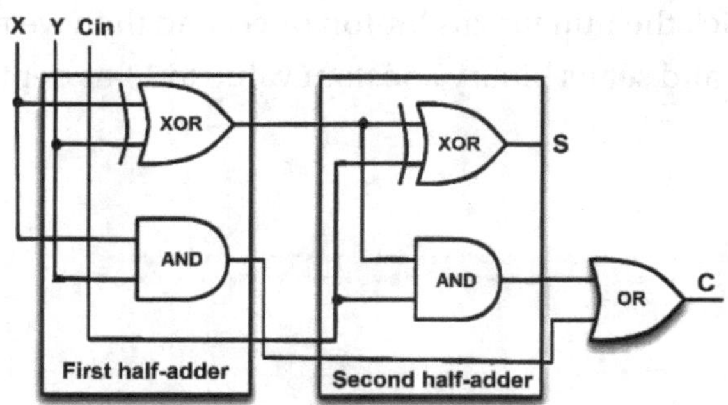

Figure 5-34. *A full adder based on half-adder structures*

So we create a new project named "Adder_structure" and also a design source file titled "top.v" and then add the following codes inside of it:

```verilog
`timescale 1ns / 1ps
module ha(
input a,b,
output s,c
    );
assign s = a ^ b;
assign c = a & b;
```

```
endmodule
/////////////////////////////////
module fa(
input x,y,cin,
output s,c
    );
wire t1,t2,t3;
ha h1(x,y,t1,t2);
ha h2(t1,cin,s,t3);
or o1(c,t3,t2);
endmodule
```

We do the same as previous procedures for running the simulation, and in the opened simulation window, we click the Restart button and then right-click the signals "x," "y," and "cin" and set their force constant parameters as depicted in Figures 5-35, 5-36, and 5-37, respectively.

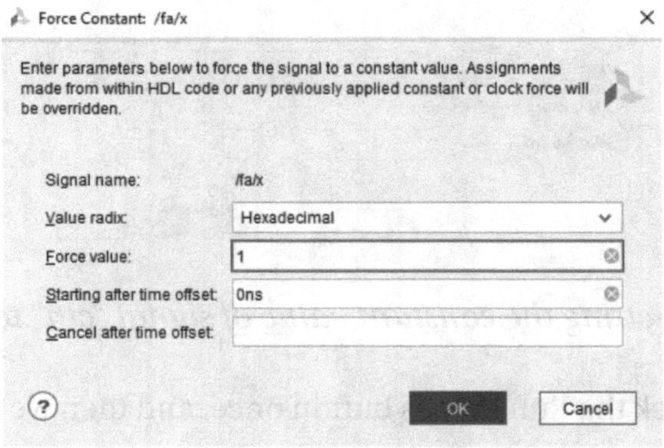

Figure 5-35. *Setting the constant value of signal "x" to 1*

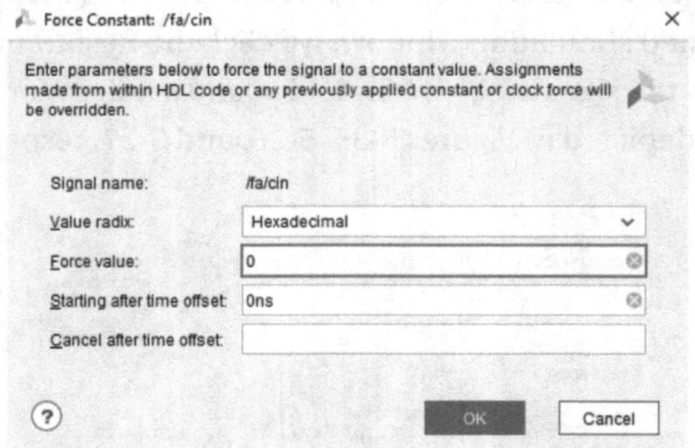

Figure 5-36. *Setting the constant value of signal "y" to 1*

Figure 5-37. *Setting the constant value of signal "cin" to 0*

Now, we click the Run for 1µs button once, and then we right-click the signal "x" and set its constant value to 0 as shown in Figure 5-38.

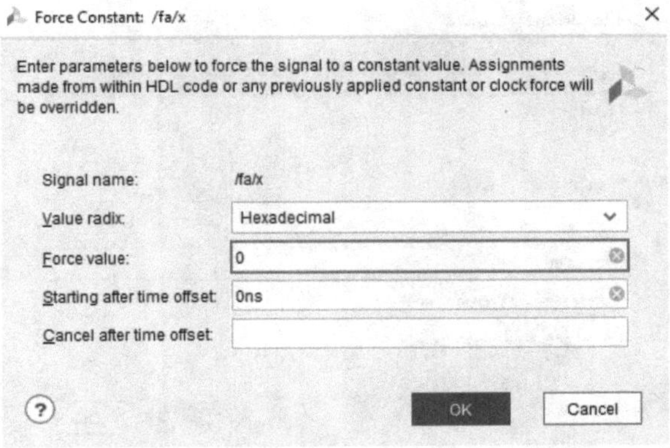

Figure 5-38. *Setting the constant value of signal "x" to 0*

Now, we click the Run for 1μs button once, and then we right-click the signals "x" and "cin" and set their constant values to 1 as illustrated in Figures 5-39 and 5-40, respectively.

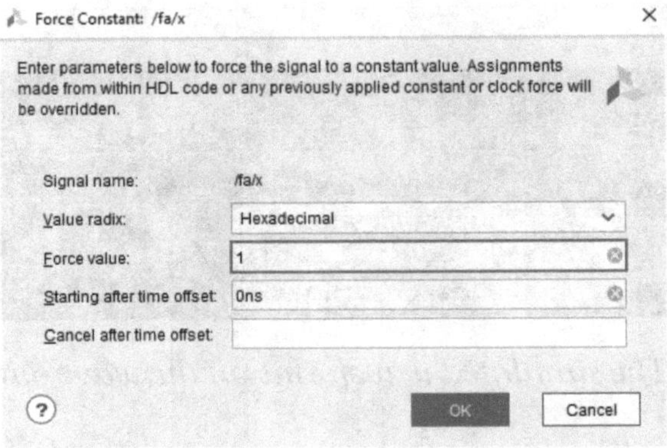

Figure 5-39. *Setting the constant value of signal "x" to 1*

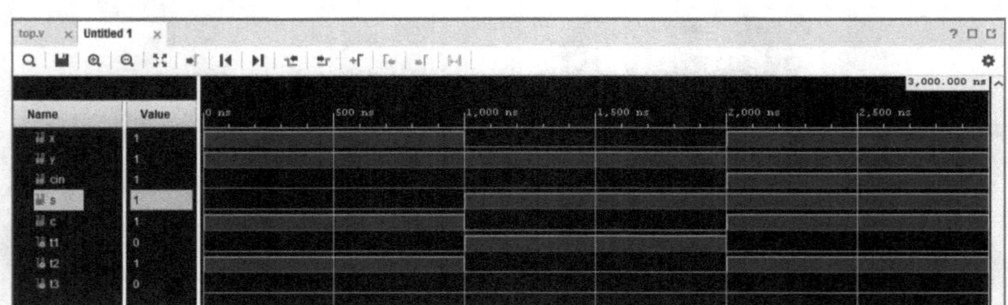

Figure 5-40. *Setting the constant value of signal "cin" to 1*

Finally, we click the Run for 1μs button once again, and then we click the Zoom Fit button to view the simulated waveforms on the wave window as shown in Figure 5-41.

Figure 5-41. *The simulated waveforms on the wave window*

The Parameter Statement

In this section, we want to implement an n-bit counter using the parameter statement. So we create a new project named "n_bit_counter" and also a design source file titled "nbit_counter.v" and then add the following codes inside of it:

```verilog
`timescale 1ns / 1ps
module nbit_counter
#(
parameter N = 4
)
(
input clk,
input start,
output [N-1:0] q
);
reg [N-1:0] temp;
initial temp = 0;
always@(posedge clk) begin
if (start == 1'b1)
    temp = temp + 1;
else
    temp = 0;
end
assign q = temp;
endmodule
```

We do the same as previous procedures for running the simulation, and in the opened simulation window, we click the Restart button and then right-click the signal "clk" and set its force clock parameters as depicted in Figure 5-42. We also right-click the signal "start" and set its force constant value to 1 as illustrated in Figure 5-43.

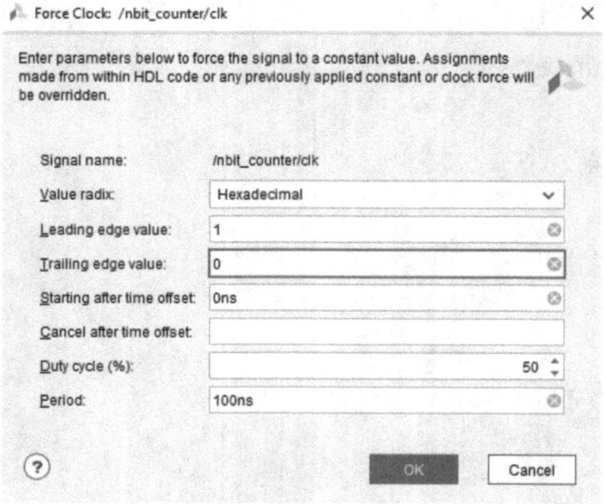

Figure 5-42. *Setting the force clock parameters for signal "clk"*

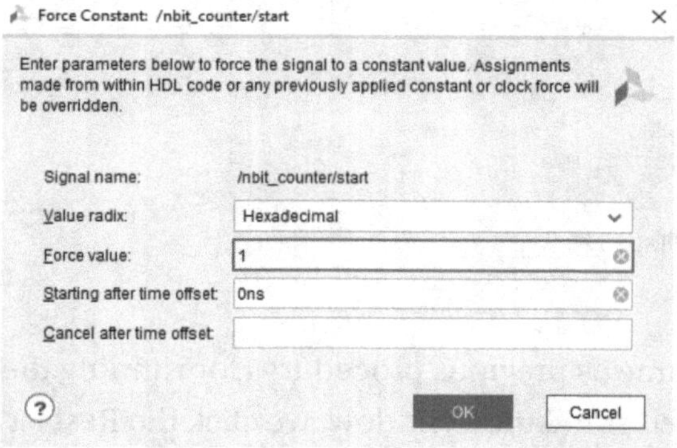

Figure 5-43. *Setting the constant value of signal "start" to 1*

Now, we click the Run for 2µs button once again, and then we click the Zoom Fit button, and also we right-click both signals "q[3:0]" and "temp[3:0]" and choose the Radix option as Binary to view the simulated waveforms on the wave window as shown in Figure 5-44.

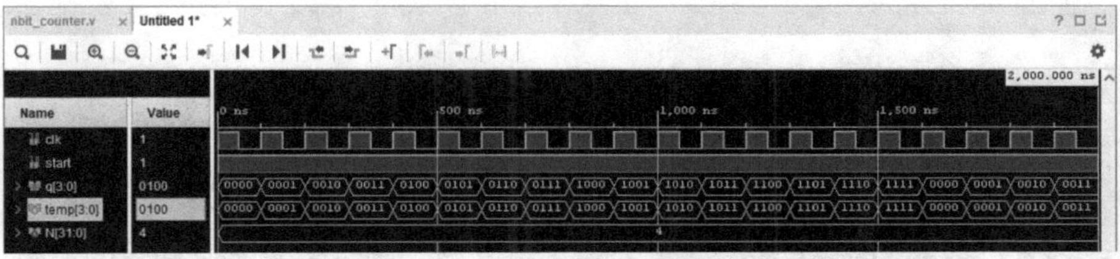

Figure 5-44. *The simulated waveforms on the wave window*

Now, we change the parameter N value from 4 to 8 as the code blow:

```
#(parameter N = 8)
```

We do the same as previous procedures for running the simulation, and in the opened simulation window, we click the Restart button and then right-click the signal "clk" and set its force clock parameters as depicted in Figure 5-42. We also right-click the signal "start" and set its force constant value to 1 as illustrated in Figure 5-43. Now, we click the Run for 100μs button once again, and then we click the Zoom Fit button, and also we right-click both signals "q[7:0]" and "temp[7:0]" and choose the Radix option as Binary to view the simulated waveforms on the wave window as shown in Figure 5-45.

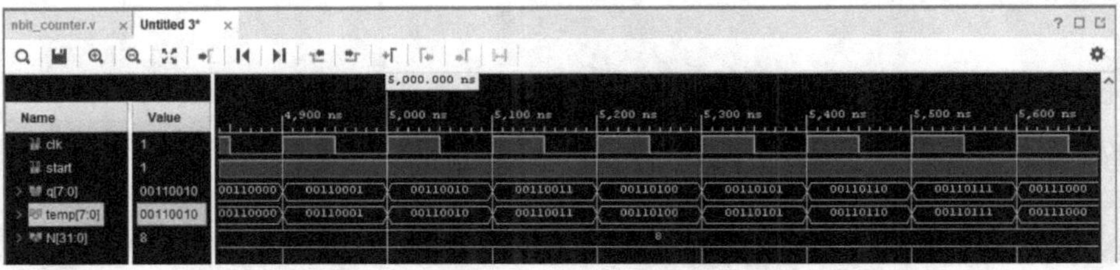

Figure 5-45. *The simulated waveforms on the wave window*

Also, we right-click the signal "q[7:0]" and choose Waveform Style as Analog to view the analog waveform of the signal "q[7:0]" as depicted in Figure 5-46.

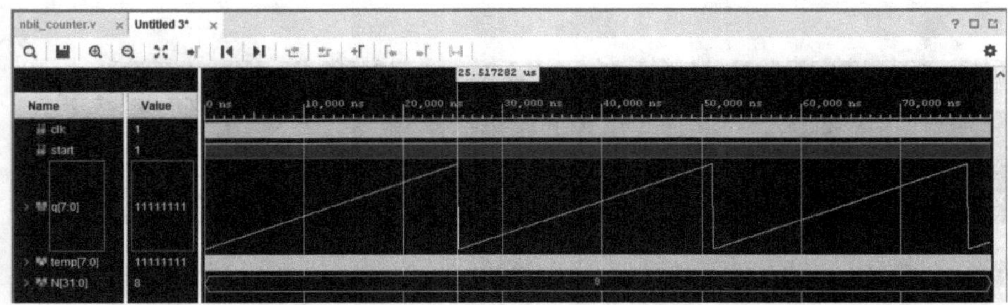

Figure 5-46. *The simulated waveforms on the wave window*

The Function Statement

In this section, we want to implement an addition and a factorial
calculation using the function statement. So we create a new project
named "Addition_Function" and also a design source file titled "funct.v"
and then add the following codes inside of it:

```verilog
`timescale 1ns / 1ps
module funct(
input [3:0] a,b,
output [4:0] c
);
function [4:0] addition(input [3:0] i1, input [3:0] i2);
addition = i1 + i2;
endfunction
assign c = addition(a,b);
endmodule
```

We do the same as previous procedures for running the simulation,
and in the opened simulation window, we click the Restart button
and then right-click the signals "a" and "b" and set their force constant
parameters as illustrated in Figures 5-47 and 5-48.

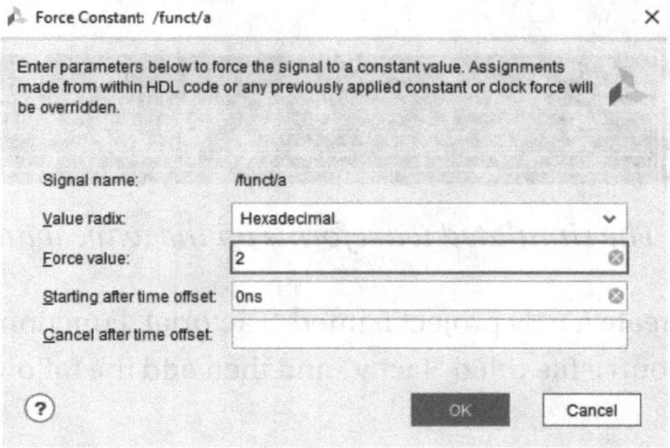

Figure 5-47. *Setting the constant value of signal "a"*

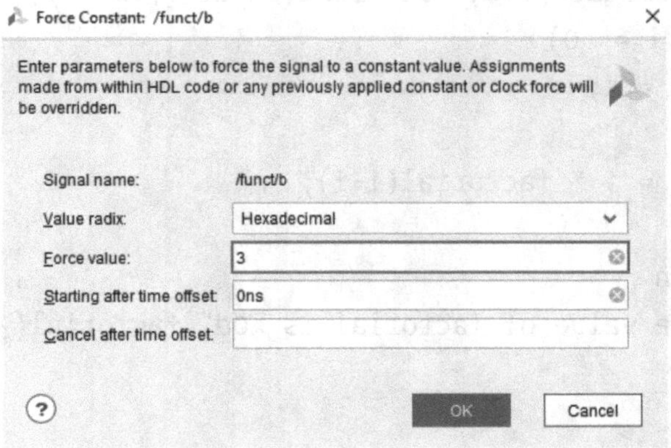

Figure 5-48. *Setting the constant value of signal "b"*

Now, we click the Run for 10μs button once, and then we click the Zoom Fit button to view the simulated waveforms on the wave window as shown in Figure 5-49.

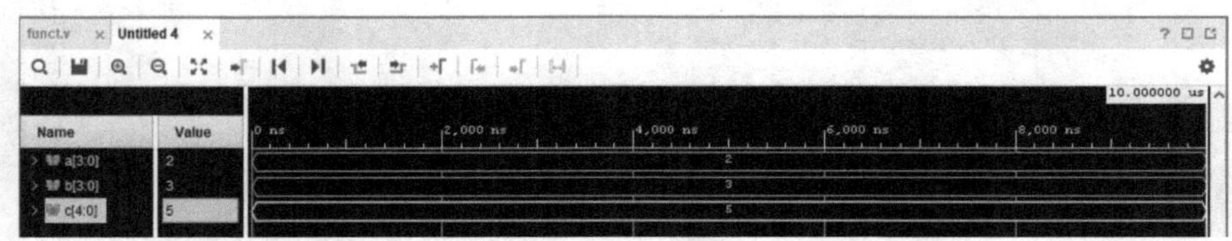

Figure 5-49. *The simulated waveforms on the wave window*

Now, we create a new project named "Factorial_Function" and
also a design source file titled "fact.v" and then add the following codes
inside of it:

```
`timescale 1ns / 1ps
module fact();
function automatic [7:0] factorial(input [7:0] i);
if (i == 1 | i == 0)
    factorial = 1;
else
    factorial = i * factorial(i-1);
endfunction
initial begin
$display("The value of factorial is %0d",factorial(3));
end
endmodule
```

We do the same as previous procedures for running the simulation,
and in the opened simulation window, we click the Restart button and
then click the Run for 10µs button, so we can view the results on the Tcl
Console as depicted in Figure 5-50.

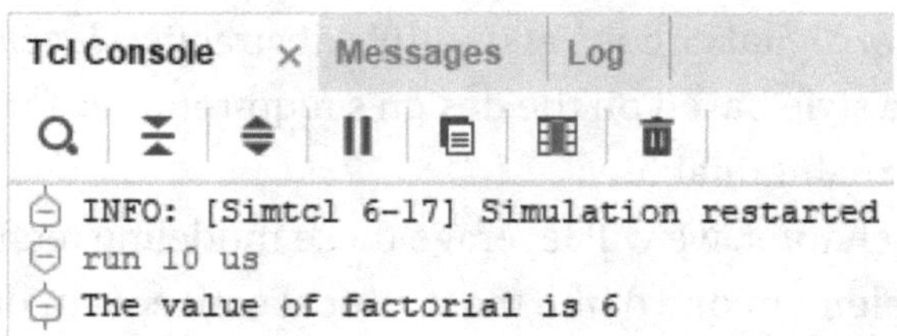

Figure 5-50. *The results on the Tcl Console*

Summary and Key Takeaways

This chapter provided a comprehensive exploration of low-level hardware modeling in Verilog, moving beyond high-level behavioral descriptions to gain finer control over digital circuit implementation. We began with gate-level modeling, constructing fundamental circuits like half-adders and full adders using primitive logic gates (AND, XOR, OR), which closely mirror physical hardware interconnections. We then delved into the even lower abstraction of switch-level modeling, where we modeled transistors as switches (PMOS, NMOS) to build basic gates like inverters, NAND, and AND gates. This level, while not synthesizable in Vivado, is crucial for custom cell design and simulation, as demonstrated by the appearance of high-impedance (z) and unknown (x) states when delays were introduced.

The chapter then shifted to structural modeling, emphasizing hierarchical design by interconnecting smaller modules (like using 2:1 muxes to build a 4:1 mux or half-adders to build a full adder). This approach promotes design reusability, modularity, and scalability. Finally, we enhanced our designs with two powerful Verilog constructs: parameters for creating flexible, configurable modules like an N-bit counter and functions for encapsulating reusable procedural blocks of code, such as for addition and factorial calculations. You should now be able to model digital circuits at multiple abstraction levels, selecting the appropriate style based on the design's requirements for control, efficiency, and maintainability.

In the next chapter, we will leverage these modeling techniques to design and implement one of the most critical concepts in digital systems: Finite State Machines (FSMs).

CHAPTER 6

Finite State Machines

In Chapter 5, we explored gate-level, switch-level, and structural modeling, focusing on low-level hardware implementation in Verilog. Now, in this chapter, we transition to Finite State Machines (FSMs), a fundamental concept in digital design that enables sequential logic control for complex systems. FSMs provide a structured approach to designing circuits with memory and predictable state transitions, making them essential for controllers, protocol handling, and decision-making logic.

This chapter begins with a simple Moore FSM, introducing the basic principles of state machines where outputs depend only on the current state. We then explore different design methodologies for Moore FSMs, including the three-process and two-process approaches, highlighting trade-offs between readability and synthesis efficiency. Modifications to the Moore FSM are examined next, demonstrating enhanced flexibility in three-process and two-process implementations.

The discussion then shifts to Mealy machines, where outputs depend on both the current state and inputs, covering three-process and two-process methodologies. Finally, we apply these concepts to a practical example—a Moore sequence detector—illustrating how FSMs can be used to recognize specific input patterns.

By the end of this chapter, you will understand the core differences between Moore and Mealy FSMs, be able to implement them using various coding styles, and apply them to real-world sequential logic problems.

© Majid Pakdel 2026
M. Pakdel, *Mastering Verilog for FPGA Design*, Maker Innovations Series,
https://doi.org/10.1007/979-8-8688-2311-4_6

Finite State Machines (FSMs) are sequential logic circuits used to control the behavior of systems and data flow paths. This chapter introduces the concept of two types of FSMs, Mealy and Moore, and the modeling styles to develop such machines. A particular FSM is defined by a list of its states and the triggering condition for each transition. The state machines are modeled using two basic types of sequential networks, which are Mealy and Moore. In a Mealy machine, the output depends on both the present (current) state and the present (current) inputs. However, in a Moore machine, the output depends only on the present state. The two-block diagram for a Mealy machine is shown in Figure 6-1.

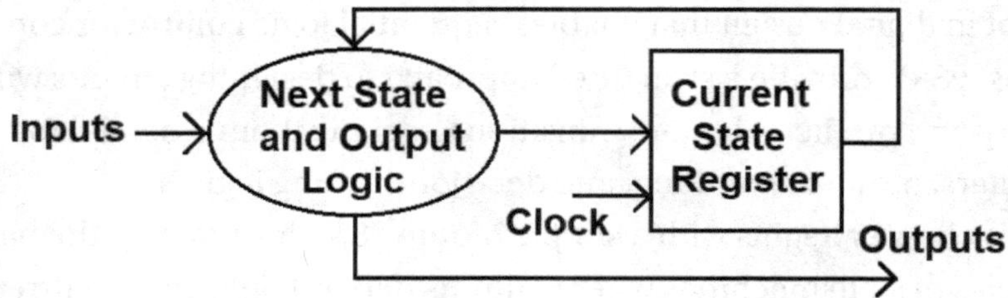

Figure 6-1. *The two-block diagram for a Mealy machine*

Also, the three-block diagram for a Mealy machine is depicted in Figure 6-2.

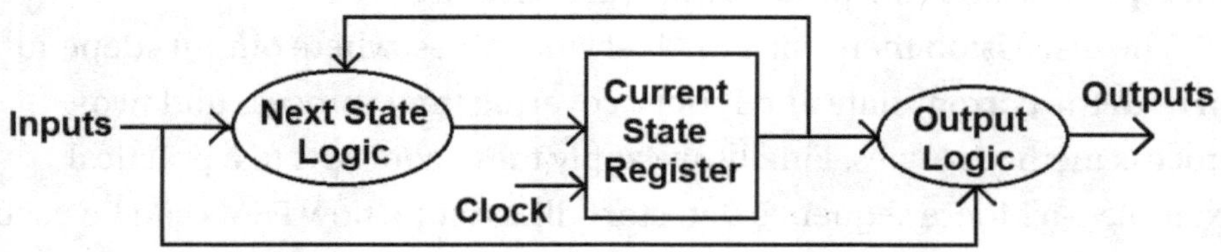

Figure 6-2. *The three-block diagram for a Mealy machine*

The three-block diagram for a Moore machine is illustrated in Figure 6-3.

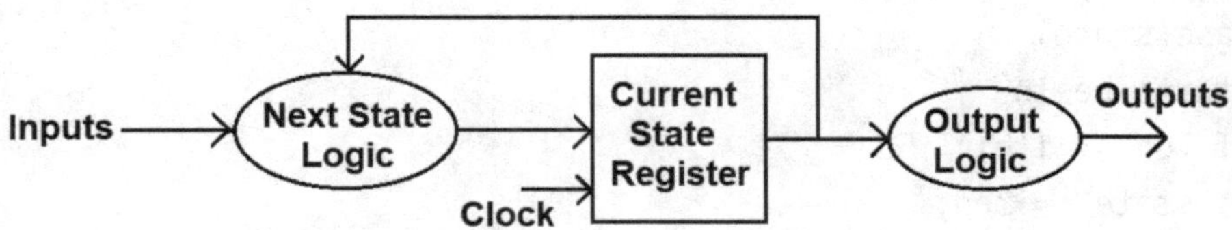

Figure 6-3. *The three-block diagram for a Moore machine*

A Simple Moore FSM

The flowchart of a simple Moore FSM for controlling the traffic lights is shown in Figure 6-4.

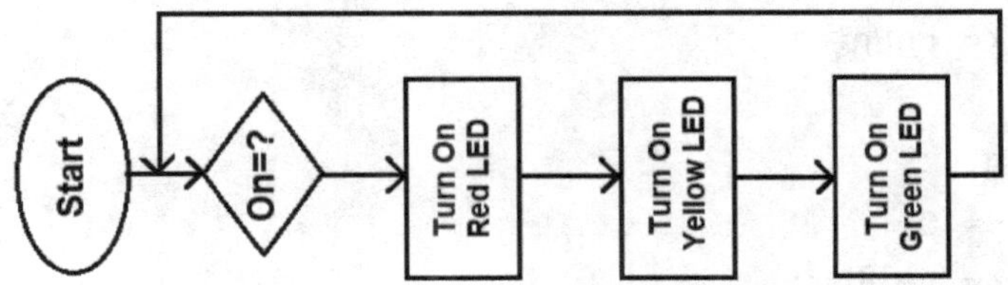

Figure 6-4. *The flowchart of a simple FSM*

Now, we create a new project named "Simple_FSM" and also a design source file titled "tlc.v" and then add the following codes inside of it:

```verilog
`timescale 1ns / 1ps
module tlc(
    input on,clk,
    output r,y,g
    );
reg tempr = 0, tempy = 0, tempg = 0;
integer count;
reg [1:0] state = 0; //00 01 10 11
parameter red = 0, green = 1, yellow = 2, start = 3;
always@(posedge clk) begin
```

```
case(state)
start: begin
if (on == 1'b1)
   state <= red;
else
   state <= start;
end
red: begin
if (count < 5) begin
   tempr <= 1'b1;
   tempy <= 1'b0;
   tempg <= 1'b0;
   count <= count + 1;
end
else begin
   count <= 0;
   state <= yellow;
end
end
yellow: begin
if (count < 5) begin
   tempr <= 1'b0;
   tempy <= 1'b1;
   tempg <= 1'b0;
   count <= count + 1;
end
else begin
   count <= 0;
   state <= green;
end
end
```

```verilog
green: begin
if (count < 5) begin
    tempr <= 1'b0;
    tempy <= 1'b0;
    tempg <= 1'b1;
    count <= count + 1;
end
else begin
    count <= 0;
    state <= start;
end
end
default: state <= start;
endcase
end
assign r = tempr;
assign y = tempy;
assign g = tempg;
endmodule
```

We select Flow ➤ Run Simulation ➤ Run Behavioral Simulation from the menu toolbar to view the waveforms on the wave window. So, in the opened simulation window, we click the Restart button and then right-click the signal "clk" and set the force clock parameters as depicted in Figure 6-5. Also, we right-click the signal "on" and set its force constant value to 1 as illustrated in Figure 6-6.

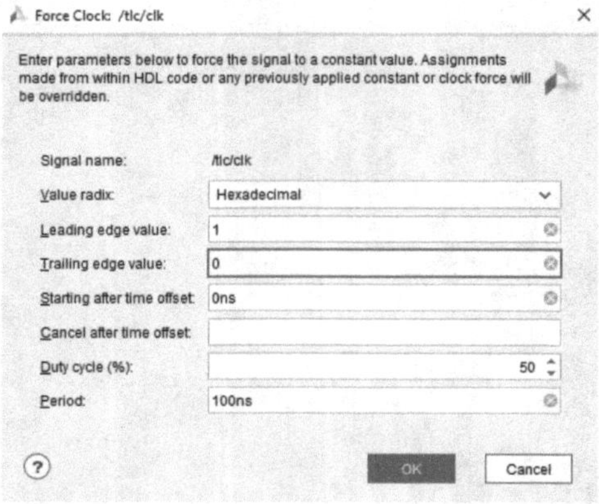

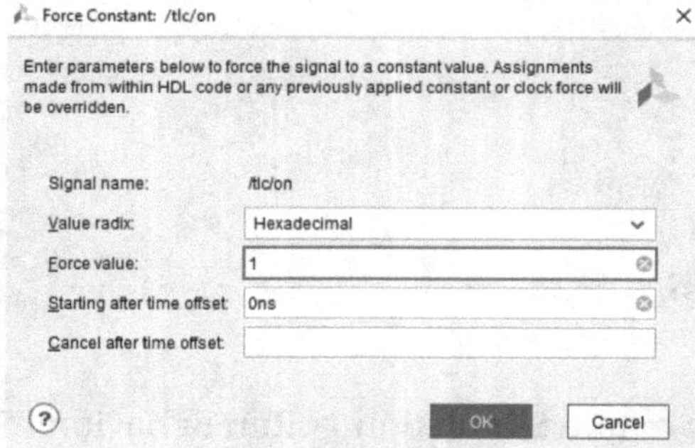

Figure 6-5. *Setting the force clock parameters for signal "clk"*

Figure 6-6. *Setting the force constant value of signal "on" to 1*

Then, we click the Run for 5µs button once, and then we click the
Zoom Fit button to view the simulated waveforms on the wave window,
and we can change the signal color as shown in Figure 6-7.

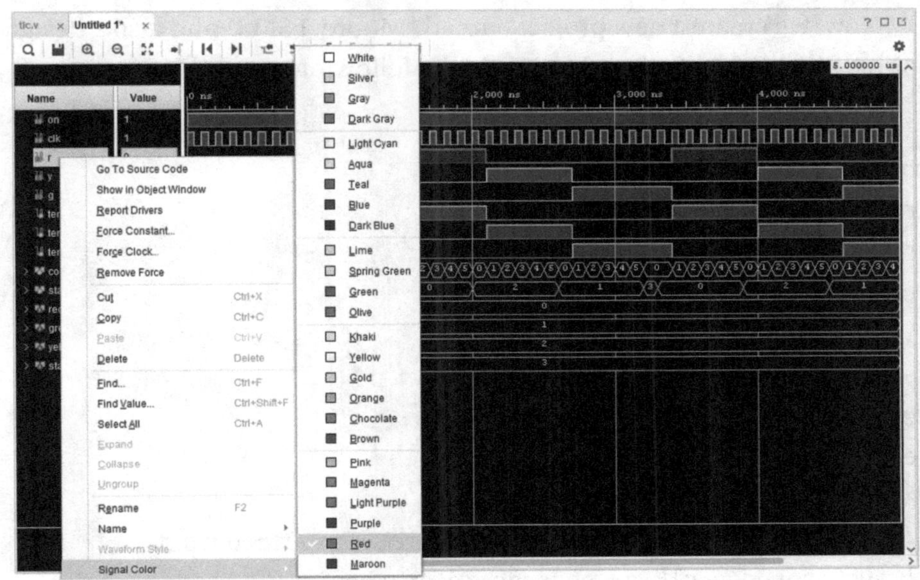

Figure 6-7. *The simulated waveforms on the wave window*

Three-Process Methodology for a Moore FSM

The state/transition diagram for a Moore FSM example is depicted in Figure 6-8.

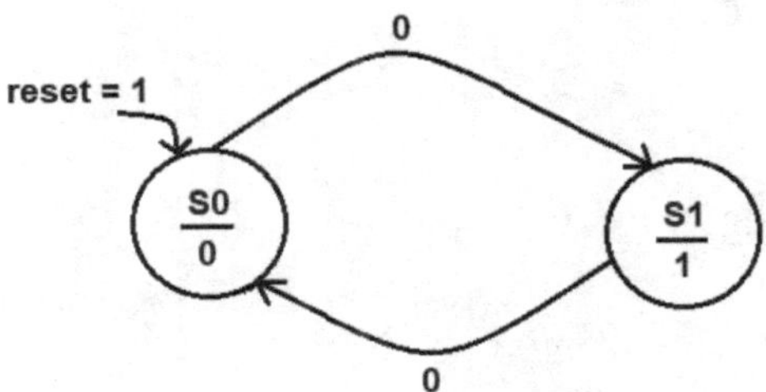

Figure 6-8. *The state/transition diagram for a Moore FSM example*

Now, we create a new project named "Moore_FSM3" and also a design source file titled "top.v" and then add the following codes inside of it:

```verilog
`timescale 1ns / 1ps
module top(
input clk,
input reset,
output dout
);
reg temp = 0;
reg state = 0;
reg nextstate = 0;
parameter s0 = 0, s1 = 1;
//Reset assertion, Compute next state, Compute output
always@(posedge clk or posedge reset) begin
if(reset == 1'b1)
    state <= s0;
else
    state <= nextstate;
end
always@(state) begin
case(state)
s0: nextstate = s1;
s1: nextstate = s0;
endcase
end
always@(state) begin
case(state)
s0: temp = 1'b0;
s1: temp = 1'b1;
```

```
endcase
end
assign dout = temp;
endmodule
```

We do the same as previous procedures for running the simulation, and in the opened simulation window, we click the Restart button and then right-click the signal "clk" and set its force clock parameters as illustrated in Figure 6-9.

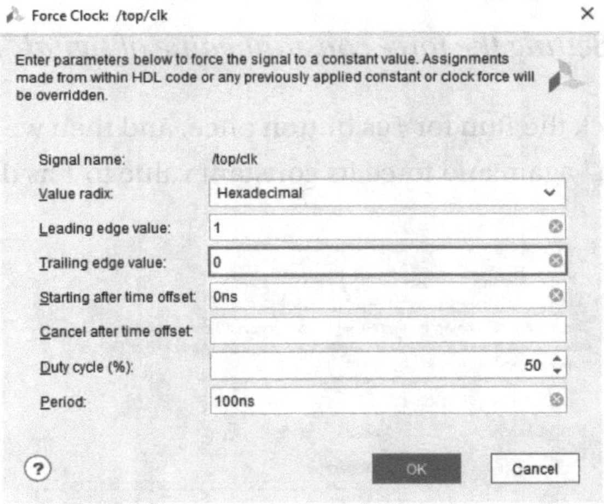

Figure 6-9. *Setting the force clock parameters for signal "clk"*

We also right-click the signal "reset" and set its force constant value to 0 as shown in Figure 6-10.

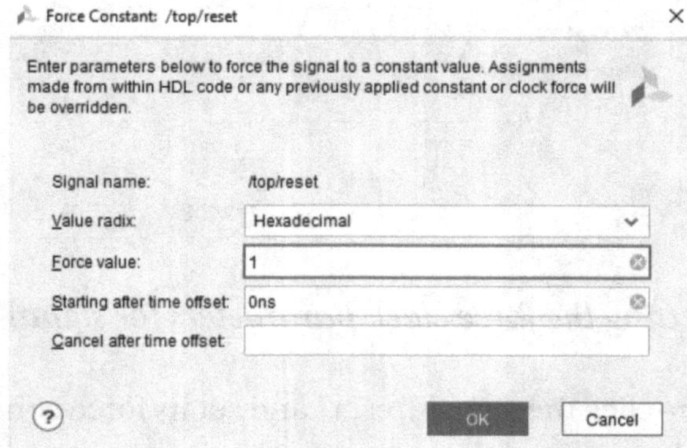

Figure 6-10. *Setting the force constant value of signal "reset" to 0*

Now, we click the Run for 1μs button once, and then we right-click the signal "reset" again and force its constant value to 1 as depicted in Figure 6-11.

Figure 6-11. *Setting the force constant value of signal "reset" to 1*

Now, we click the Run for 1μs button once again, and then we click the Zoom Fit button to view the simulated waveforms on the wave window as illustrated in Figure 6-12.

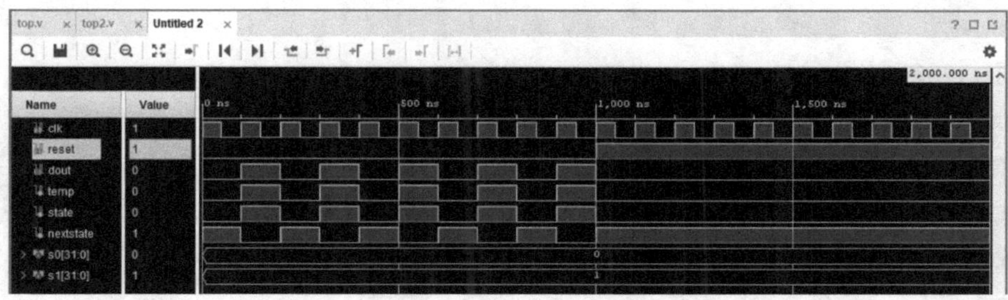

Figure 6-12. *The simulated waveforms on the wave window*

Two-Process Methodology for a Moore FSM

In this section we again consider the state/transition diagram for a Moore
FSM example, which is shown in Figure 6-8. We create a new design source
file titled "top2.v" and then add the following codes inside of it:

```verilog
`timescale 1ns / 1ps
module top2(
input clk,
input reset,
output dout
);
reg temp = 0;
reg state = 0;
reg nextstate = 0;
parameter s0 = 0, s1 = 1;
//Reset assertion, Compute next state, Compute output
always@(posedge clk or posedge reset) begin
if(reset == 1'b1)
    state <= s0;
else
    state <= nextstate;
```

```
end
always@(state) begin
case(state)
s0: begin
nextstate = s1;
temp = 1'b0;
end
s1: begin
nextstate = s0;
temp = 1'b1;
end
endcase
end
assign dout = temp;
endmodule
```

We right-click the Verilog file "top2.v" and select the Set as Top option as depicted in Figure 6-13.

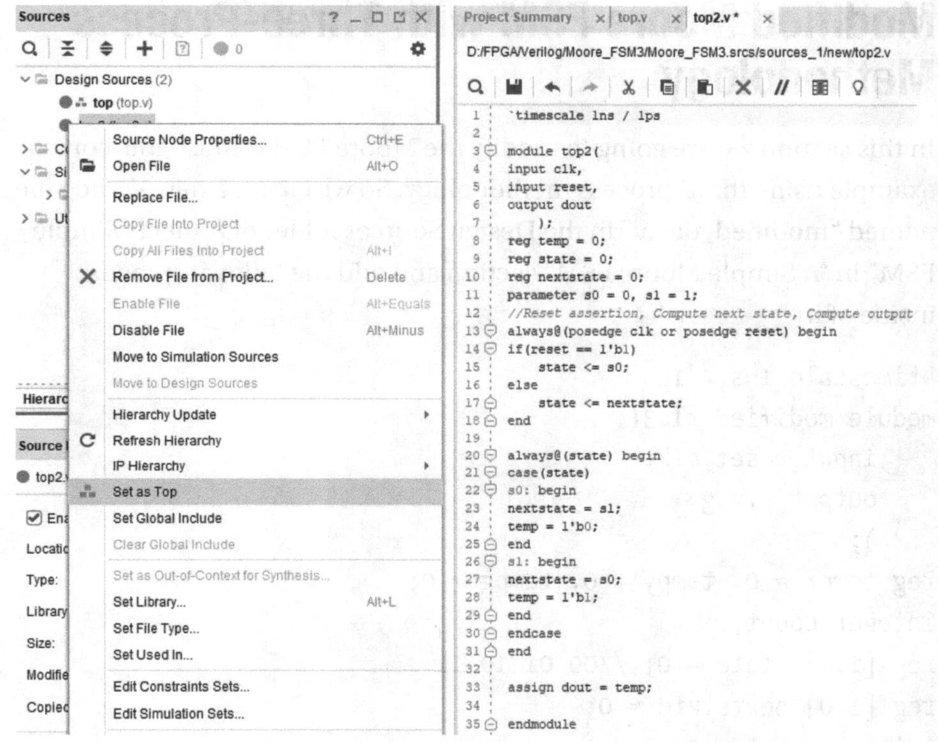

Figure 6-13. *Selecting the Set as Top option*

We do the same as previous procedures for running the simulation, and in the opened simulation window, we click the Restart button and then right-click the signal "clk" and set the force clock parameters as illustrated in Figure 6-9. We also right-click the signal "reset" and set its force constant value to 0 as shown in Figure 6-10. Now, we click the Run for 1μs button once, and then we right-click the signal "reset" again and force its constant value to 1 as depicted in Figure 6-11. Now, we click the Run for 1μs button once again, and then we click the Zoom Fit button to view the simulated waveforms on the wave window as illustrated in Figure 6-12.

Modified Moore FSM with Three-Process Methodology

In this section we are going to modify the Moore FSM traffic lights control example using three-process methodology. So we create a new Verilog file named "modified_tlc3.v" in the Design Sources folder of project "Simple_FSM" in "A Simple Moore FSM" section and add the following codes inside of it:

```verilog
`timescale 1ns / 1ps
module modified_tlc3(
    input reset,clk,
    output r,y,g
    );
reg tempr = 0, tempy = 0, tempg = 0;
integer count;
reg [1:0] state = 0; //00 01 10 11
reg [1:0] nextstate = 0;
initial count = 0;
parameter red = 0, green = 1, yellow = 2, start = 3;
always@(posedge clk or posedge reset) begin
if (reset == 1'b1)
    state <= start;
else
    state <= nextstate;
end
//Next state decoder
always@(posedge clk) begin
case(state)
start: nextstate = red;
red: begin
if (count < 5)
```

```verilog
      count = count + 1;
else begin
   nextstate = yellow;
   count = 0;
end
end
yellow: begin
if (count < 5)
   count = count + 1;
else begin
   nextstate = green;
   count = 0;
end
end
green: begin
if (count < 5)
   count = count + 1;
else begin
   nextstate = start;
   count = 0;
end
end
endcase
end
always@(state) begin
case(state)
start: begin
tempr = 1'b0;
tempy = 1'b0;
tempg = 1'b0;
end
```

```
red: begin
tempr = 1'b1;
tempy = 1'b0;
tempg = 1'b0;
end
yellow: begin
tempr = 1'b0;
tempy = 1'b1;
tempg = 1'b0;
end
green: begin
tempr = 1'b0;
tempy = 1'b0;
tempg = 1'b1;
end
default: state <= start;
endcase
end
assign r = tempr;
assign y = tempy;
assign g = tempg;
 endmodule
```

We do the same as previous procedures for running the simulation, and in the opened simulation window, we click the Restart button and then right-click the signal "reset" and set the force constant value to 0 as illustrated in Figure 6-14. We also right-click the signal "clk" and set the force clock parameters as shown in Figure 6-15.

Force Constant: /modified_tlc3/reset

Enter parameters below to force the signal to a constant value. Assignments made from within HDL code or any previously applied constant or clock force will be overridden.

Signal name: /modified_tlc3/reset

Value radix: Hexadecimal

Force value: 0

Starting after time offset: 0ns

Cancel after time offset:

OK   Cancel

Figure 6-14. *Setting the force constant value of signal "reset" to 0*

Force Clock: /modified_tlc3/clk

Enter parameters below to force the signal to a constant value. Assignments made from within HDL code or any previously applied constant or clock force will be overridden.

Signal name: /modified_tlc3/clk

Value radix: Hexadecimal

Leading edge value: 1

Trailing edge value: 0

Starting after time offset: 0ns

Cancel after time offset:

Duty cycle (%):   50

Period: 100ns

OK   Cancel

Figure 6-15. *Setting the force clock parameters for signal "clk"*

Now, we click the Run for 4µs button once, and then we right-click the signal "reset" again and force its constant value to 1 as depicted in Figure 6-16.

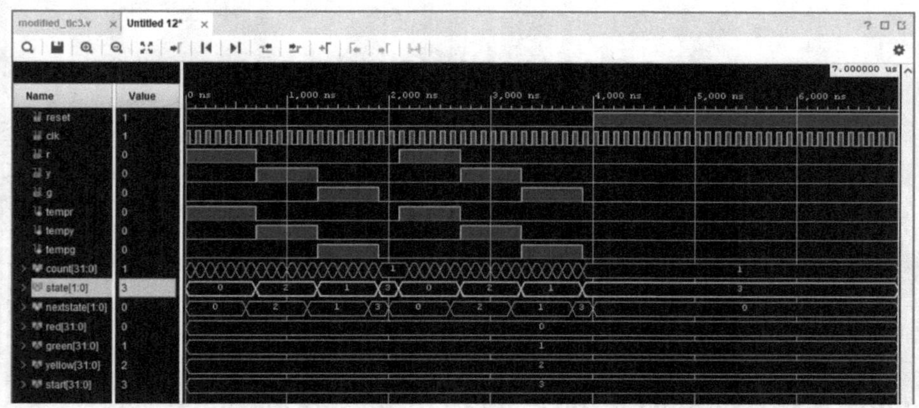

Figure 6-16. *Setting the force constant value of signal "reset" to 1*

Now, if we click the Run for 3μs button once again and then we click the Zoom Fit button to view the simulated waveforms on the wave window, we will get the results as illustrated in Figure 6-17.

Figure 6-17. *The simulated waveforms on the wave window*

Modified Moore FSM with Two-Process Methodology

In this section we are going to modify the Moore FSM traffic lights control example using two-process methodology. So we create a new Verilog file named "modified_tlc2.v" in the Design Sources folder of project "Simple_FSM" in "A Simple Moore FSM" section and add the following codes inside of it:

```verilog
`timescale 1ns / 1ps
module modified_tlc2(
    input reset,clk,
    output r,y,g
    );
reg tempr = 0, tempy = 0, tempg = 0;
integer count;
reg [1:0] state = 0; //00 01 10 11
reg [1:0] nextstate = 0;
initial count = 0;
parameter red = 0, green = 1, yellow = 2, start = 3;
always@(posedge clk or posedge reset) begin
if (reset == 1'b1)
   state <= start;
else
   state <= nextstate;
end
//Next state decoder
always@(posedge clk) begin
case(state)
start: begin
tempr = 1'b0;
tempy = 1'b0;
```

```
tempg = 1'b0;
nextstate = red;
end
red: begin
tempr = 1'b1;
tempy = 1'b0;
tempg = 1'b0;
if (count < 5)
   count = count + 1;
else begin
   nextstate = yellow;
   count = 0;
end
end
yellow: begin
tempr = 1'b0;
tempy = 1'b1;
tempg = 1'b0;
if (count < 5)
   count = count + 1;
else begin
   nextstate = green;
   count = 0;
end
end
green: begin
tempr = 1'b0;
tempy = 1'b0;
tempg = 1'b1;
if (count < 5)
   count = count + 1;
else begin
```

```
    nextstate = start;
    count = 0;
end
end
endcase
end
assign r = tempr;
assign y = tempy;
assign g = tempg;
endmodule
```

We do the same as previous procedures for running the simulation, and in the opened simulation window, we click the Restart button and then right-click the signal "reset" and set the force constant value to 0 as illustrated in Figure 6-14. We also right-click the signal "clk" and set the force clock parameters as shown in Figure 6-15. Now, we click the Run for 4μs button once, and then we right-click the signal "reset" again and force its constant value to 1 as depicted in Figure 6-16. Now, if we click the Run for 3μs button once again and then click the Zoom Fit button to view the simulated waveforms on the wave window, we will get the results as illustrated in Figure 6-18.

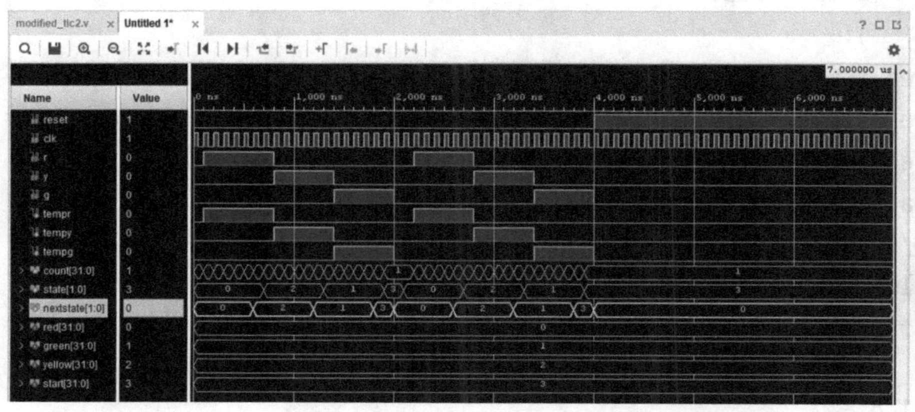

Figure 6-18. *The simulated waveforms on the wave window*

Three-Process Methodology for Mealy Machines

In this section, we will implement a three-process Mealy machine. Figure 6-19 shows a simple Mealy machine example.

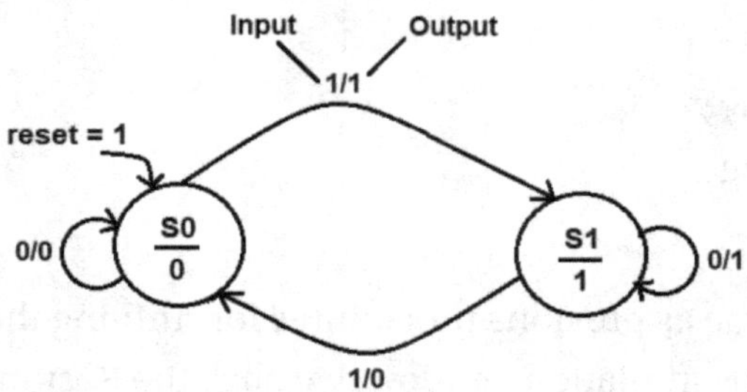

Figure 6-19. *A simple Mealy machine example*

So we create a new project named "Mealy3" and also create a design source file titled "mealy.v" and add the following codes inside of it:

```verilog
`timescale 1ns / 1ps
module mealy(
    input clk,din,reset,
    output dout
    );
reg temp = 0;
reg state = 0;
reg nextstate = 0;
parameter s0 = 0, s1 = 1;
//Reset Logic
always@(posedge clk or posedge reset) begin
if (reset == 1'b1)
    state <= s0;
else
```

```verilog
      state <= nextstate;
end
//Next state decoder logic
always@(state or din) begin
case(state)
s0: begin
if(din == 1'b0)
   nextstate = s0;
else
   nextstate = s1;
end
s1: begin
if(din == 1'b0)
   nextstate = s1;
else
   nextstate = s0;
end
endcase
end
always@(state or din) begin
case(state)
s0: begin
if(din == 1'b0)
   temp = 0;
else
   temp = 1;
end
s1: begin
if(din == 1'b0)
   temp = 1;
else
```

```
    temp = 0;
end
endcase
end
assign dout = temp;
endmodule
```

We do the same as previous procedures for running the simulation, and in the opened simulation window, we click the Restart button and right-click the signals "clk" and "din" and set the force clock parameters as shown in Figures 6-20 and 6-21, respectively. Then, we right-click the signal "reset" and set the force constant value to 0 as illustrated in Figure 6-22.

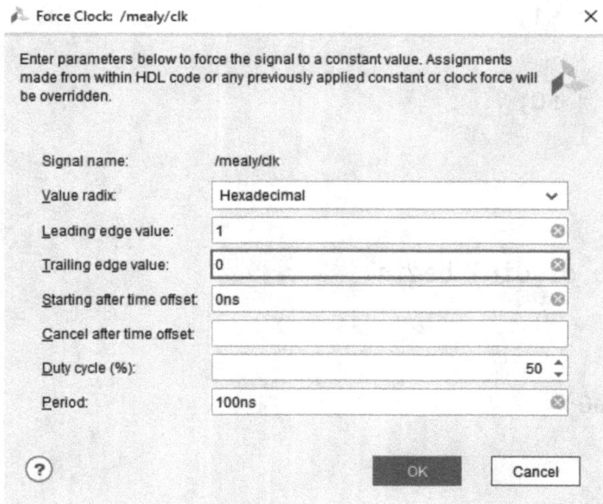

Figure 6-20. *Setting the force clock parameters for signal "clk"*

Force Clock: /mealy/din

Enter parameters below to force the signal to a constant value. Assignments made from within HDL code or any previously applied constant or clock force will be overridden.

Signal name: /mealy/din
Value radix: Hexadecimal
Leading edge value: 1
Trailing edge value: 0
Starting after time offset: 0ns
Cancel after time offset:
Duty cycle (%):   50
Period: 400ns

OK   Cancel

Figure 6-21. *Setting the force clock parameters for signal "din"*

Force Constant: /mealy/reset

Enter parameters below to force the signal to a constant value. Assignments made from within HDL code or any previously applied constant or clock force will be overridden.

Signal name: /mealy/reset
Value radix: Hexadecimal
Force value: 0
Starting after time offset: 0ns
Cancel after time offset:

OK   Cancel

Figure 6-22. *Setting the force constant value of signal "reset" to 0*

Now, we click the Run for 2µs button once, and then we right-click the signal "reset" again and force its constant value to 1 as depicted in Figure 6-23.

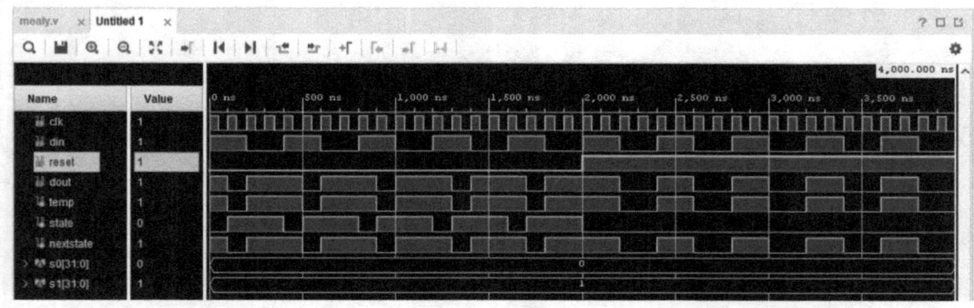

Figure 6-23. *Setting the force constant value of signal "reset" to 1*

Now, if we click the Run for 2µs button once again and then we click
the Zoom Fit button to view the simulated waveforms on the wave window,
we will get the results as illustrated in Figure 6-24.

Figure 6-24. *The simulated waveforms on the wave window*

Two-Process Methodology for Mealy Machines

In this section, we will implement a two-process Mealy machine for the
simple Mealy machine example in Figure 6-19. So we create another
Verilog file titled "mealy2.v" in the Design Sources folder of the project
"Mealy3" in the previous section and add the following codes inside of it:

```verilog
`timescale 1ns / 1ps
module mealy2(
    input clk,din,reset,
    output dout
    );
reg temp = 0;
reg state = 0;
reg nextstate = 0;
parameter s0 = 0, s1 = 1;
//Reset Logic
always@(posedge clk or posedge reset) begin
if (reset == 1'b1)
    state <= s0;
else
    state <= nextstate;
end
//Next state decoder logic
always@(state or din) begin
case(state)
s0: begin
if(din == 1'b0) begin
    nextstate = s0;
    temp = 0;
end
else begin
    nextstate = s1;
    temp = 1;
end
end
s1: begin
if(din == 1'b0) begin
```

```
    nextstate = s1;
     temp = 1;
end
else
begin
   nextstate = s0;
   temp = 0;
end
end
endcase
end
assign dout = temp;
endmodule
```

We do the same as previous procedures for running the simulation, and in the opened simulation window, we click the Restart button and right-click the signals "clk," "din," and "reset" and set the force clock parameters as shown in Figures 6-25, 6-26, and 6-27, respectively.

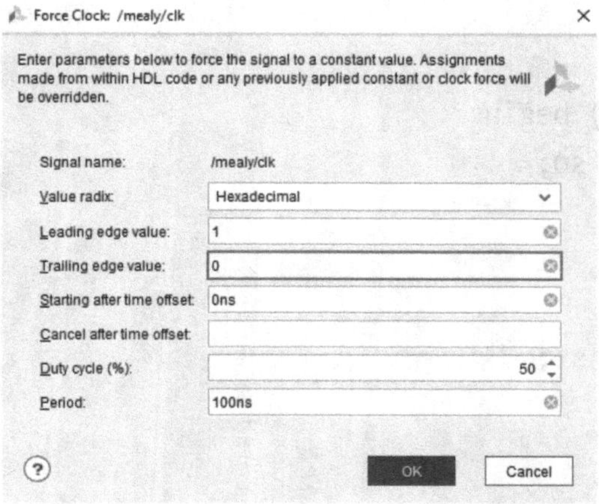

Figure 6-25. *Setting the force clock parameters for signal "clk"*

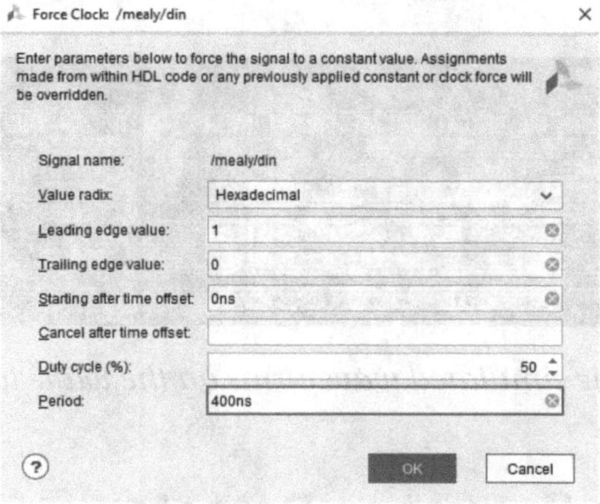

Figure 6-26. *Setting the force clock parameters for signal "din"*

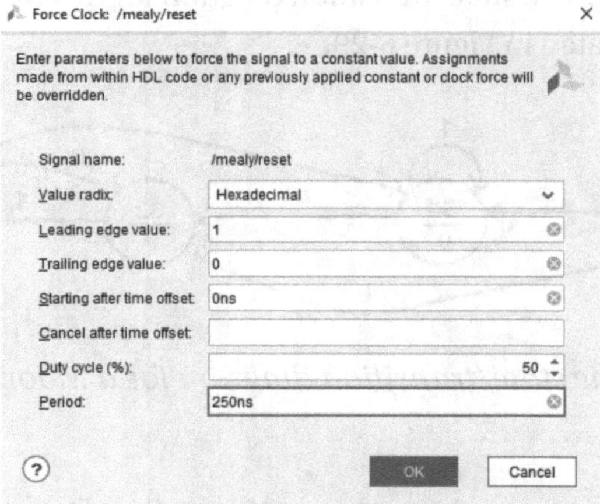

Figure 6-27. *Setting the force clock parameters for signal "reset"*

Now, if we click the Run for 2μs button once and then we click the
Zoom Fit button to view the simulated waveforms on the wave window, we
will get the results as depicted in Figure 6-28.

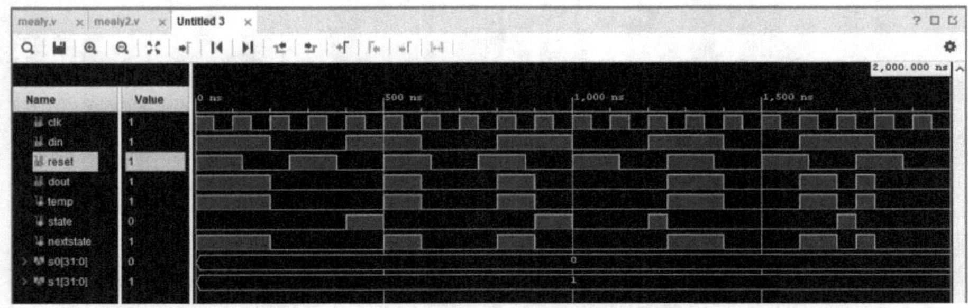

Figure 6-28. *The simulated waveforms on the wave window*

The Moore Sequence Detector

In this section, we will implement a Moore sequence detector to detect the sequence 101. The state/transition diagram for this Moore sequence detector is illustrated in Figure 6-29.

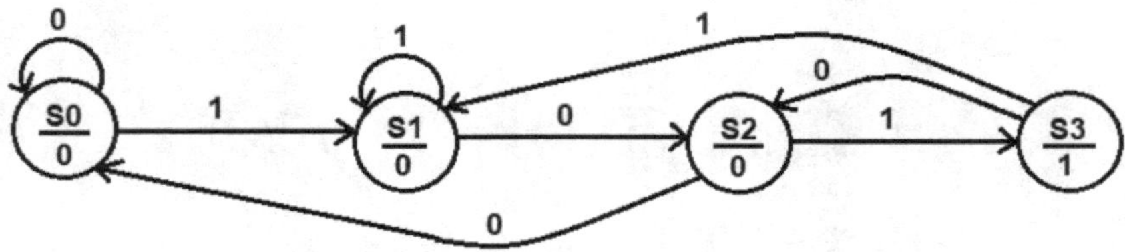

Figure 6-29. *The state/transition diagram for a Moore sequence detector*

So we create a new project named "Moore_Seq_Det" and also create a design source file titled "moore.v" and add the following codes inside of it:

```verilog
`timescale 1ns / 1ps
module moore(
    input clk,din,
    output dout
    );
```

```verilog
reg temp = 0;
reg [1:0] state = 0;
reg [1:0] nextstate = 0; //Since we do not have the reset logic
parameter s0 = 0, s1 = 1, s2 = 2, s3 = 3;
always@(posedge clk) begin
   state <= nextstate;
end
//Next state decoder logic
always@(posedge clk) begin
case(state)
s0: begin
if (din == 1'b0) begin
  nextstate = s0;
  temp = 0;
end
else begin
  nextstate = s1;
  temp = 0;
end
end
s1: begin
if (din == 1'b0) begin
  nextstate = s2;
  temp = 0;
end
else begin
  nextstate = s1;
  temp = 0;
end
end
s2: begin
```

```verilog
if (din == 1'b0) begin
   nextstate = s0;
   temp = 0;
end
else begin
   nextstate = s3;
   temp = 1;
end
end
s3: begin
if (din == 1'b0) begin
   nextstate = s2;
   temp = 0;
end
else begin
   nextstate = s1;
   temp = 0;
end
end
endcase
end
assign dout = temp;
endmodule
```

We do the same as previous procedures for running the simulation, and in the opened simulation window, we click the Restart button, and then we right-click the signal "clk" and set the force clock parameters as shown in Figure 6-30. We also right-click the signal "din" and set the force constant value to 1 as depicted in Figure 6-31. Now, we click the Run for 200ns button once, and then we right-click the signal "din" and set the force constant value to 0 as illustrated in Figure 6-32. Once again, we click the Run for 200ns button, and then we right-click the signal "din" and set the force constant value to 1 as shown in Figure 6-31. Once again, we click the Run for 200ns button, and then we click the Zoom Fit button to view the simulated waveforms on the wave window, so we will get the results as depicted in Figure 6-33.

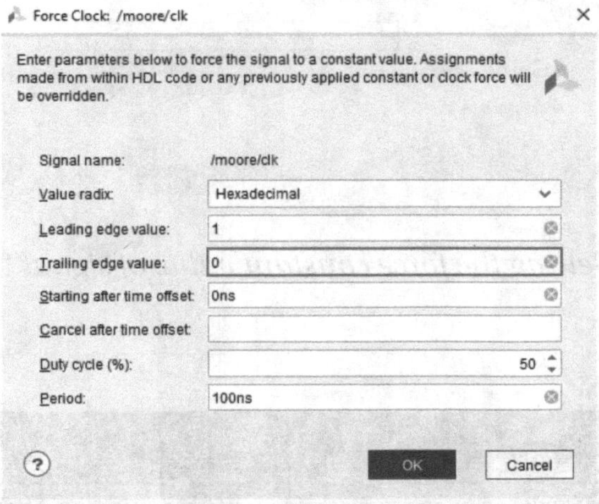

Figure 6-30. *Setting the force clock parameters for signal "clk"*

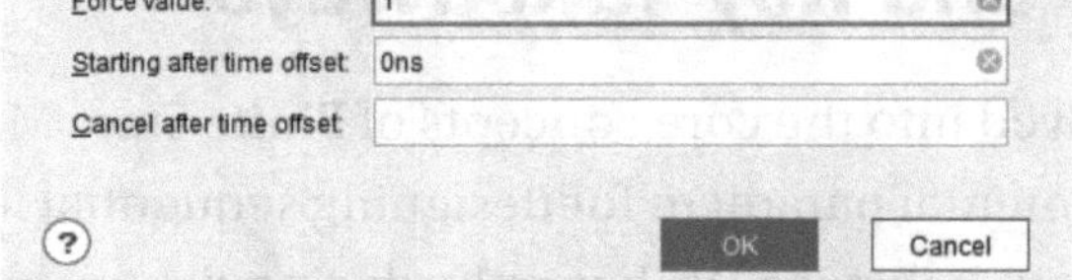

Figure 6-31. *Setting the force constant value of signal "din" to 1*

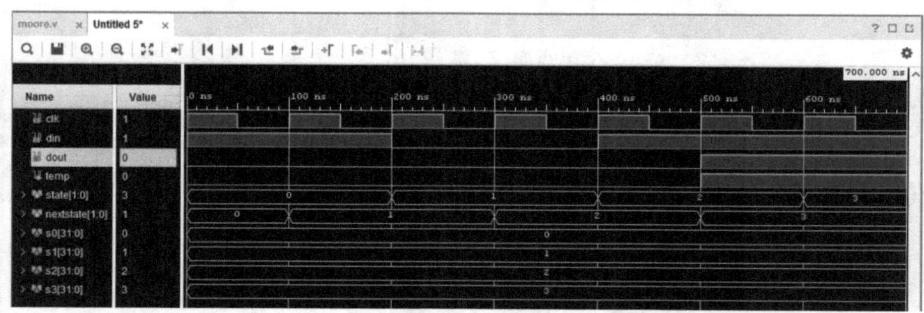

Figure 6-32. *Setting the force constant value of signal "din" to 0*

Figure 6-33. *The simulated waveforms on the wave window*

Summary and Key Takeaways

This chapter delved into the core concepts of Finite State Machines
(FSMs), a fundamental paradigm for designing sequential logic circuits
that control system behavior. We began by distinguishing between the two
primary types of FSMs: the Moore machine, where outputs depend solely
on the current state, and the Mealy machine, where outputs depend on
both the current state and the inputs. A practical traffic lights controller
served as our initial introduction to building a simple Moore FSM.

We then explored the two primary coding methodologies for implementing FSMs in Verilog. The three-process methodology provides a highly structured and readable approach by separating the state register, next-state logic, and output logic into distinct always blocks. In contrast, the two-process methodology combines the next-state and output logic, often leading to more concise code. We applied both methodologies to implement Moore and Mealy machines, including modified versions of the traffic lights controller, allowing you to compare their trade-offs in clarity and efficiency. Finally, we applied these concepts to a practical Moore sequence detector, demonstrating how an FSM can be designed to recognize a specific input pattern (101), solidifying the real-world application of these design techniques. By now you should be able to differentiate between Moore and Mealy machines, model them effectively using both two- and three-process styles, and apply FSMs to solve sequential control problems.

In the next chapter, we will move from designing individual modules to building more complex systems, exploring Vivado's block design interface and the use of Intellectual Property (IP) cores to create sophisticated digital designs efficiently.

CHAPTER 7

Block Design and IPs

In Chapter 6, we explored Finite State Machines (FSMs), learning how to model sequential logic for control systems and pattern recognition. Now, in this chapter, we shift our focus to modular design and Intellectual Property (IP) cores, which enable efficient system integration by reusing pre-verified hardware blocks. IP-based design is a cornerstone of modern digital systems, allowing designers to build complex applications faster while minimizing errors.

This chapter begins with predefined IP cores, including a binary counter, a sinusoidal waveform generator, and a multiplier, demonstrating how to integrate and customize existing IPs for specific applications. We then transition to creating custom IPs from scratch, applying this knowledge to design a D-flip-flop IP and use it in a larger system.

Next, we explore hierarchical design techniques with a 4-bit ripple carry adder and a function generator, highlighting how IPs simplify large-scale projects. We also discuss port polarity in Vivado, ensuring correct signal interfacing between modules. Finally, we bridge hardware and software co-design by implementing a digital filter using MATLAB, showcasing how algorithmic IPs can be optimized for FPGA deployment.

By the end of this chapter, you will be proficient in IP-based design, from integrating existing cores to developing custom modules, enabling you to construct scalable and reusable digital systems efficiently.

© Majid Pakdel 2026
M. Pakdel, *Mastering Verilog for FPGA Design*, Maker Innovations Series,
https://doi.org/10.1007/979-8-8688-2311-4_7

"IP" stands for Intellectual Property. IPs are the libraries for HDL (hardware design language) modules that are available for use. Users and companies build IPs for use, so that designs are easier and faster to build. Block design significantly reduces time to design a system.

The Binary Counter IP

To start, we want to create a 4-bit binary counter with a built-in IP using block design. So we create a new project named "IP_project1" and then click the Create Block Design option with the design name of "design_1" as shown in Figure 7-1.

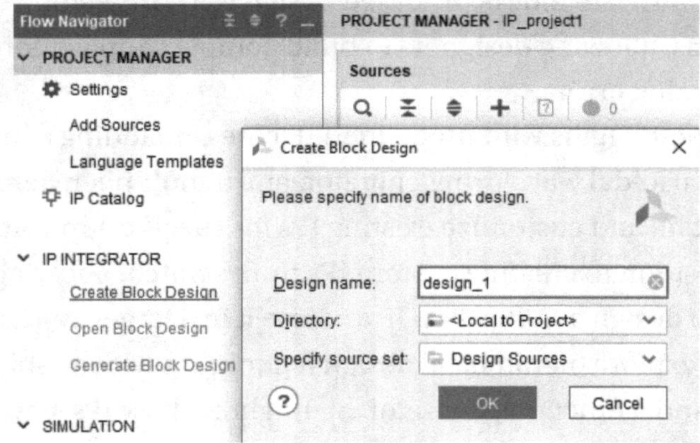

Figure 7-1. *Creating a block design*

Now, we click the add (+) button and enter "binary" in the search area to find the binary counter IP as depicted in Figure 7-2.

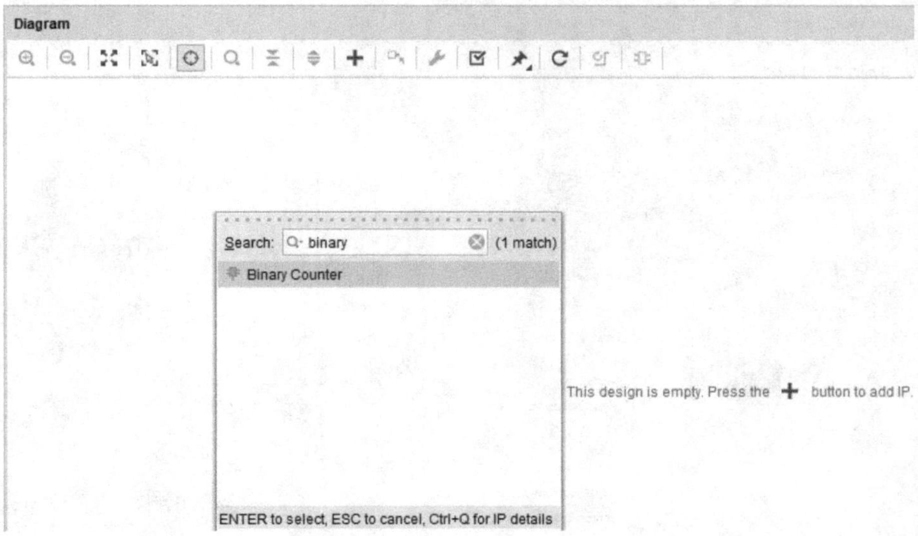

Figure 7-2. *Searching for the binary counter IP*

We double-click the binary counter IP and set its Basic and Control tab parameters as illustrated in Figures 7-3 and 7-4, respectively.

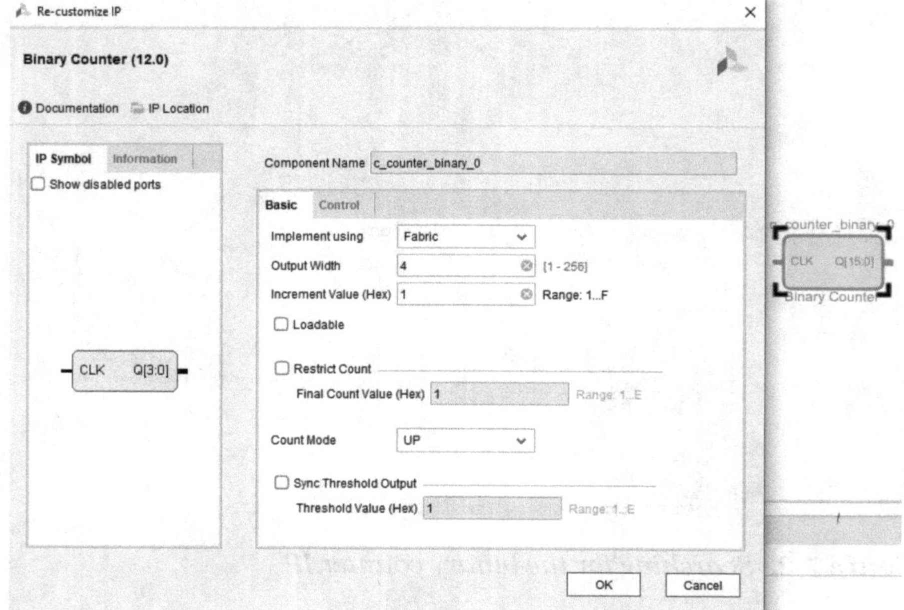

Figure 7-3. *Setting the binary counter IP Basic tab parameters*

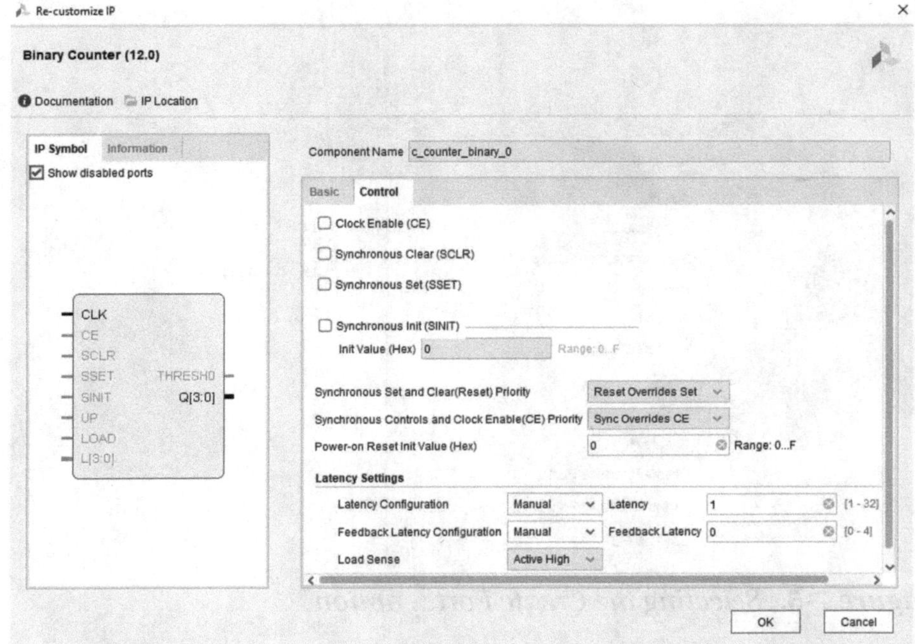

Figure 7-4. *Setting the binary counter IP Control tab parameters*

We right-click in the block diagram window and select the Create
Port... option as shown in Figure 7-5.

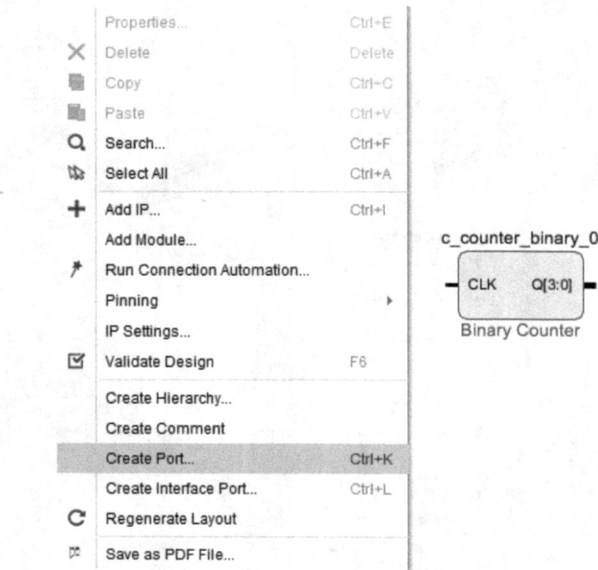

Figure 7-5. *Selecting the Create Port... option*

Then, we set the Create Port window parameters as depicted in Figure 7-6.

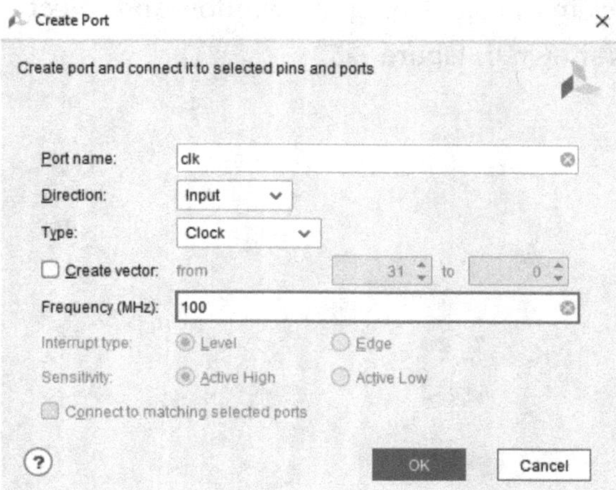

Figure 7-6. *Setting the Create Port window parameters*

Now, we connect the port "clk" to the clock pin of the binary counter. We can do the same procedure for the port "Q_0[3:0]." However, we can also select the pin "Q[3:0]" in the binary counter and press Ctrl + T on the keyboard; we can easily do that as illustrated in Figure 7-7.

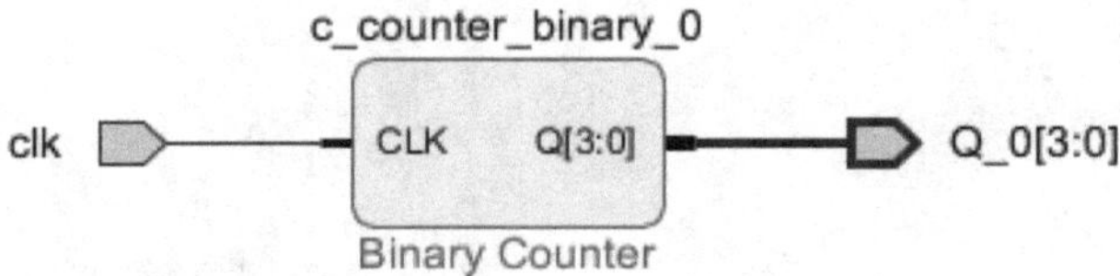

Figure 7-7. *The binary counter with connected ports*

We also click the port "Q_0" and set its name as "q" as shown in Figure 7-8.

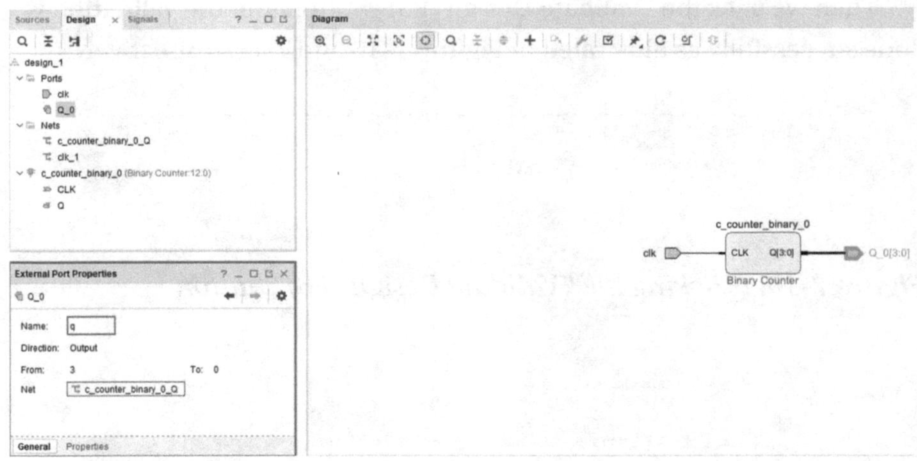

Figure 7-8. *Setting the port "Q_0" name as "q"*

In the Diagram window, we click the "Optimize Routing" button as depicted in Figure 7-9.

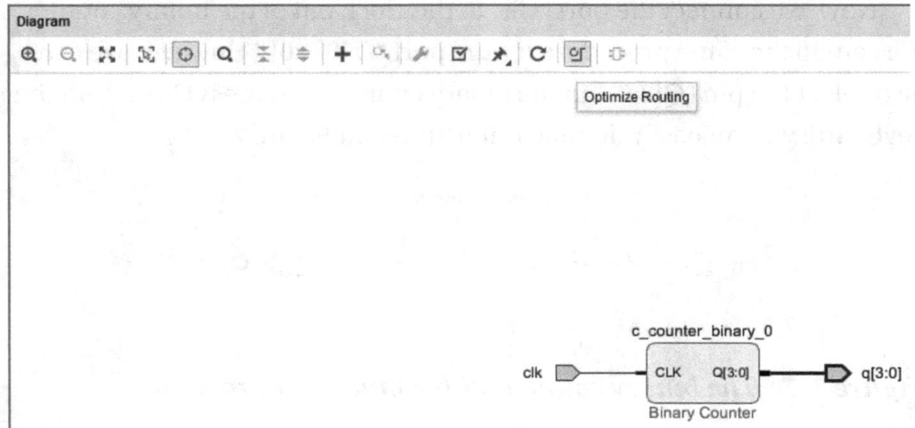

Figure 7-9. *Clicking the "Optimize Routing" button*

Then we click the "Validate Design (F6)" button and the validation is done successfully as illustrated in Figures 7-10 and 7-11, respectively.

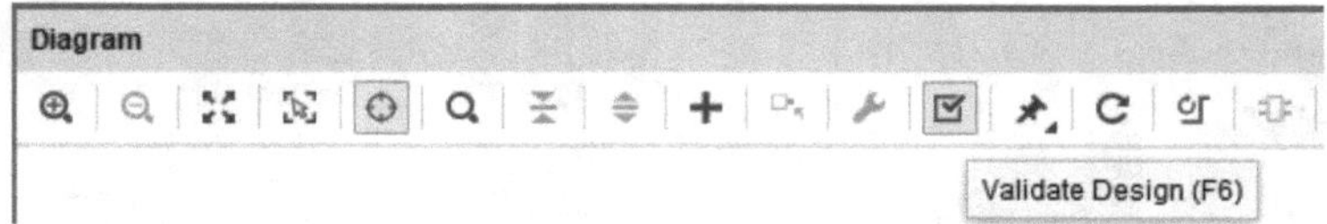

Figure 7-10. *Clicking the "Validate Design (F6)" button*

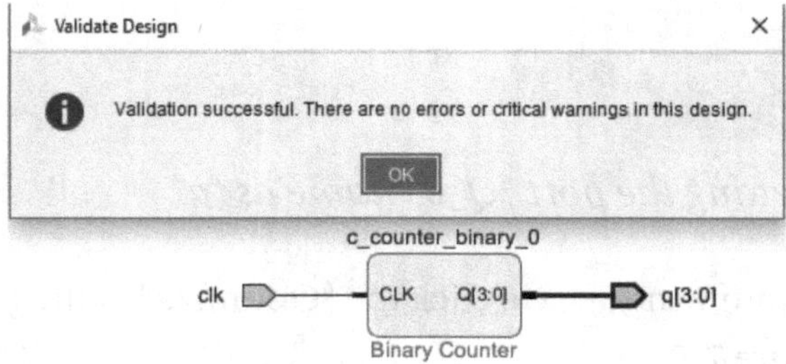

Figure 7-11. *Successful design validation*

Now, we right-click "design_1" and select the "Create HDL Wrapper…" option, and then in the opened window, we let Vivado manage wrapper and auto-update as shown in Figures 7-12 and 7-13, respectively.

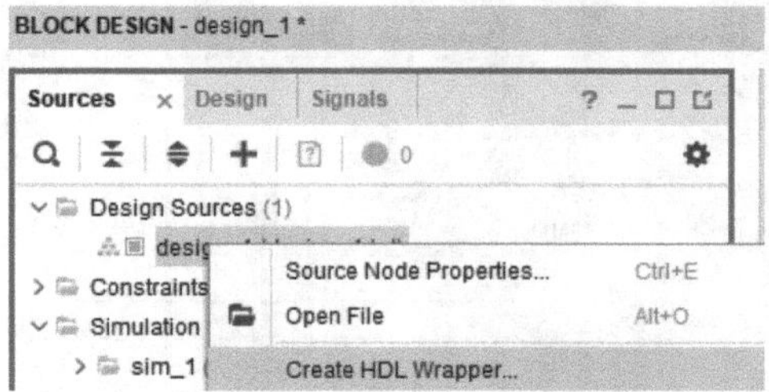

Figure 7-12. *Selecting the "Create HDL Wrapper…" option*

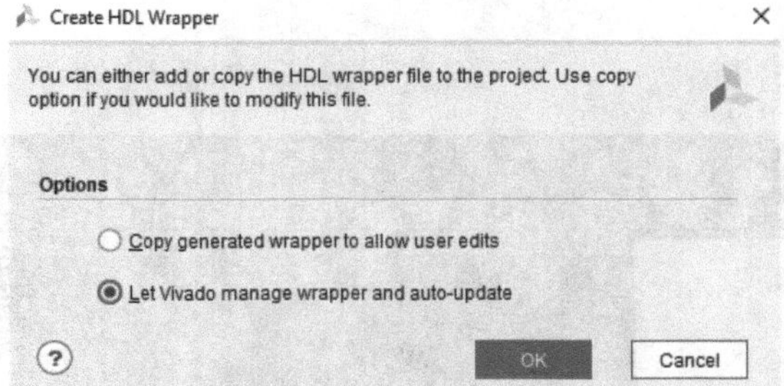

Figure 7-13. *Letting Vivado manage wrapper and auto-update*

We select Flow ➤ Run Simulation ➤ Run Behavioral Simulation from the menu toolbar to view the waveforms on the wave window. So, in the opened simulation window, we click the Restart button and then right-click the signal "clk" and set the force clock parameters as depicted in Figure 7-14. Now, we click the Run for 200ns button, and then we click the Zoom Fit button to view the simulated waveforms on the wave window. We also right-click the signal "q[3:0]" and choose the Radix option as Unsigned Decimal, so we will get the results as illustrated in Figure 7-15.

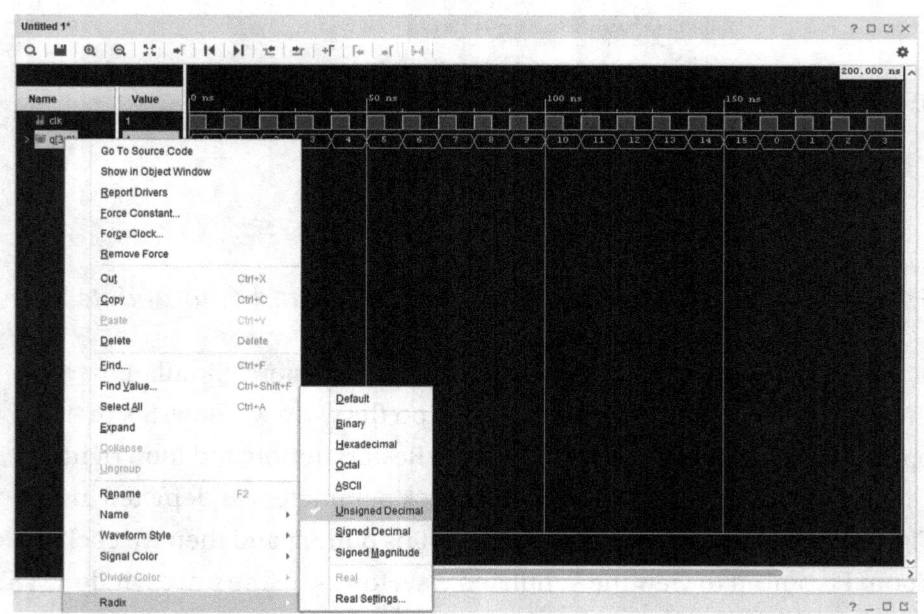

Figure 7-14. *Setting the force clock parameters for signal "clk"*

Figure 7-15. *Choosing the Radix option as Unsigned Decimal*

We also right-click the signal "q[3:0]" and choose Waveform Style as Analog, to view the signal "q[3:0]" as an analog waveform. Then we select Waveform Style ➤ Analog Settings… as shown in Figure 7-16.

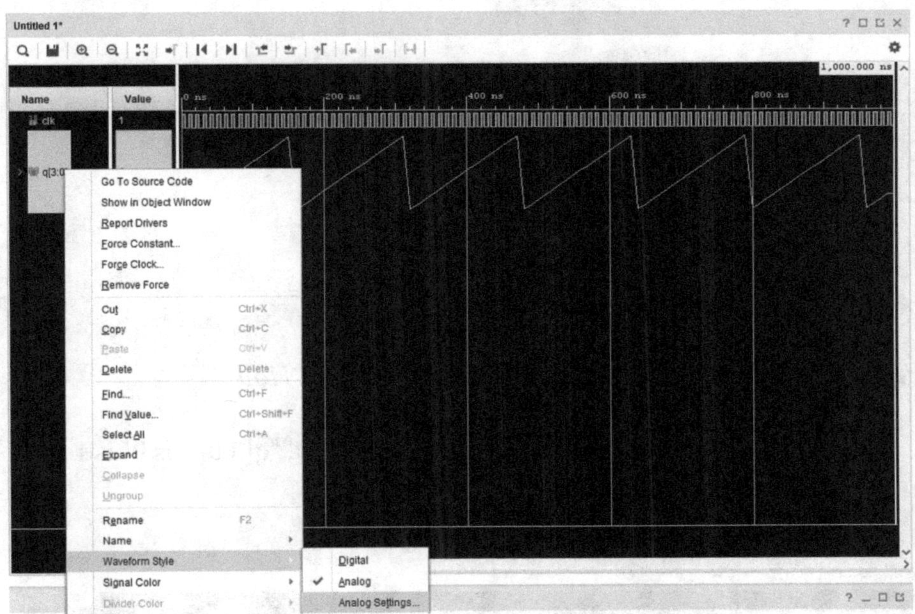

Figure 7-16. *Choosing Waveform Style of signal "q[3:0]" as Analog*

In the opened Analog Settings window, we set the interpolation style as "Hold" as depicted in Figure 7-17.

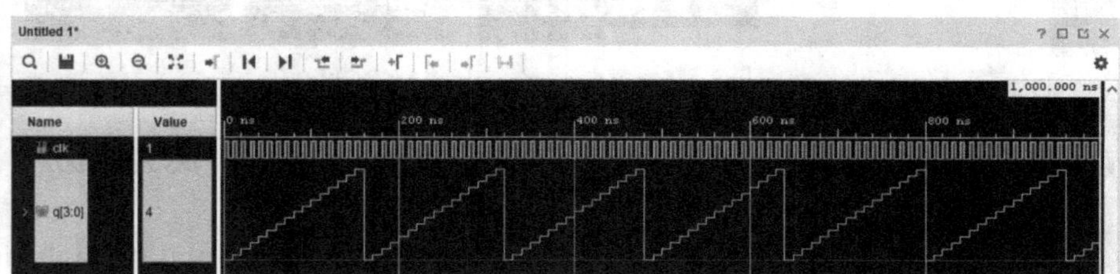

Figure 7-17. *Setting the interpolation style as "Hold"*

So we can view the staircase waveform of signal "q[3:0]" as illustrated in Figure 7-18.

Figure 7-18. *The staircase waveform of signal "q[3:0]"*

The Sinusoidal Waveform Generator IP

In this section, we want to create a sinusoidal waveform generator using a DDS compiler IP. So we create a new project named "IP_sine_gen" and then click the Create Block Design option with the design name of "design_1." Now, we click the add (+) button and enter "dds" in the search area to find the DDS compiler IP as depicted in Figure 7-19.

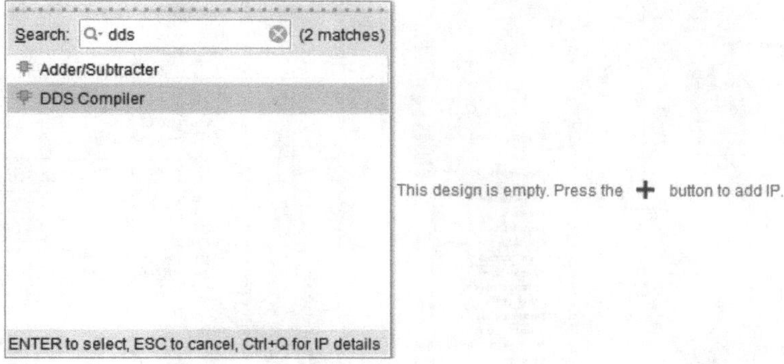

Figure 7-19. *Searching for the DDS compiler IP*

We double-click the DDS compiler IP and set its Configuration tab parameters as illustrated in Figure 7-20. Now, we can view the summary of settings in the Summary tab of the DDS Compiler window as shown in Figure 7-21. We also set the Implementation, Detailed Implementation, and Output Frequencies tabs' parameters as depicted in Figures 7-22, 7-23, and 7-24, respectively.

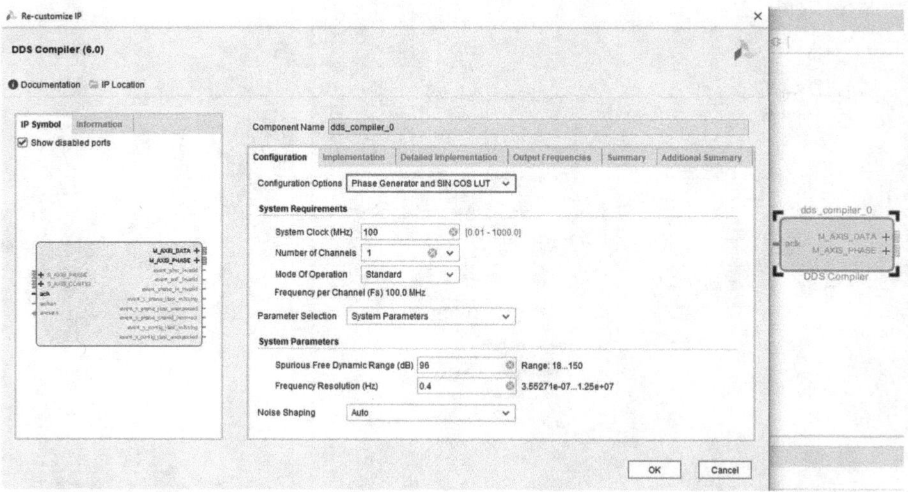

Figure 7-20. *Setting the DDS compiler IP Configuration tab parameters*

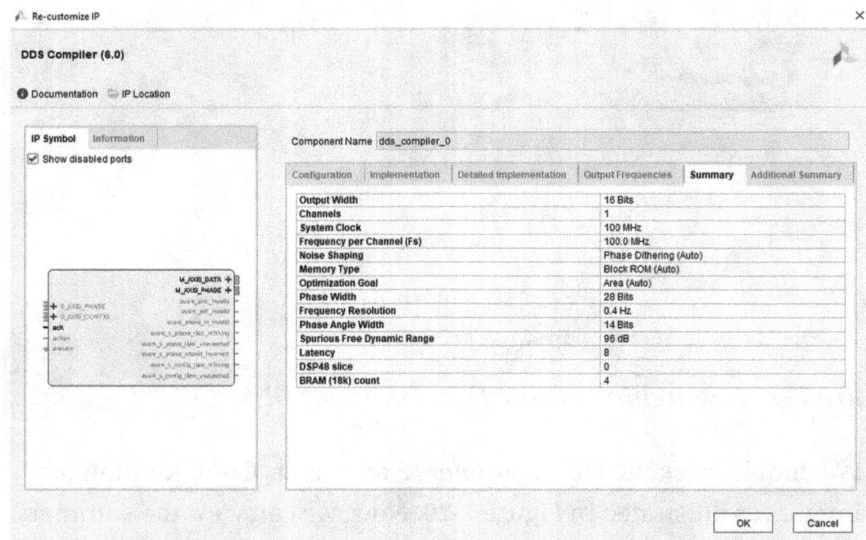

Figure 7-21. *The summary of DDS compiler IP settings*

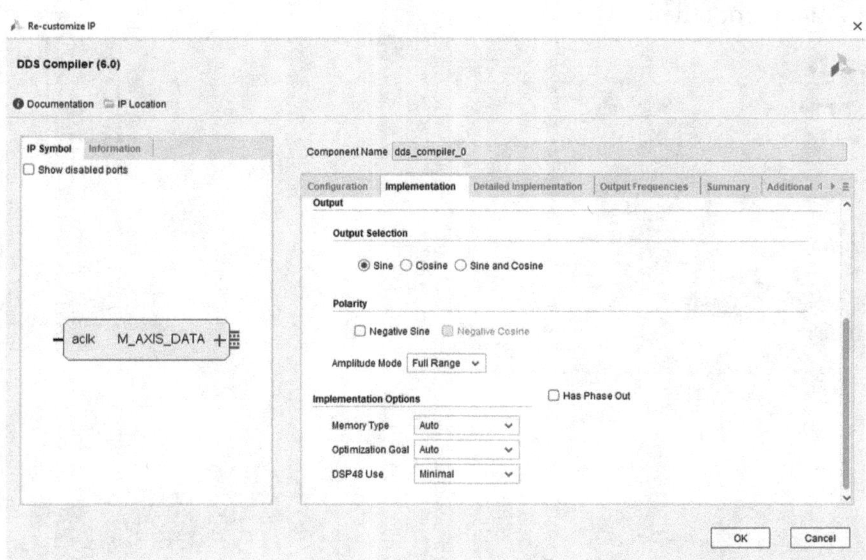

Figure 7-22. *Setting the DDS compiler IP Implementation tab parameters*

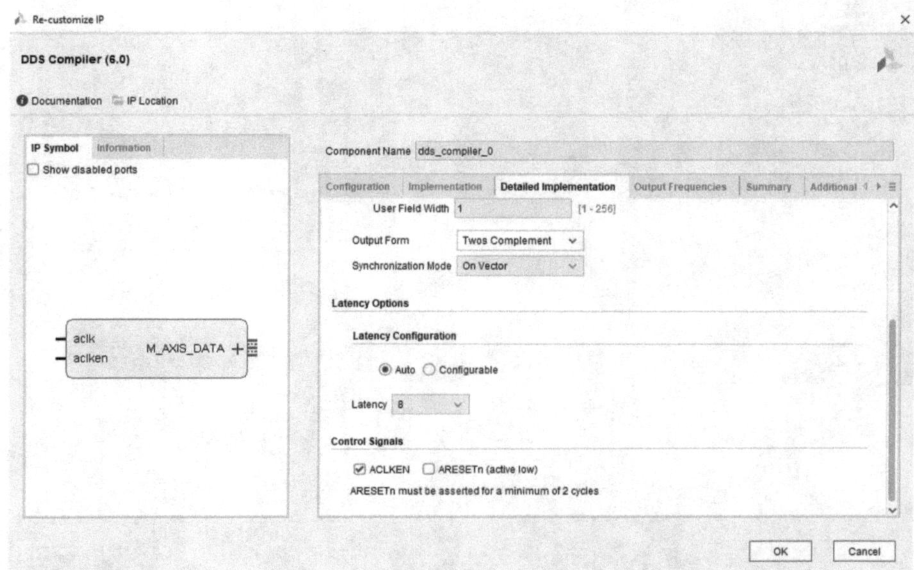

Figure 7-23. *Setting the DDS compiler IP Detailed Implementation tab parameters*

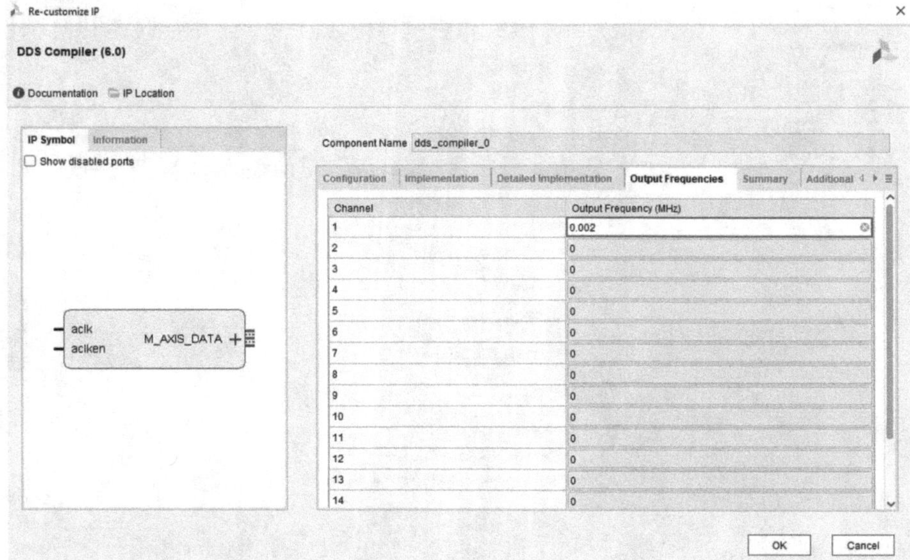

Figure 7-24. *Setting the DDS compiler IP Output Frequencies tab parameters*

We select the pins of the DDS compiler IP and press Ctrl + T on the keyboard to create the connected ports and then click the Optimize Routing button as illustrated in Figure 7-25.

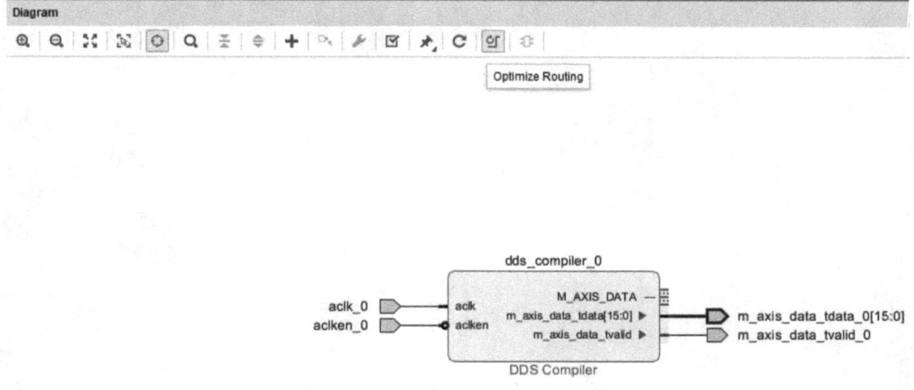

Figure 7-25. *Clicking the Optimize Routing button*

Also, we click the "Validate Design (F6)" button, and the validation is done successfully as illustrated in Figure 7-26.

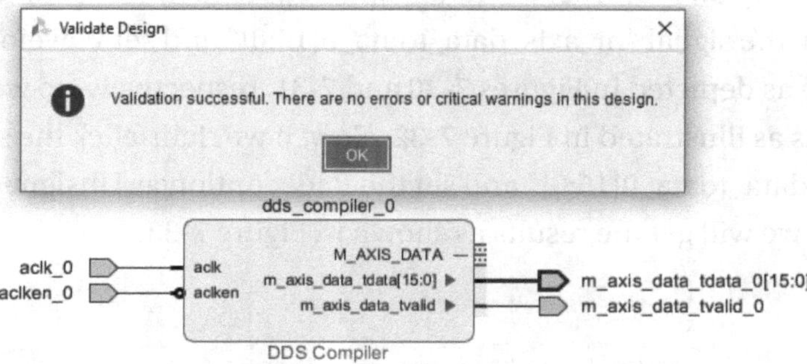

Figure 7-26. *Successful design validation*

Now, we right-click "design_1" and select the "Create HDL wrapper..." option, and then in the opened window, we let Vivado manage wrapper and auto-update as shown in Figure 7-27.

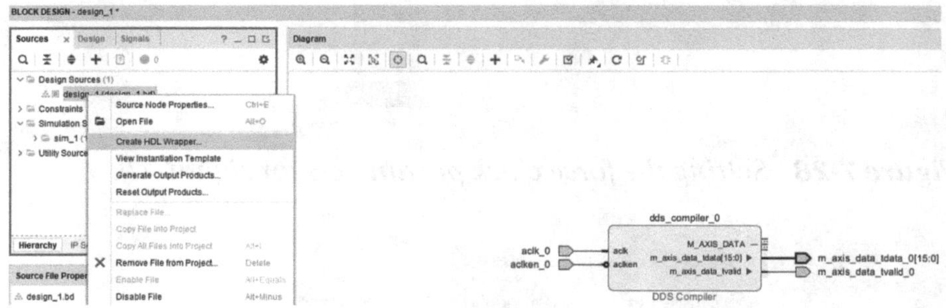

Figure 7-27. *Selecting the "Create HDL Wrapper..." option*

We select Flow ➤ Run Simulation ➤ Run Behavioral Simulation from the menu toolbar to view the waveforms on the wave window. So, in the opened simulation window, we click the Restart button and then right-click the signal "clk" and set the force clock parameters as depicted in Figure 7-28. We right-click the signal "aclken_0" and set the force constant value to 1 as shown in Figure 7-29. Then, we click the Run for 100µs button once, and then we click the Zoom Fit button to view the simulated waveforms on the wave window, and we right-click the signal "m_axis_data_tdata_0[15:0]" and set the Radix option as Signed Decimal. We also right-click the signal "m_axis_data_tdata_0[15:0]" and set Waveform Style as Analog as depicted in Figures 7-30 and 7-31, respectively, so we will get the results as illustrated in Figure 7-32. Now, if we right-click the signal "m_axis_data_tdata_0[15:0]" and set the Radix option as Unsigned Decimal, we will get the results as shown in Figure 7-33.

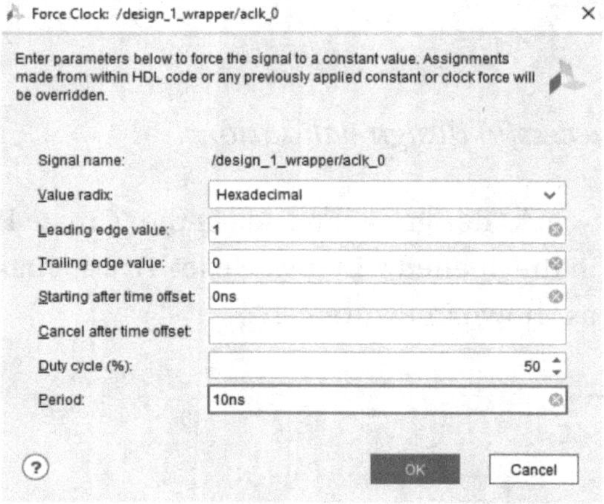

Figure 7-28. *Setting the force clock parameters for signal "clk"*

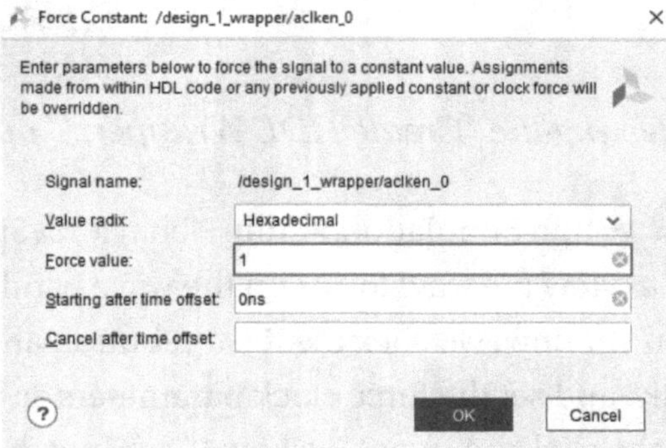

Figure 7-29. *Setting the force constant value of signal "aclken_0" to 1*

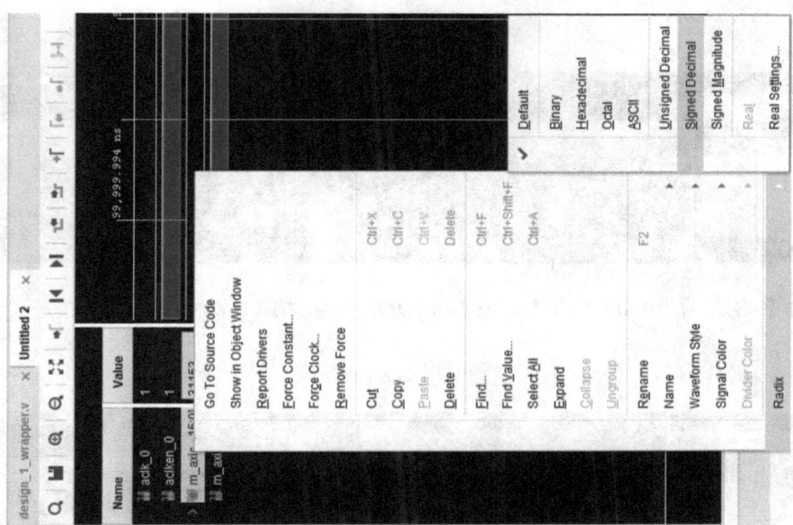

Figure 7-30. *Setting the Radix option as Signed Decimal for signal "m_axis_data_tdata_0"*

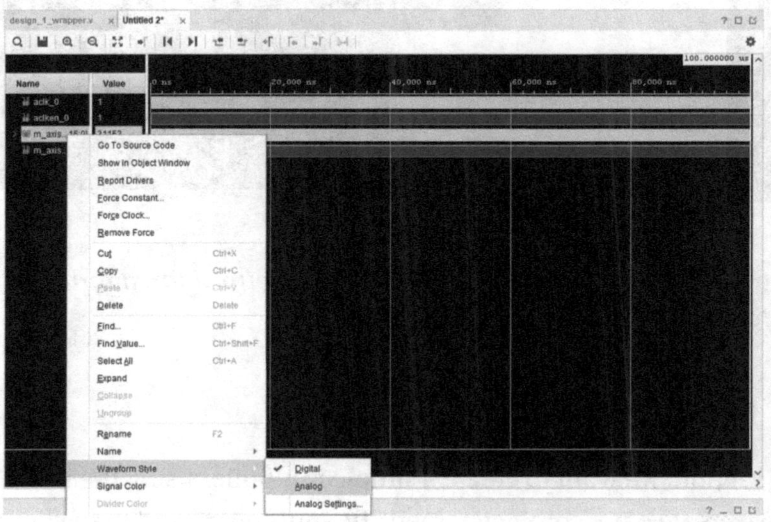

Figure 7-31. *Setting Waveform Style as Analog for signal "m_axis_ data_tdata_0"*

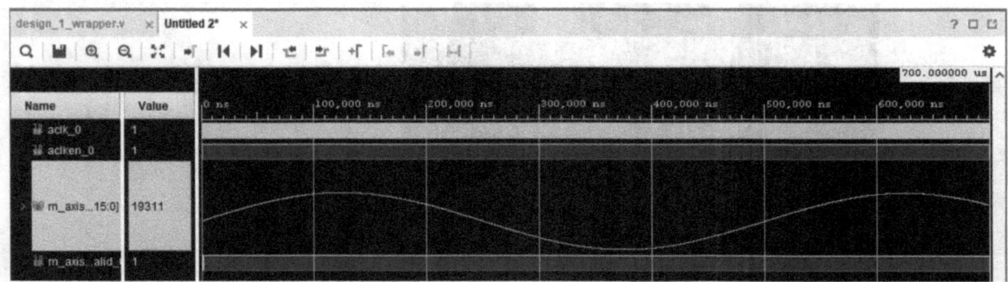

Figure 7-32. *The simulated waveforms on the wave window*

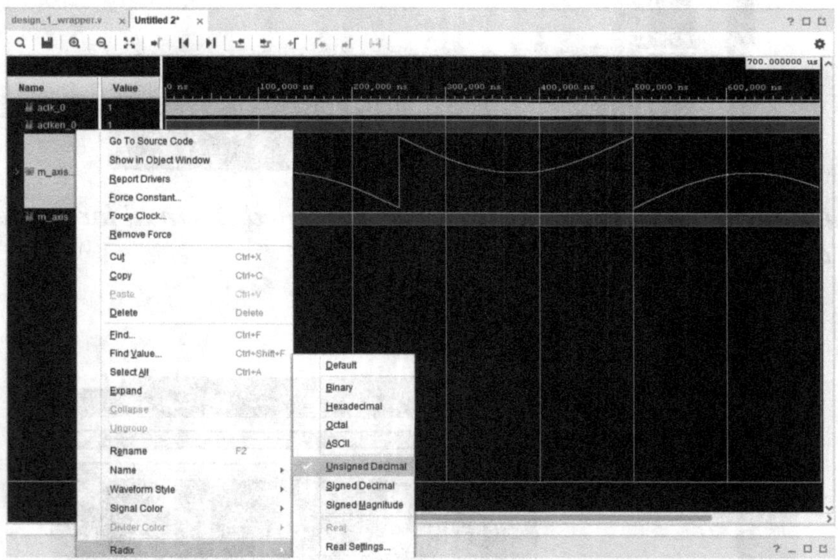

Figure 7-33. *Setting Radix as Unsigned Decimal for signal "m_axis_data_tdata_0"*

The Multiplier IP

In this section, we want to create a simple multiplier using the multiplier IP. So we create a new project named "IP_multiplier" and then click the Create Block Design option with the design name of "design_1." Now, we click the add (+) button and enter "multiplier" in the search area to find the multiplier IP as depicted in Figure 7-34.

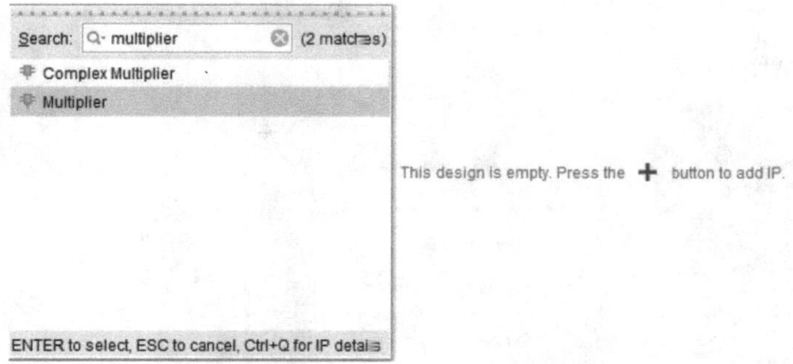

Figure 7-34. *Searching for the multiplier IP*

We double-click the multiplier IP and set its Basic tab parameters as illustrated in Figure 7-35.

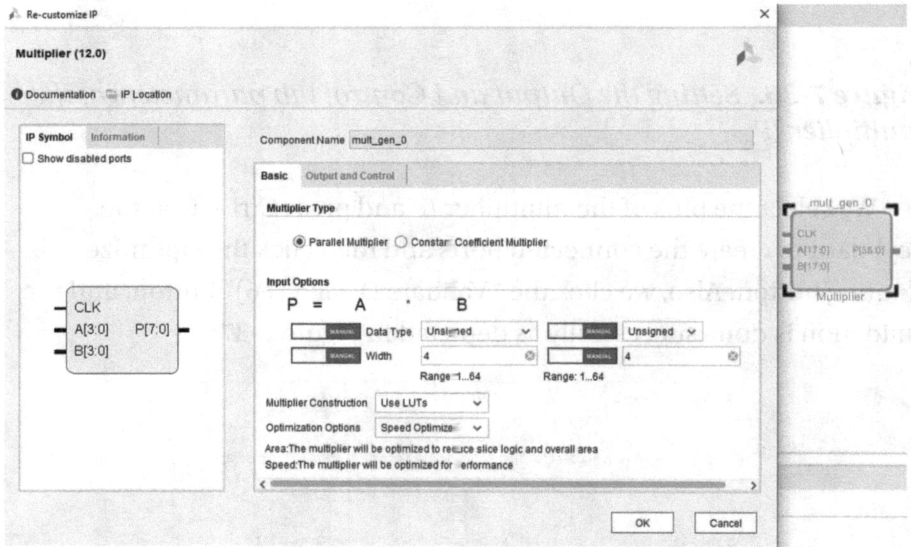

Figure 7-35. *Setting the Basic tab parameters of the multiplier IP*

We also set the Output and Control tab parameters of the multiplier IP as shown in Figure 7-36.

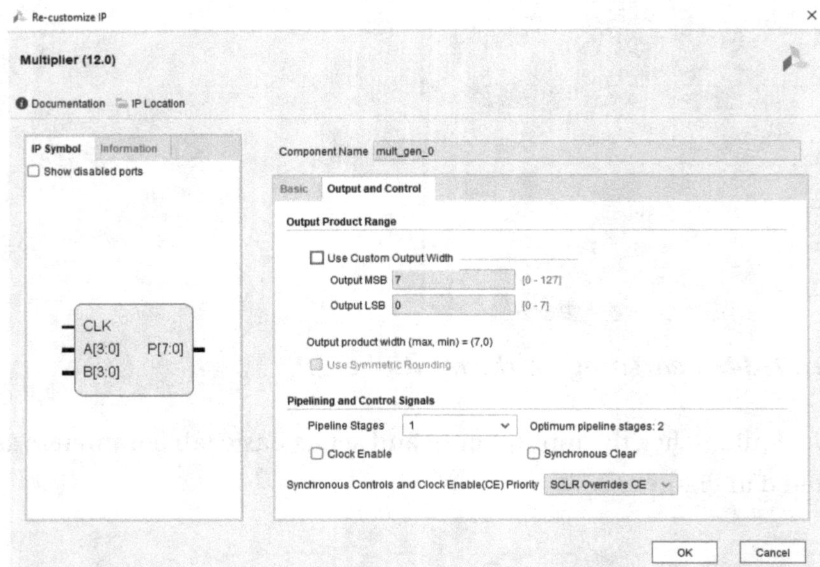

Figure 7-36. *Setting the Output and Control tab parameters of the multiplier IP*

We select the pins of the multiplier IP and press Ctrl + T on the keyboard to create the connected ports and then click the Optimize Routing button. Also, we click the "Validate Design (F6)" button, and the validation is done successfully as depicted in Figure 7-37.

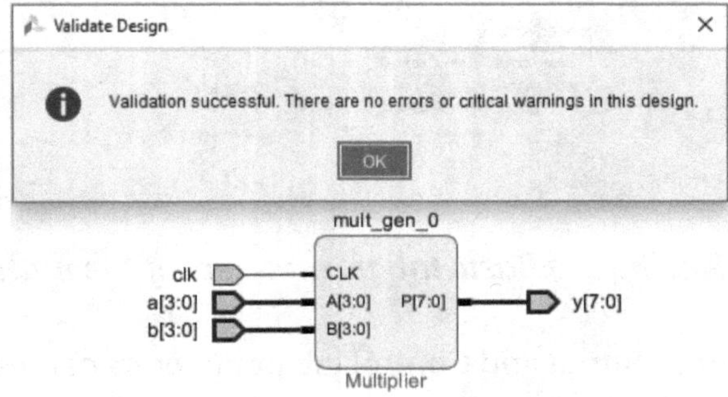

Figure 7-37. *Successful design validation*

Now, we right-click "design_1" and select the "Create HDL Wrapper..." option as shown in Figure 7-38.

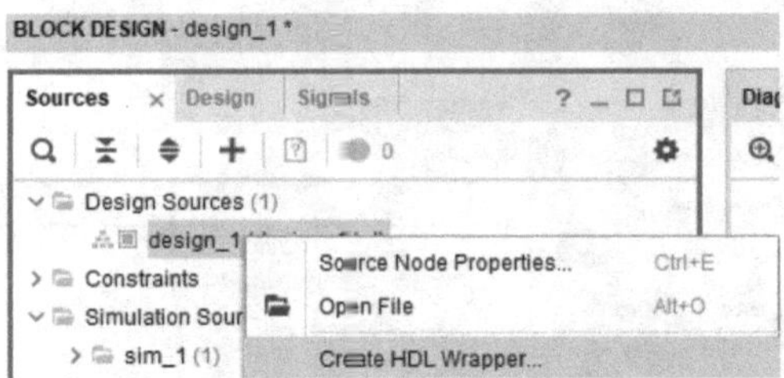

Figure 7-38. Selecting the "Create HDL Wrapper..." option

Now in the opened window, we let Vivado manage wrapper and auto-update as shown in Figure 7-39.

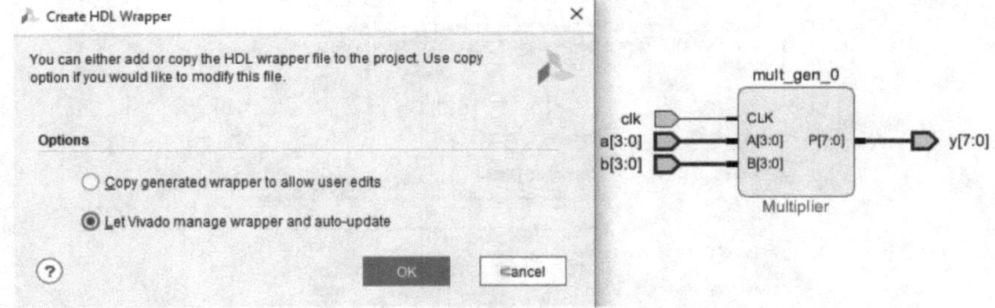

Figure 7-39. Letting Vivado manage wrapper and auto-update

We select Flow ➤ Run Simulation ➤ Run Behavioral Simulation from the menu toolbar to view the waveforms on the wave window. So, in the opened simulation window, we click the Restart button and then right-click the signals "a" and "b" and set their force constant values to unsigned decimal 4 as depicted in Figures 7-40 and 7-41, respectively. We also right-click the signal "clk" and set the force clock parameters as illustrated in Figure 7-42.

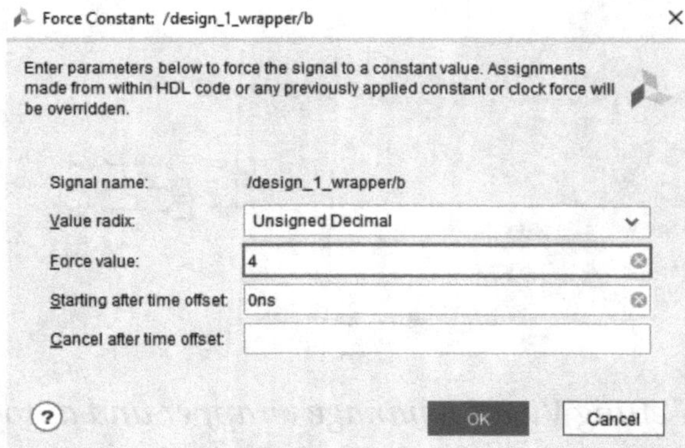

Figure 7-40. *Setting the force constant value of signal "a" to 4*

Figure 7-41. *Setting the force constant value of signal "b" to 4*

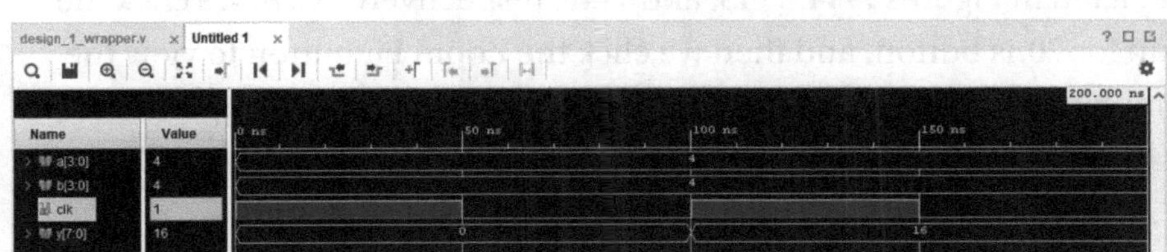

Figure 7-42. *Setting the force clock parameters for signal "clk"*

Now, we click the Run for 200ns button, and then we click the Zoom Fit button to view the simulated waveforms on the wave window. We also right-click the signal "y[7:0]" and choose the Radix option as Unsigned Decimal, so we will get the results as shown in Figure 7-43

Figure 7-43. *The simulated waveforms on the wave window*

Creating a New IP

In this section, we want to create a new IP for a full adder. So we create a new project named "Create_IP_FA" and also create a design source file titled "fa.v" and add the following codes inside of it:

```verilog
`timescale 1ns / 1ps
module fa(
    input a,b,cin,
    output s,cout
    );
assign s = a ^ b ^ cin;
assign cout = (a & b) | (a & cin) | (b & cin);
endmodule
```

We choose Flow ➤ Run Simulation ➤ Run Behavioral Simulation from the menu toolbar to view the waveforms on the wave window. So, in the opened simulation window, we click the Restart button and then right-click the signals "a," "b," and "cin" and set the force clock parameters as depicted in Figures 7-44, 7-45, and 7-46, respectively. Now, we click the Run for 20ns button, and then we click the Zoom Fit button to view the simulated waveforms on the wave window as illustrated in Figure 7-47.

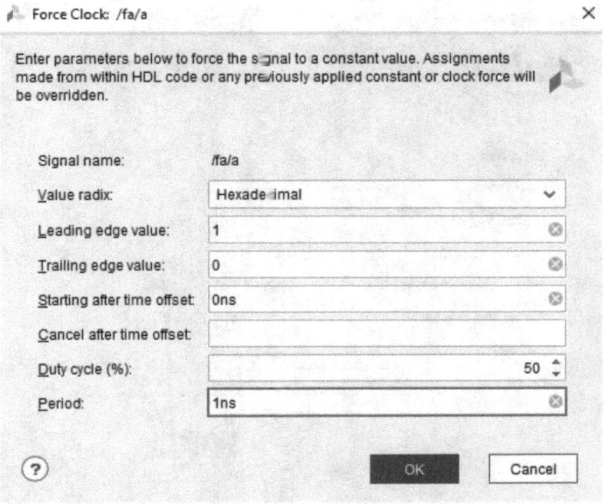

Figure 7-44. *Setting the force clock parameters for signal "a"*

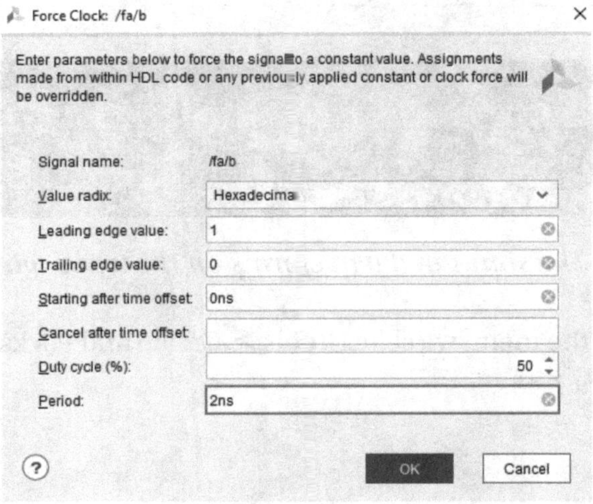

Figure 7-45. *Setting the force clock parameters for signal "b"*

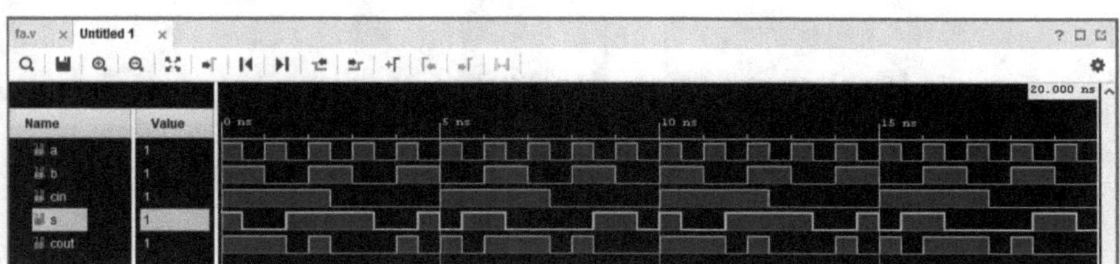

Figure 7-46. *Setting the force clock parameters for signal "cin"*

Figure 7-47. *The simulated waveforms on the wave window*

Now, from the menu we select Tools ➤ Create and Package New IP... as shown in Figure 7-48.

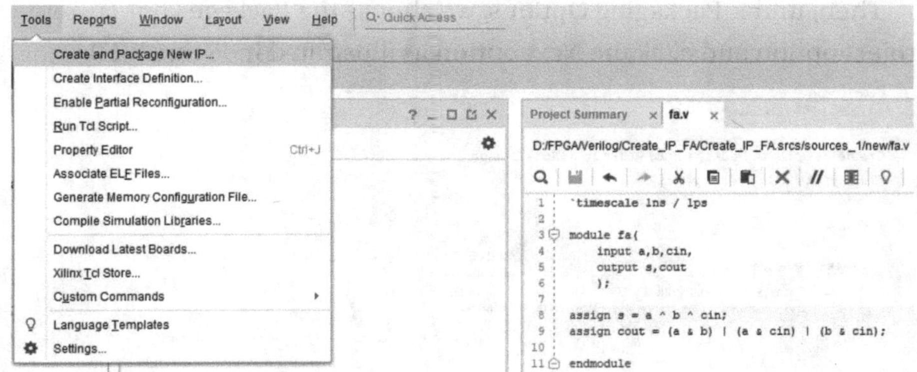

Figure 7-48. *Selecting the Create and Package New IP... option*

In the opened Create and Package New IP window, we click the Next button as depicted in Figure 7-49.

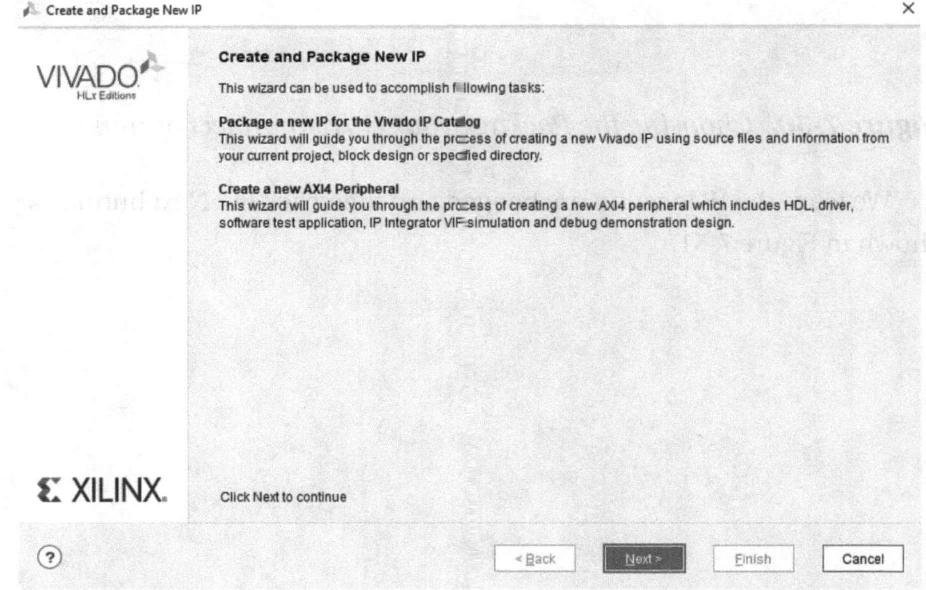

Figure 7-49. *Clicking the Next button*

Then, under Packaging Options, we choose the Package your current project option and click the Next button as illustrated in Figure 7-50.

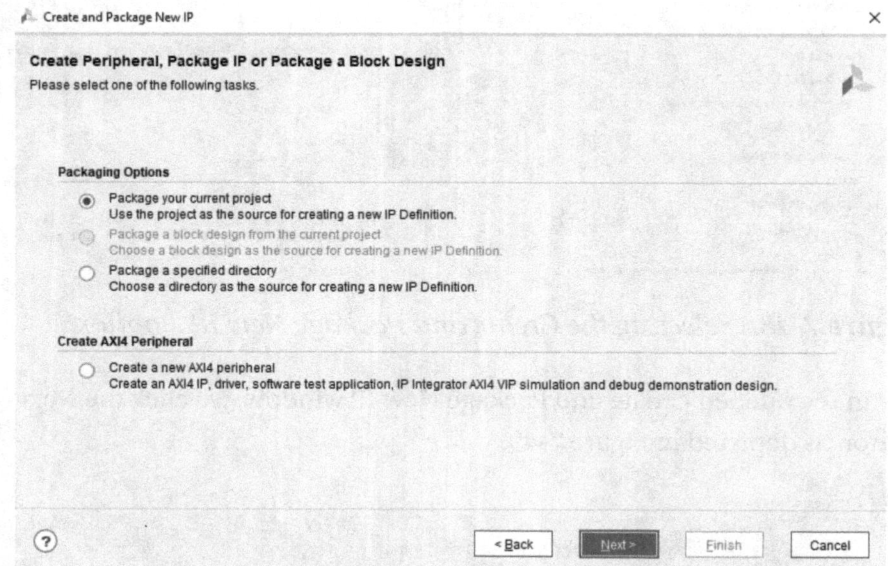

Figure 7-50. *Choosing the Package your current project option*

We leave the IP location unchanged and then click the Next button as shown in Figure 7-51.

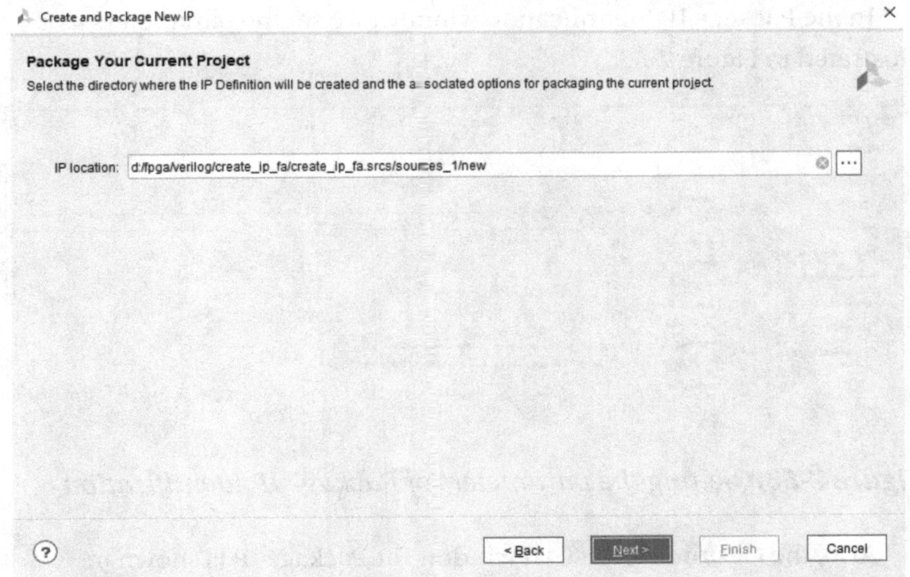

Figure 7-51. *Setting the IP location*

In the New IP Creation summary window, we click the Finish button as depicted in Figure 7-52.

Create and Package New IP

VIVADO
HLx Editions

New IP Creation

The following pieces of information will be gathered:

o Identification information based on top module name
o Family compatibility based on part in the project
o File(s) from Synthesis and Simulation file sets
o Ports from the file containing the top module
o Parameters from the file containing the top module
o Bus Interfaces based on port names
o Address Spaces and Memory Maps based on inferred bus interfaces

Following file will be created on disk along with corresponding customization files:
d:/fpga/verilog/create_ip_fa/create_ip_fa.srcs/sources_1/new/component.xml

Σ XILINX.   Click Finish to continue

< Back   Next >   Finish   Cancel

Figure 7-52. *Clicking the Finish button*

In the Package IP Identification window, we set the parameters as illustrated in Figure 7-53.

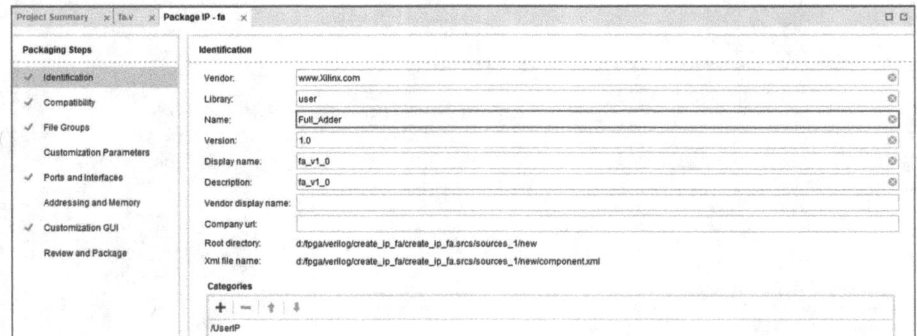

Figure 7-53. *Setting the parameters of Package IP Identification*

Also, the Customization GUI window for Package IP is shown in Figure 7-54, and finally in the Review and Package window, we click the Package IP button and it is done successfully as depicted in Figure 7-55.

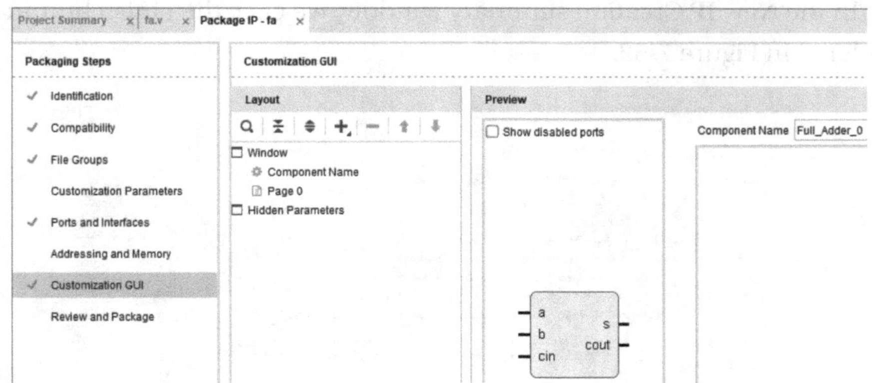

Figure 7-54. *The Customization GUI window for Package IP*

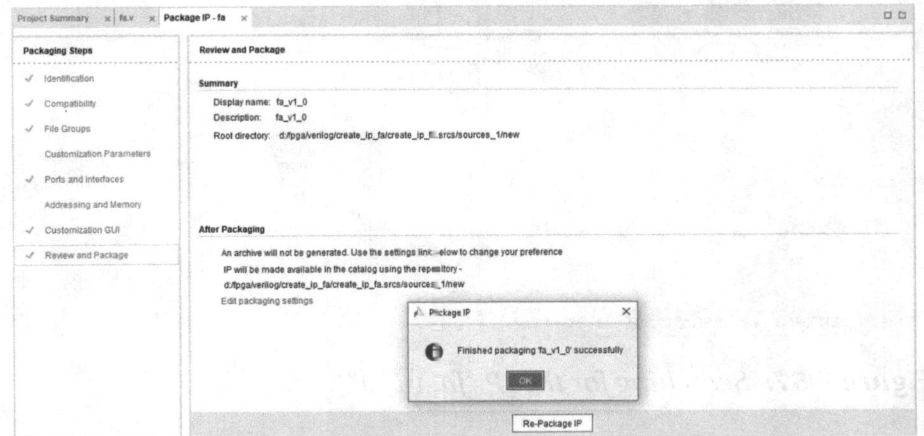

Figure 7-55. *Packaging IP successfully*

Now, we double-click the Create Block Design option in the Project Manager section with the design name of "design_1" as shown in Figure 7-56.

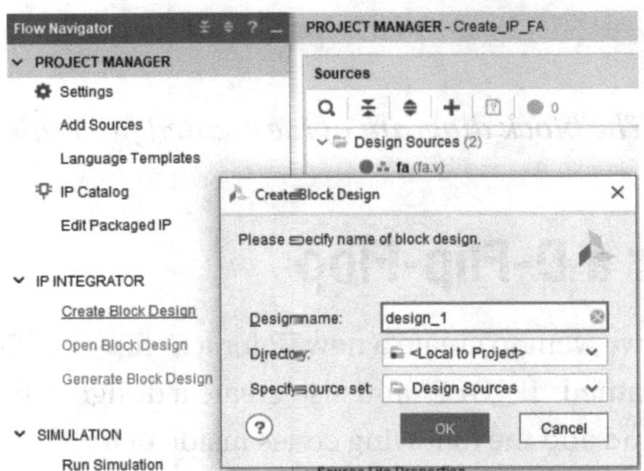

Figure 7-56. *Creating a block design*

Now, we click the add (+) button and enter "full" in the search area to find the IP "fa_v1_0" as depicted in Figure 7-57.

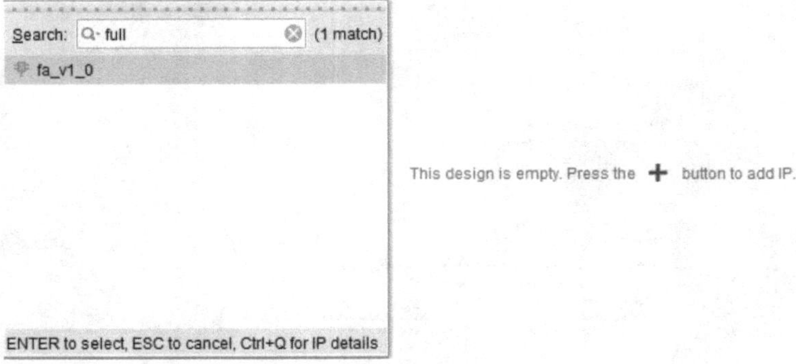

Figure 7-57. *Searching for the IP "fa_v1_0"*

The block diagram of the created full adder is illustrated in Figure 7-58.

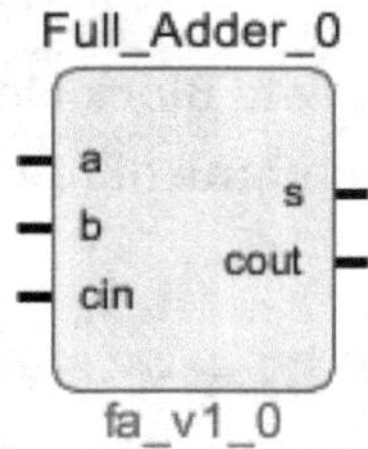

Figure 7-58. *The block diagram of the created full adder*

The IP for a D-Flip-Flop

In this section, we want to create a new IP for a D-flip-flop. So we create a new project named "IP_DFF" and also create a design source file titled "D_flipflop.v" and add the following codes inside of it:

```
`timescale 1ns / 1ps
module D_flipflop(
    input clk,din,
    output q
    );
```

```
reg temp;
initial temp = 0;
always@(posedge clk) begin
temp <= din;
end
assign q = temp;
endmodule
```

We select Flow ➤ Run Simulation ➤ Run Behavioral Simulation from
the menu toolbar to view the waveforms on the wave window. So, in the
opened simulation window, we click the Restart button, and then we
right-click the signal "clk" and set the force clock parameters as depicted
in Figure 7-59. We also right-click the signal "din" and set the force clock
parameters as depicted in Figure 7-60. Now, we click the Run for 2μs
button, and then we click the Zoom Fit button to view the simulated
waveforms on the wave window as illustrated in Figure 7-61.

Figure 7-59. *Setting the force clock parameters for signal "clk"*

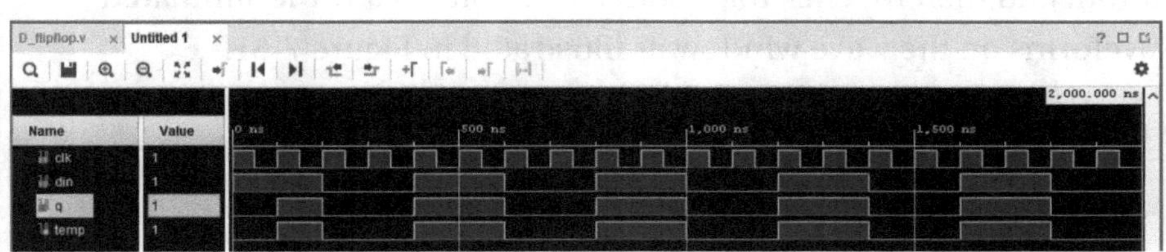

Figure 7-60. *Setting the force clock parameters for signal "din"*

Figure 7-61. *The simulated waveforms on the wave window*

Now, we select the "Create and Package New IP..." option from the Tools menu as shown in Figure 7-62.

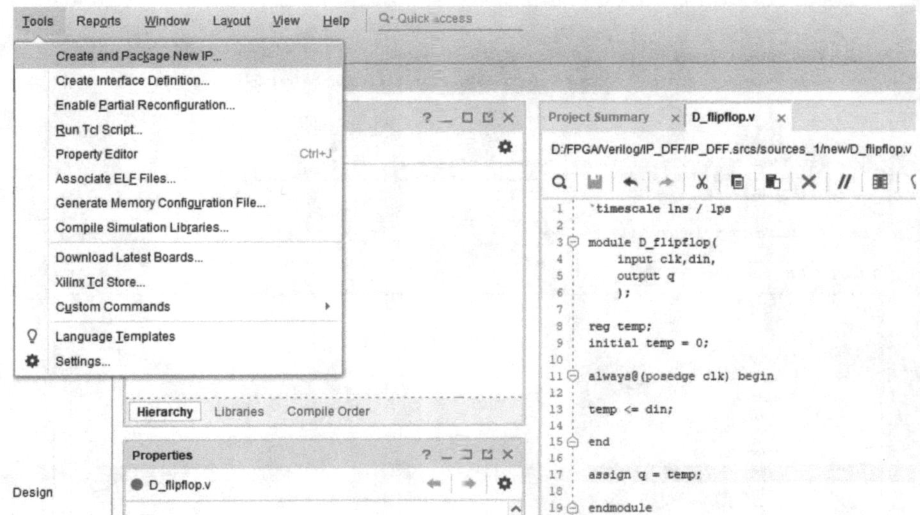

Figure 7-62. *Selecting the Create and Package New IP... option*

Now, we do not want to use the default IP location, and instead we want to use a new directory to save our new IP, and then we click the Next button as depicted in Figures 7-63 and 7-64, respectively.

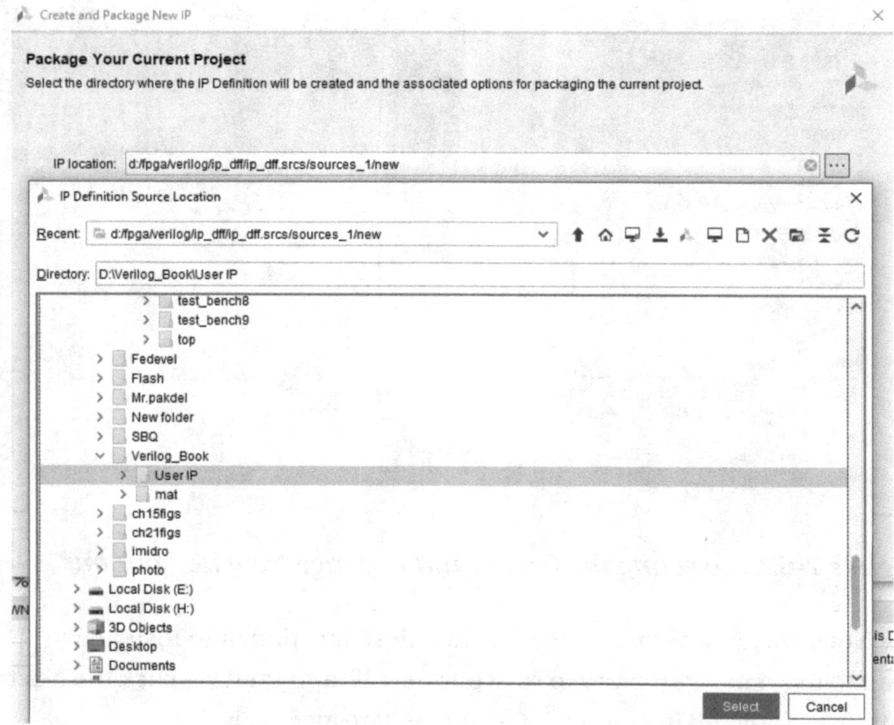

Figure 7-63. *Using a new directory to save our new IP*

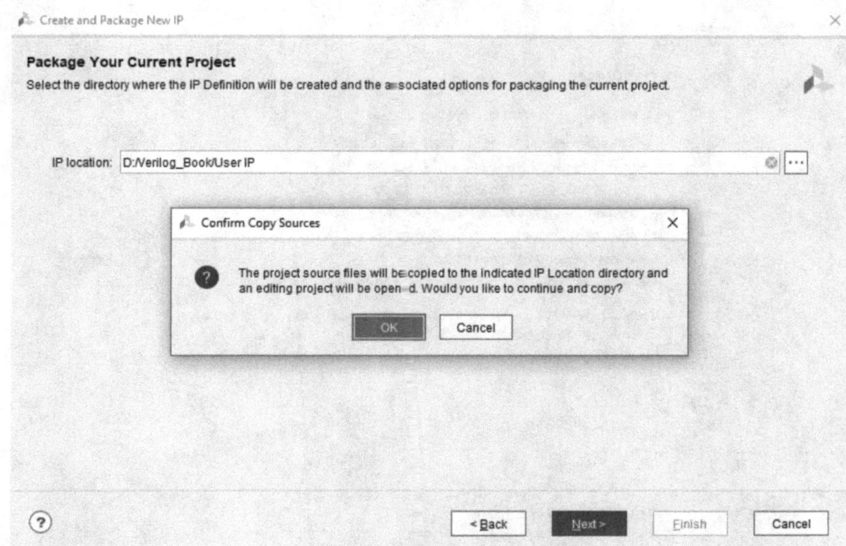

Figure 7-64. *A new IP location for creating a new IP*

Finally, in the New IP Creation summary window, we click the Finish button as illustrated in Figure 7-65.

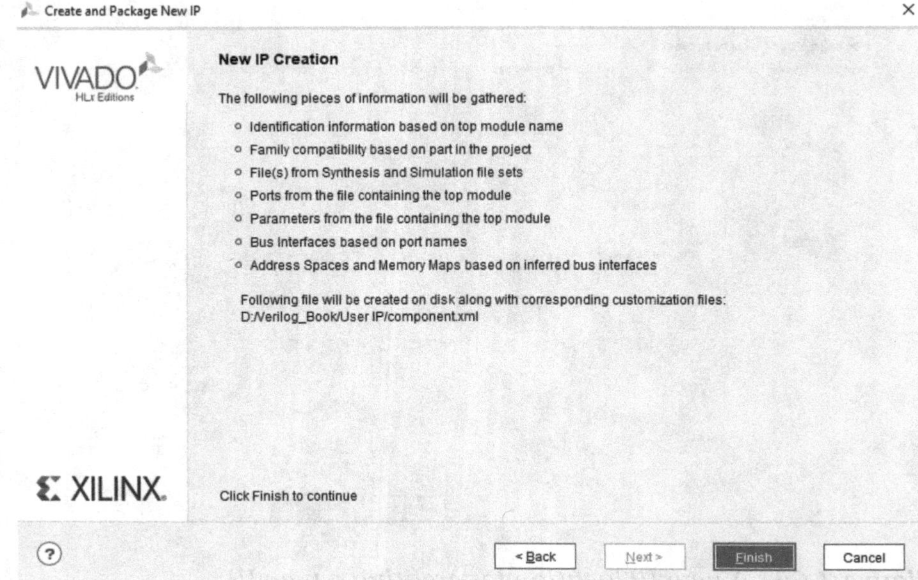

Figure 7-65. *The New IP Creation summary window*

Also, the Customization GUI window for Package IP is shown in
Figure 7-66, and finally in the Review and Package window, we click the
Package IP button and it is done successfully as depicted in Figure 7-67.

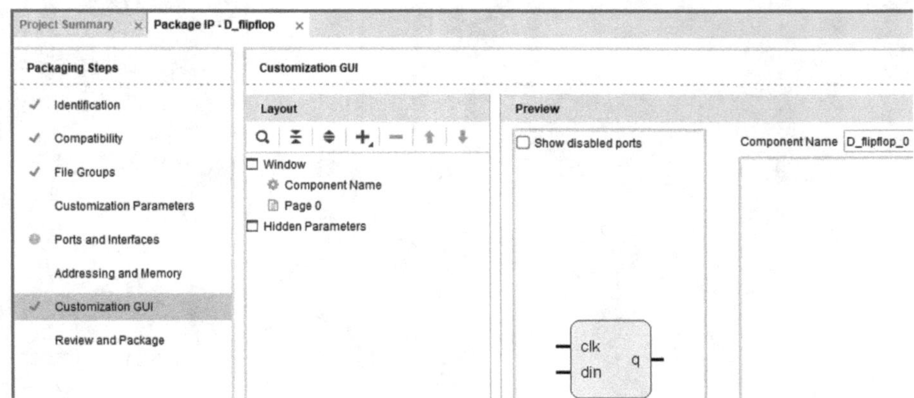

Figure 7-66. *The Customization GUI window for Package IP*

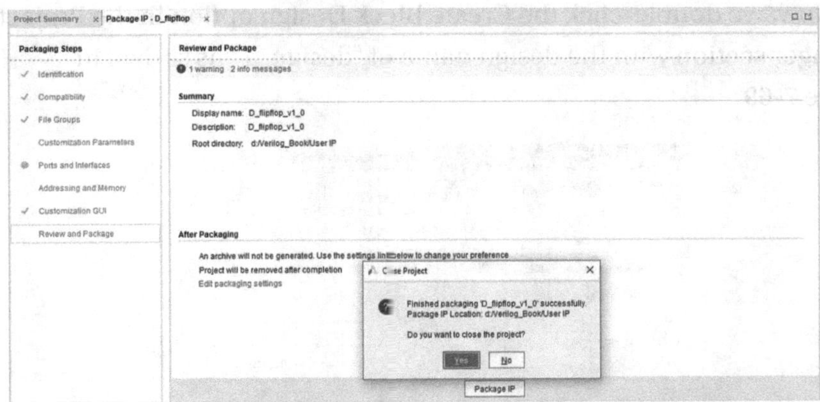

Figure 7-67. *Packaging IP successfully*

Using the Created D-Flip-Flop IP

In this section, we want to use the created D-flip-flop IP. So we create a new project named "Use_IP_DFF" as illustrated in Figure 7-68.

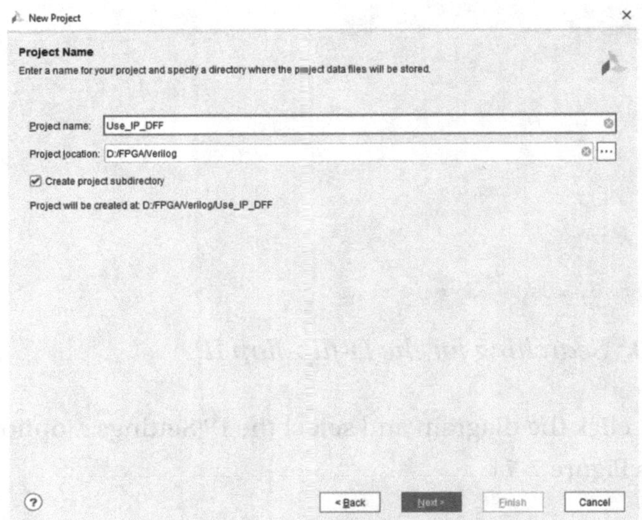

Figure 7-68. *Creating a new project named "Use_IP_DFF"*

Now, we double-click the Create Block Design option in the Project Manager section with the design name of "design_1" as shown in Figure 7-69.

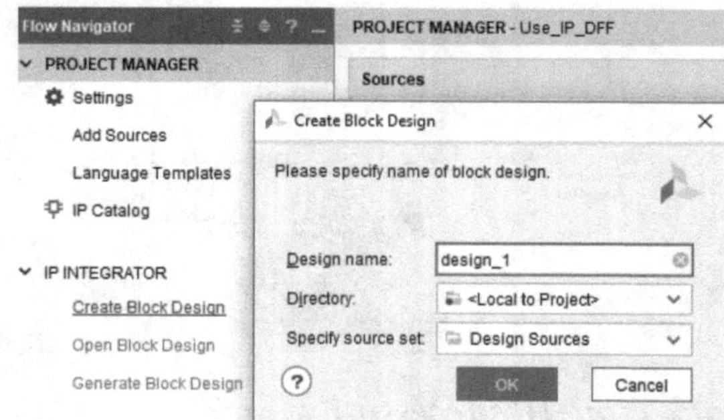

Figure 7-69. *Creating a block design*

Now, we click the add (+) button and enter "d_flipflop" in the search area to find the created D-flip-flop IP; however, we cannot find it as depicted in Figure 7-70.

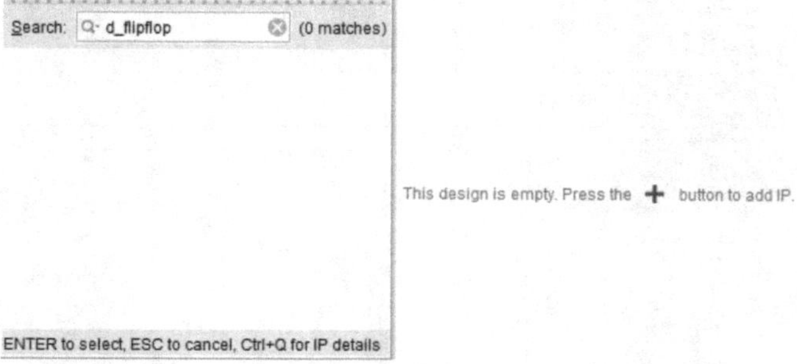

Figure 7-70. *Searching for the D-flip-flop IP*

We right-click the diagram and select the IP Settings... option as illustrated in Figure 7-71.

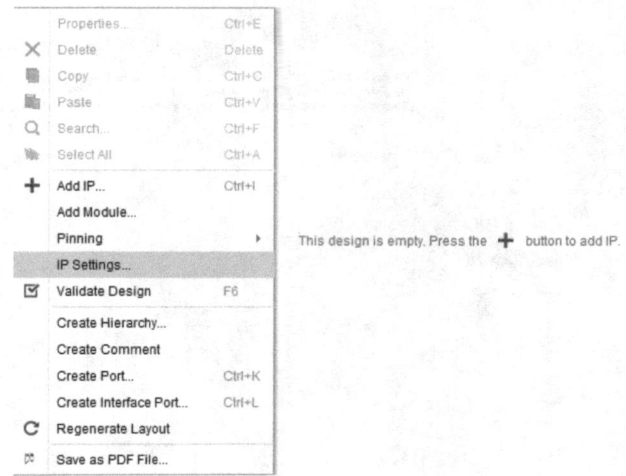

Figure 7-71. *Selecting the IP Settings... option*

In the Settings window, we choose Project Settings ➤ IP ➤ Repository, and then we click the add (+) button in IP Repositories to add the created IP directory as shown in Figures 7-72 and 7-73, respectively.

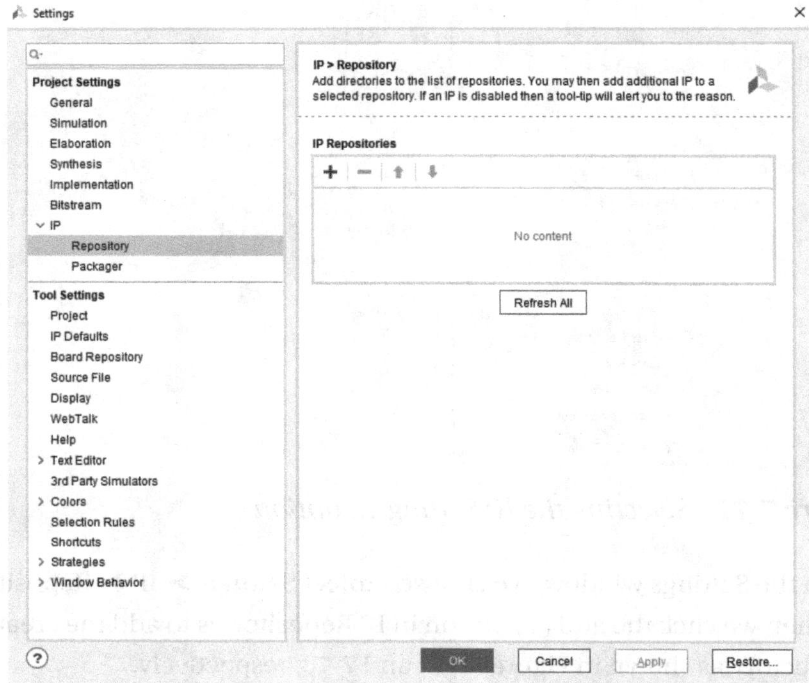

Figure 7-72. *Clicking the add (+) button in IP Repositories*

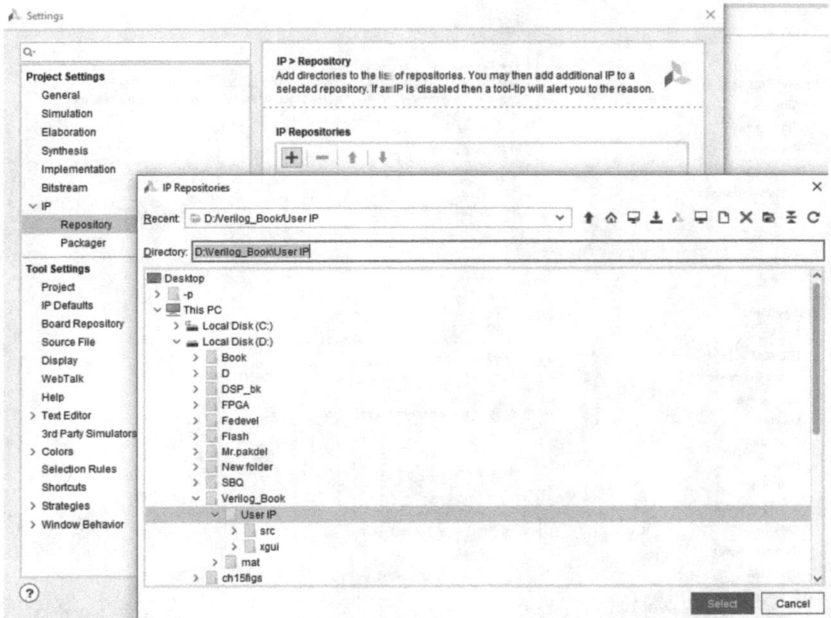

Figure 7-73. *Adding the created IP directory*

If we click the OK button, we can view that the repository is added to the project as depicted in Figure 7-74

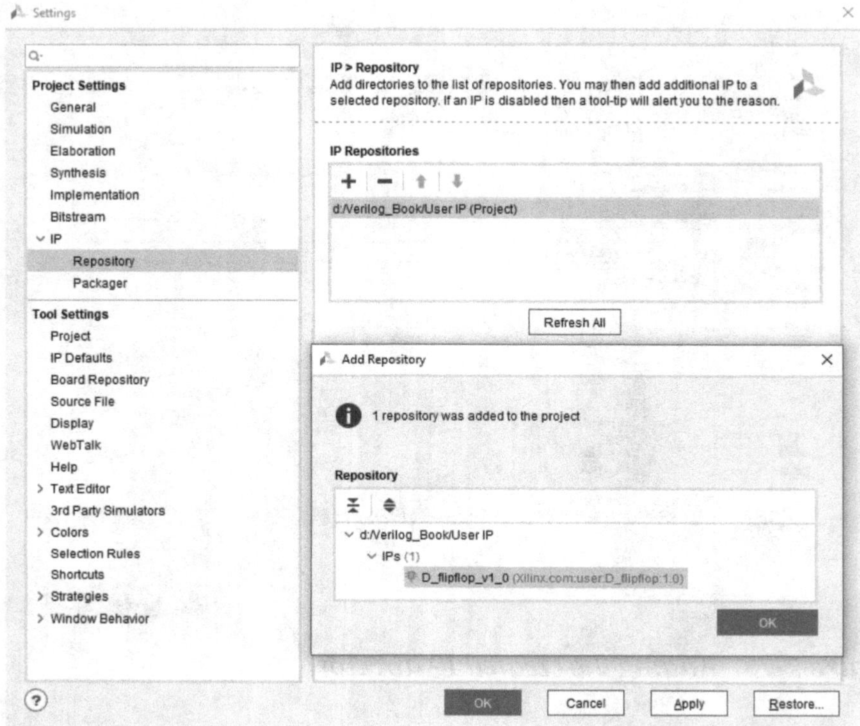

Figure 7-74. *The added repository to the project*

Now, if we enter "d_flipflop" in the search area, we can select the created D-flip-flop IP as depicted in Figure 7-75.

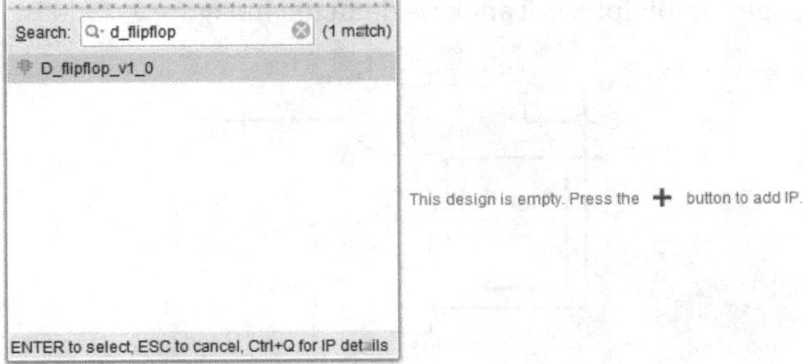

Figure 7-75. *Selecting the created D-flip-flop IP*

Now, we can add the created D-flip-flop to the Diagram window as illustrated in Figure 7-76.

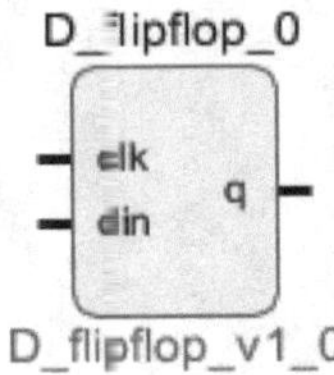

Figure 7-76. *Adding the created D-flip-flop to the Diagram window*

The 4-Bit Ripple Carry Adder

In this section, we want to create a 4-bit ripple carry adder as shown in Figure 7-77.

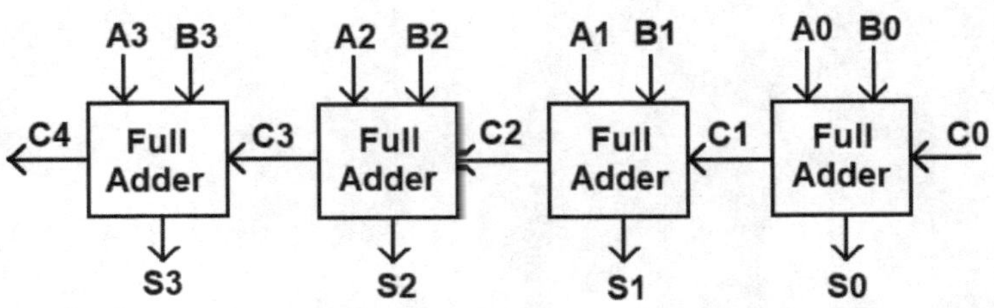

Figure 7-77. *A 4-bit ripple carry adder*

The logic circuit for a full adder is depicted in Figure 7-78.

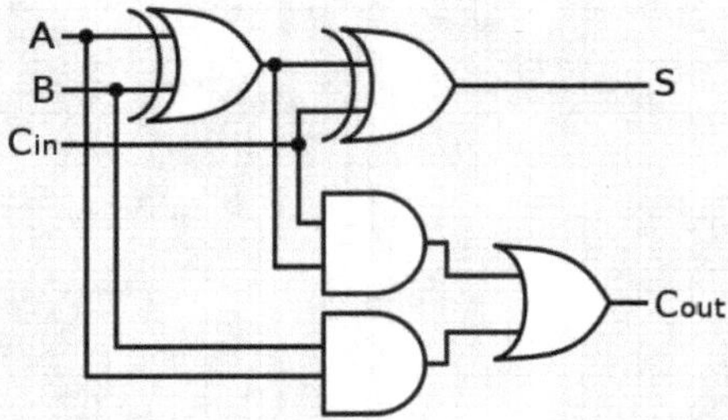

Figure 7-78. *The logic circuit for a full adder*

Now, we create a new project named "RC_Adder4" and also create a design source file titled "fulladder.v" and add the following codes inside of it as illustrated in Figures 7-79 and 7-80, respectively:

```
`timescale 1ns / 1ps
module fulladder(
    input a,b,cin,
    output s,cout
    );
assign s = a ^ b ^ cin;
assign cout = (a & b) | (a & cin) | (b & cin);
endmodule
```

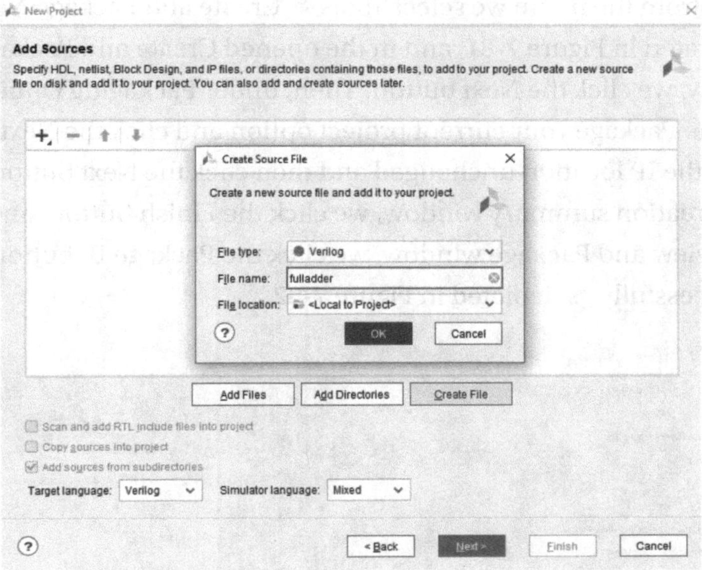

Figure 7-79. *Creating a design source file titled "fulladder.v"*

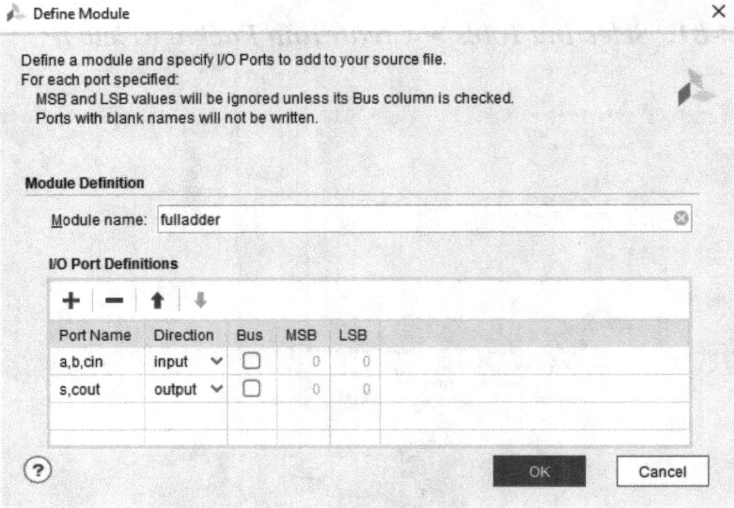

Figure 7-80. *I/O Port Definitions in the Define Module window*

Now, from the menu we select Tools ➤ Create and Package New IP... as demonstrated in Figure 7-81, and in the opened Create and Package New IP window, we click the Next button. Then, under Packaging Options, we choose the Package your current project option and click the Next button. We leave the IP location unchanged and then click the Next button. In the New IP Creation summary window, we click the Finish button, and finally in the Review and Package window, we click the Package IP button and it is done successfully as depicted in Figure 7-82.

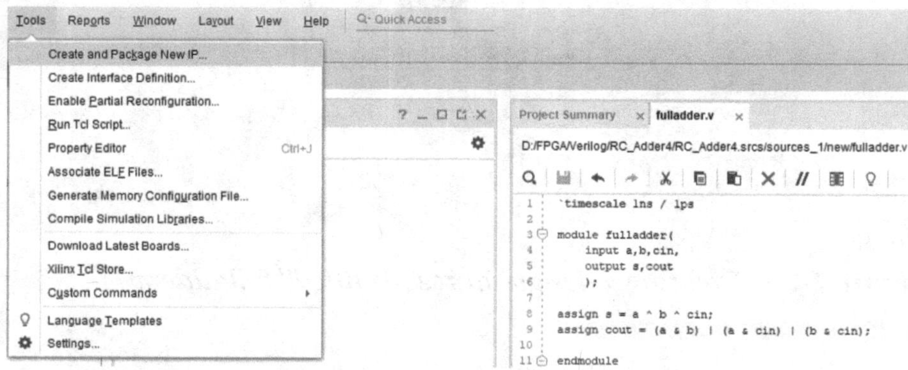

Figure 7-81. *Selecting Tools ➤ Create and Package New IP...*

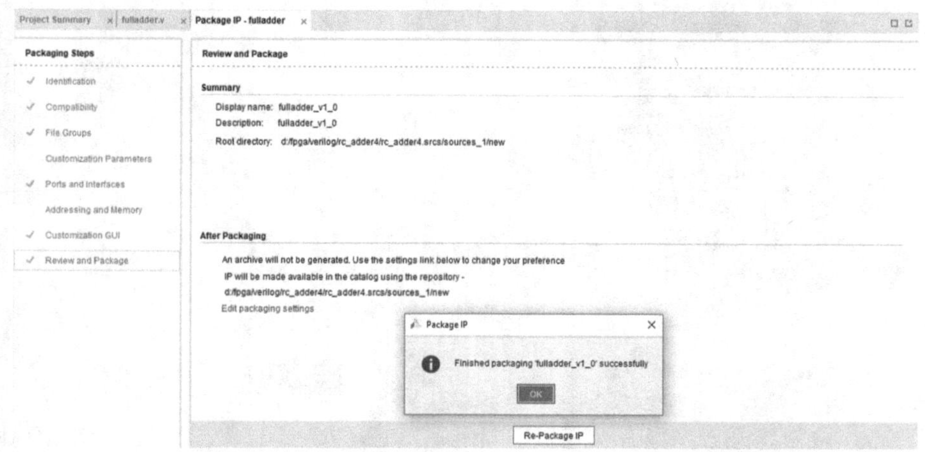

Figure 7-82. *Successful packaging of the full adder IP*

In the Project Manager section, we double-click the Create Block Design option to create a block design named "design_1" as illustrated in Figure 7-83.

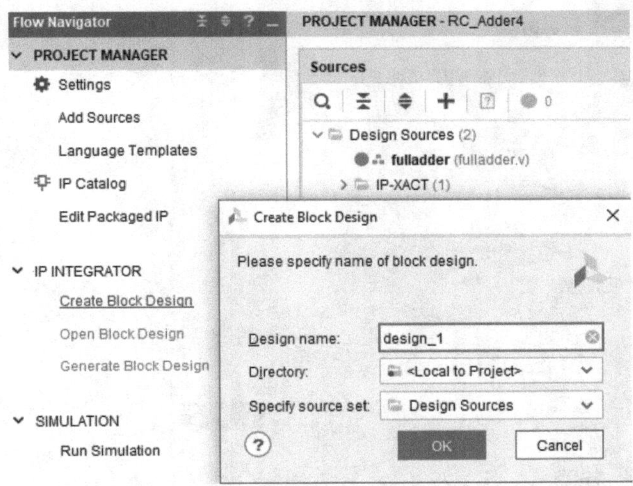

Figure 7-83. *Creating a block design named "design_1"*

In the Diagram window, we right-click and select the Create Port… option as shown in Figure 7-84.

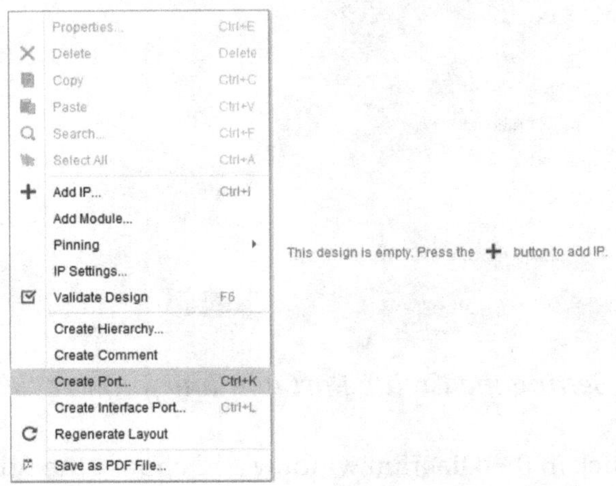

Figure 7-84. *Selecting the Create Port… option*

Now, we set the Create Port window for ports "a" and "b" as depicted in Figures 7-85 and 7-86, respectively.

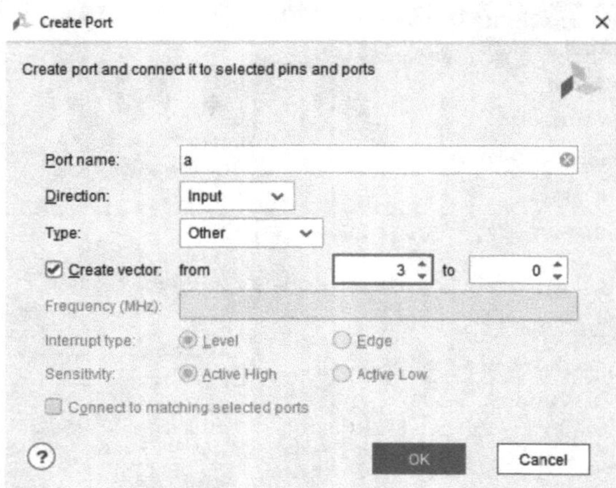

Figure 7-85. *Setting the Create Port window for port "a"*

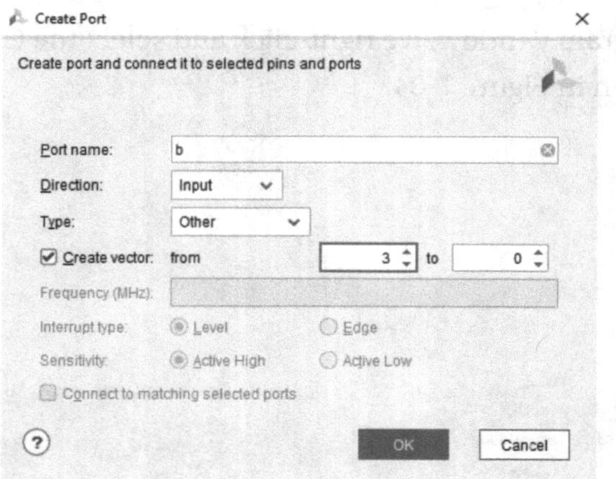

Figure 7-86. *Setting the Create Port window for port "b"*

We right-click in the Diagram window and choose the Add IP... option as illustrated in Figure 7-87.

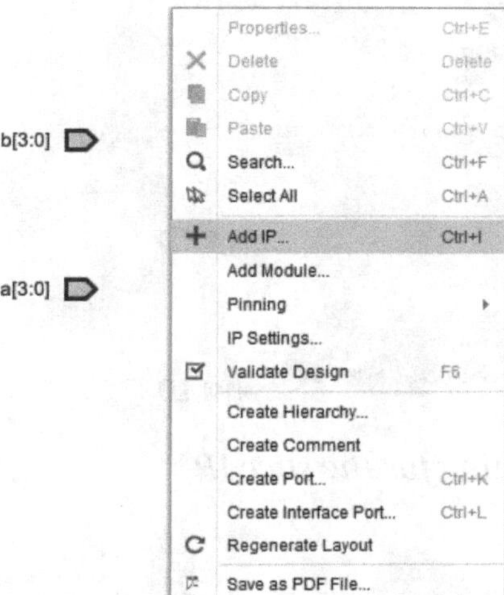

Figure 7-87. *Selecting the Add IP... option*

Then, in the search area of the opened window, we enter "full" to find our created full adder IP as shown in Figure 7-88.

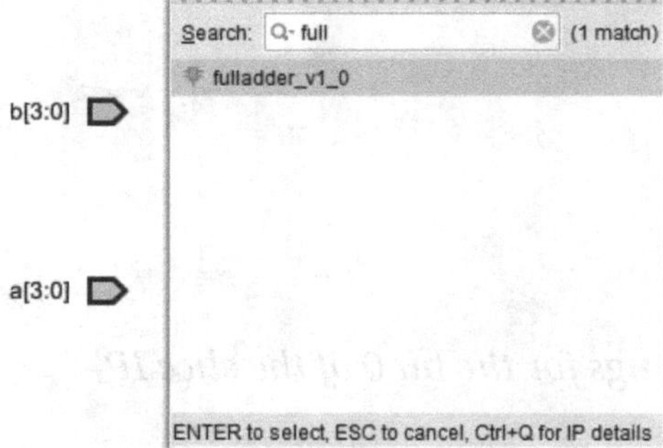

Figure 7-88. *Searching for our created full adder IP*

Now, we search for the slice IP and set the bit 0 of it as depicted in Figures 7-89 and 7-90, respectively.

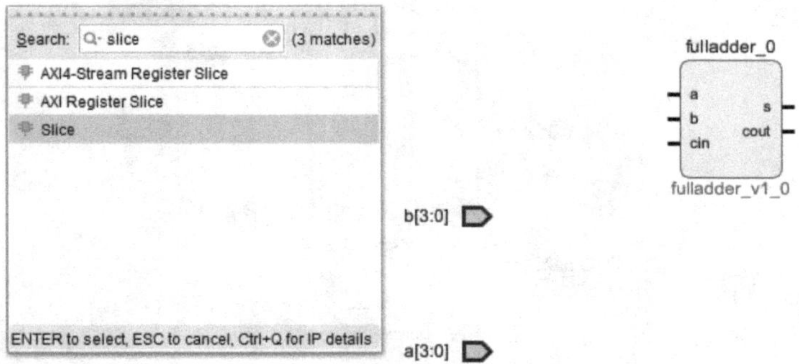

Figure 7-89. *Searching for the slice IP*

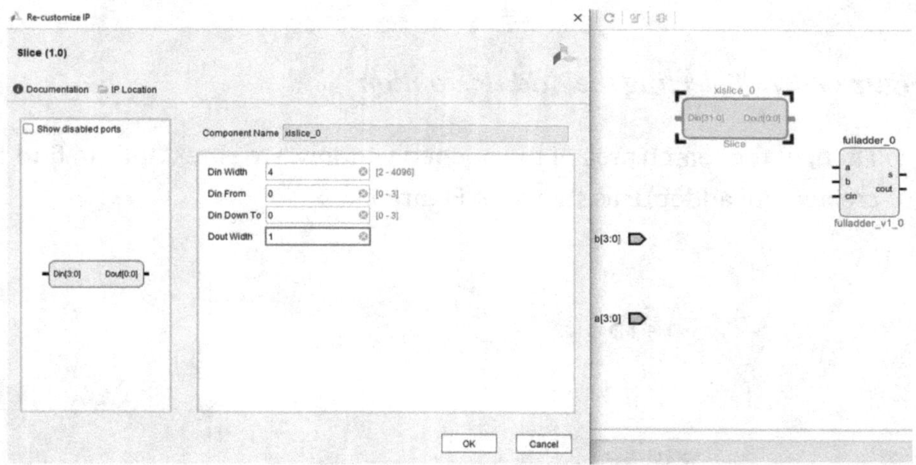

Figure 7-90. *Settings for the bit 0 of the slice IP*

We copy and paste the slice IP and set the bits 1, 2, and 3 of it as illustrated in Figures 7-91, 7-92, and 7-93, respectively.

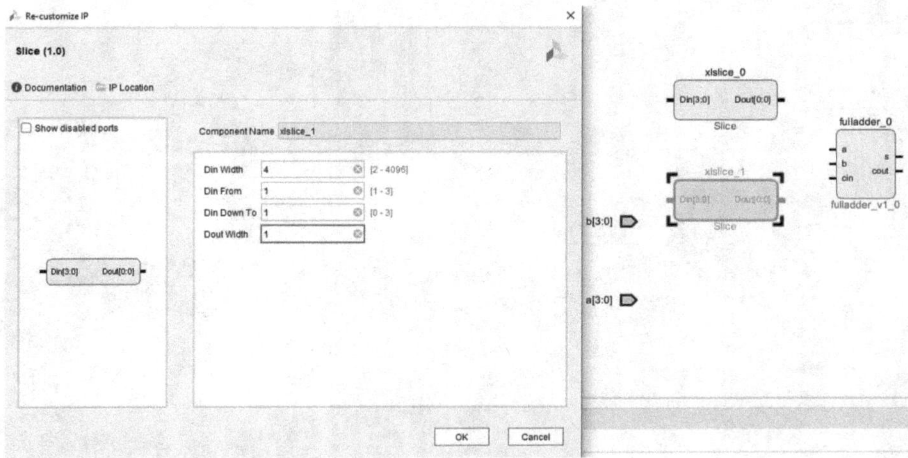

Figure 7-91. *Settings for the bit 1 of the slice IP*

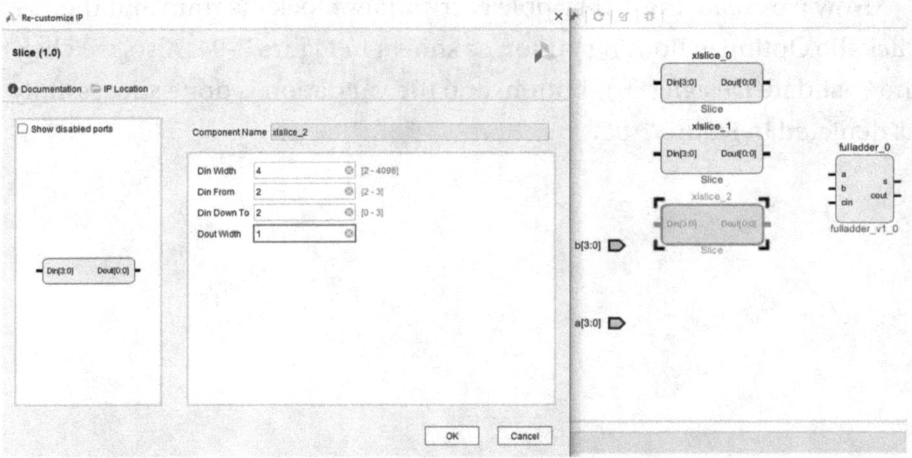

Figure 7-92. *Settings for the bit 2 of the slice IP*

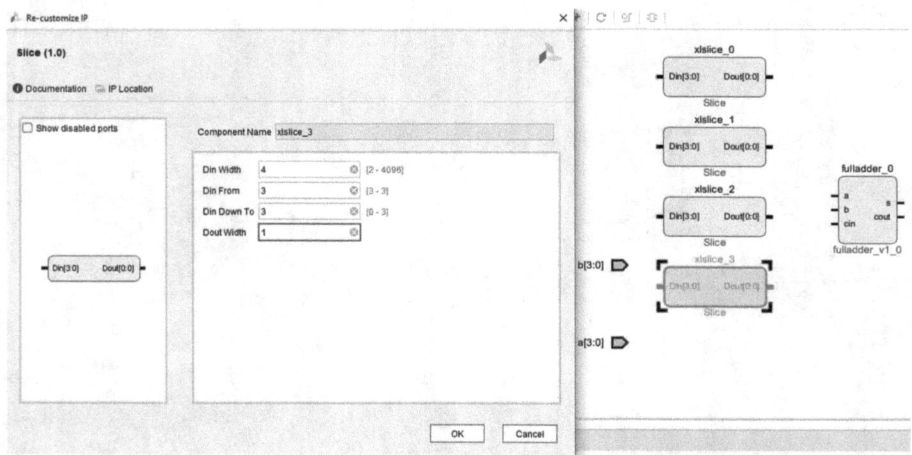

Figure 7-93. *Settings for the bit 3 of the slice IP*

Now we create the 4-bit ripple carry adder block diagram and then click the Optimize Routing button as shown in Figure 7-94. Also, we click the "Validate Design (F6)" button, and the validation is done successfully as depicted in Figure 7-95.

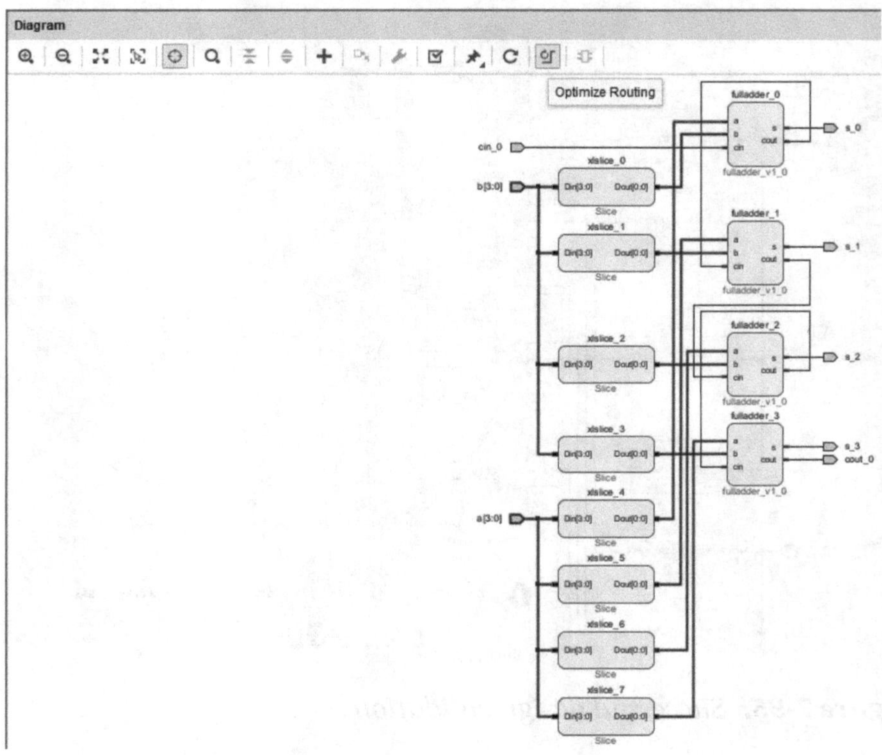

Figure 7-94. *Clicking the Optimize Routing button*

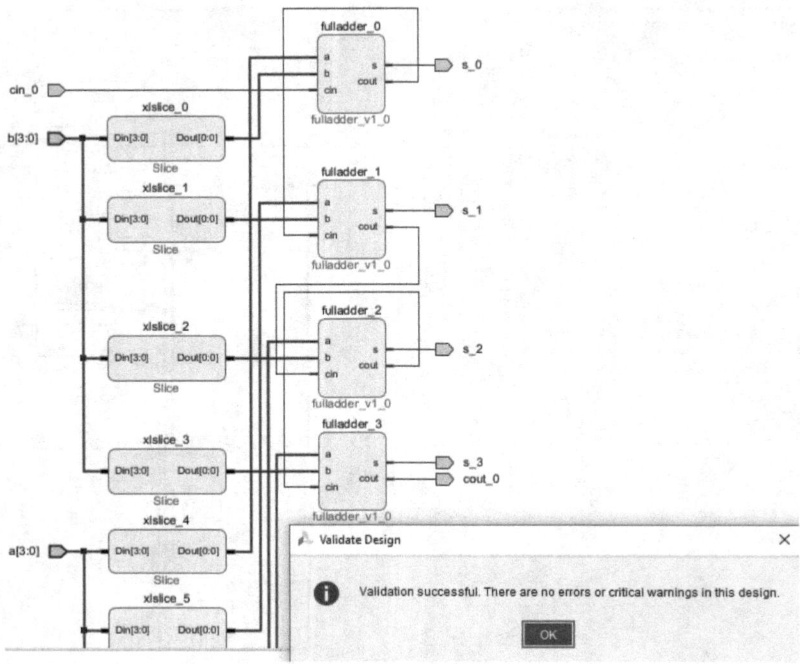

Figure 7-95. *Successful design validation*

Now, we right-click "design_1" and select the "Create HDL Wrapper…" option, and then in the opened window we let Vivado manage wrapper and auto-update as shown in Figure 7-96.

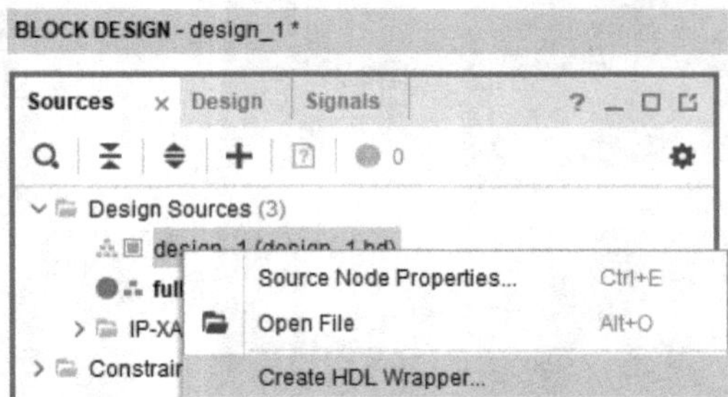

Figure 7-96. *Selecting the "Create HDL Wrapper…" option*

We select Flow ➤ Run Simulation ➤ Run Behavioral Simulation from the menu toolbar to view the waveforms on the wave window. So, in the opened simulation window, we click the Restart button, and then we right-click the signals "a" and "b" and set the force constant binary values of them to "1000" and "0011" as depicted in Figures 7-97 and 7-98, respectively.

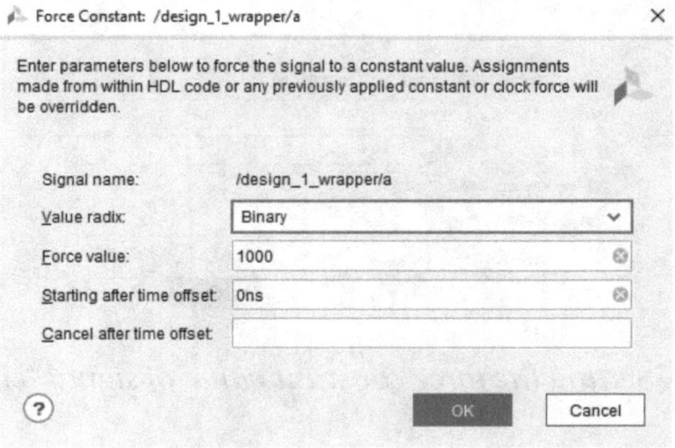

Figure 7-97. *Setting the force constant binary value of signal "a" to "1000"*

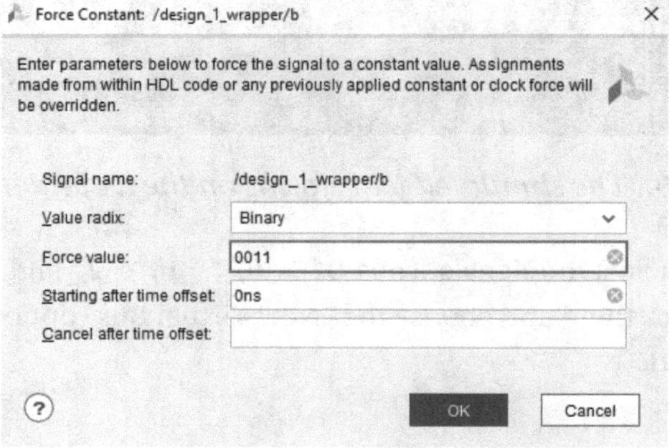

Figure 7-98. *Setting the force constant binary value of signal "b" to "0011"*

We also right-click the signal "cin_0" and set the force constant value of it to 0 as illustrated in Figure 7-99. Now, we click the Run for 1µs button, and then we click the Zoom Fit button to view the simulated waveforms on the wave window as shown in Figure 7-100.

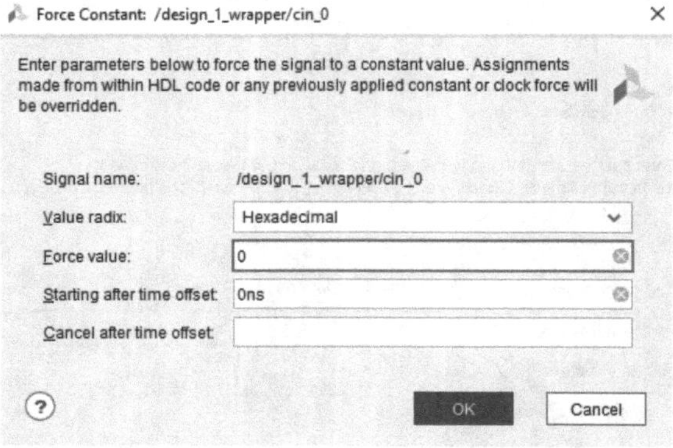

Figure 7-99. *Setting the force constant value of signal "cin_0" to 0*

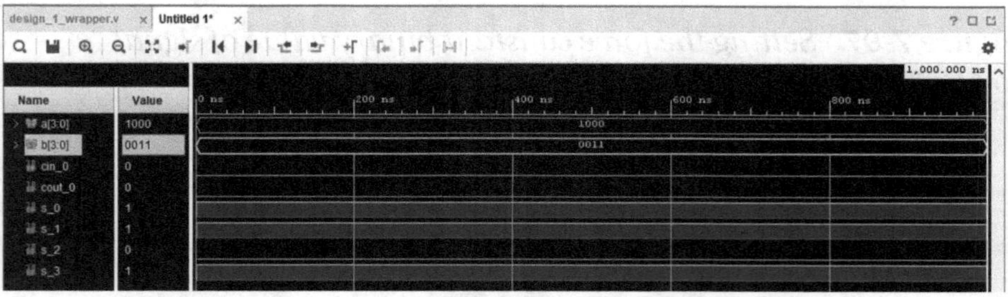

Figure 7-100. *The simulated waveforms on the wave window*

Now, we select the signals "cout_0," "s_0," "s_1", "s_2," and "s_3" and then right-click them and choose the "New Virtual Bus" option as depicted in Figure 7-101.

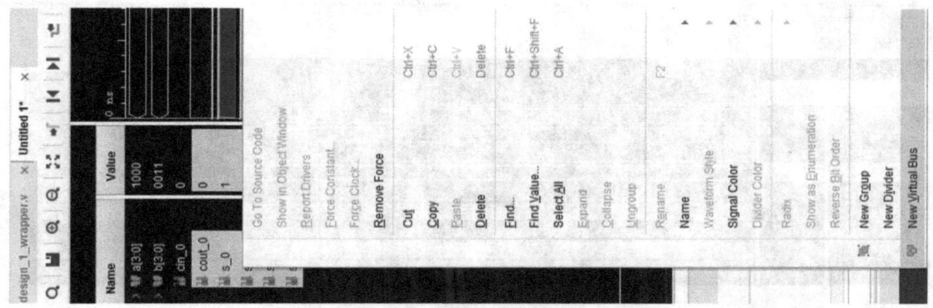

Figure 7-101. *Choosing the "New Virtual Bus" option*

We also right-click "New Virtual Bus" and select the Radix option as Binary as illustrated in Figure 7-102. Now, we can view the result as shown in Figure 7-103.

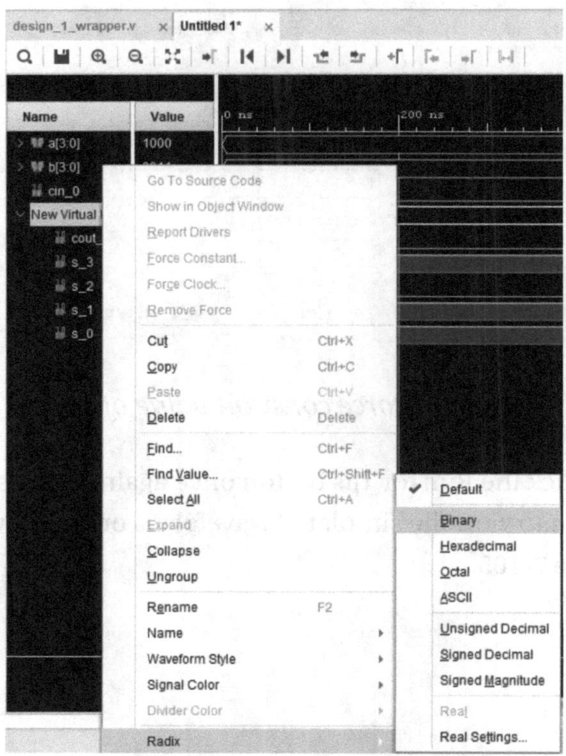

Figure 7-102. *Selecting the Radix option as Binary*

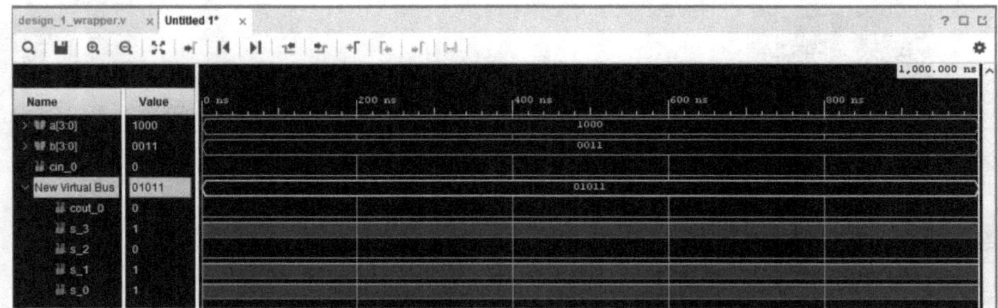

Figure 7-103. *The simulated waveforms on the wave window*

We right-click the signal "cin_0" and set the force constant value of it to 1 as depicted in Figure 7-104.

Figure 7-104. *Setting the force constant value of signal "cin_0" to 1*

Then, we click the Run for 1μs button once again, and also, we click the Zoom Fit button to view the simulated waveforms on the wave window as shown in Figure 7-105.

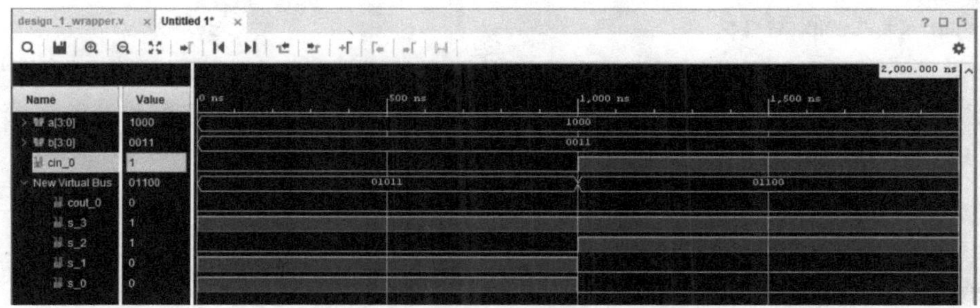

Figure 7-105. *The simulated waveforms on the wave window*

The Function Generator

In this section, we want to create a function generator. So we create a new project named "Function_Generator" and also a design source file titled "top.v", and then we add the following codes inside of it:

```verilog
`timescale 1ns / 1ps
module top(
output [3:0] dout,
input clk,
input [1:0] sel
    );
reg [3:0] temp;
integer i,j;
initial begin
temp = 0;
i = 0;
j = 0;
end
always@(posedge clk) begin
case(sel)
2'b00: begin
```

```verilog
temp <= temp + 1;
end
2'b01: begin
if(i < 15) begin
   i <= i + 1;
   temp <= temp + 1;
end
else if(i >= 15 && i < 30) begin
   i <= i + 1;
   temp <= temp - 1;
end
else begin
   i <= 0;
   temp <= 0;
end
end
2'b10: begin
if (j < 5) begin
   j <= j + 1;
   temp <= 4'b0000;
end
else if(j >= 5 && j < 10) begin
   j <= j + 1;
   temp <= 4'b1111;
end
else begin
   j <= 0;
   temp <= 4'b0000;
end
end
default: temp <= 4'bxxxx;
```

```
endcase
end
assign dout = temp;
endmodule
```

We choose Flow ➤ Run Simulation ➤ Run Behavioral Simulation from the menu toolbar to view the waveforms on the wave window. So, in the opened simulation window, we click the Restart button, and then we right-click the signal "clk" and set the force clock parameters as depicted in Figure 7-106.

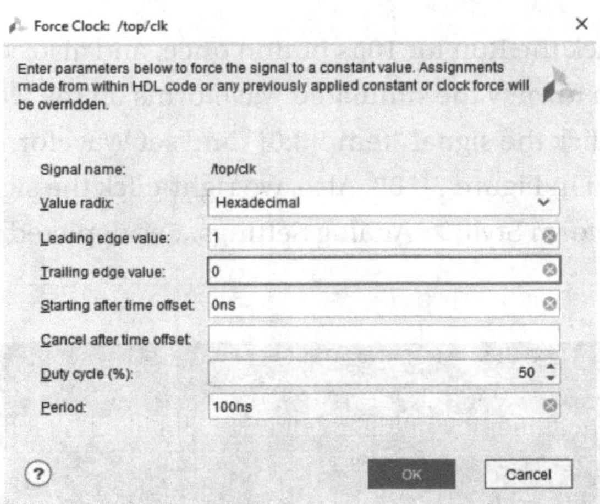

Figure 7-106. *Setting the force clock parameters for signal "clk"*

We also right-click the signal "sel" and set its force constant value to 00 as illustrated in Figure 7-107.

Figure 7-107. *Setting the force constant value of signal "sel" to 00*

Then, we click the Run for 10μs button once, and also, we click the Zoom Fit button to view the simulated waveforms on the wave window. Then we right-click the signal "temp[3:0]" and set Waveform Style as Analog as shown in Figure 7-108. Also, we right-click the signal "temp[3:0]" and select Waveform Style ➤ Analog Settings... as depicted in Figure 7-109.

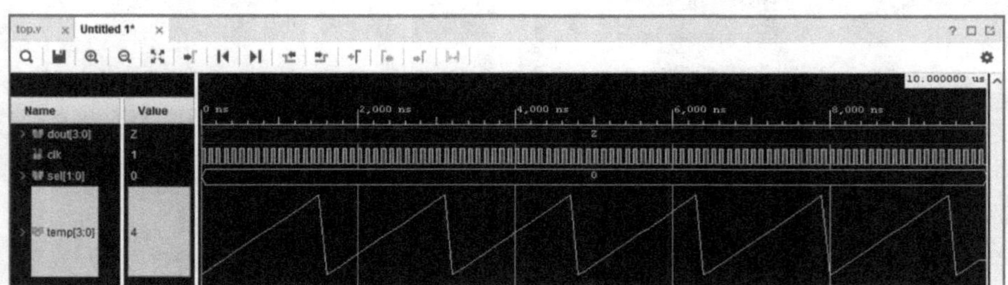

Figure 7-108. *The simulated waveforms on the wave window*

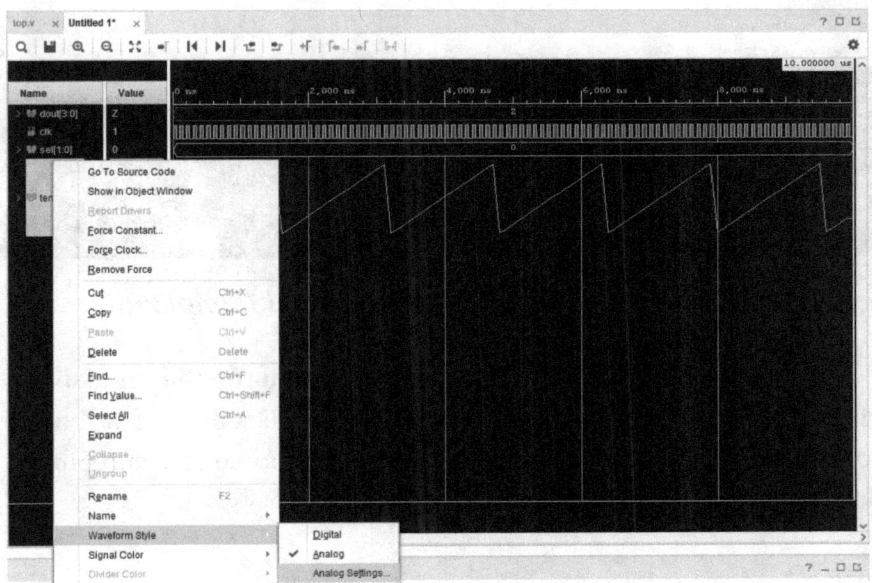

Figure 7-109. *Selecting Waveform Style ➤ Analog Settings...*

In the Analog Settings window, we select the interpolation style as Hold as illustrated in Figure 7-110. Now, we can view the staircase waveform of signal "temp[3:0]" as shown in Figure 7-111.

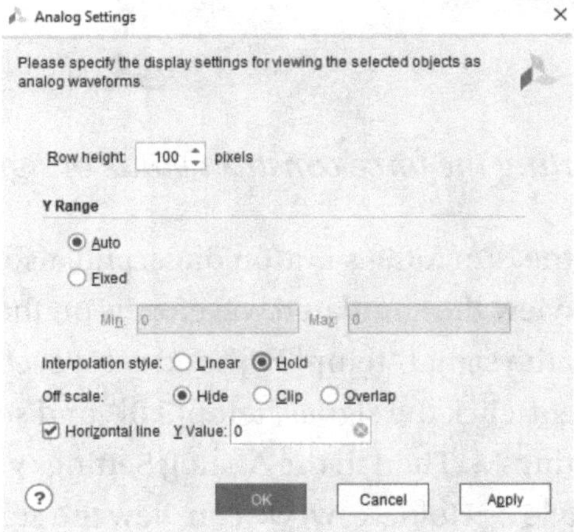

Figure 7-110. *Selecting the interpolation style as Hold*

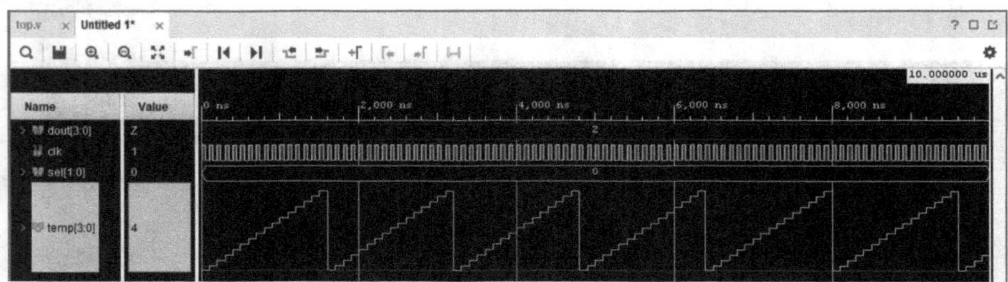

Figure 7-111. *The staircase waveform of signal "temp[3:0]"*

Now, we close the simulation wave window and run the simulation again, and in the opened simulation window, we click the Restart button, and then we right-click the signal "sel" and set the force constant binary value to 01 as depicted in Figure 7-112.

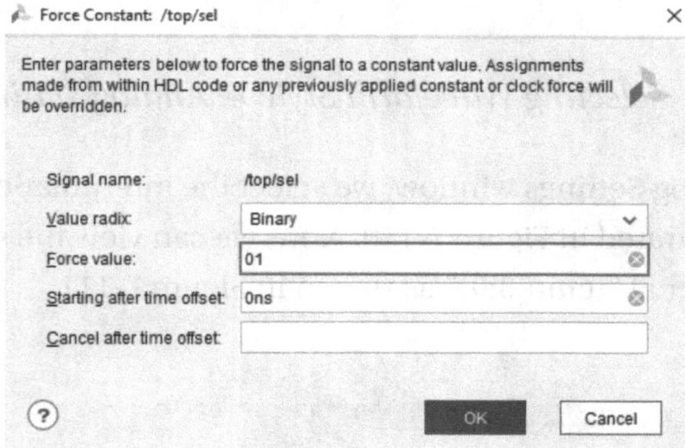

Figure 7-112. *Setting the force constant value of signal "sel" to 01*

Then, we click the Run for 9μs button once, and also, we click the Zoom Fit button to view the simulated waveforms on the wave window. Then we right-click the signal "temp[3:0]" and set Waveform Style as Analog. Also, we right-click the signal "temp[3:0]" and select Waveform Style ➤ Analog Settings.... Then in the Analog Settings window, we select the interpolation style as Hold. Now, we can view the staircase waveform of signal "temp[3:0]" as shown in Figure 7-113.

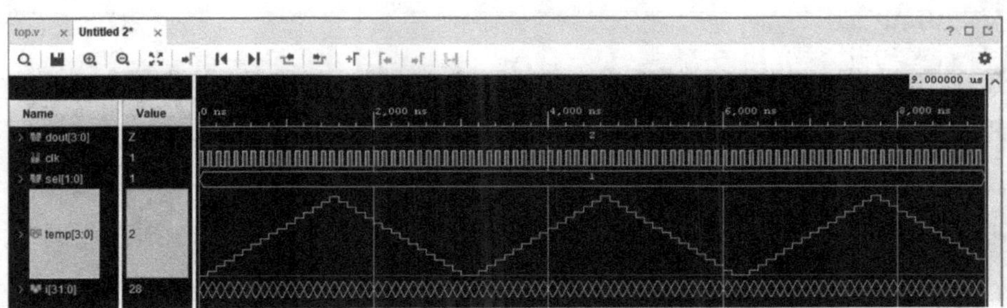

Figure 7-113. *The staircase waveform of signal "temp[3:0]"*

Now, we right-click the signal "sel" and set the force constant binary value to 00 depicted in Figure 7-114. Then, we click the Run for 7µs button once again, and also, we click the Zoom Fit button to view the simulated waveforms on the wave window as illustrated in Figure 7-115.

Figure 7-114. *Setting the force constant value of signal "sel" to 00*

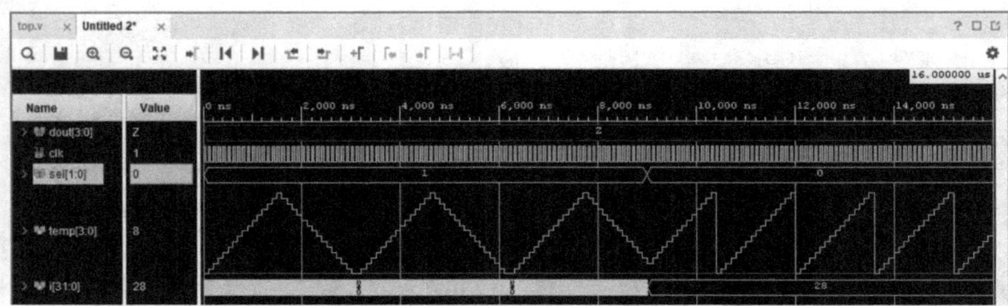

Figure 7-115. *The staircase waveform of signal "temp[3:0]"*

Now, we close the simulation wave window and run the simulation again, and in the opened simulation window, we click the Restart button, and then we right-click the signal "sel" and set the force constant binary value to 10 as depicted in Figure 7-116.

Figure 7-116. *Setting the force constant binary value to 10*

Then, we click the Run for 4μs button once, and also, we click the Zoom Fit button to view the simulated waveforms on the wave window. Then we right-click the signal "temp[3:0]" and set Waveform Style as Analog. Also, we right-click the signal "temp[3:0]" and select Waveform Style ➤ Analog Settings…. Then in the Analog Settings window, we select the interpolation style as Hold. Now, we can view the staircase waveform of signal "temp[3:0]" as shown in Figure 7-117.

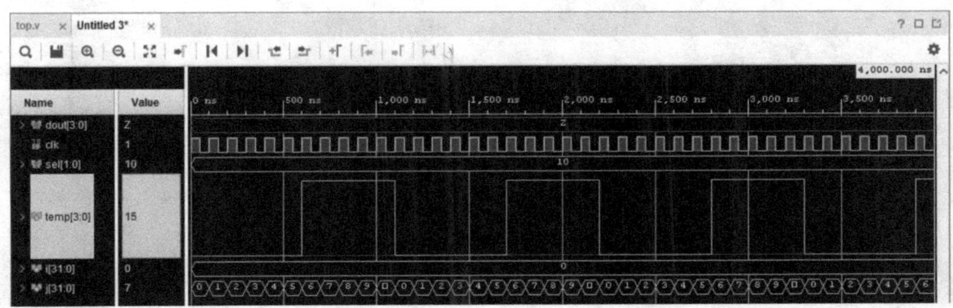

Figure 7-117. *The staircase waveform of signal "temp[3:0]"*

Now, from the menu we select Tools ➤ Create and Package New IP... as demonstrated in Figure 7-118, and in the opened Create and Package New IP window, we click the Next button. Then, under Packaging Options, we choose the Package your current project option and click the Next button. We leave the IP location unchanged and then click the Next button. In the New IP Creation summary window, we click the Finish button, and finally in the Review and Package window, we click the Package IP button and it is done successfully as depicted in Figure 7-119. In the Project Manager section, we double-click the Create Block Design option to create a block design named "design_1" as illustrated in Figure 7-120.

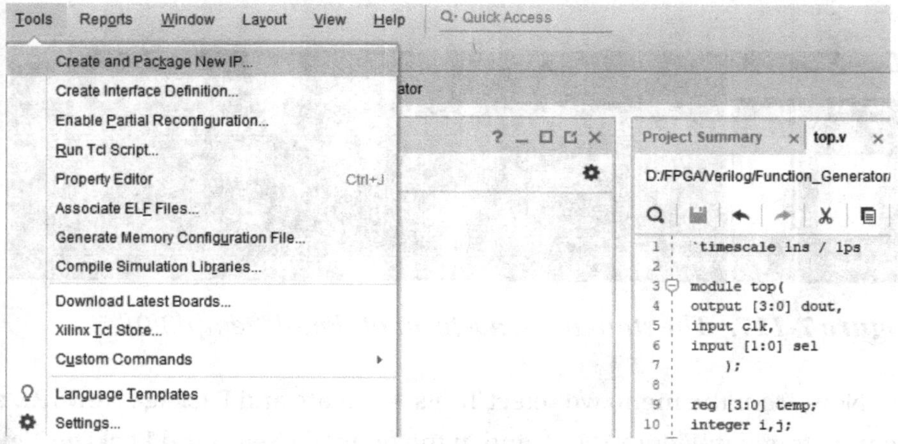

Figure 7-118. *Selecting Tools ➤ Create and Package New IP...*

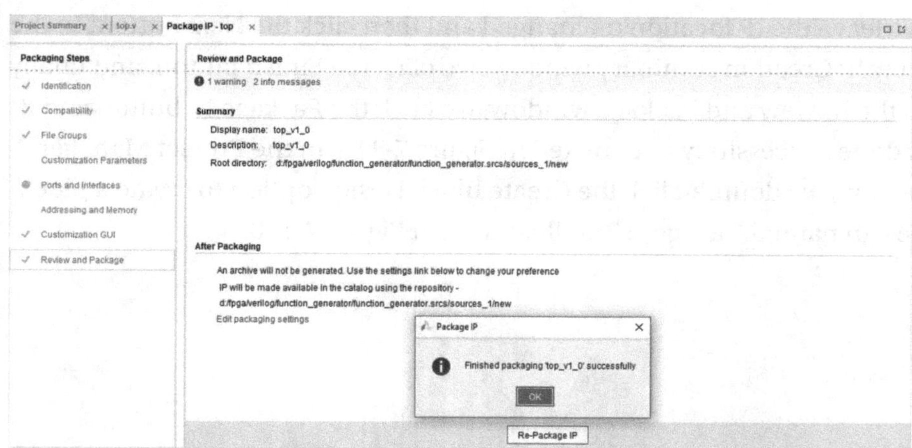

Figure 7-119. *Successful packaging of the full adder IP*

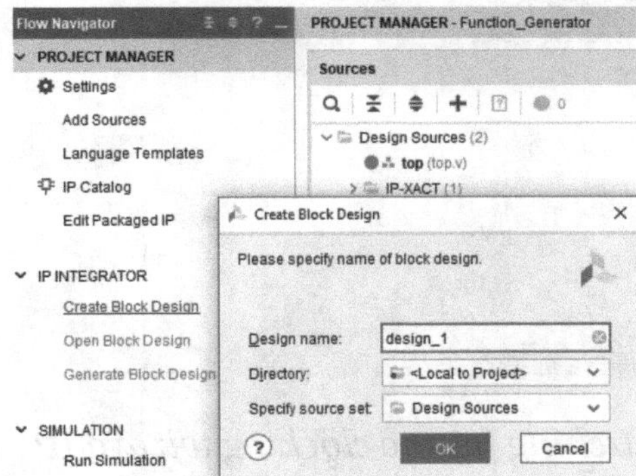

Figure 7-120. *Creating a block design named "design_1"*

Now, we search for the created function generator IP as shown in Figure 7-121. We also search for the clocking wizard IP as depicted in Figure 7-122.

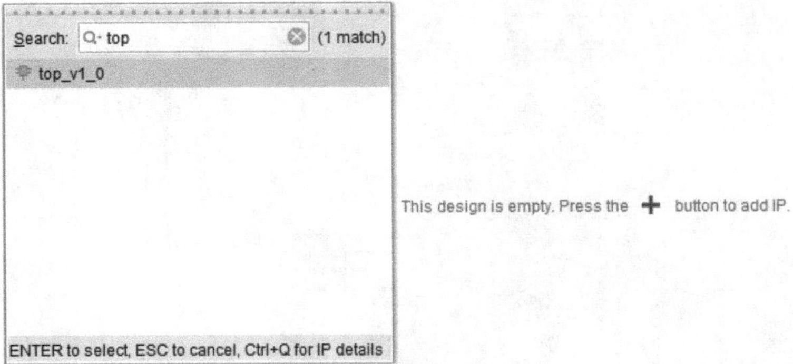

Figure 7-121. *Searching for the created function generator IP*

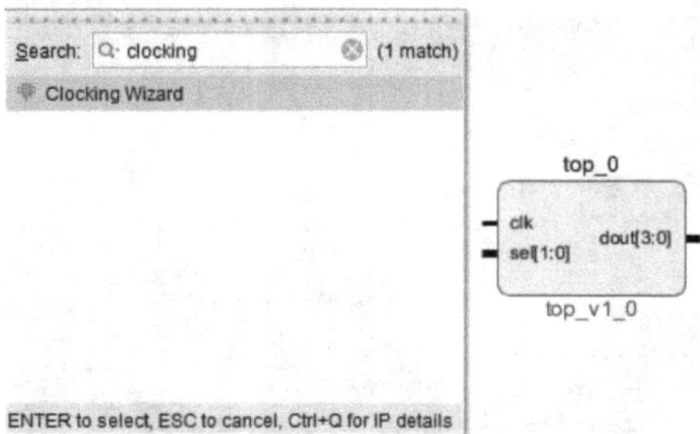

Figure 7-122. *Searching for the clocking wizard IP*

Now, we double-click the clocking wizard IP, and in the Output Clocks tab, we set the parameters as illustrated in Figure 7-123.

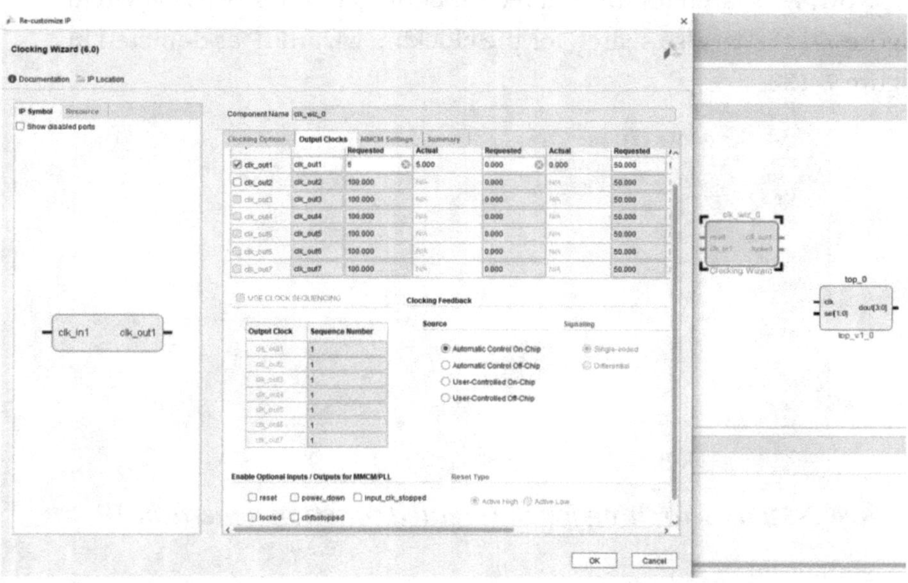

Figure 7-123. *Setting the Output Clocks tab parameters of the clocking wizard IP*

Now we create the function generator block diagram and then click the Optimize Routing button. Also, we click the "Validate Design (F6)" button, and the validation is done successfully as depicted in Figure 7-124.

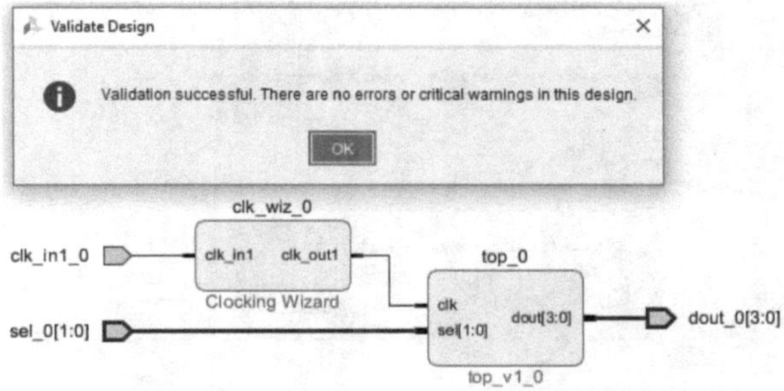

Figure 7-124. *Successful design validation*

Now, we right-click "design_1" and select the "Create HDL Wrapper..." option, and then in the opened window we let Vivado manage wrapper and auto-update as shown in Figures 7-125 and 7-126, respectively.

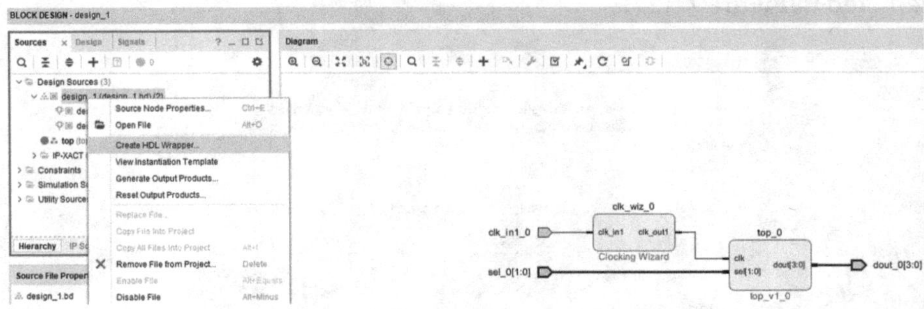

Figure 7-125. *Selecting the "Create HDL Wrapper..." option*

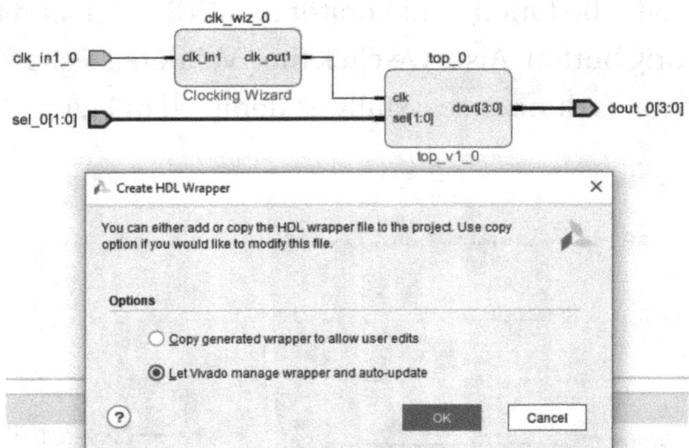

Figure 7-126. *Letting Vivado manage wrapper and auto-update*

We select Flow ➤ Run Simulation ➤ Run Behavioral Simulation from the menu toolbar to view the waveforms on the wave window. So, in the opened simulation window, we click the Restart button, and then we right-click the signal "clk_in1_0" and set the force clock parameters of it as depicted in Figure 7-127.

Figure 7-127. *Setting the force clock parameters of signal "clk_in1_0"*

We also right-click the signal "sel_0" and set the force constant binary value of it to 00 as illustrated in Figure 7-128.

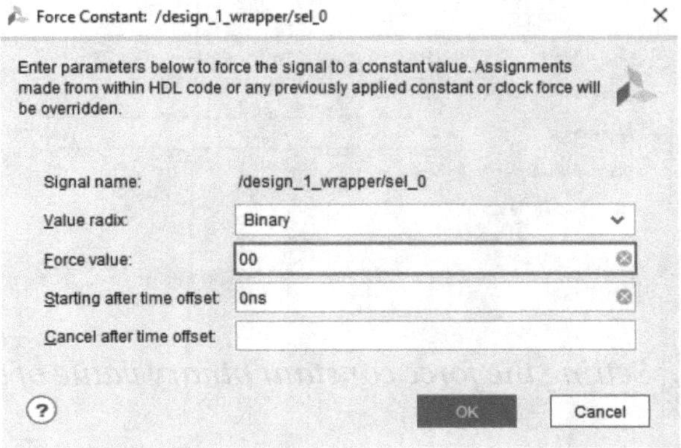

Figure 7-128. *Setting the force constant binary value of signal "sel_0" to 00*

Then, we click the Run for 15μs button once and then right-click the signal "sel_0" and set the force constant binary value of it to 01 as illustrated in Figure 7-129. Now, we click the Run for 25μs button once again and then right-click the signal "sel_0" and set the force constant binary value of it to 10 as shown in Figure 7-130.

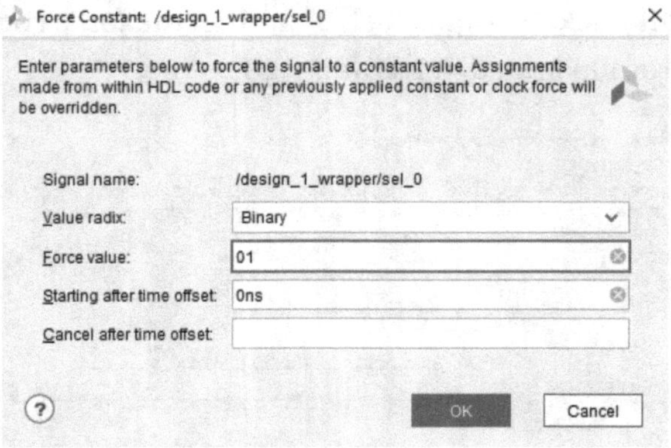

Figure 7-129. *Setting the force constant binary value of signal "sel_0" to 01*

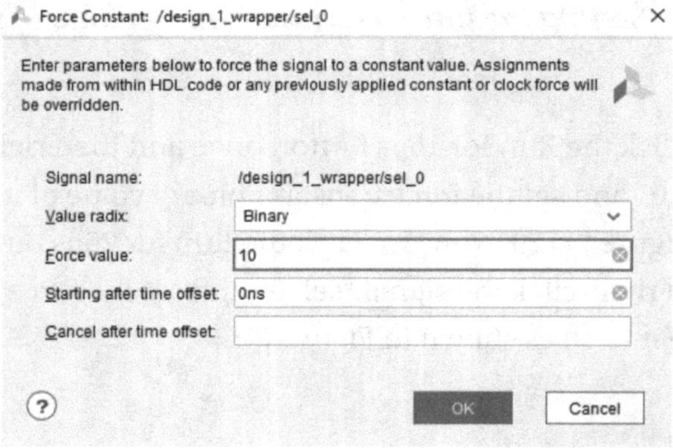

Figure 7-130. *Setting the force constant binary value of signal "sel_0" to 10*

Also, we click the Run for 9µs button once again, and we click the Zoom Fit button to view the simulated waveforms on the wave window. Then we right-click the signal "dout_0[3:0]" and set Waveform Style as Analog. Also, we right-click the signal "dout_0[3:0]" and select Waveform Style ➤ Analog Settings…. Then in the Analog Settings window, we select the interpolation style as Hold. Now, we can view the staircase waveform of signal "dout_0[3:0]" as depicted in Figure 7-131.

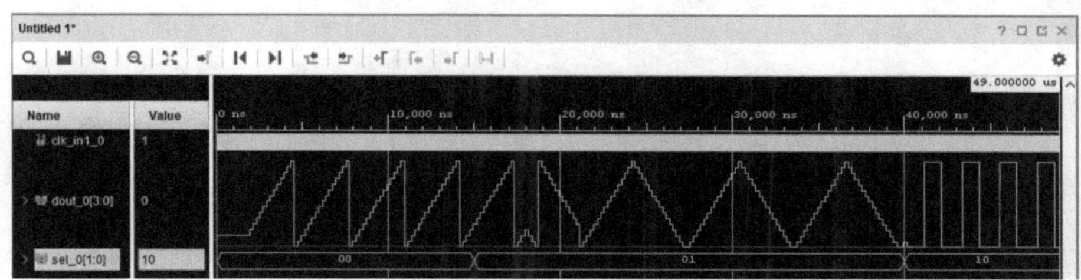

Figure 7-131. *The staircase waveform of signal "dout_0[3:0]"*

Polarity of the Ports in Vivado

In this section, we want to correct the port polarity bug in Vivado. So we create a new project named "Bug" and also a design source file titled "D_flipflop.v", and then we add the following codes inside of it as illustrated in Figures 7-132 and 7-133, respectively:

```verilog
`timescale 1ns / 1ps
module D_filpflop(
    input clk,din,rst,
    output q,qbar
    );
reg temp;
initial temp = 0;
always@(posedge clk) begin
if (rst)
   temp <= 1'bx;
else
   temp <= din;
end
assign q = temp;
assign qbar = ~temp;
endmodule
```

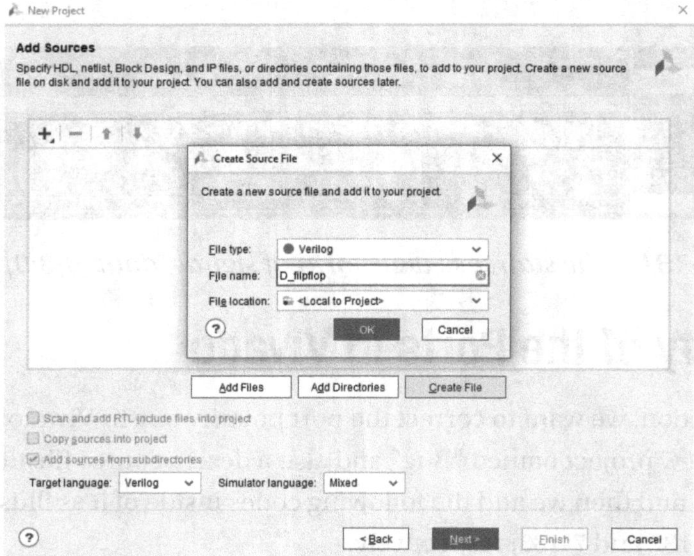

Figure 7-132. *Creating a design source file titled "D_flipflop.v"*

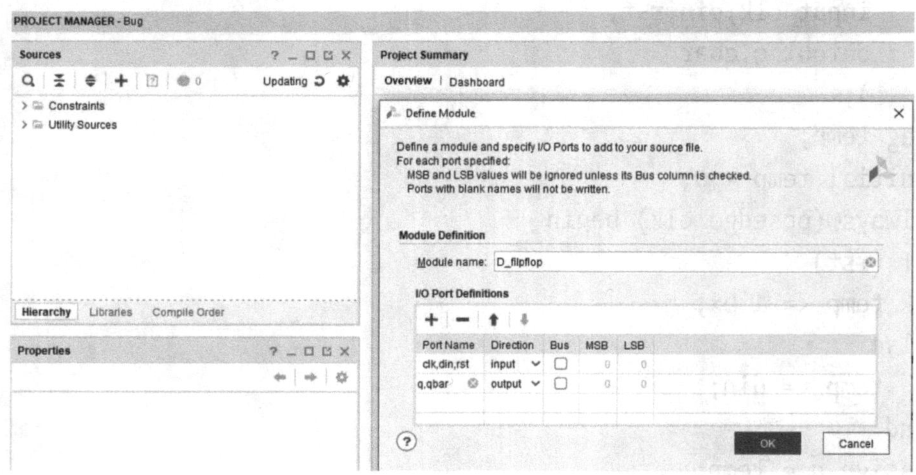

Figure 7-133. *Adding I/O ports for the module "D_flipflop"*

We choose Flow ➤ Run Simulation ➤ Run Behavioral Simulation from the menu toolbar to view the waveforms on the wave window. So, in the opened simulation window, we click the Restart button, and then we right-click the signal "clk" and set the force clock parameters of it as shown in Figure 7-134.

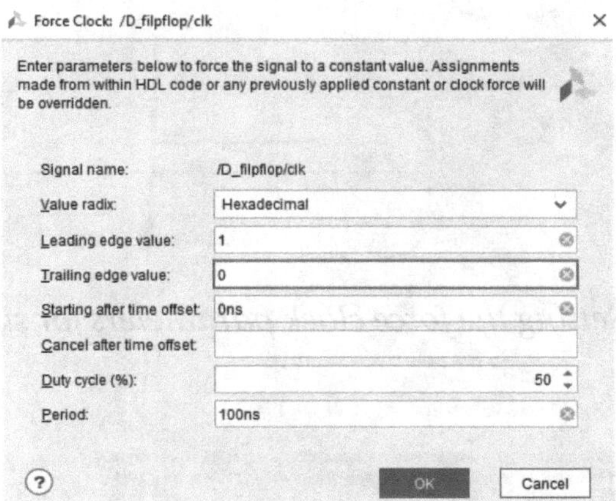

Figure 7-134. *Setting the force clock parameters for signal "clk"*

We also right-click the signals "din" and "rst" and set the force clock parameters of them as depicted in Figures 7-135 and 7-136, respectively.

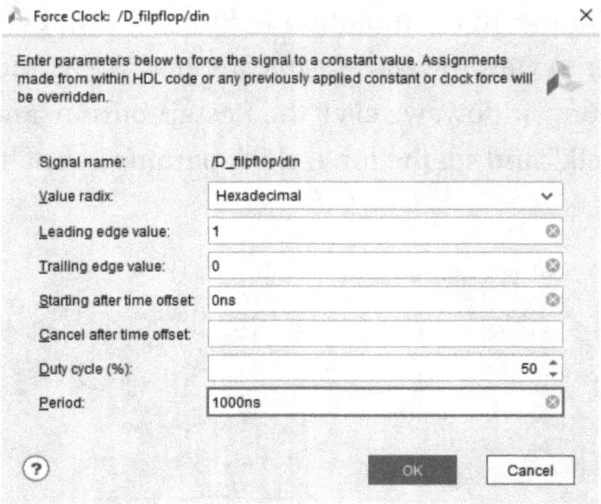

Figure 7-135. *Setting the force clock parameters for signal "din"*

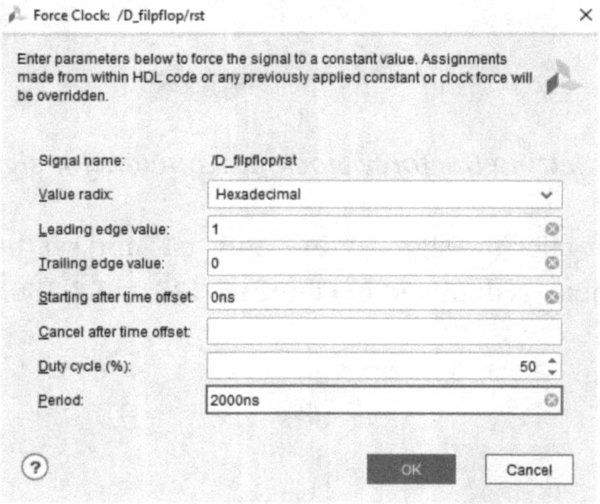

Figure 7-136. *Setting the force clock parameters for signal "rst"*

Then, we click the Run for 6µs button once, and also, we click the Zoom Fit button to view the simulated waveforms on the wave window as illustrated in Figure 7-137.

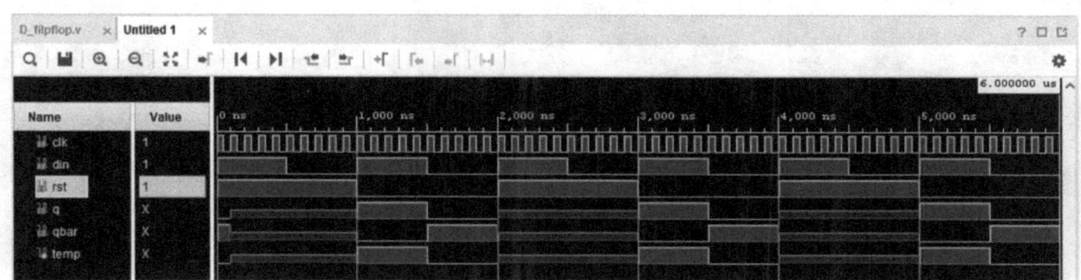

Figure 7-137. *The simulated waveforms on the wave window*

Now, from the menu we select Tools ➤ Create and Package New IP… as demonstrated in Figure 7-138, and in the opened Create and Package New IP window, we click the Next button. Then, under Packaging Options, we choose the Package your current project option and click the Next button. We leave the IP location unchanged and then click the Next button. In the New IP Creation summary window, we click the Finish button, and in the Customization GUI window, we can observe that the polarity of pin "rst" is inverted or in the active low mode as shown in Figure 7-139.

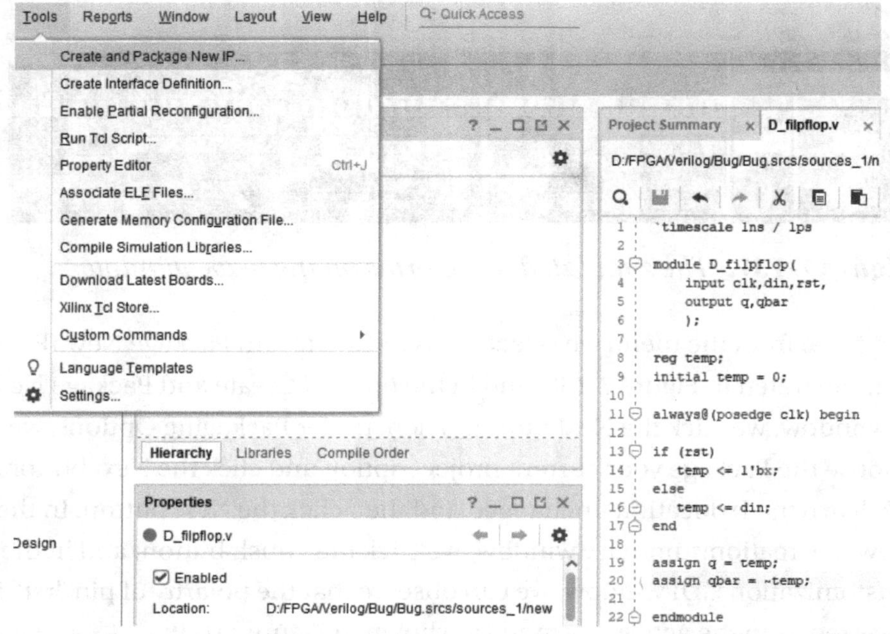

Figure 7-138. *Selecting Tools ➤ Create and Package New IP…*

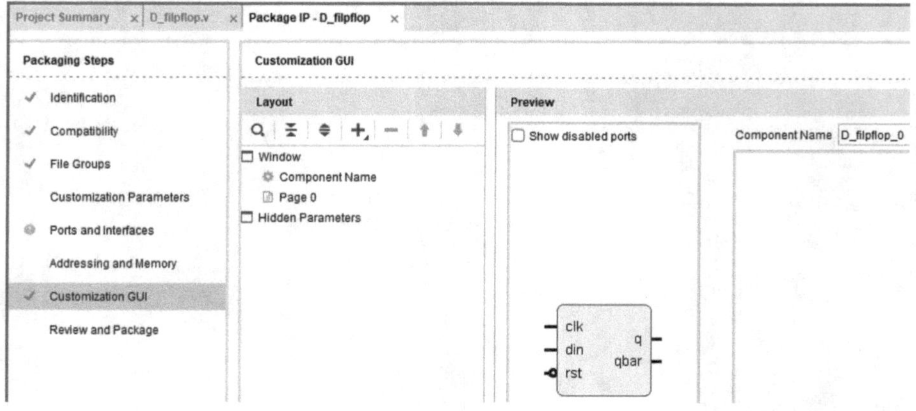

Figure 7-139. *The inverted polarity of pin "rst"*

In the Ports and Interfaces window, we right-click the port "rst" and select the Add Bus Interface... option as depicted in Figure 7-140.

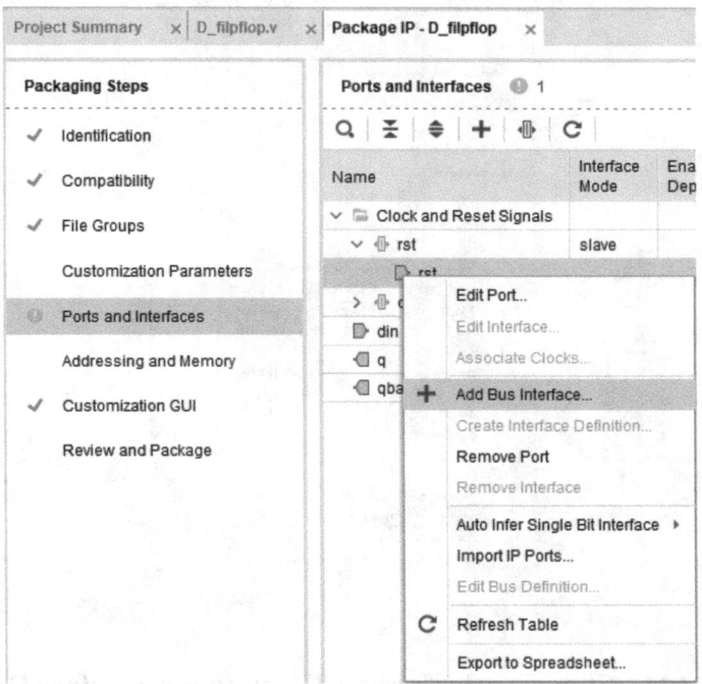

Figure 7-140. *Selecting the Add Bus Interface... option*

In the opened Add Interface window, we enter the name as "rst" and its mode as slave, and also, we click the three dots button of Interface Definition to open the Interface Definition Chooser window. Then under Signal we choose the "reset_rtl" option as illustrated in Figure 7-141.

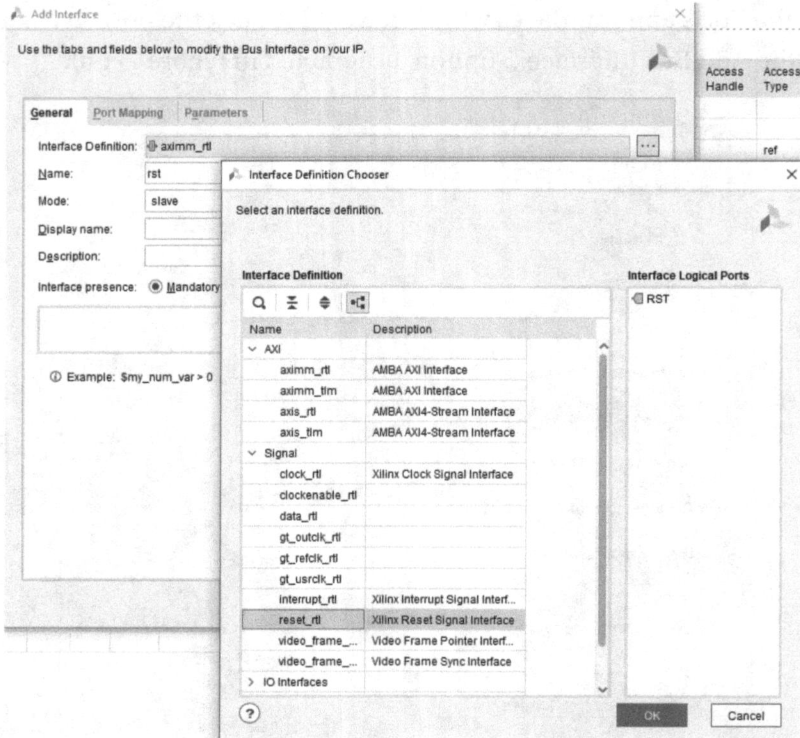

Figure 7-141. *Choosing the "reset_rtl" option for Interface Definition*

Now, we click the Port Mapping tab of the Add Interface window to view the mapping IP's physical port "rst" to the logical port "RST" as shown in Figure 7-142. In the Parameters tab of the Add Interface window, we right-click the User Set folder and select the Add Bus Parameter... option as depicted in Figure 7-143.

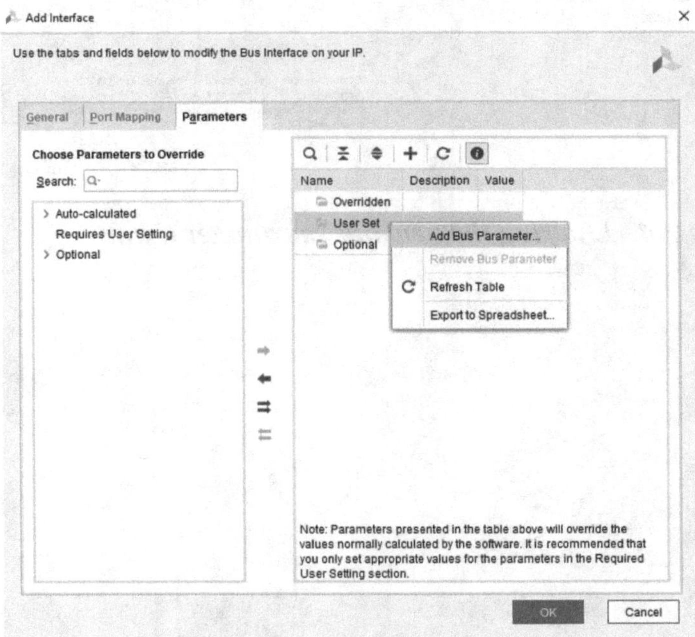

Figure 7-142. *The Port Mapping tab of the Add Interface window*

Figure 7-143. *Selecting the Add Bus Parameter… option*

We enter the new bus parameter name as "POLARITY" in the Add Parameter window and then click the "OK" button as illustrated in Figure 7-144. We also enter "ACTIVE_HIGH" for the value of parameter "POLARITY" as shown in Figure 7-145.

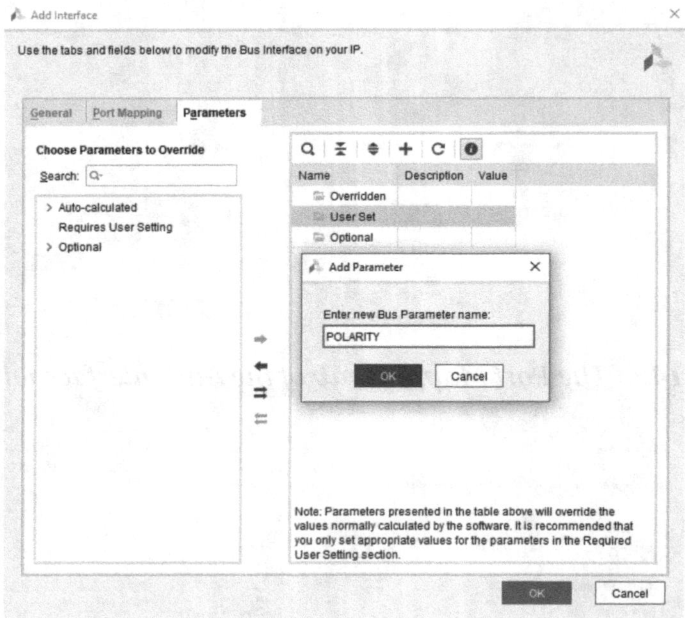

Figure 7-144. *Entering the new bus parameter name*

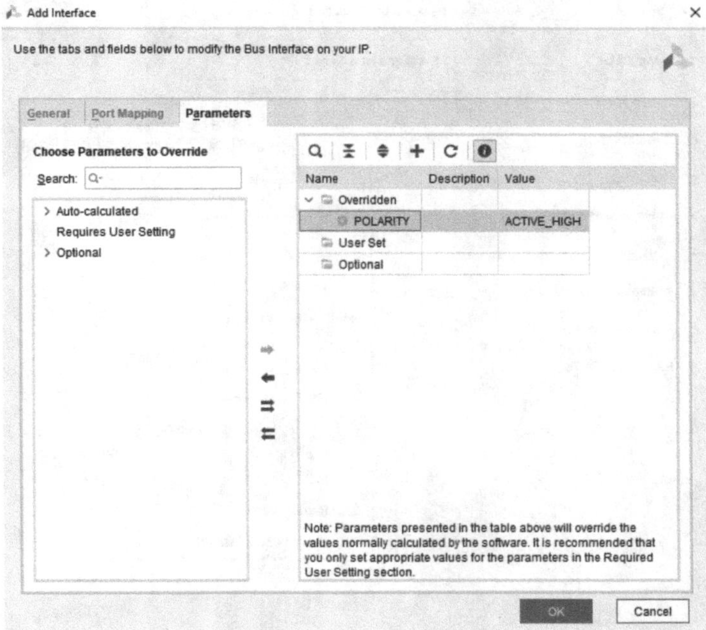

Figure 7-145. *Entering "ACTIVE_HIGH" for the value of the added parameter*

Then, we select the Auto Infer Single Bit Interface option as Reset as depicted in Figure 7-146.

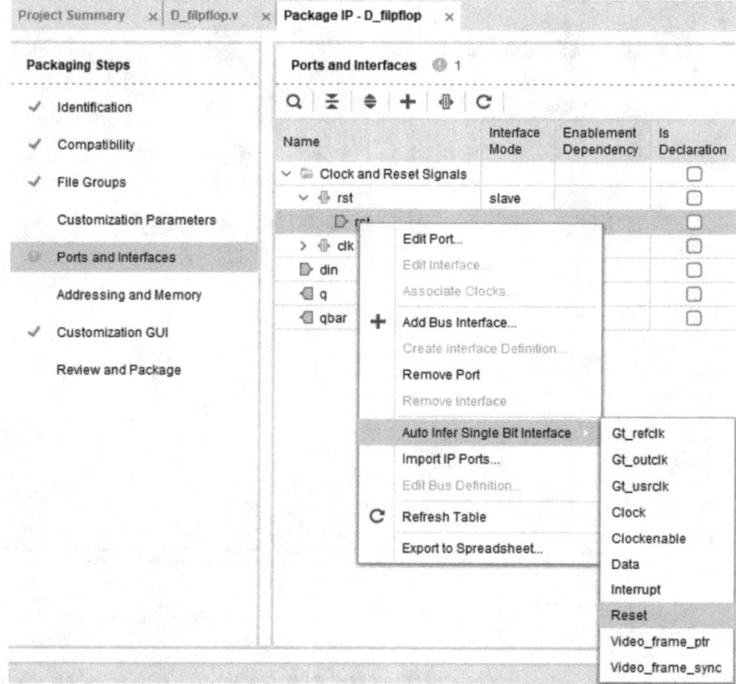

Figure 7-146. *Selecting the Auto Infer Single Bit Interface option as Reset*

Now, if we go ahead to the Customization GUI window, we can observe that the pin "rst" is now in the active high mode and it is not inverted as depicted in Figure 7-147.

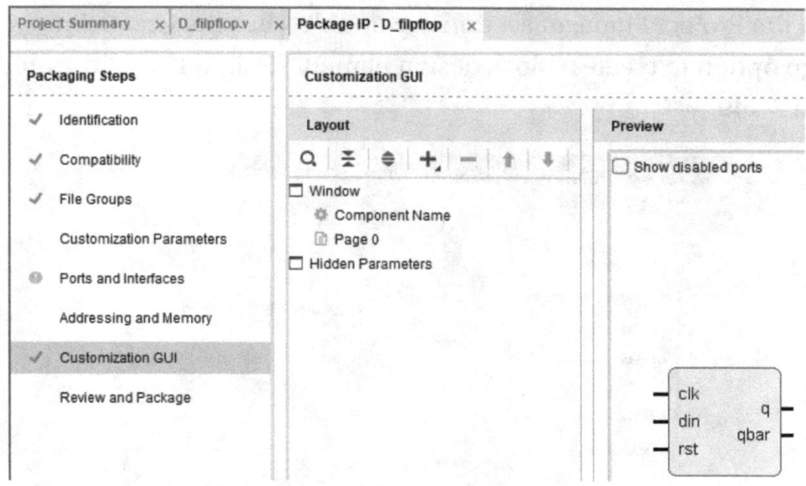

Figure 7-147. *The active high mode for the pin "rst"*

Finally in the Review and Package window, we click the Package IP button, and it is done successfully as depicted in Figure 7-148.

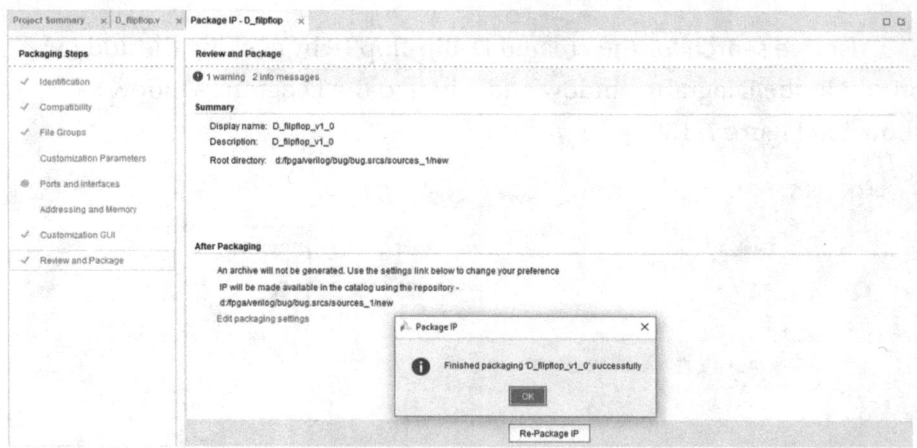

Figure 7-148. *Successful packaging of the D-flip-flop IP*

In the Project Manager section, we double-click the Create Block Design option to create a block design named "design_1" as illustrated in Figure 7-149.

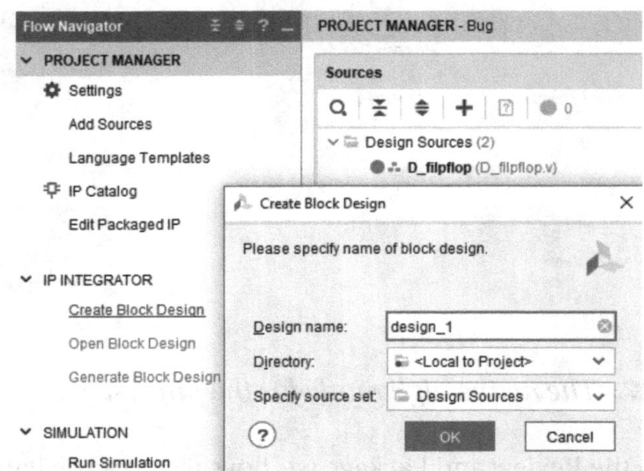

Figure 7-149. *Creating a block design named "design_1"*

Also, we search for the created D-flip-flop IP by clicking the add (+) button in the Diagram window and add it to the Diagram window as shown in Figure 7-150.

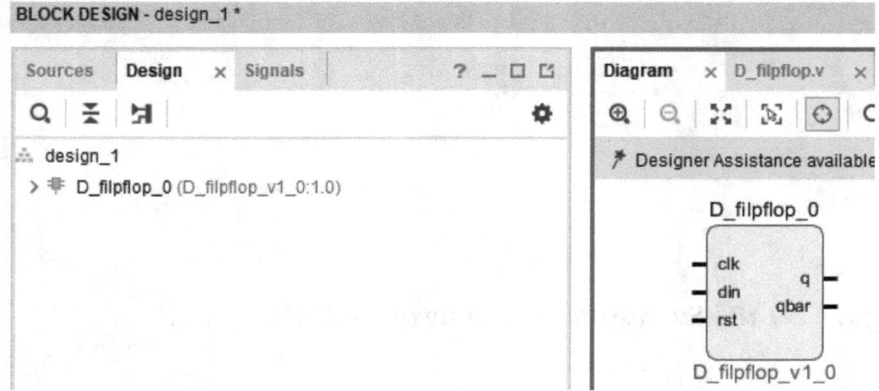

Figure 7-150. *The D-flip-flop IP added to the Diagram window*

Digital Filter Design Using MATLAB

In this section, we are going to design a low-pass digital filter using MATLAB in Vivado. So, in the MATLAB Command Window, we enter the following command:

```
>> fdatool
```

Therefore, the Filter Designer window is opened, and we set the parameters and then click the Set quantization parameters button as depicted in Figure 7-151.

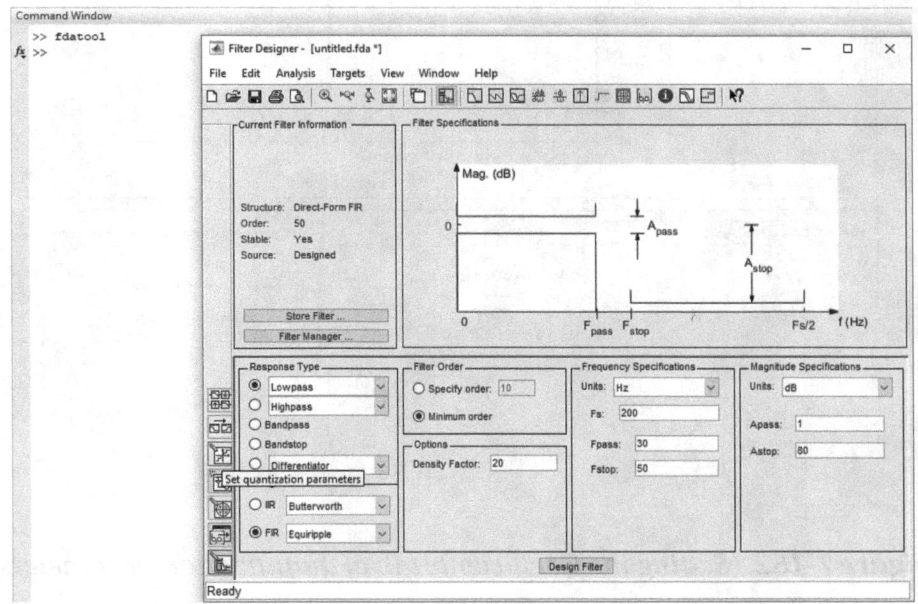

Figure 7-151. *Setting the Filter Designer parameters*

In the opened window, we set the Coefficients, Input/Output, and Filter Internals tabs of quantization parameters and then click the Apply button as illustrated in Figures 7-152, 7-153, and 7-154, respectively. Now, we click the Filter Coefficients button to view the filter coefficients as shown in Figure 7-155. If in the Coefficients tab we check the Use unsigned representation option, we can observe the unsigned filter coefficients as depicted in Figure 7-156. Finally, we choose File in the menu and select the Export... option as illustrated in Figure 7-157. We set Export To as Coefficient File (ASCII) and Format as Decimal and then click the Export button to save it as the file "lp.fcf" as shown in Figure 7-158.

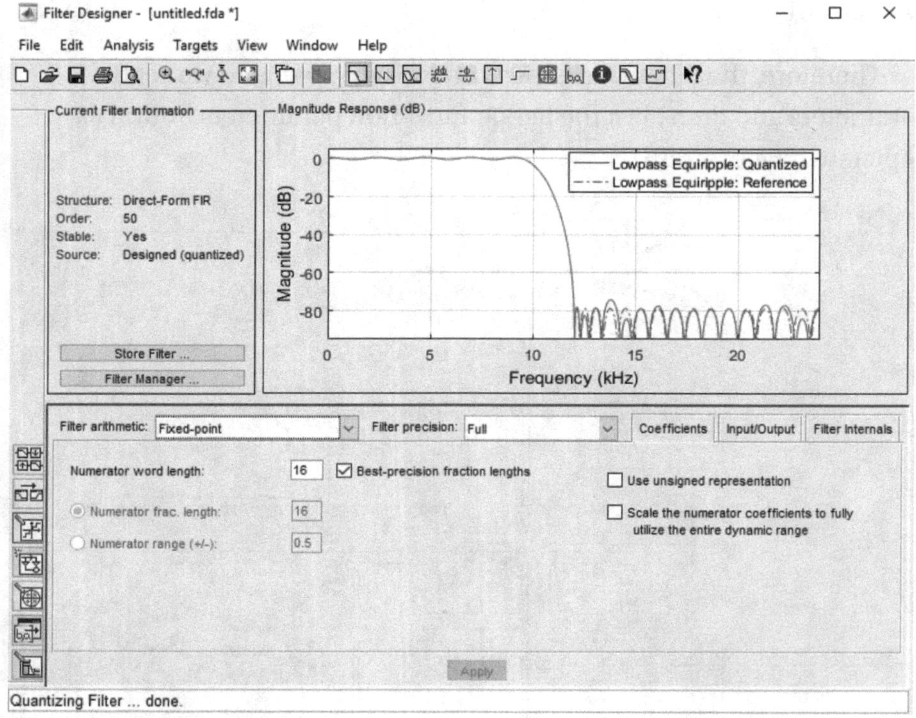

Figure 7-152. *Setting the Coefficients tab of quantization parameters*

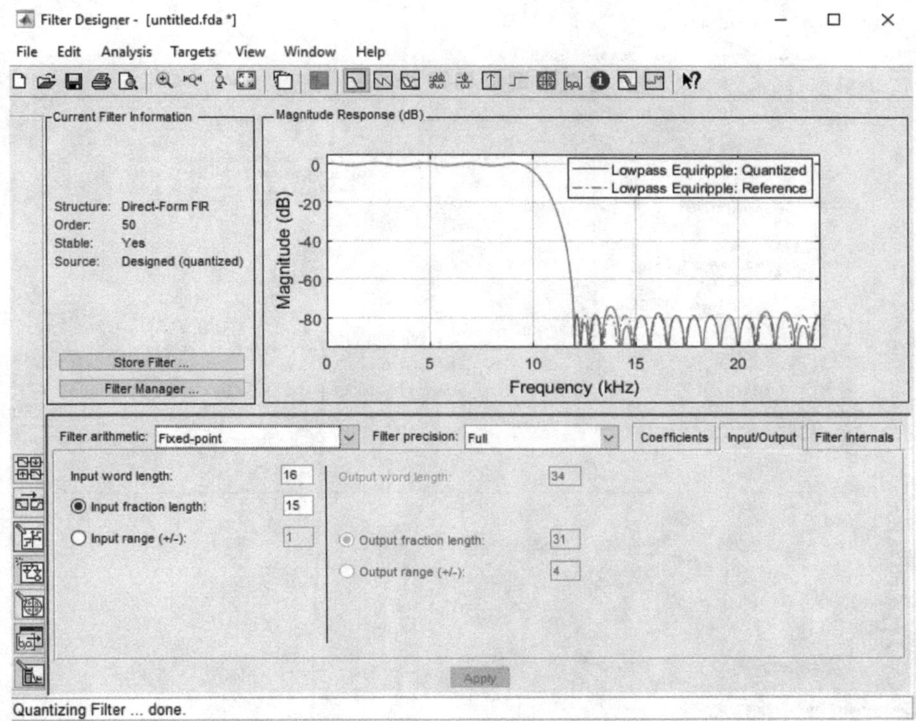

Figure 7-153. *Setting the Input/Output tab of quantization parameters*

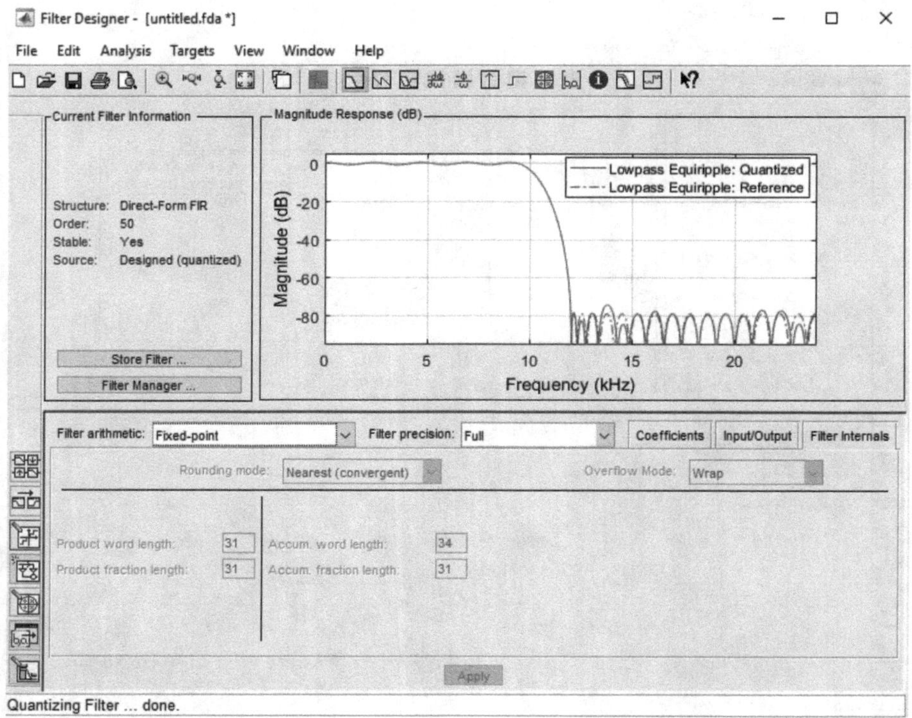

Figure 7-154. *Setting the Filter Internals tab of quantization parameters*

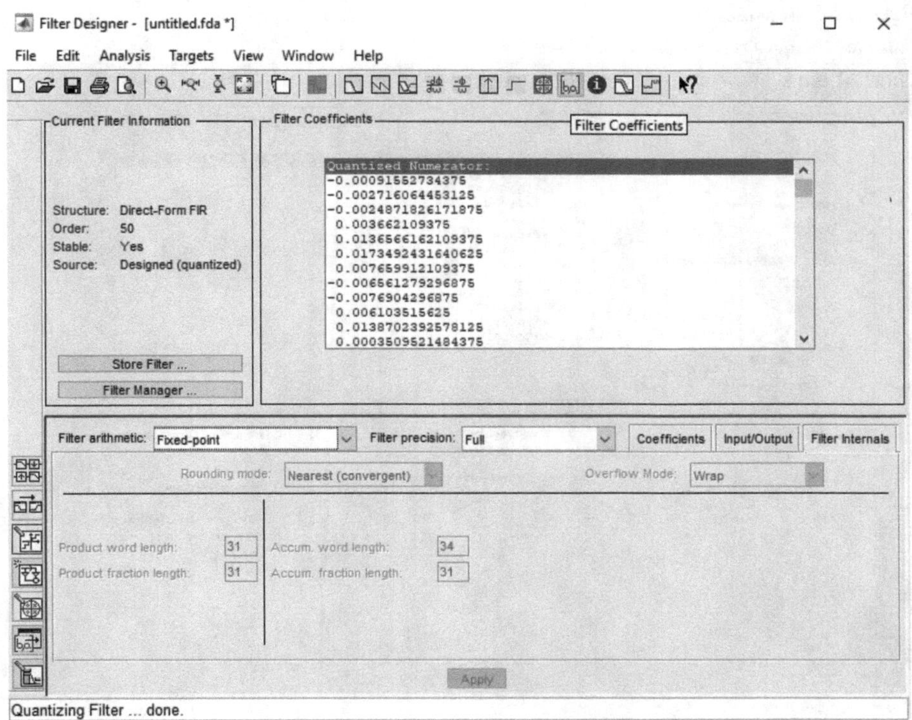

Figure 7-155. *Viewing the filter coefficients*

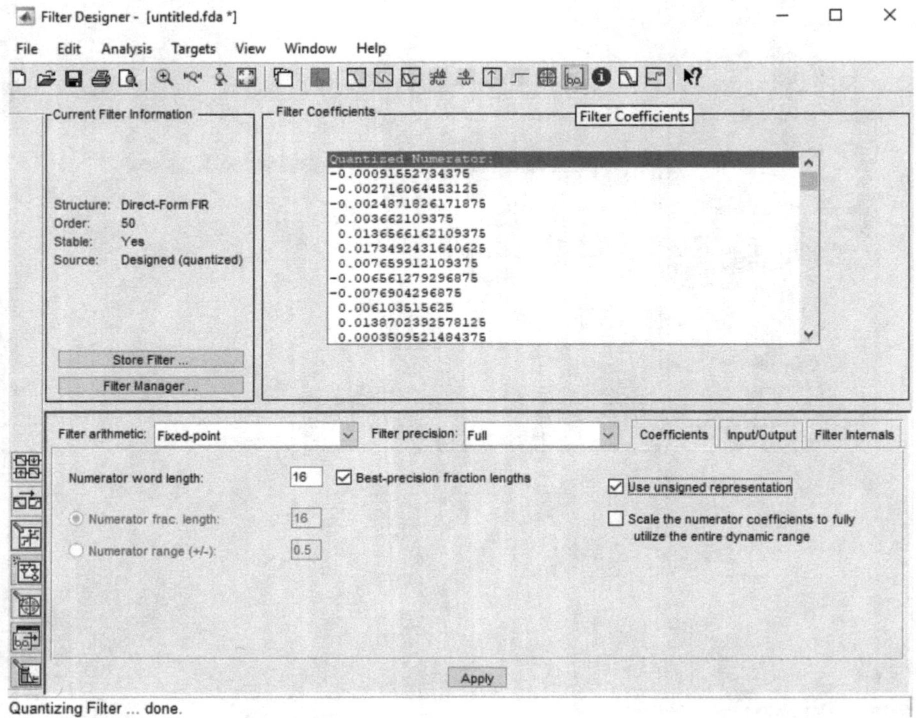

Figure 7-156. *Selecting the Use unsigned representation option*

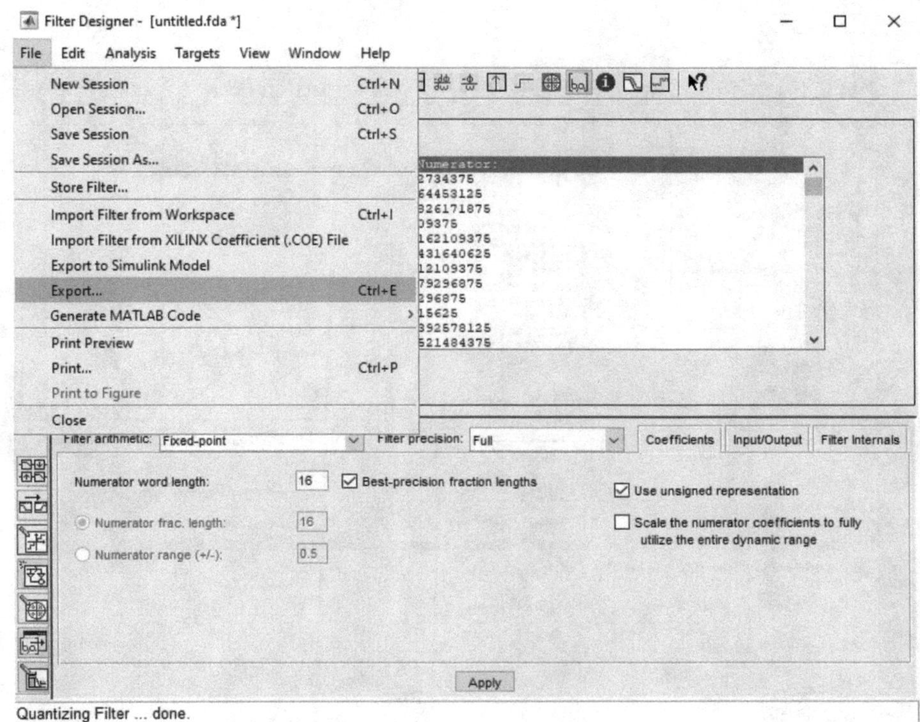

Figure 7-157. *Selecting the Export... option*

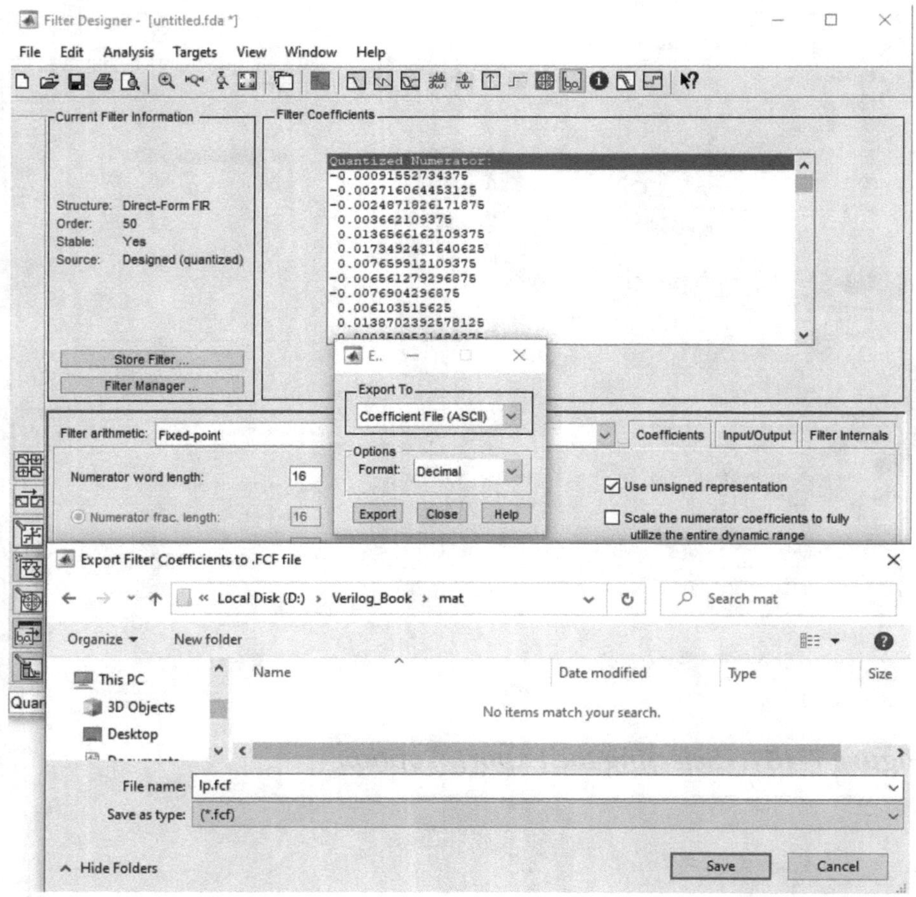

Figure 7-158. *Saving the filter coefficients file as "lp.fcf"*

We open the exported filter coefficients file ("lp.fcf") with Notepad and set it as depicted in Figure 7-159.

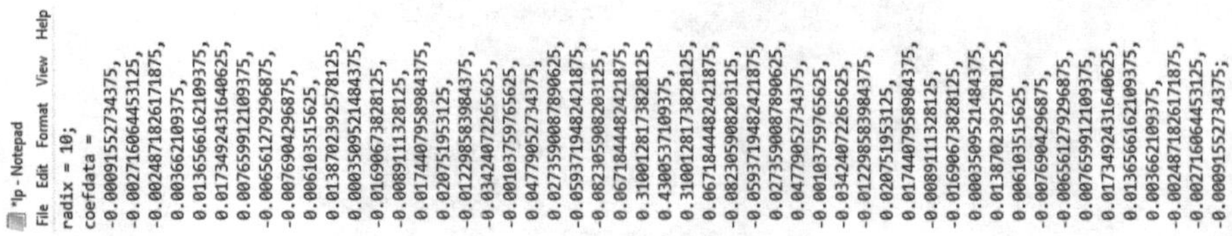

Figure 7-159. *Settings of the filter coefficients file ("lp.fcf")*

We also save the edited filter coefficients file ("lp.fcf") as a text file named "lp.coe" as illustrated in Figure 7-160. We also copy and paste the edited file "lp.fcf" and rename it as "lp.coe".

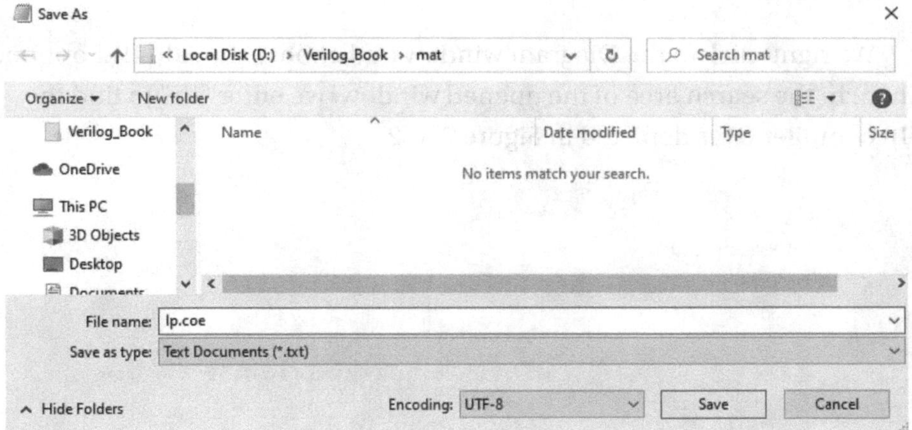

Figure 7-160. *Saving the edited filter coefficients text file as "lp.coe"*

So we create a new project named "Digital_Filter" and create a block design titled "design_1" as shown in Figure 7-161.

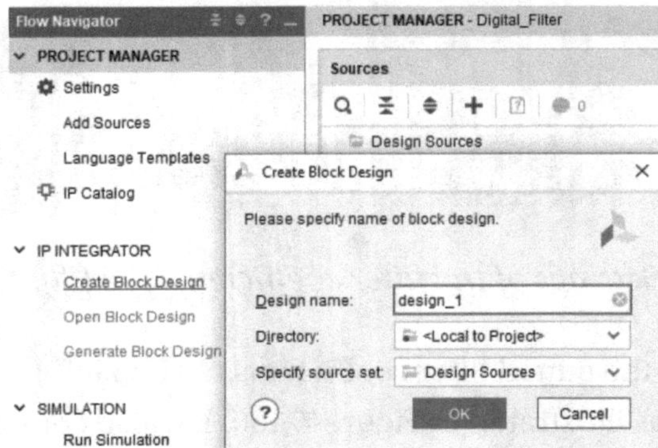

Figure 7-161. *Creating a block design titled "design_1"*

We right-click in the Diagram window and choose the Add IP... option. Then, in the search area of the opened window, we enter "fir" to find the FIR compiler IP as depicted in Figure 7-162.

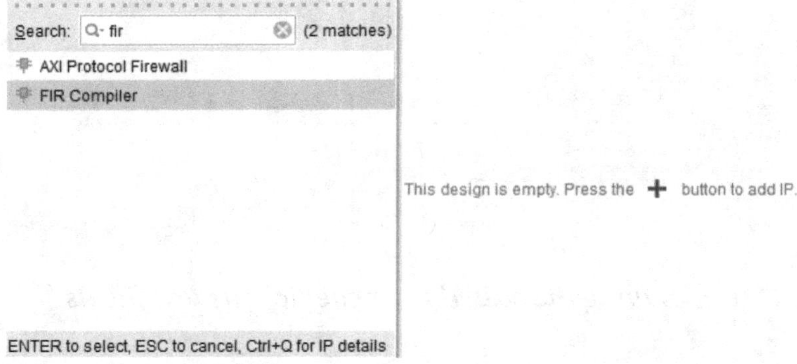

Figure 7-162. *Searching for the FIR compiler IP*

We double-click the FIR compiler IP to view the Filter Options tab and IP symbol as well as the frequency response as illustrated in Figures 7-163 and 7-164, respectively.

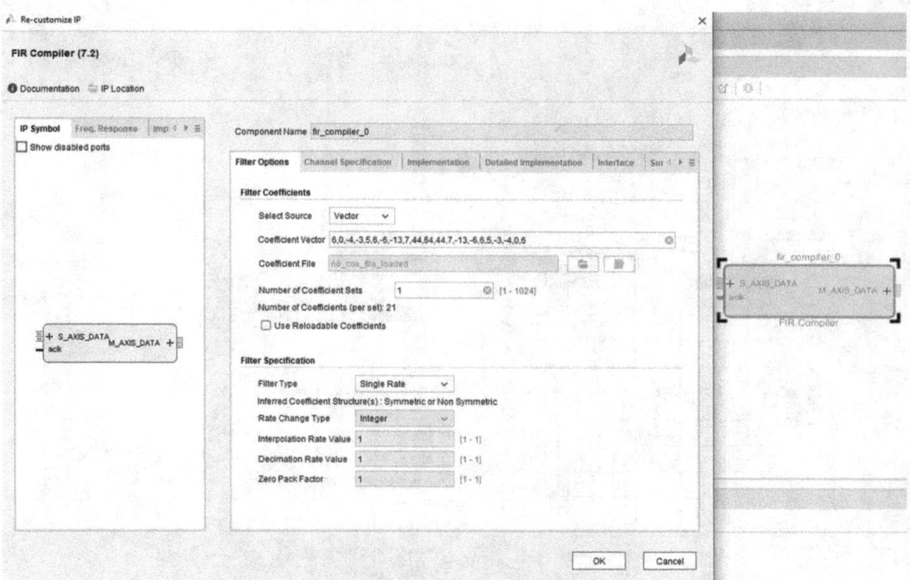

Figure 7-163. *The Filter Options tab and IP symbol of the FIR compiler IP*

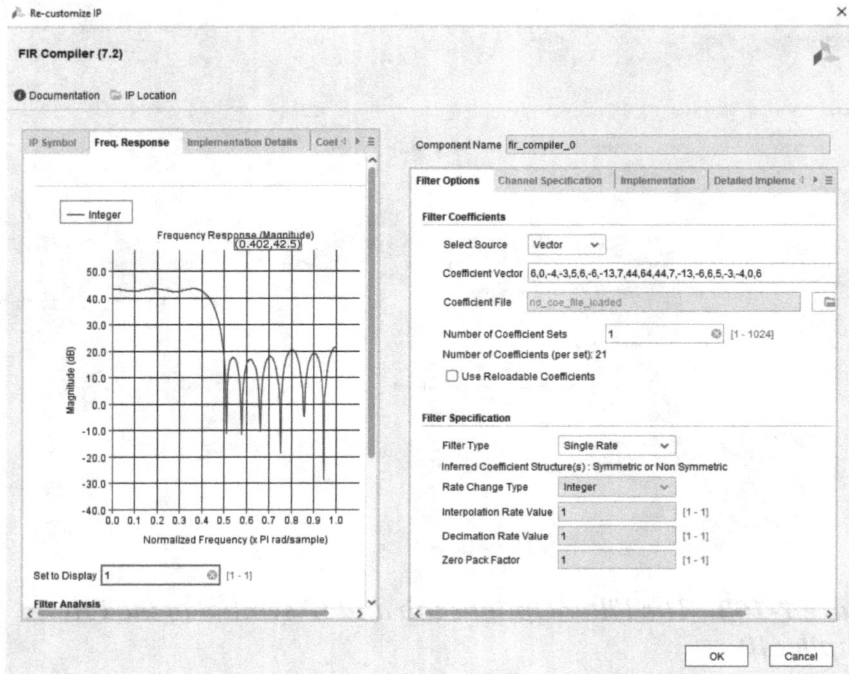

Figure 7-164. *The frequency response of the FIR compiler IP*

In the Filter Options tab, we select the source as COE File and choose the coefficient file "lp.coe" we created using MATLAB and then click the OK button as shown in Figures 7-165 and 7-166, respectively.

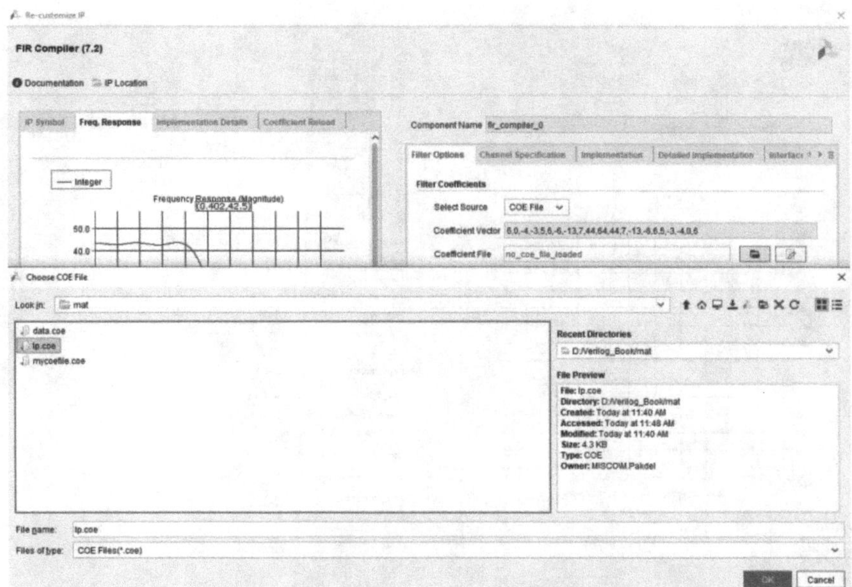

Figure 7-165. *Choosing the coefficient file "lp.coe"*

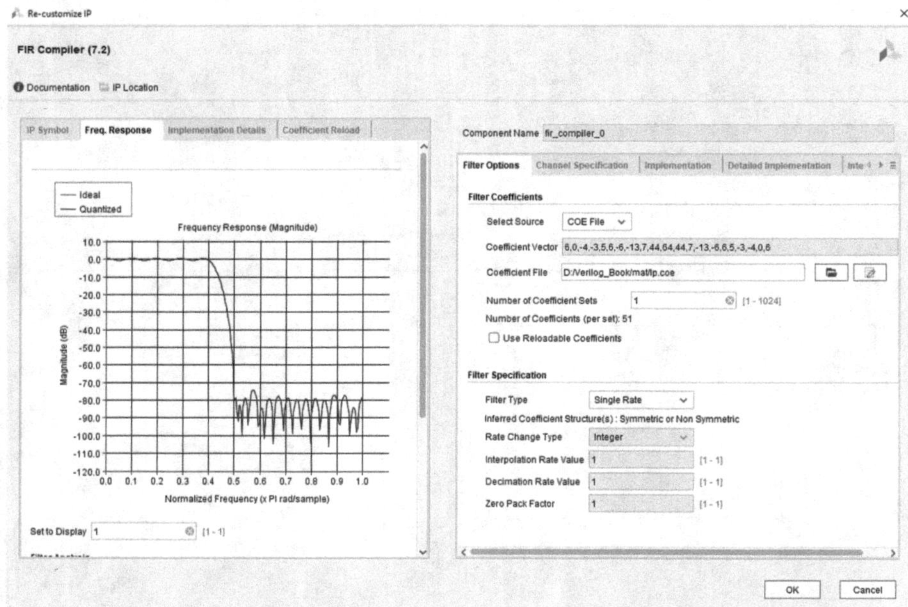

Figure 7-166. *Clicking the OK button*

In the Channel Specification tab of FIR Compiler, we set the input sampling frequency to 200Hz as depicted in Figure 7-167.

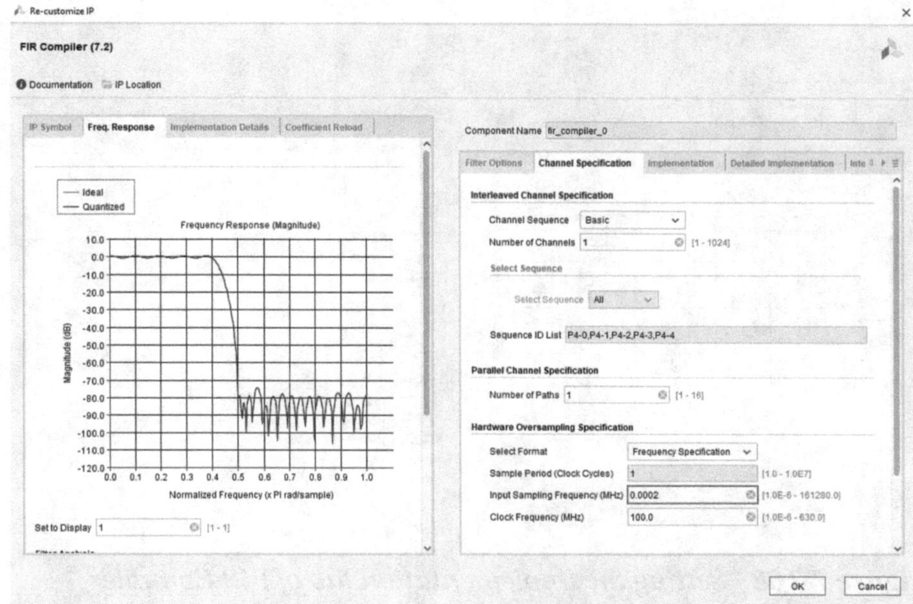

Figure 7-167. *Setting the Channel Specification tab of FIR Compiler*

In the Implementation and Detailed Implementation tabs of FIR Compiler, we set the parameters as illustrated in Figures 7-168 and 7-169, respectively.

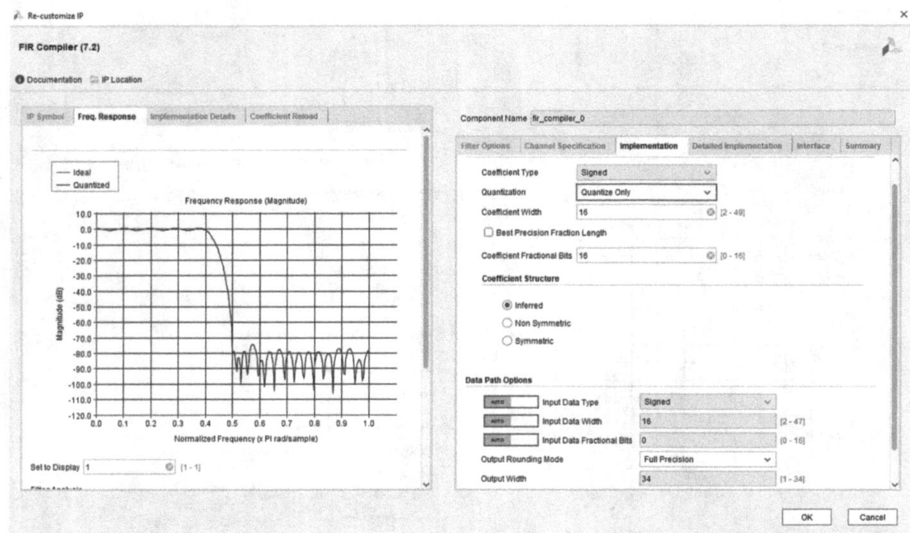

Figure 7-168. *Setting the Implementation tab of FIR Compiler*

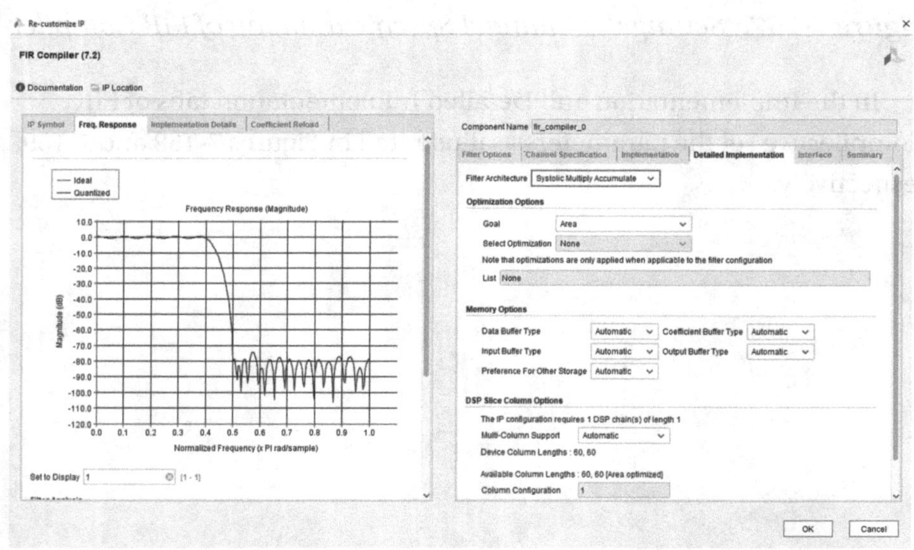

Figure 7-169. *Setting the Detailed Implementation tab of FIR Compiler*

We also set the Interface tab of the FIR compiler IP as shown in
Figure 7-170.

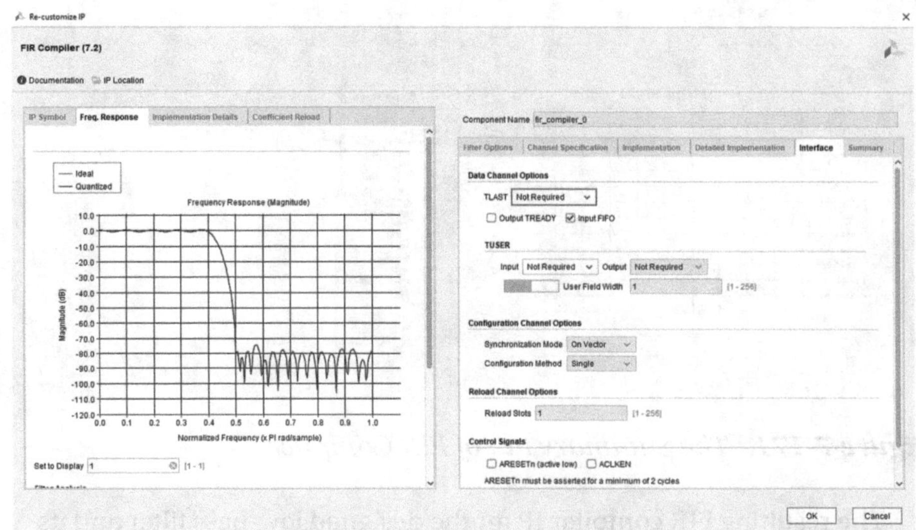

Figure 7-170. *Setting the Interface tab of FIR Compiler*

Now, we can observe the Summary tab of FIR Compiler as depicted in
Figure 7-171.

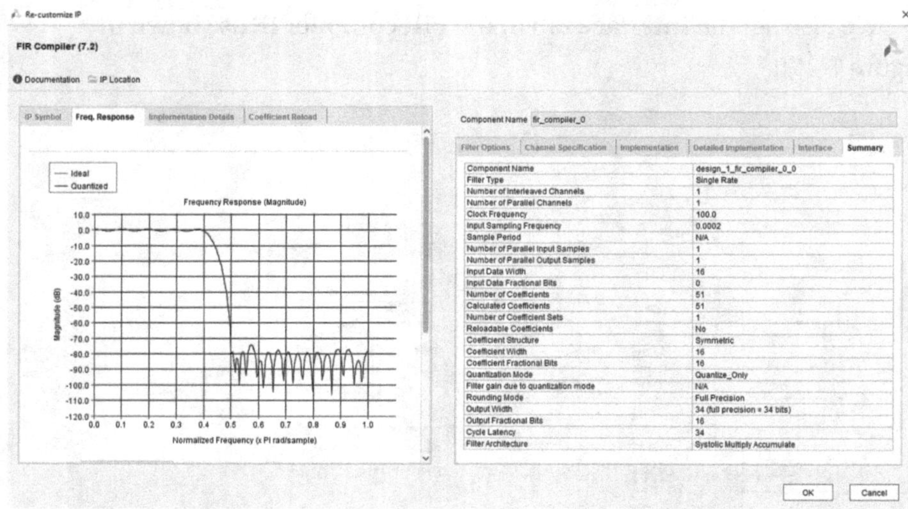

Figure 7-171. *The Summary tab of FIR Compiler*

The resulting FIR compiler IP for the designed low-pass filter and its input and output pins are illustrated in Figure 7-172.

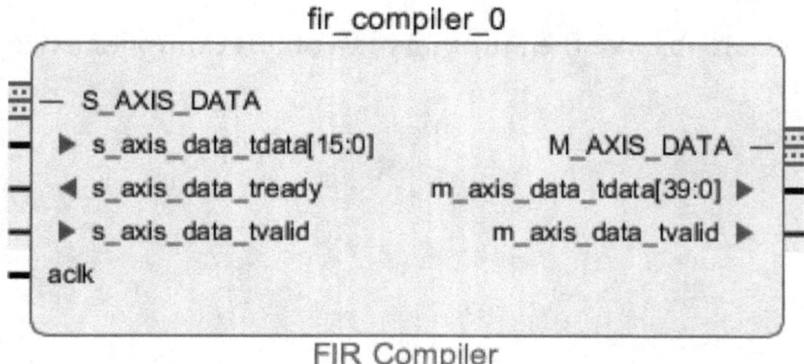

Figure 7-172. *The resulting FIR compiler IP for the designed low-pass filter*

Summary and Key Takeaways

In this chapter, we delved into the practical aspects of block design and Intellectual Property (IP), a fundamental methodology for modern digital design. We began by learning how to integrate and customize predefined IP cores, including a binary counter, a sinusoidal waveform generator (DDS compiler), and a multiplier, using Vivado's block design interface. This process involved configuring IP parameters, creating external ports, and validating the design.

We then transitioned from using IPs to creating them, walking through the steps to package your own Verilog modules—such as a full adder and a D-flip-flop—as reusable IP cores. This was followed by learning how to add these custom IPs to your project's repository and utilize them in a new block design. The chapter also covered hierarchical design techniques by constructing a 4-bit ripple carry adder from multiple full adder IPs and a more complex function generator IP that could produce different waveforms.

A crucial troubleshooting skill was addressed by exploring how to correct port polarity in the IP packaging GUI to ensure signals like reset behave as intended. Finally, we bridged the gap between algorithm and hardware by designing a digital low-pass filter in MATLAB, exporting its coefficients, and implementing it in Vivado using the FIR compiler IP. This demonstrated a complete workflow for deploying complex, algorithm-based IPs onto an FPGA.

By mastering these skills, you are now equipped to efficiently build complex systems by leveraging both existing and custom IP cores, significantly reducing design time and increasing reliability through modular, reusable components. In the next chapter, we will apply these foundational concepts to implement various communication interfaces and tackle a series of practical, miscellaneous projects.

CHAPTER 8

Communication Interfaces and Miscellaneous Projects

In Chapter 7, we explored block design and IP cores, learning how to integrate and create reusable hardware modules for efficient system development. Building on these concepts, this chapter focuses on communication protocols and practical FPGA interfacing techniques, which are essential for real-world embedded systems and digital design applications.

This chapter covers a range of communication interfaces, beginning with the UART protocol, a fundamental serial communication standard widely used in microcontroller–FPGA interactions. We then explore pulse-width modulation (PWM) for analog signal generation and LCD interfacing for display control. Next, we discuss Built-In Self-Test (BIST) techniques for verifying hardware functionality, followed by I2C-based EEPROM (Electrically Erasable PROM) interfacing, demonstrating how to store and retrieve data from external memory.

© Majid Pakdel 2026
M. Pakdel, *Mastering Verilog for FPGA Design*, Maker Innovations Series,
https://doi.org/10.1007/979-8-8688-2311-4_8

The chapter also addresses RTL synthesis considerations, ensuring that designs are optimized for hardware implementation. Finally, we examine SPI communication for DAC (digital-to-analog converter) and ADC (analog-to-digital converter) interfacing, highlighting how FPGAs can interact with analog components for data conversion and signal processing.

By the end of this chapter, you will have hands-on experience with essential communication protocols and peripheral interfacing, enabling you to design robust, real-world FPGA-based systems. So, in this chapter, we are going to implement communication interfaces as well as some miscellaneous projects on FPGA.

The UART Interface

The UART interface is used in short distances (1m–10m), and its maximum speed is 500kb/s. Also, it is one-to-one communication for the RS232 protocol, and it can be used to interface with up to 256 devices in the RS485 protocol. The flowchart for implementing the UART interface (for sending the ASCII hex code 41, which is the character A) is shown in Figure 8-1.

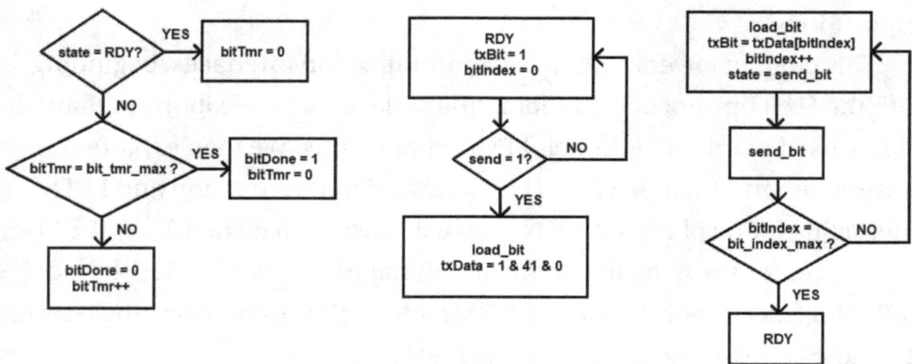

Figure 8-1. *The flowchart for implementing the UART interface*

So we create a new project named "UART" and also a design source file titled "top.v" and then add the following codes inside of it:

```verilog
`timescale 1ns / 1ps
module top(
input send, //When to start transmission of data this pin
            must be high
input clk, //100 MHZ
output uart_tx // it is connected to the transmit pin of RS232
            and output of FPGA
    );
// 100MHz/9600 = 10416
parameter bit_tmr_max = 10416;
parameter bit_index_max = 10; //Single frame of UART consists
                                of 10 bits data

parameter rdy = 0, load_bit = 1, send_bit = 2;


reg [13:0] bitTmr = 0;
reg bitDone;
reg [3:0] bitIndex;
reg txBit = 1'b1;
reg [9:0] txData;
reg [1:0] state = rdy;

//Generating bit rate
always@(posedge clk) begin

if (state == rdy)
    bitTmr <= 0;
else begin
    if(bitTmr == bit_tmr_max) begin
        bitDone <= 1'b1;
        bitTmr <= 0;
```

```verilog
        end
    else begin
        bitTmr <= bitTmr + 1;
        bitDone <= 1'b0;
    end
end
end

//Next state process
always@(posedge clk) begin
case(state)
rdy : begin
txBit = 1'b1;
bitIndex <= 0;
if(send == 1'b1) begin
   state <= load_bit;
   txData = {1'b1,8'h41,1'b0}; //stop bit = 1,8-bit data,
                               start bit = 0
end
else
   state <= rdy;
end

load_bit : begin
bitIndex <= bitIndex + 1;
txBit <= txData[bitIndex]; //txBit is as output of uart_tx
state <= send_bit;
end

send_bit : begin
if(bitDone == 1'b1) begin
    if(bitIndex == bit_index_max)
        state <= rdy;
```

```
    else
        state <= load_bit;
end
end
default : state <= rdy;

endcase
end
assign uart_tx = txBit;
endmodule
```

We select Flow ➤ Run Simulation ➤ Run Behavioral Simulation from the menu toolbar to view the waveforms on the wave window. So, in the opened simulation window, we click the Restart button and then right-click the signal "send" and set its constant value to zero and also right-click the signal "clk" and set the force clock period to 10ns (the clock frequency is 100MHz). Then we run the simulation for 20ns, and after that we right-click the signal "send" and set its constant value to one and again run the simulation for 1000µs (1ms). Now, we click the Zoom Fit button to view the simulated waveforms on the wave window as depicted in Figure 8-2.

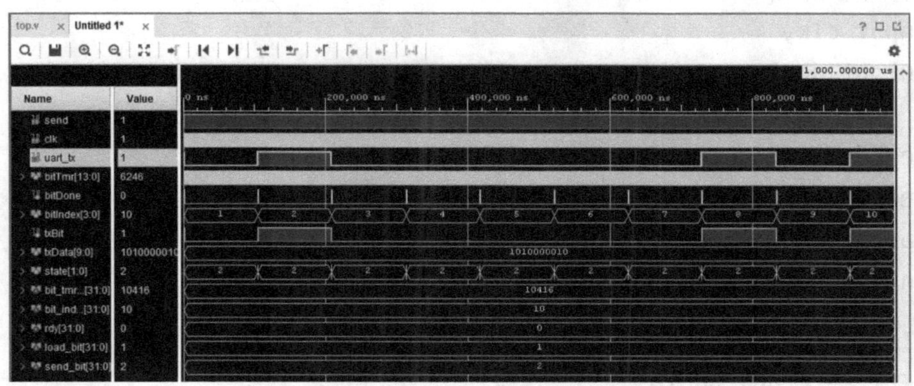

Figure 8-2. *The simulated waveforms on the wave window*

The PWM Implementation

Pulse-width modulation (PWM) is a way of digitally encoding analog signal levels. So the duty cycle of a square wave is modulated to encode a specific analog signal level as illustrated in Figure 8-3.

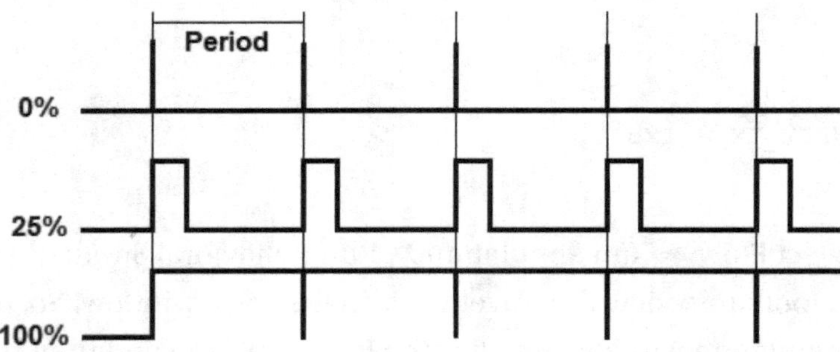

Figure 8-3.   *The duty cycle of a square wave*

So we create a new project named "PWM_LED" and also a design source file titled "pwm.v" and then add the following codes inside of it:

```verilog
`timescale 1ns / 1ps
module pwm(
input clk,
output dout
    );
reg dt = 0;
reg done = 0;
parameter max_period = 5000;
integer step,i = 0;

always@(posedge clk) begin
if(i <= step) begin
    dt <= 1;
    i <= i + 1;
```

```verilog
    done <= 0;
end
else if (i > step && i < max_period) begin
  i <= i + 1;
  dt <= 0;
  done <= 0;
end
else
  i <= 0;
  done <= 1; //handshaking signal
end

always@(posedge clk) begin
if (done == 1) begin
   if (step < max_period)
       step <= step + 50;
   else
       step = 0;
end
end
assign dout = dt;
endmodule
```

We select Flow ➤ Run Simulation ➤ Run Behavioral Simulation from the menu toolbar to view the waveforms on the wave window. So, in the opened simulation window, we click the Restart button, and then we right-click the signal "clk" and set the force clock period to 10ns (the clock frequency is 100MHz). Then we run the simulation for 800µs. Now, we click the Zoom Fit button to view the simulated waveforms on the wave window as depicted in Figure 8-4.

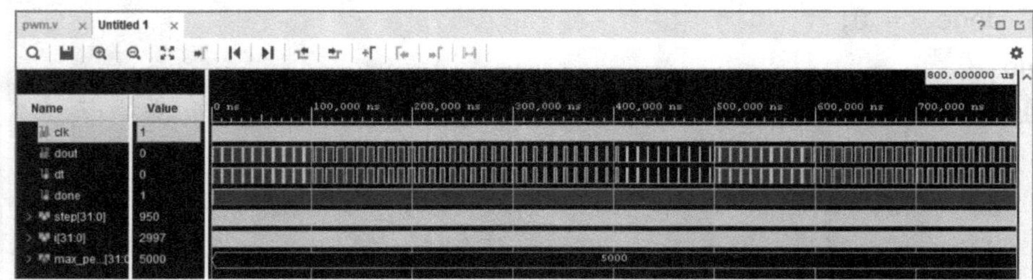

Figure 8-4. *The simulated waveforms on the wave window*

The LCD Interface Implementation

An LCD is used to display a character. A character is represented as an
ASCII value. To display the character, only the ASCII value is sent to the
LCD, and ASCII has 8 bits. The pin diagram for a 16 × 2 LCD is illustrated in
Figure 8-5.

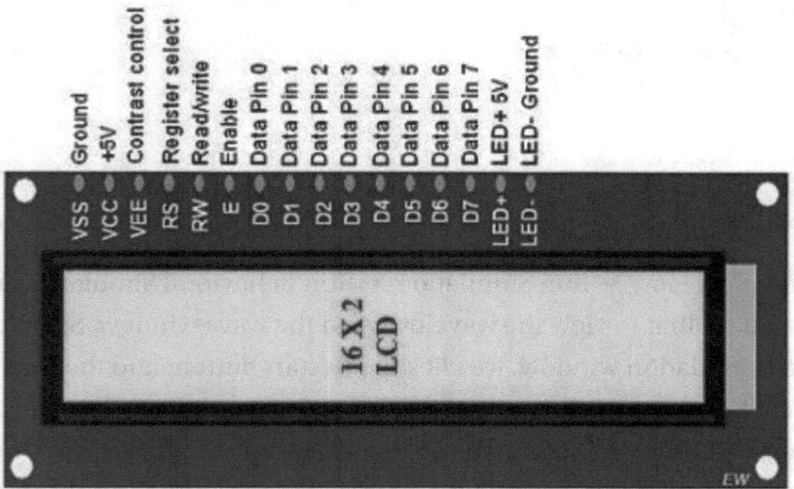

Figure 8-5. *The pin diagram for a 16 × 2 LCD*

If the logic state of RS (Register Select) is 1, the data register is selected. If the logic state of RS is 0, the command register is selected. When the data is sent to data pins of the LCD, the high-to-low pulse will be given in the E (Enable) pin. The ASCII values for commands used in the code are as below:

38 = Function Set: 8-bit, 2-line, 5 × 7 dots

0C = Display On, Cursor Off

06 = Entry Mode

01 = Clear Display

C0 = Place Cursor to 2nd Line

Also, the ASCII values for data used in the code are as follows:

41 = A, 42 = B, 43 = C

So we create a new project named "LCD" and also a design source file titled "lcd.v" and then add the following codes inside of it:

```verilog
`timescale 1ns / 1ps
module lcd(
input clk,
output rs,rw,en,
output [7:0] dout
    );

reg rst = 0,rwt = 0,ent = 0;
reg [7:0] temp;
integer count = 0;
reg [7:0] data [7:0];

initial begin
//commands to start LCD, rs = 0 : command signal
data[0] = 8'h38; //Function Set: 8-bit, 2-Line, 5*7 Dots
```

```verilog
data[1] = 8'h0c; //Display on, Cursor off
data[2] = 8'h06; //Entry Mode
data[3] = 8'h01; //Clear Display
data[4] = 8'hc0; //Place Cursor to 2nd Line

//data to be displayed on LCD, rs = 1 : data signal
data[5] = 8'h41; //character A (ASCII)
data[6] = 8'h42; //character B (ASCII)
data[7] = 8'h43; //character C (ASCII)
end

//clk = 100 MHz, LCD ferq = 100 kHz => count_max =
(100M/100k)/2 = 500
always@(posedge clk) begin
if(count < 500)
   count <= count + 1;
else begin
   count <= 0;
   ent <= ~ent;
end
end
reg [2:0] j = 0;

always@(negedge ent) begin
if(j <= 4) begin
   rst <= 0;
   rwt <= 0;
   temp <= data[j];
   j <= j + 1;
end
else if(j > 4 && j < 8) begin
   rst <= 1;
   rwt <= 0;
```

```
   temp <= data[j];
   j <= j + 1;
end
else
   j <= 0;
end

assign rs = rst;
assign rw = rwt;
assign en = ent;
assign dout = temp;
endmodule
```

We select Flow ➤ Run Simulation ➤ Run Behavioral Simulation from the menu toolbar to view the waveforms on the wave window. So, in the opened simulation window, we click the Restart button, and then we right-click the signal "clk" and set the force clock period to 10ns as shown in Figure 8-6.

Force Clock: /lcd/clk

Enter parameters below to force the signal to a constant value. Assignments made from within HDL code or any previously applied constant or clock force will be overridden.

Signal name: /lcd/clk
Value radix: Hexadecimal
Leading edge value: 1
Trailing edge value: 0
Starting after time offset: 0ns
Cancel after time offset:
Duty cycle (%):   50
Period: 10ns

OK   Cancel

Figure 8-6. *Setting the force clock parameters for signal "clk"*

Then we run the simulation for 170µs. Now, we click the Zoom Fit button to view the simulated waveforms on the wave window as depicted in Figure 8-7.

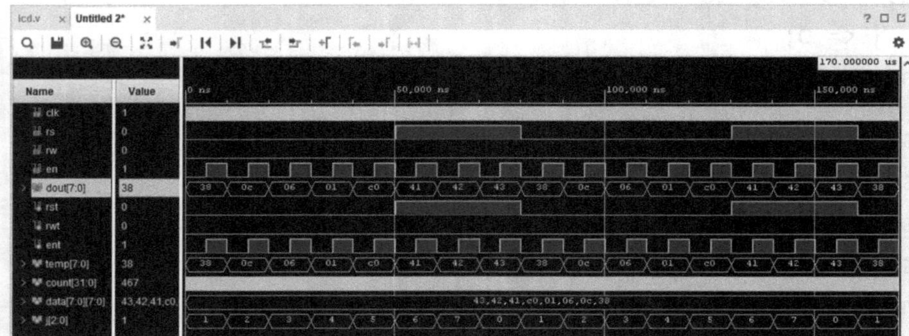

Figure 8-7. *The simulated waveforms on the wave window*

The Built-In Self-Test (BIST) for LEDs and Switches

A Built-In Self-Test (BIST) is a mechanism that permits a machine to test itself. The main purpose of a BIST is to reduce complexity, cost, and reliance upon external test equipment. In this section we use the BIST technique for LEDs and switches on the FPGA development board. So we create a new project named "BIST" and also a design source file titled "bist.v" and then add the following codes inside of it:

```
`timescale 1ns / 1ps
module bist(
input clk,
input [15:0] sw,
output [15:0] led
    );
//Slower Clock
```

```verilog
//parameter delay = 10_000_000; //In real
parameter delay = 10; //For simulation purpose
reg sclk = 0; //slower clock
integer count = 0;

always@(posedge clk) begin
if (count < delay)
    count <= count + 1;
else begin
    sclk = ~sclk;
    count <= 0;
end
end

//to identify whether user has pressed the switch
reg flag = 0;
always@(posedge sclk) begin
if(sw == 16'h0000)
    flag <= 0;
else
    flag <= 1;
end

//Output decoding process
reg [15:0] temp = 0;
integer cnt = 0;
always@(posedge sclk) begin
case(flag)
0: begin
if(cnt <= 15) begin
   temp <= {1'b1,temp[15:1]};
   cnt <= cnt + 1;
end
```

```
else if(cnt == 16) begin
   cnt <= cnt + 1;
   temp <= 0;
end
else if(cnt > 16 && cnt <= 32) begin
   cnt <= cnt + 1;
   temp <= {temp[14:0],1'b1};
end
else begin
   cnt <= 0;
   temp <= 0;
end
end
1: temp = sw;
endcase
end
assign led = temp;
endmodule
```

We select Flow ➤ Run Simulation ➤ Run Behavioral Simulation from the menu toolbar to view the waveforms on the wave window. So, in the opened simulation window, we click the Restart button, and then we right-click the signal "clk" and set the force clock period to 100ns as illustrated in Figure 8-8.

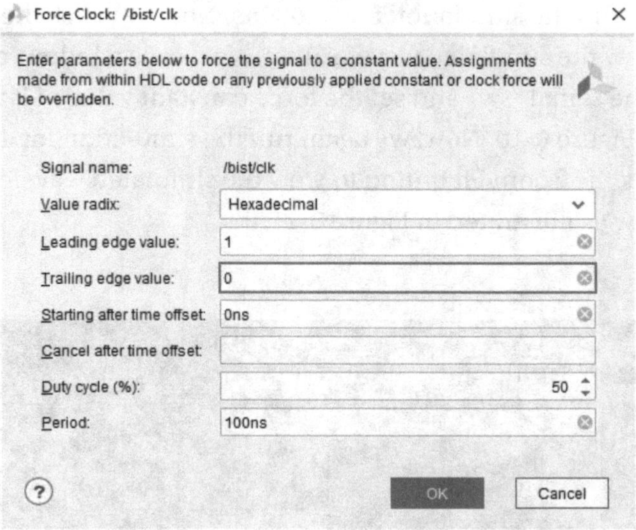

Figure 8-8. *Setting the force clock parameters for signal "clk"*

We also right-click the signal "sw" and set the force constant value of it to 0 as shown in Figure 8-9.

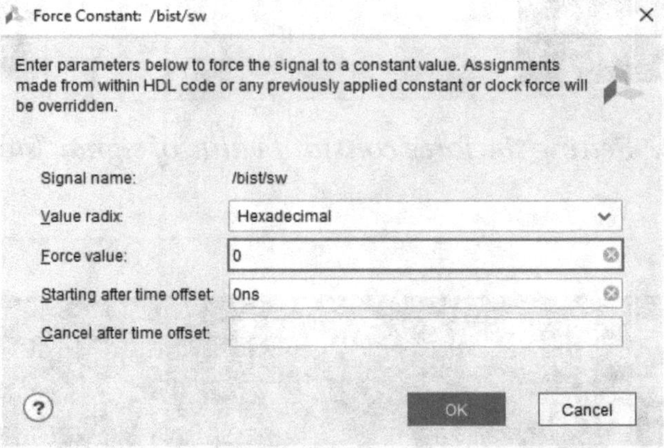

Figure 8-9. *Setting the force constant value of signal "sw" to 0*

Then we run the simulation for 82,500ns. Now, we click the Zoom Fit button to view the simulated waveforms on the wave window, and then we right-click the signal "sw" and set the force constant value of it to 34h as depicted in Figure 8-10. Now, we again run the simulation for 4,500ns, and then we click the Zoom Fit button to view the simulated waveforms on the wave window as illustrated in Figure 8-11.

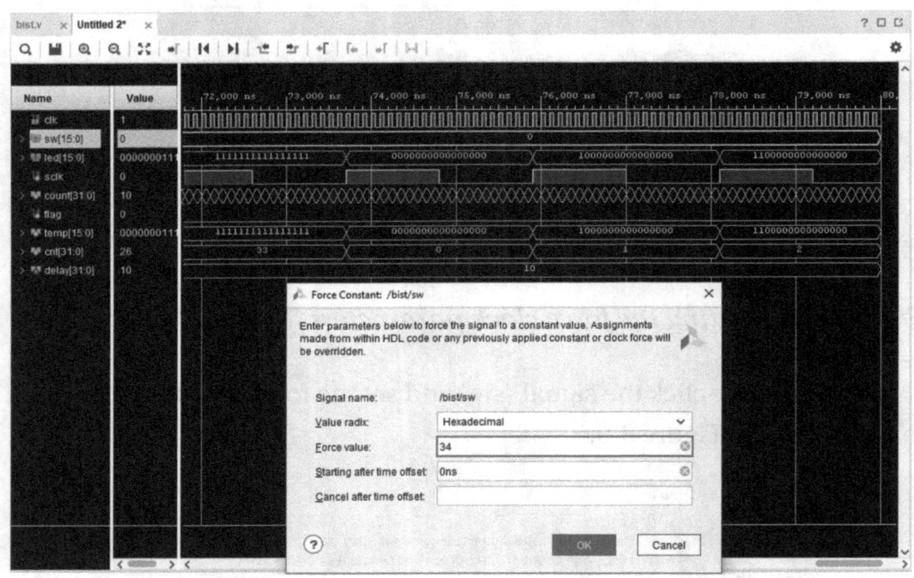

Figure 8-10. *Setting the force constant value of signal "sw" to 34h*

Figure 8-11. *The simulated waveforms on the wave window*

Interfacing EEPROM to FPGA with the 2C Protocol

The Microchip 24AA64/24LC64 (24XX64*) is a 64-kbit Electrically Erasable PROM (EEPROM). This device is organized as 8 blocks of 1K × 8-bit memory with a 2-wire serial interface (I2C). The maximum clock frequency is 400kHz. The data transfer sequence on the serial bus is shown in Figure 8-12.

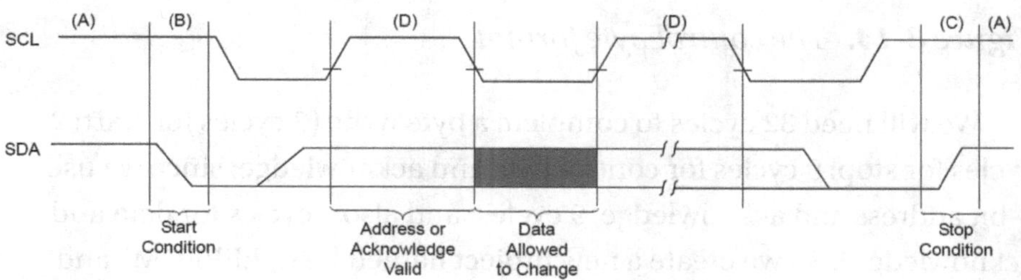

Figure 8-12. *The data transfer sequence on the serial bus*

In Figure 8-12, we have (A), (B), (C), and (D), which indicate bus not busy, start data transfer, stop data transfer, and data valid, respectively. The byte write procedure is depicted in Figure 8-13.

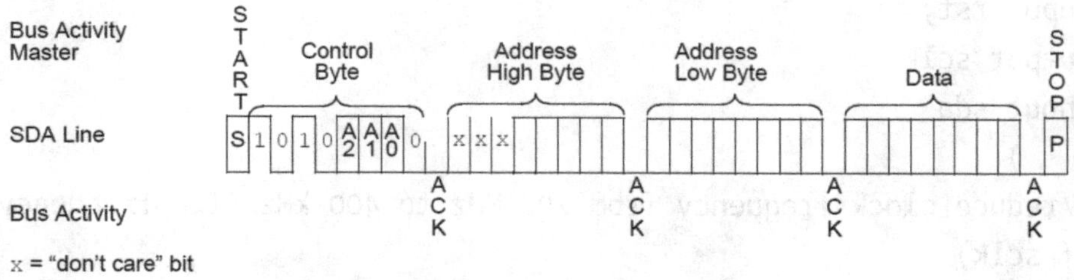

Figure 8-13. *The byte write procedure*

Also, the control byte format is illustrated in Figure 8-14.

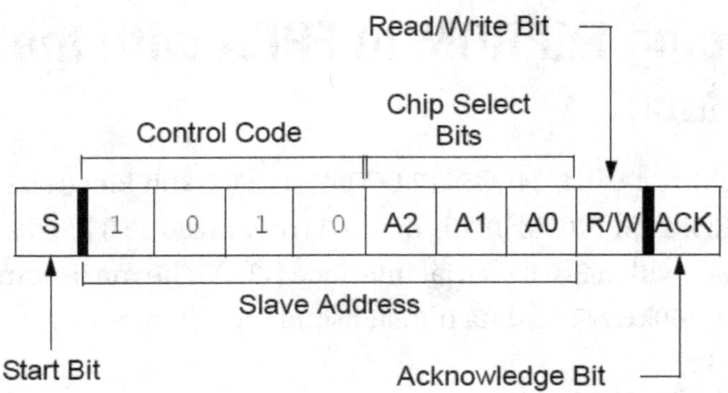

Figure 8-14. *The control byte format*

We will need 32 cycles to complete a byte write (3 cycles for start; 2 cycles for stop; 9 cycles for control byte and acknowledge; since we use 8-bit address and acknowledge, 9 cycles; and also 9 cycles for data and acknowledge). So we create a new project named "I2C_EEPROM" and also a design source file titled "i2c.v" and then add the following codes inside of it:

```verilog
`timescale 1ns / 1ps
module i2c(
input clk,
input rst,
output sclk,
inout sda
    );
//reduce clock frequency from 100 MHz to 400 kHz (I2C frequency
of sclk)
//(100M/400k)/2 = 125: count_max
//SCLK for our EEPROM
integer clk_counter = 0;
reg tclk = 0;
```

```verilog
always@(posedge clk) begin
if (clk_counter <= 125)
   clk_counter <= clk_counter + 1;
else begin
   clk_counter <= 0;
   tclk = ~tclk;
end
end

integer data_counter = 0;
always@(posedge tclk or posedge rst) begin
if (rst == 1'b1)
    data_counter <= 0;
else begin
    if(data_counter < 32)
       data_counter <= data_counter + 1;
    else
       data_counter <= 0;
end
end

reg tnclk = 0; //Used only for start and stop otherwise we use
tclk--(tnclk or tclk = SCL pin)
reg tdata = 0;   // (tdata = SDA pin)
always@(posedge tclk or posedge rst) begin
if (rst) begin
    tnclk <= 1;
    tdata <= 1;
end begin
case(data_counter)
//Start Condition
0: begin tdata <= 1; tnclk <= 1; end
```

```
1: tdata <= 0;
2: tnclk <= 0;
//Data Transaction Slave Address = 10100000
3: tdata <= 1;
4: tdata <= 0;
5: tdata <= 1;
6: tdata <= 0;
7: tdata <= 0;
8: tdata <= 0;
9: tdata <= 0;
10: tdata <= 0;

//Wait for ACK
11: tdata <= 1'bz;

//Memory location address
12: tdata <= 0;
13: tdata <= 0;
14: tdata <= 0;
15: tdata <= 0;
16: tdata <= 0;
17: tdata <= 0;
18: tdata <= 0;
19: tdata <= 0;

//Wait for ACK
20: tdata <= 1'bz;

//Data
21: tdata <= 1;
22: tdata <= 0;
23: tdata <= 1;
24: tdata <= 0;
```

```verilog
25: tdata <= 1;
26: tdata <= 0;
27: tdata <= 1;
28: tdata <= 0;

//Wait for ACK
29: tdata <= 1'bz;

//Stop Condition
30: begin tdata <= 0; tnclk <= 1; end
31: tdata <= 1;

default: tdata <= 1'bz;

endcase
end
end
assign sda = tdata;
assign sclk = (data_counter >= 3) & (data_counter < 30) ? tclk
: tnclk;
endmodule
```

We select Flow ➤ Run Simulation ➤ Run Behavioral Simulation from the menu toolbar to view the waveforms on the wave window. So, in the opened simulation window, we click the Restart button, and then we right-click the signal "clk" and set the force clock period to 10ns as illustrated in Figure 8-15.

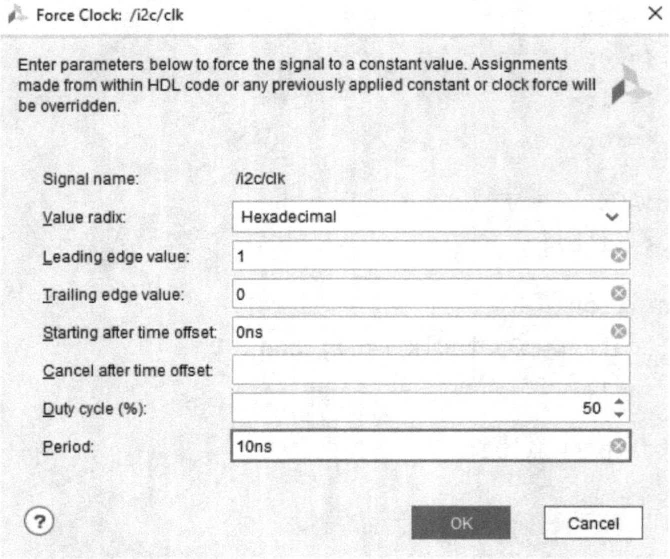

Force Clock: /i2c/clk

Enter parameters below to force the signal to a constant value. Assignments made from within HDL code or any previously applied constant or clock force will be overridden.

Signal name: /i2c/clk

Value radix: Hexadecimal

Leading edge value: 1

Trailing edge value: 0

Starting after time offset: 0ns

Cancel after time offset:

Duty cycle (%):   50

Period: 10ns

OK   Cancel

Figure 8-15. *Setting the force clock parameters for signal "clk"*

We also right-click the signal "rst" and set the force constant value of it to 1 as shown in Figure 8-16.

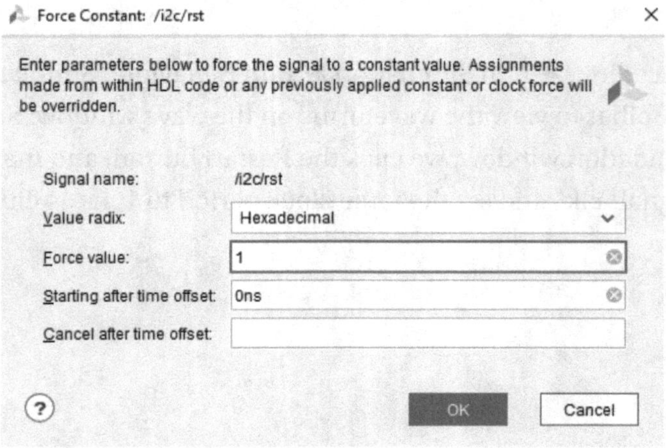

Force Constant: /i2c/rst

Enter parameters below to force the signal to a constant value. Assignments made from within HDL code or any previously applied constant or clock force will be overridden.

Signal name: /i2c/rst

Value radix: Hexadecimal

Force value: 1

Starting after time offset: 0ns

Cancel after time offset:

OK   Cancel

Figure 8-16. *Setting the force constant value of signal "rst" to 1*

Now, we run the simulation for 100ns, and then we right-click the signal "rst" and set the force constant value of it to 0 as depicted in Figure 8-17.

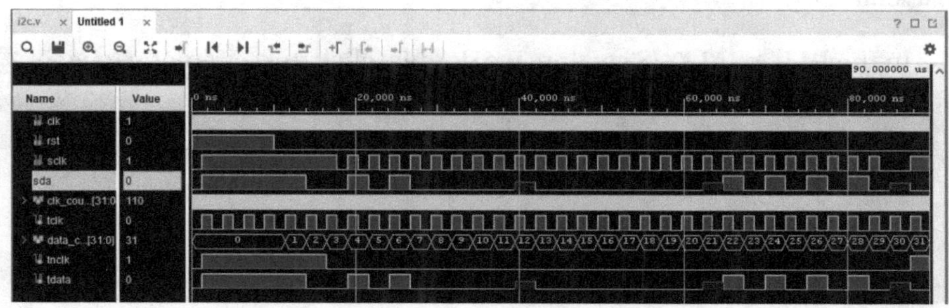

Figure 8-17. *Setting the force constant value of signal "rst" to 0*

Now, we again run the simulation for 90,000ns, and then we click the Zoom Fit button to view the simulated waveforms on the wave window as illustrated in Figure 8-18.

Figure 8-18. *The simulated waveforms on the wave window*

RTL for Synthesis

The if–else statement is used in combination with procedural assignment, which is used in a sequential circuit with nested if–else statements as well. We also can use it in combinatorial loops. So we create a new project named "project_IF_ELSE" and also a design source file titled "top.v" and then add the following codes for a combinational circuit of a 2 × 1 multiplexer inside of it:

```verilog
`timescale 1ns / 1ps
module top(
input a,ce,clk,rst,b,sel,
output reg y
    );
always@(a or b) begin
if(sel)
  y = a;
else
  y = b;
end
endmodule
```

In the RTL ANALYSIS section, we double-click the schematic to view the schematic of RTL analysis as shown in Figure 8-19.

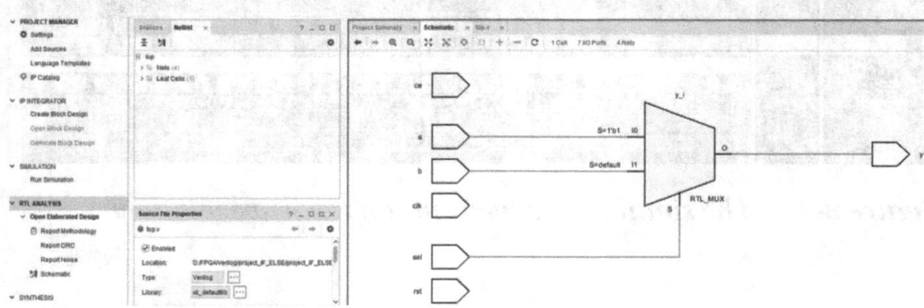

Figure 8-19. *The schematic of RTL analysis*

Now, we want to implement a D-flip-flop using a sequential circuit with synchronous active low reset and an if–else statement. Suppose we have not used the else statement as below:

```
`timescale 1ns / 1ps
module top(
input a,ce,clk,rst,b,sel,
output reg y
    );
always@(posedge clk) begin
if(rst == 1'b1) //synchronous reset (active low)
    y = din;
end
endmodule
```

If we reload the schematic, we can observe that the reset (rst) pin is connected to the clock enable (CE) pin as depicted in Figure 8-20.

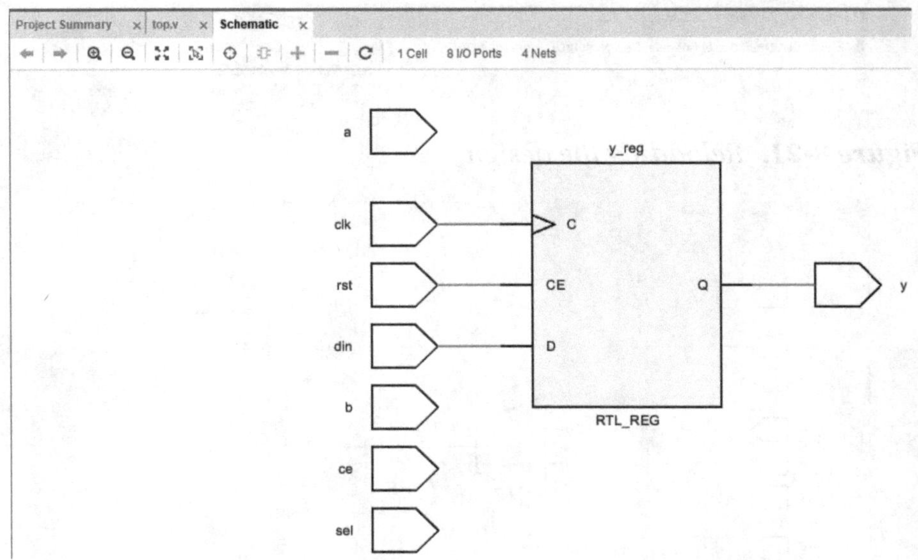

Figure 8-20. *Connection of the reset pin to CE*

Now, we add the else statement to the code as below:

```verilog
`timescale 1ns / 1ps
module top(
input a,ce,clk,rst,b,sel,
output reg y
    );
always@(posedge clk) begin
if(rst == 1'b1) //synchronous reset (active low)
    y = din;
else
    y = 0;
end
endmodule
```

If we reload the design, we can view the new schematic as illustrated in Figures 8-21 and 8-22, respectively.

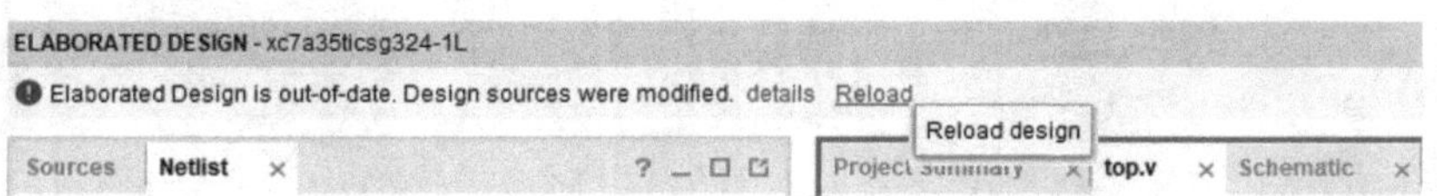

Figure 8-21. *Reloading the design*

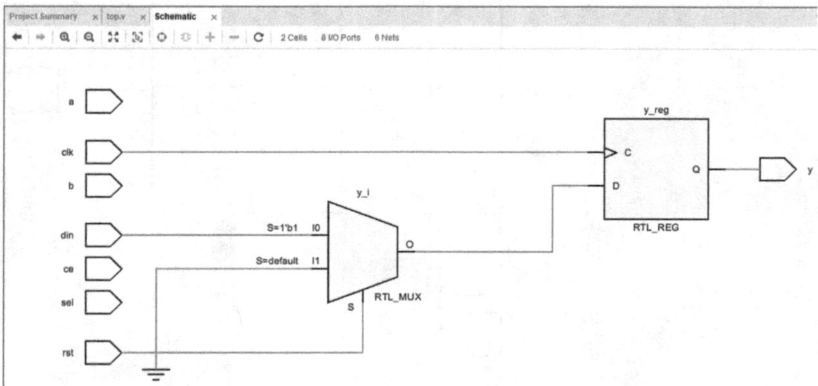

Figure 8-22. *The new RTL schematic*

Now, we change our codes as below:

```verilog
`timescale 1ns / 1ps
module top(
input a,ce,clk,rst,b,sel,
output reg y
    );
always@(posedge clk) begin
if(rst == 1'b0) //synchronous reset (active low)
   y = 0;
else
   y = din;
end
endmodule
```

If we reload the design, we can view the new and improved schematic as illustrated in Figure 8-23.

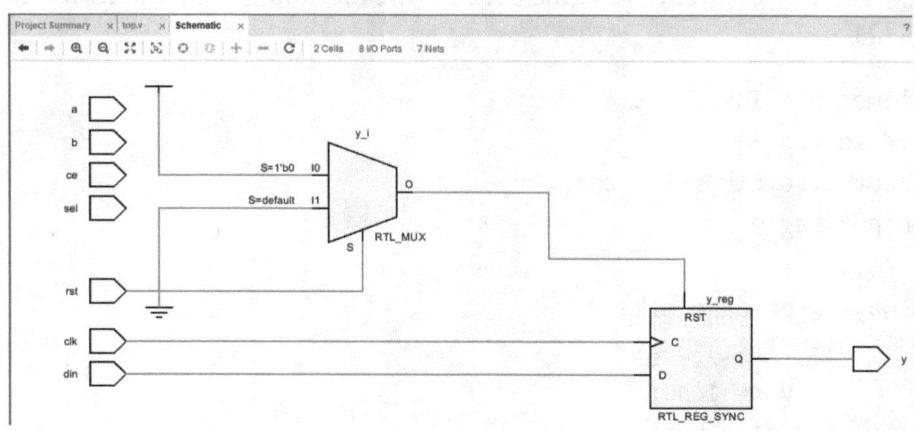

Figure 8-23. *The improved RTL schematic*

We can go ahead and select Language Templates in the Project Manager section and search for the D-flip-flop and find coding examples under the Synthesis Constructs section as shown in Figure 8-24.

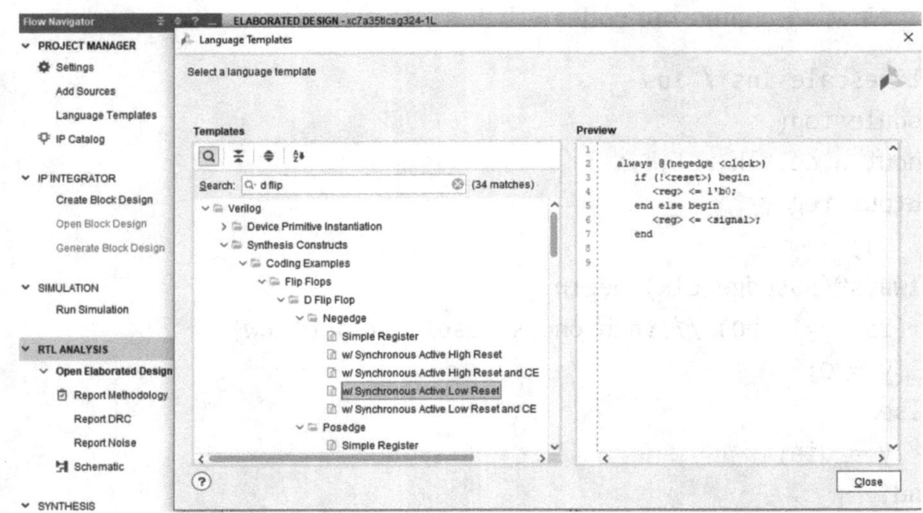

Figure 8-24. *Finding coding examples under the Synthesis Constructs section*

Then we copy and paste the codes to the file "top.v" and modify them as below:

```verilog
`timescale 1ns / 1ps
module top(
input a,ce,clk,rst,b,sel,
output reg y
    );
always @(posedge clk)
    if (!rst) begin
        y <= 1'b0;
    end else begin
        y <= din;
    end
endmodule
```

If we reload the design, we can view the modified schematic as illustrated in Figure 8-25.

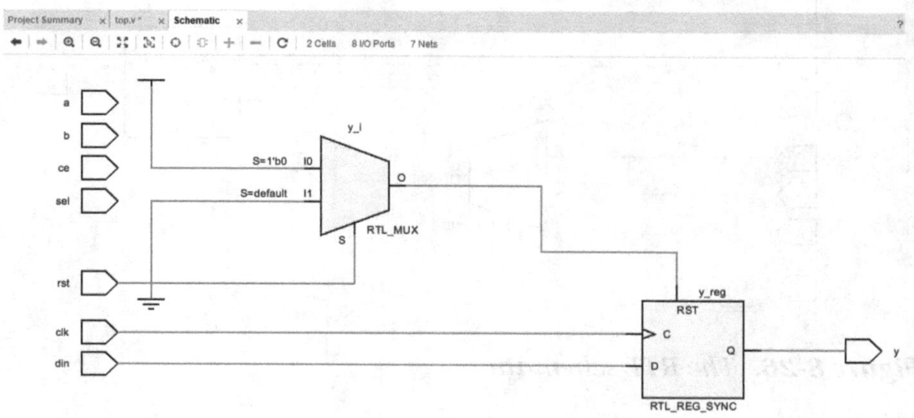

Figure 8-25. *The modified RTL schematic*

As you can see in Figure 8-25, we get the same schematic of Figure 8-23. Now, if we consider the active high synchronous reset scenario, the codes will be as follows:

```
`timescale 1ns / 1ps
module top(
input a,ce,clk,rst,b,sel,
output reg y
    );
always@(posedge clk) begin
if(rst == 1'b0) //synchronous reset (active high)
   y = din;
else
   y = 0;
end
endmodule
```

If we reload the design, we can view the schematic as shown in Figure 8-26.

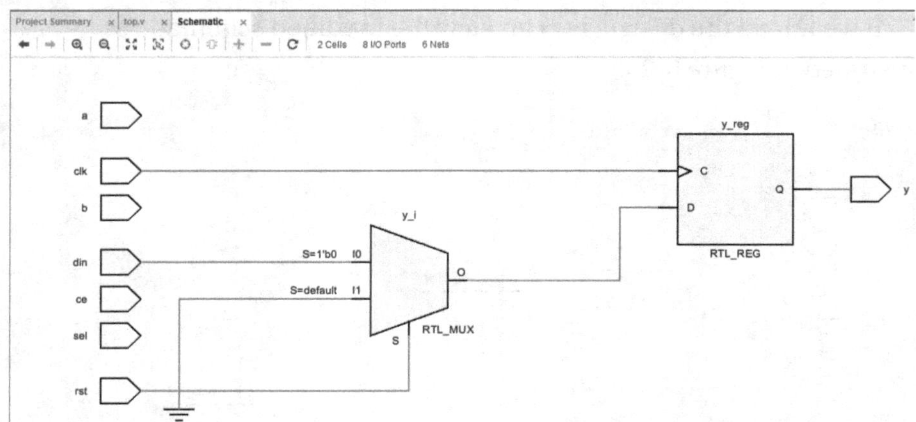

Figure 8-26. *The RTL schematic*

Again, we can go ahead and select Language Templates in the Project Manager section and search for the D-flip-flop and find coding examples under the Synthesis Constructs section as shown in Figure 8-27.

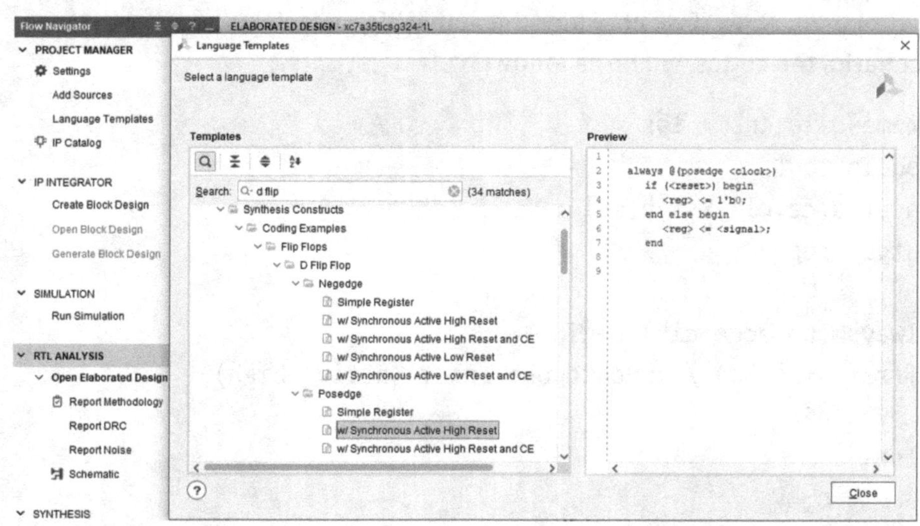

Figure 8-27. *Finding coding examples under the Synthesis Constructs section*

Then we copy and paste the codes to the file "top.v" and modify them as below:

```verilog
`timescale 1ns / 1ps
module top(
input a,ce,clk,rst,b,sel,
output reg y
    );
always @(posedge clk)
      if (rst) begin
          y <= 1'b0;
      end else begin
          y <= din;
      end
endmodule
```

So we just reverse our code, and if we reload the design, we can view the schematic as depicted in Figure 8-28.

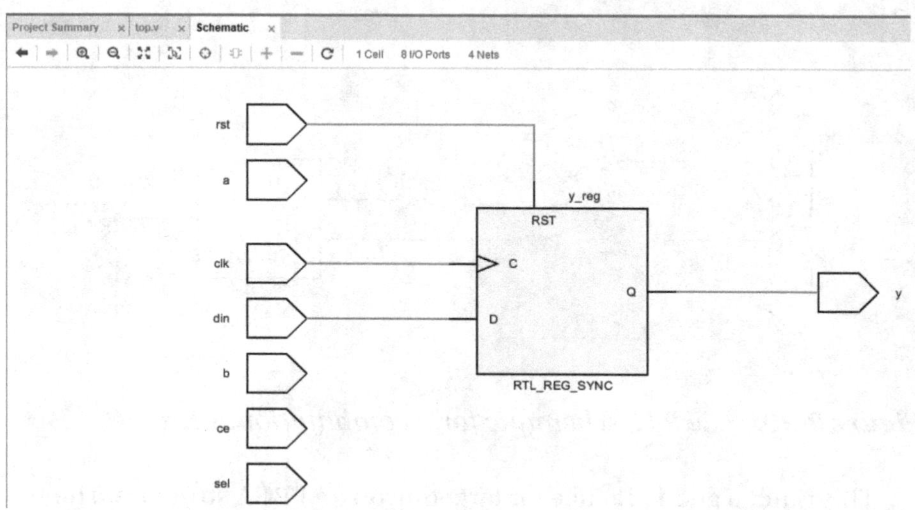

Figure 8-28. *The desired RTL schematic*

Now, consider the following combinational code:

```verilog
`timescale 1ns / 1ps
module top(
input a,ce,clk,rst,b,sel,
output reg y
    );
always@(a or b) begin
if(sel)
  y = y ^ a; //XOR
else
  y = y;
end
endmodule
```

If we reload the design, we can view the schematic as shown in Figure 8-29.

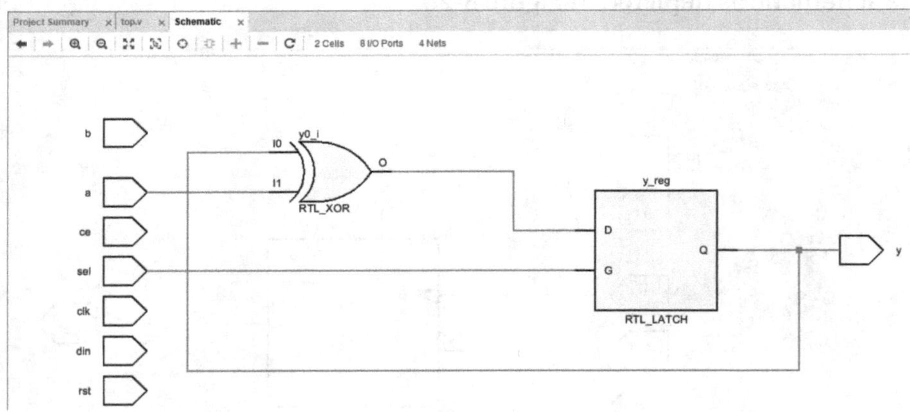

Figure 8-29.   *The RTL schematic for a combinational circuit*

This is not a good practice for targeting on an FPGA structure. The scenario of the solution is to add a resistor in the feedback route. Also, you can register the output and then perform the output only on the edge of the clock or perform the next process. So we do the following modification in our codes:

```verilog
`timescale 1ns / 1ps
module top(
input a,ce,clk,rst,b,sel,
output reg y
    );
reg temp;
always @(posedge clk) begin
temp <= y;
end
always@(a or temp) begin
if(sel)
  y = temp ^ a;
else
  y = temp;
end
endmodule
```

If we reload the design, we can observe the schematic as shown in Figure 8-30.

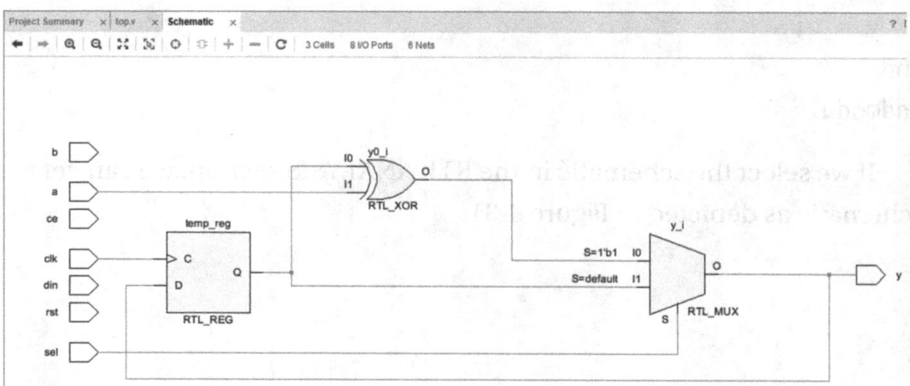

Figure 8-30. *The modified RTL schematic*

As a summary, we should try to always add all the possible cases for the if–else statement. We should not forget to use else for the if–else statement. Also, when we have combinational loops, we should register our outputs. If you have multiple pins such as reset (rst) and clock enable (CE), you better use the language template. Finally, if you want to write a code for active high reset, try to write the code only on that case, and if you start to write a complimentary statement (active low reset), it will give us a behavior that is not acceptable. We should also avoid latches with the if statement. For example, consider the following codes:

```verilog
`timescale 1ns / 1ps
module top(
input a,b,c,
input [1:0] sel,
output reg y
    );
always@(*) begin
if(sel == 2'b00)
    y = a;
else if(sel == 2'b01)
    y = b;
else if(sel == 2'b10)
    y = c;
end
endmodule
```

If we select the schematic in the RTL ANALYSIS section, we can get the schematic as depicted in Figure 8-31.

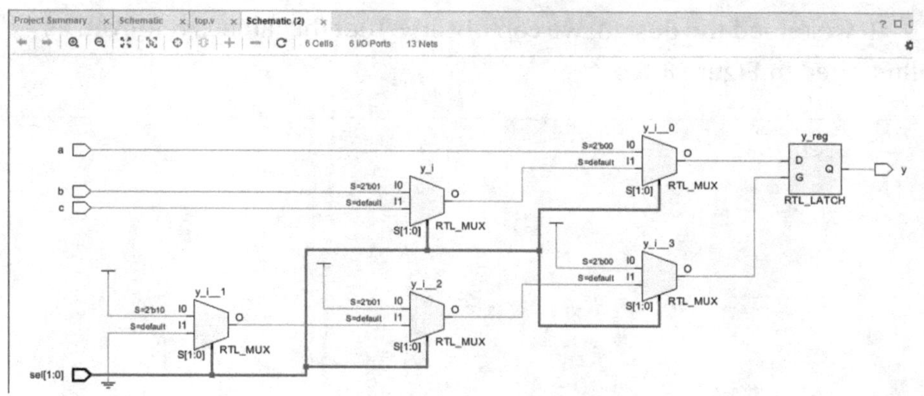

Figure 8-31. *The RTL schematic*

As you can see in Figure 8-31, we will have a latch, which is not acceptable. Now, we add the else statement and modify the codes as below:

```
`timescale 1ns / 1ps
module top(
input a,b,c,
input [1:0] sel,
output reg y
    );
always@(*) begin
if(sel == 2'b00)
    y = a;
else if(sel == 2'b01)
    y = b;
else if(sel == 2'b10)
    y = c;
else
    y = a;
end
endmodule
```

If we reload the design, we can observe that the latch is removed as illustrated in Figure 8-32.

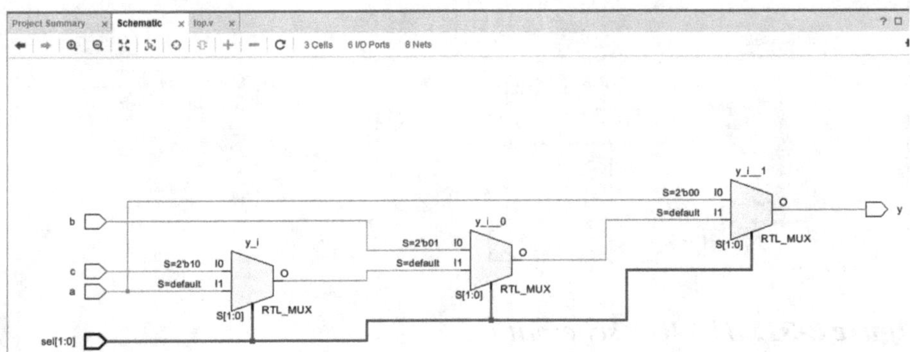

Figure 8-32. *The RTL schematic with the removed latch*

Now, we consider the same example by the case statement. We should cover all the cases and also the default in our codes. Firstly, we use the following codes:

```
`timescale 1ns / 1ps
module top(
input a,b,c,
input [1:0] sel,
output reg y
    );
always@(*) begin
case(sel)
2'b00: y = a;
2'b01: y = b;
2'b10: y = c;
endcase
end
endmodule
```

If we reload the design, we can observe the schematic as shown in Figure 8-33.

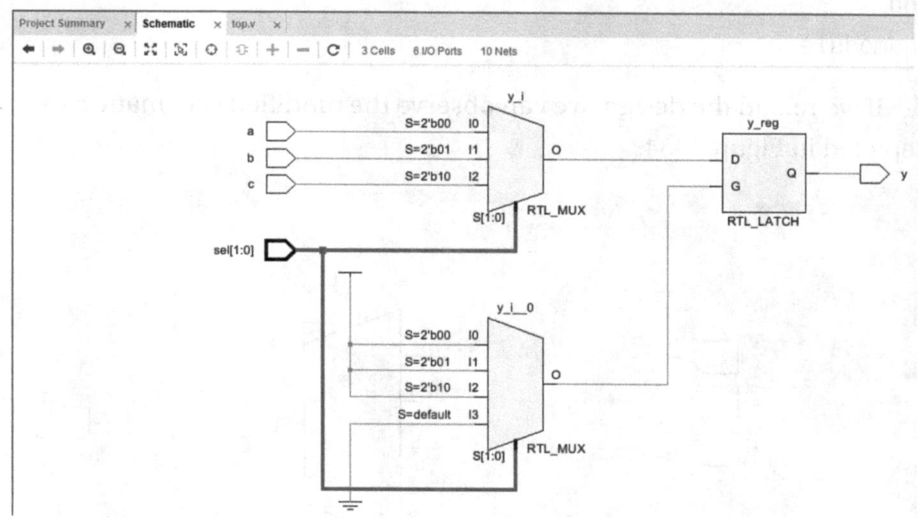

Figure 8-33. *The RTL schematic*

As you can view in Figure 8-33, we will have a latch, which is not acceptable. Now, we add all cases and modify the codes as below:

```
`timescale 1ns / 1ps
module top(
input a,b,c,
input [1:0] sel,
output reg y
    );
always@(*) begin
case(sel)
2'b00: y = a;
2'b01: y = b;
2'b10: y = c;
```

```
2'b11: y = a;
endcase
end
endmodule
```

If we reload the design, we can observe the modified schematic as depicted in Figure 8-34.

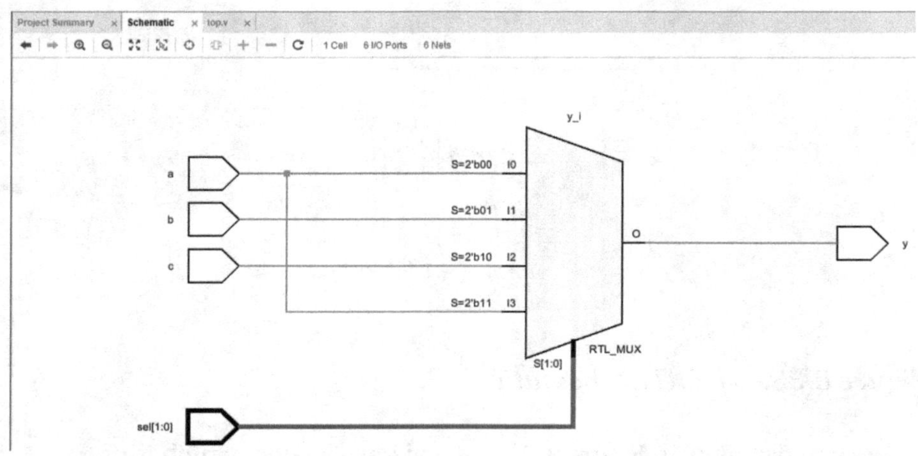

Figure 8-34. *The modified RTL schematic*

Now, we delete the added case and use the default instead of that as the following codes:

```
`timescale 1ns / 1ps
module top(
input a,b,c,
input [1:0] sel,
output reg y
    );
always@(*) begin
case(sel)
2'b00: y = a;
```

```
2'b01: y = b;
2'b10: y = c;
default: y = a;
endcase
end
endmodule
```

If we reload the design, we can observe that we get the same schematic as illustrated in Figure 8-34. So, if all the cases have not been defined in the case statement, we should use the default method.

SPI for DAC

PmodDA4 is an 8-channel, 12-bit DAC with SPI, and its pinout table as well as schematic are demonstrated in Table 8-1 and Figure 8-35, respectively.

Table 8-1. *The pinout description table*

Pin	Signal	Description
1	~CS	Chip Select
2	MOSI	Master-Out-Slave-In
3	NC	Not Connected
4	SCLK	Serial Clock
5	GND	Power Supply Ground
6	VCC	Power Supply (3.3V/5V)

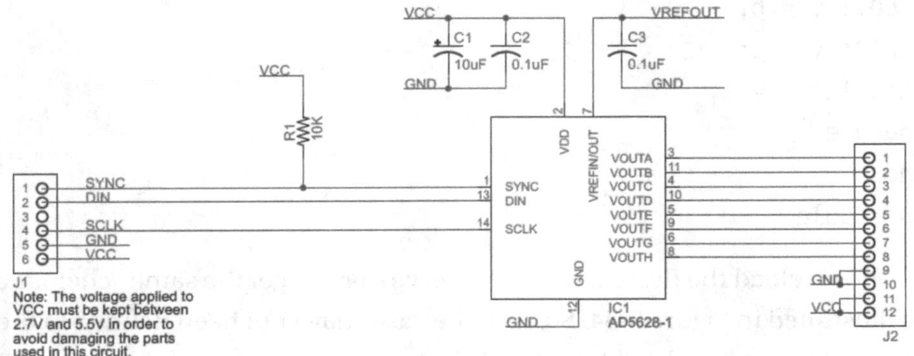

Figure 8-35. *The schematic of PmodDA4*

It is recommended that PmodDA4 is operated at 3.3V. The maximum clock frequency for SCLK is 1.8MHz, and we will use 1MHz for SCLK. Since the FPGA clock is 100MHz, firstly we will convert it to 1MHz. PmodDA4 communicates with FPGA via the SPI protocol. By driving the Chip Select (CS) line to a logic-level low voltage, users may send a series of 32 bits of information with the data clocked in to the appropriate register on the falling edge of the Serial Clock (SCLK). Once the 32nd bit of information has been clocked in, the command that was sent in the data stream is executed. An example data stream of how the 32 bits are to be sent to the module is provided from the AD5628 datasheet as illustrated in Figure 8-36.

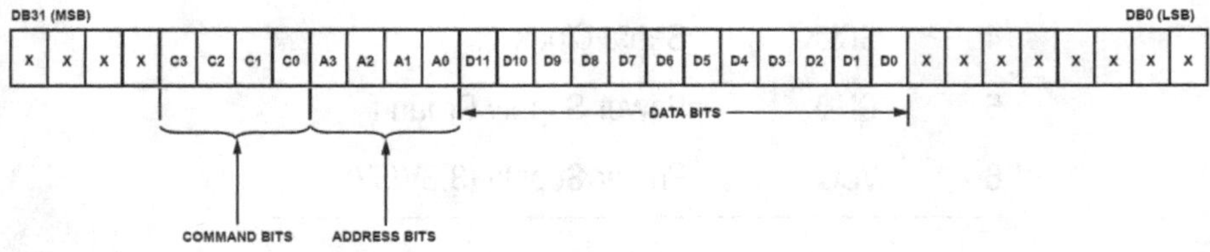

Figure 8-36. *The AD5628 input register contents*

Users should note that PmodDA4 by default attempts to use an external reference voltage. However, as there is no external reference

354

voltage provided on PmodDA4, users must write to the register to program the chip to use its internal reference voltage of 1.25V. The data stream required to change this is provided in Table 8-2. Also, the 32-bit input shift register contents for the reference setup command are given in Table 8-3.

Table 8-2. *Internal reference register*

Internal REF Register (DB0)	Action
0	Reference off (default)
1	Reference on

Table 8-3. *The 32-bit input shift register contents for the reference setup command*

MSB DB31 to DB28	DB27	DB26	DB25	DB24	DB23	DB22	DB21	DB20	DB19 to DB1	LSB DB0
X	1	0	0	0	X	X	X	X	X	1/0
Don't cares	Command bits (C3 to C0)				Address bits (A3 to A0)-don't cares				Don't cares	Internal REF Register

We should use a flowchart, and that is the first step in developing our interface project. If you have a flowchart, the programming in Verilog will be very easy. So understanding the flowchart is very important in designing any interface code, and you can write an FSM easily out of the flowchart. The flowchart for SPI of FPGA and PmodDA4 is shown in Figure 8-37.

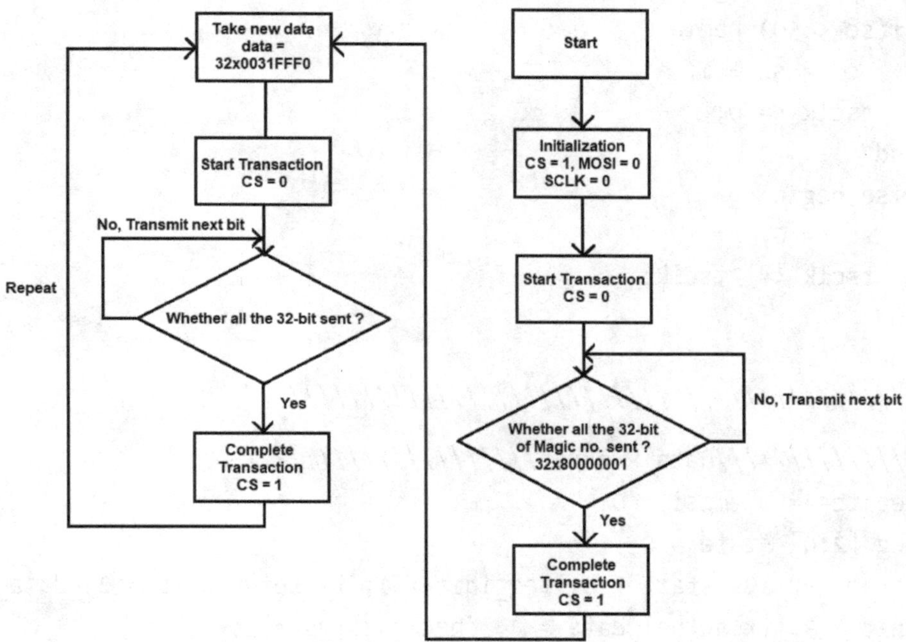

Figure 8-37. *The flowchart for SPI*

So we create a new project named "SPI_PmodDA4" and also a design source file titled "spi_interface.v" and then add the following codes inside of it:

```verilog
`timescale 1ns / 1ps
module spi_interface(
input clk,start,
output mosi,cs,sclk
```

```verilog
    );
//Generating Slower Clock Process////////////
//100 MHz -> 1 MHz (100/2 = 50 : max_sc)
integer sc = 0; //slower clock count
reg tsclk = 0;
always@(posedge clk) begin
if(sc < 50) begin
   sc <= sc + 1;
   tsclk <= 0;
end
else begin
   sc <= 0;
   tsclk <= ~tsclk;
end
end
/////////////////////////////////////////////
/////////////Data Process//////////////////////
reg tcs = 0,tmosi = 0;
reg [2:0] state = 0;
parameter sys_start = 0, reg_init = 1, tx_setup_data = 2, data_
init = 3, tx_actual_data = 4, check_status = 5;
reg [31:0] setup,data;
integer dc = 0;
always@(posedge tsclk) begin
case(state)
//Used to identify start of transaction by the user
sys_start: begin
tcs <= 1'b1;
if(start == 1'b1)
   state <= reg_init;
else
```

```verilog
    state <= sys_start;
end
///////Initialization of Registers////////////
reg_init: begin
tcs <= 1'b0;
tmosi <= 1'b0;
setup <= 32'h8000_0001;
state <= tx_setup_data;
end

tx_setup_data: begin
tcs <= 1'b0;
if (dc < 32) begin
   tmosi <= setup[31-dc]; // initial value of dc = 0
   dc <= dc + 1;
end
else begin
   dc <= 0;
   tcs <= 1'b1;
   state <= data_init;
end
end

data_init: begin
tmosi <= 1'b0;
data <= 32'h030F_FF00;
//data <= {12'h030,datain,8'h00}
tcs <= 1'b0;
state <= tx_actual_data;
end

tx_actual_data: begin
tcs <= 1'b0;
```

```
if (dc < 32) begin
   tmosi <= data[31-dc]; // initial value of dc = 0
   dc <= dc + 1;
end
else begin
   dc <= 0;
   tcs <= 1'b1;
   state <= check_status;
end
end

check_status: begin
if (start == 1'b1)
    state <= data_init;
else
   state <= sys_start;
end

endcase
end
assign sclk = tsclk;
assign mosi = tmosi;
assign cs = tcs;
endmodule
```

We select Flow ➤ Run Simulation ➤ Run Behavioral Simulation from the menu toolbar to view the waveforms on the wave window. So, in the opened simulation window, we click the Restart button, and then we right-click the signal "clk" and set the force clock period to 100ns as illustrated in Figure 8-38.

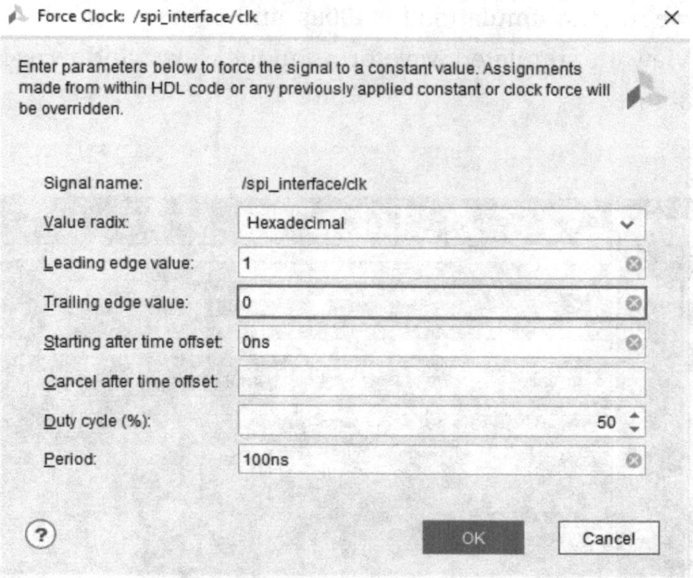

Figure 8-38. *Setting the force clock parameters for signal "clk"*

We also right-click the signal "start" and set the force constant value of it to 1 as shown in Figure 8-39.

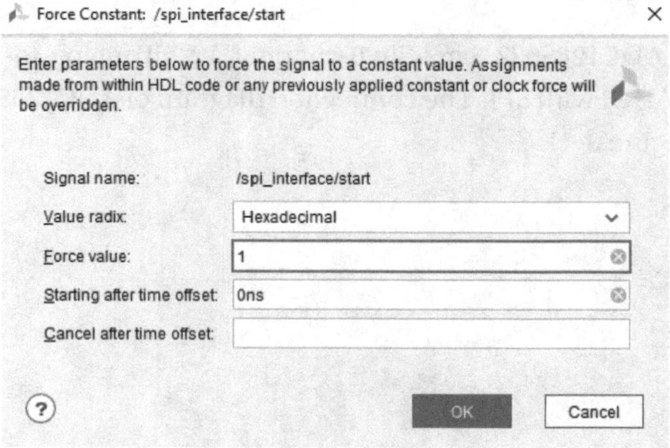

Figure 8-39. *Setting the force constant value of signal "start" to 1*

Now, we run the simulation for 400µs, and then we click the Zoom Fit button to view the simulated waveforms on the wave window as illustrated in Figure 8-40.

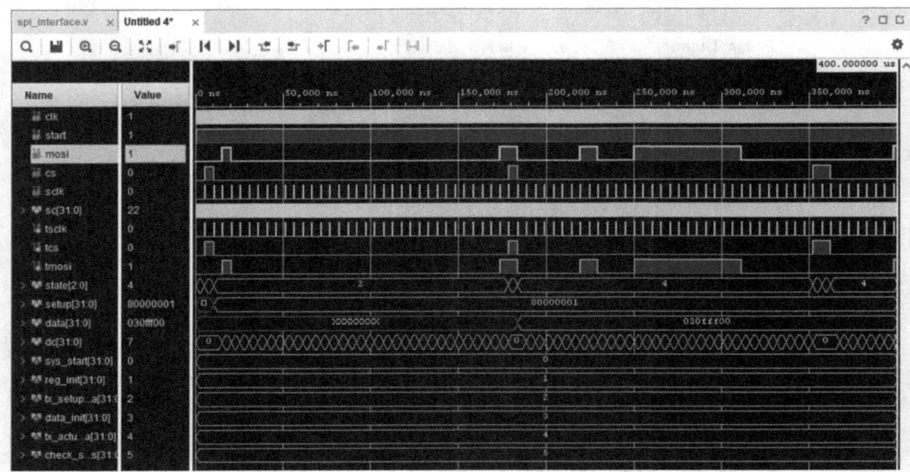

Figure 8-40. *The simulated waveforms on the wave window*

SPI for ADC

We will use ADC128S022 that is an 8-channel, 12-bit analog-to-digital converter (ADC) with SPI. The connection diagram of ADC128S022 is shown in Figure 8-41.

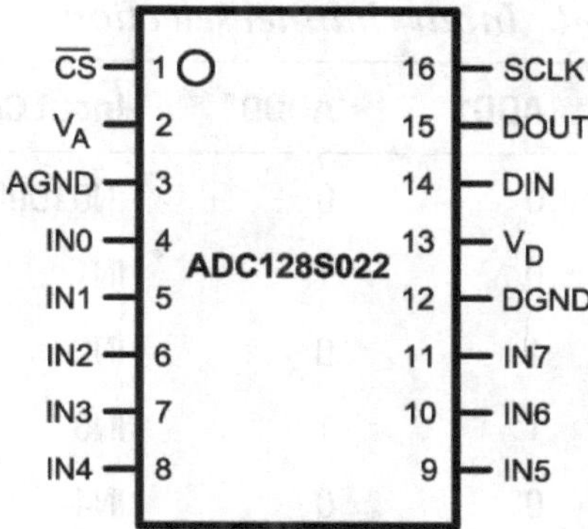

Figure 8-41. *The connection diagram of ADC128S022*

The ADC128S022 operational timing diagram is depicted in Figure 8-42.

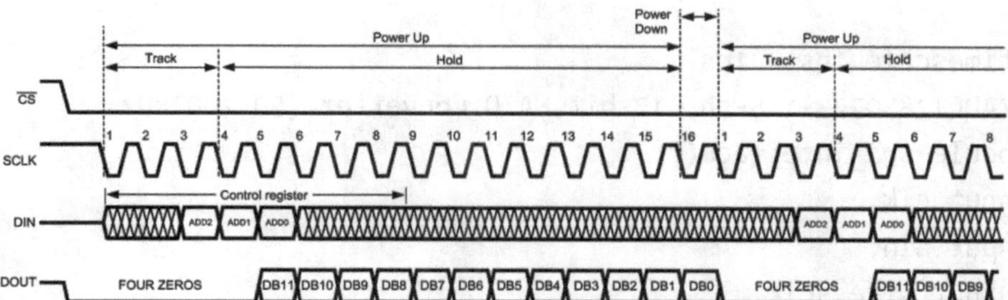

Figure 8-42. *The ADC128S022 operational timing diagram*

The maximum clock frequency for SCLK is 3.2MHz, DIN is the programming pin, and DOUT is the pin from which 12-bit analog-to-digital data is coming out. Also, the input channel selection is provided in Table 8-4. So we create a new project named "SPI_ADC" and also a design source file titled "spi_interface.v" and then add the following codes inside of it:

Table 8-4. *Input channel selection*

ADD2	ADD1	ADD0	Input Channel
0	0	0	IN0 (Default)
0	0	1	IN1
0	1	0	IN2
0	1	1	IN3
1	0	0	IN4
1	0	1	IN5
1	1	0	IN6
1	1	1	IN7

```verilog
`timescale 1ns / 1ps
//ADC128S022 -> 8-ch, 12-bit, A/D Converter (50-200)kHz
module spi_interface(
input clk,
input din,
output wire sclk,
output reg dout,
output reg cs
    );

reg ADD2,ADD1,ADD0;

reg [3:0] count;
reg [11:0] dataout0;
reg [11:0] dataout2;
reg [11:0] data_temp;
reg clock_out;
```

```verilog
initial
begin
count = 4'd0;
cs = 1;
ADD2 = 0;
ADD1 = 1;
ADD0 = 0;
clock_out = 0;
dataout0 = 12'd0;
dataout2 = 12'd0;
data_temp = 12'd0;
end

////Reduce Clock Frequency/////
//100 MHz -> 100 kHz : clk_cnt_max = (100M/100k)/2 = 500
integer clk_cnt = 0;
reg tclk = 0;
always@(posedge clk)
begin
if(clk_cnt < 500)
    clk_cnt <= clk_cnt + 1;
else begin
    tclk <= ~tclk;
    clk_cnt <= 0;
end
end

always@(negedge tclk)
begin
if (count == 1)
    cs <= 0;
end
```

```verilog
assign sclk = cs ? 1 : tclk; // hardwire sclk to clk if cs = 0
otherwise sclk = cs = 1

always@(posedge tclk)
begin
count <= count + 4'd1;
end

always@(posedge tclk)
begin
case(count)
3: begin
dout <= ADD2;
end
4: begin
dout <= ADD1;
end
5: begin
dout <= ADD0;
ADD1 <= !ADD1;
end
endcase
end
always@(posedge tclk)
begin
case(count)
4: begin
if(ADD1 == 1)
    dataout2 <= data_temp;
else
    dataout0 <= data_temp;
end
```

```verilog
5: data_temp[11] <= din;
6: data_temp[10] <= din;
7: data_temp[9] <= din;
8: data_temp[8] <= din;
9: data_temp[7] <= din;
10: begin
data_temp[6] <= din;
clock_out <= 1;
end
11: begin
data_temp[5] <= din;
clock_out <= 0;
end
12: data_temp[4] <= din;
13: data_temp[3] <= din;
14: data_temp[2] <= din;
15: data_temp[1] <= din;
0: data_temp[0] <= din;
endcase
end
endmodule
```

We select Flow ➤ Run Simulation ➤ Run Behavioral Simulation from the menu toolbar to view the waveforms on the wave window. So, in the opened simulation window, we click the Restart button, and then we right-click the signal "clk" and set the force clock period to 100ns as illustrated in Figure 8-43.

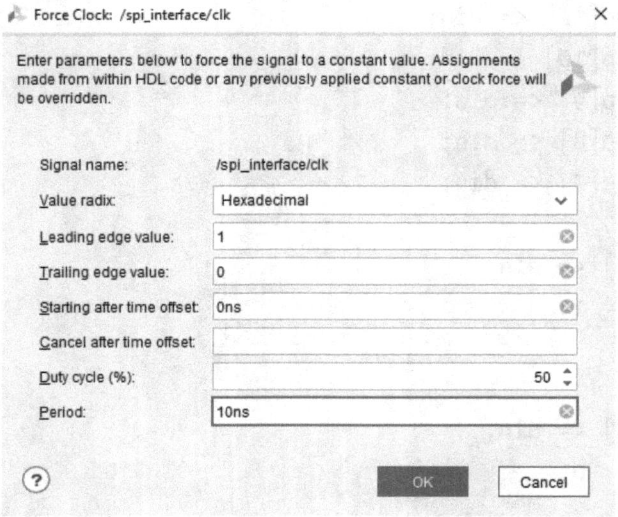

Figure 8-43. *Setting the force clock parameters for signal "clk"*

We also right-click the signal "din" and set the force constant value of it to 1 as shown in Figure 8-44.

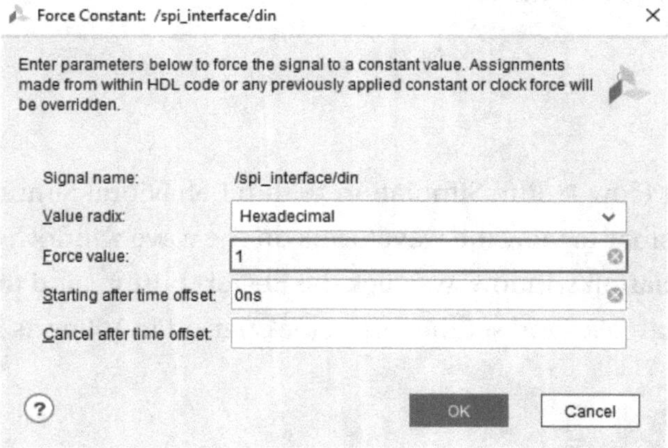

Figure 8-44. *Setting the force constant value of signal "din" to 1*

Now, we run the simulation for 400µs, and then we click the Zoom Fit button to view the simulated waveforms on the wave window as illustrated in Figure 8-45. As you can view on the wave window, we read the ADC value (din = fffh) from two ADC channels (IN0 and IN2) simultaneously, and the results are demonstrated in dataout0[11:0] and dataout2[11:0], respectively.

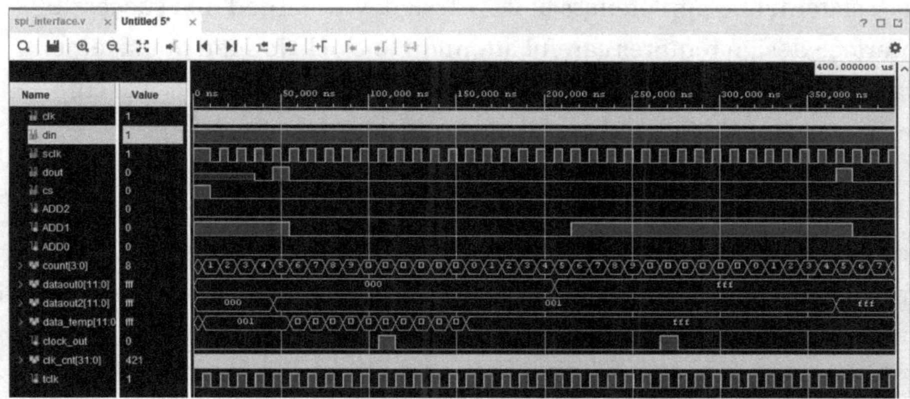

Figure 8-45. *The simulated waveforms on the wave window*

Summary and Key Takeaways

In this chapter, we explored essential communication interfaces and practical FPGA projects that bridge digital design with real-world applications. We began with the fundamental UART interface, implementing serial communication for character transmission. The chapter then progressed to PWM generation for analog signal control, LCD interfacing for display systems, and Built-In Self-Test (BIST) techniques for hardware verification. We delved into the I2C protocol for EEPROM interfacing, demonstrating external memory operations, and examined critical RTL synthesis considerations for optimized hardware implementation. Finally, we covered SPI for both DAC (digital-to-analog) and ADC (analog-to-digital) conversion, completing the communication protocol spectrum.

The key technical insights include understanding timing diagrams for protocol implementation, mastering state machine design for interface controllers, and recognizing the importance of proper reset strategies and case statement completeness in RTL design. We learned that successful interface design requires careful attention to clock domain management, signal timing constraints, and protocol-specific requirements like chip select handling in SPI and acknowledge bits in I2C.

These communication interfaces form the backbone of embedded systems, enabling FPGAs to interact with peripherals, sensors, memory devices, and other system components. The hands-on projects demonstrated how theoretical protocol knowledge translates into practical implementations, emphasizing the importance of simulation validation before hardware deployment.

In the next chapter, we will advance to processor design by implementing a RISC-V processor, bringing together the digital design concepts covered throughout this book to create a complete computing system.

CHAPTER 9

Implementation of a RISC-V Processor

In Chapter 8, we explored communication interfaces and hardware interfacing techniques, demonstrating how FPGAs interact with peripherals using protocols like UART, SPI, and I2C. Now, in this chapter, we take a significant step forward by applying these foundational concepts to processor design, focusing on the implementation of a RISC-V architecture—an open source instruction set architecture (ISA) that has revolutionized modern computing.

This chapter begins with a simple implementation scheme of a RISC-V processor, introducing the core components and design philosophy behind RISC architectures. We then dive into the detailed Verilog implementation, covering the datapath, control unit, and instruction execution flow. Finally, we validate our design through simulation, ensuring correct functionality and performance.

By combining the low-level hardware skills from previous chapters with this processor implementation, you will gain a comprehensive understanding of how software instructions translate to hardware operations. This knowledge bridges the gap between digital design and computer architecture, preparing you for more advanced projects in custom computing systems and FPGA-based SoC (System-on-Chip) development.

© Majid Pakdel 2026
M. Pakdel, *Mastering Verilog for FPGA Design*, Maker Innovations Series,
https://doi.org/10.1007/979-8-8688-2311-4_9

So, in this chapter, we are going to implement a simple RISC-V processor using Verilog in Vivado. We will use Chapter 4, Section 4.4, of the book *Computer Organization and Design, RISC-V Edition*, second edition, authored by David A. Patterson and John L. Hennessy as the reference.

A Simple Implementation Scheme of a RISC-V Processor

The block diagram for a simple implementation scheme of a RISC-V processor is shown in Figure 9-1.

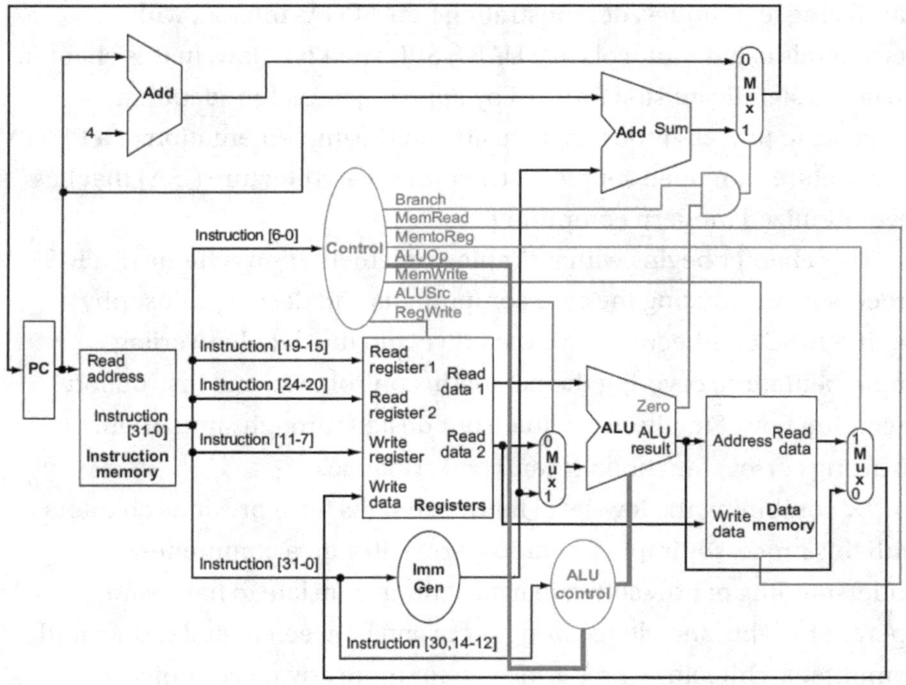

Figure 9-1. *A simple implementation scheme of a RISC-V processor*

The RISC-V Processor Verilog Implementation

So we create a new project named "RISCV_Processor" and also a design source file titled "top.v" and then add the following codes inside of it:

```verilog
`timescale 1ns / 1ps
//Program Counter
module Program_Counter(clk, reset, PC_in, PC_out);
input clk, reset;
input [31:0] PC_in;
output reg [31:0] PC_out;

always@(posedge clk or posedge reset)
begin
if(reset)
    PC_out <= 32'b00;
else
    PC_out <= PC_in;
end

endmodule

// PC + 4
module PCplus4(fromPC, NextoPC);
input [31:0] fromPC;
output [31:0] NextoPC;

assign NextoPC = 4 + fromPC;

endmodule

/*

// Instruction Memory
```

```verilog
module Instruction_Mem(clk, reset, read_address,
instruction_out);
input clk, reset;
input [31:0] read_address;
output reg [31:0] instruction_out;
integer k;
reg [31:0] I_Mem[63:0];

always@(posedge clk or posedge reset)
begin
if(reset)
begin
    for(k=0;k<64;k=k+1) begin
      I_Mem[k] <= 32'b00;
    end
end
else
    instruction_out <= I_Mem[read_address];
end

endmodule
*/

// Instruction Memory
module Instruction_Mem(clk, reset, read_address,
instruction_out);
input clk, reset;
input [31:0] read_address;
output reg [31:0] instruction_out;
integer k;
reg [31:0] I_Mem[63:0];
initial instruction_out <= 0;
```

```verilog
//R-type
always@(posedge clk)
begin
    instruction_out <= I_Mem[read_address];
end

always@(posedge clk or posedge reset)
begin
if(reset)
begin
    for(k=0;k<64;k=k+1) begin
       I_Mem[k] <= 32'b00;
    end
end
else begin
//R-type
I_Mem[0] <= 32'b0000_0000_0000_0000_0000_0000_0000_0000;
// no operation
I_Mem[4] <= 32'b0000000_11001_10000_000_01101_0110011;
// add x13, x16, x25
I_Mem[8] <= 32'b0100000_00011_01000_000_00101_0110011;
// sub x5, x8, x3
I_Mem[12] <= 32'b0000000_00011_00010_111_00001_0110011;
// and x1, x2, x3
I_Mem[16] <= 32'b0000000_00101_00011_110_00100_0110011;
// or x4, x3, x5

//I-type
I_Mem[20] <= 32'b000000000011_10101_000_10110_0010011;
//addi x22, x21, 3
I_Mem[24] <= 32'b000000000001_01000_110_01001_0010011;
//ori x9, x8, 1
```

```verilog
//L-type
I_Mem[28] <= 32'b000000001111_00101_010_01000_0000011;
//lw x8, 15(x5)
I_Mem[32] <= 32'b000000000011_00011_010_01001_0000011;
//lw x9, 3(x3)

//S-type
I_Mem[36] <= 32'b0000000_01111_00101_010_01100_0100011;
//sw x15, 12(x5)
I_Mem[40] <= 32'b0000000_01110_00110_010_01010_0100011;
//sw x14, 10(x6)

//SB-type
I_Mem[44] <= 32'h00948663; //beq x9, x9, 12
end
end

endmodule

/*
//Register File
module Reg_File(clk, reset, RegWrite, Rs1, Rs2, Rd, Write_data,
read_data1, read_data2);
input clk, reset, RegWrite;
input [4:0] Rs1, Rs2, Rd;
input[31:0] Write_data;
output [31:0] read_data1, read_data2;
integer k;
reg [31:0] Registers[31:0];

always@(posedge clk or posedge reset)
begin
if(reset)
begin
```

```verilog
    for(k=0;k<64;k=k+1) begin
        Registers[k] <= 32'b00;
    end
end
else if(RegWrite)
    Registers[Rd] <= Write_data;
end

assign read_data1 = Registers[Rs1];
assign read_data2 = Registers[Rs2];

endmodule
*/

//Register File
module Reg_File(clk, reset, RegWrite, Rs1, Rs2, Rd, Write_data,
read_data1, read_data2);
input clk, reset, RegWrite;
input [4:0] Rs1, Rs2, Rd;
input[31:0] Write_data;
output reg[31:0] read_data1, read_data2;
reg [31:0] Registers[31:0];

initial begin
read_data1 <= 0;
read_data2 <= 0;
end

initial begin
Registers[0] = 0;
Registers[1] = 4;
Registers[2] = 2;
Registers[3] = 24;
Registers[4] = 4;
```

```
Registers[5] = 1;
Registers[6] = 44;
Registers[7] = 4;
Registers[8] = 2;
Registers[9] = 1;
Registers[10] = 23;
Registers[11] = 4;
Registers[12] = 90;
Registers[13] = 10;
Registers[14] = 20;
Registers[15] = 30;
Registers[16] = 40;
Registers[17] = 50;
Registers[18] = 60;
Registers[19] = 70;
Registers[20] = 80;
Registers[21] = 80;
Registers[22] = 90;
Registers[23] = 70;
Registers[24] = 60;
Registers[25] = 65;
Registers[26] = 4;
Registers[27] = 32;
Registers[28] = 12;
Registers[29] = 34;
Registers[30] = 5;
Registers[31] = 10;
end

always@(posedge clk or posedge reset)
begin
if(RegWrite) begin
```

```verilog
      Registers[Rd] <= Write_data;
      read_data1 <= Registers[Rs1];
      read_data2 <= Registers[Rs2];
end
end
endmodule

//Immediate Generator
module ImmGen(Opcode, instruction, ImmExt);
input [6:0] Opcode;
input [31:0] instruction;
output reg [31:0] ImmExt;

initial ImmExt <= 0;

always@(*)
begin
    case(Opcode)
    7'b0000011 : ImmExt <= {{20{instruction[31]}},
    instruction[31:20]};
    7'b0100011 : ImmExt <= {{20{instruction[31]}},
    instruction[31:25], instruction[11:7]};
    7'b0100011 : ImmExt <= {{19{instruction[31]}},
    instruction[31], instruction[30:25], instruction[11:8],
    1'b0};
    endcase
end

endmodule

//Control Unit
module Control_Unit(instruction, Branch, MemRead, MemtoReg,
ALUOp, MemWrite, ALUSrc, RegWrite);
input [6:0] instruction;
```

```verilog
output reg Branch, MemRead, MemtoReg, MemWrite, ALUSrc,
RegWrite;
output reg [1:0] ALUOp;

initial begin
Branch <= 0;
MemRead <= 0;
MemtoReg <= 0;
MemWrite <= 0;
ALUSrc <= 0;
RegWrite <= 0;
ALUOp <= 0;
end

always@(*)
begin
   case(instruction)
   7'b0110011 : {ALUSrc, MemtoReg, RegWrite, MemRead, MemWrite,
   Branch, ALUOp} <= 8'b001000_01;
   7'b0000011 : {ALUSrc, MemtoReg, RegWrite, MemRead, MemWrite,
   Branch, ALUOp} <= 8'b111100_00;
   7'b0100011 : {ALUSrc, MemtoReg, RegWrite, MemRead, MemWrite,
   Branch, ALUOp} <= 8'b100010_00;
   7'b1100011 : {ALUSrc, MemtoReg, RegWrite, MemRead, MemWrite,
   Branch, ALUOp} <= 8'b000001_01;

   endcase
end

endmodule

//ALU
module ALU_unit(A, B, Control_in, ALU_Result, zero);
input [31:0] A, B;
```

```verilog
input [3:0] Control_in;
output reg zero;
output reg [31:0] ALU_Result;

initial begin
zero <= 0;
ALU_Result <= 0;
end

always@(Control_in or A or B)
begin
    case(Control_in)
    4'b0000 : begin zero <= 0; ALU_Result <= A & B; end
    4'b0001 : begin zero <= 0; ALU_Result <= A | B; end
    4'b0010 : begin zero <= 0; ALU_Result <= A + B; end
    4'b0110 : begin if(A==B) zero <= 1; else zero <= 0;
    ALU_Result <= A - B; end
    endcase
end

endmodule

// ALU Control
module ALU_Control(ALUOp, fun7, fun3, Control_out);
input fun7;
input [2:0] fun3;
input [1:0] ALUOp;
output reg [3:0] Control_out;

initial Control_out = 0;

always@(*)
begin
    case({ALUOp, fun7, fun3})
```

```verilog
      6'b00_0_000 : Control_out <= 4'b0010;
      6'b01_0_000 : Control_out <= 4'b0110;
      6'b10_0_000 : Control_out <= 4'b0010;
      6'b10_1_000 : Control_out <= 4'b0110;
      6'b10_0_111 : Control_out <= 4'b0000;
      6'b10_0_110 : Control_out <= 4'b0001;
    endcase
end

endmodule


// Data Memory
module Data_Memory(clk, reset, MemWrite, MemRead, read_address,
Write_data, MemData_out);
input clk, reset, MemWrite, MemRead;
input [31:0] read_address, Write_data;
output [31:0] MemData_out;
integer k;
reg [31:0] D_Memory[63:0];

always@(posedge clk or posedge reset)
begin
if(reset)
begin
    for(k=0;k<64;k=k+1) begin
       D_Memory[k] <= 32'b00;
    end
end

else if(MemWrite) begin
    D_Memory[read_address] <= Write_data;

end
```

```verilog
end

assign MemData_out = (MemRead) ? D_Memory[read_address]
: 32'b00;

endmodule

//Multiplexers
//Mux 1
module Mux1(sel1, A1, B1, Mux1_out);
input sel1;
input [31:0] A1, B1;
output [31:0] Mux1_out;

assign Mux1_out = (sel1 == 1'b0) ? A1 : B1;

endmodule
//Mux 2
module Mux2(sel2, A2, B2, Mux2_out);
input sel2;
input [31:0] A2, B2;
output[31:0] Mux2_out;

assign Mux2_out = (sel2 == 1'b0) ? A2 : B2;

endmodule
//Mux 3
module Mux3(sel3, A3, B3, Mux3_out);
input sel3;
input [31:0] A3, B3;
output [31:0] Mux3_out;

assign Mux3_out = (sel3 == 1'b0) ? A3 : B3;

endmodule
```

```
// AND logic
module AND_logic(branch, zero, and_out);
input branch, zero;
output and_out;

assign and_out = branch & zero;

endmodule

// Adder
module Adder(in_1, in_2, Sum_out);
input [31:0] in_1, in_2;
output [31:0] Sum_out;

assign Sum_out = in_1 + in_2;

endmodule

// All modules instantiate here...
module top(clk, reset);
input clk, reset;

wire [31:0] PC_top, instruction_top, Rd1_top, Rd2_top, ImmExt_
top, mux1_top, Sum_out_top, NextoPC_top, PCin_top, address_top,
Memdata_top, WiteBack_top;
wire RegWrite_top, ALUSrc_top, zero_top, branch_top, sel2_top,
MemtoReg_top, MemWrite_top, MemRead_top;
wire [1:0] ALUOp_top;
wire [3:0] control_top;

// Program Counter
Program_Counter PC(.clk(clk), .reset(reset), .PC_in(PCin_top),
.PC_out(PC_top));
```

```verilog
// PC + 4
PCplus4 PC_Adder(.fromPC(PC_top), .NextoPC(NextoPC_top));

// Instruction Memory
Instruction_Mem Inst_Memory(.clk(clk), .reset(reset), .read_
address(PC_top), .instruction_out(instruction_top));

//Register File
Reg_File Reg_File(.clk(clk), .reset(reset), .RegWrite(RegWrite_
top), .Rs1(instruction_top[19:15]), .Rs2(instruction_
top[24:20]), .Rd(instruction_top[11:7]), .Write_data(WiteBack_
top), .read_data1(Rd1_top), .read_data2(Rd2_top));

// Immediate Generator
ImmGen ImmGen(.Opcode(instruction_top[6:0]),
.instruction(instruction_top), .ImmExt(ImmExt_top));

// Control Unit
Control_Unit Control_Unit(.instruction(instruction_top[6:0]),
.Branch(branch_top), .MemRead(MemRead_top), .MemtoReg(MemtoReg_
top), .ALUOp(ALUOp_top), .MemWrite(MemWrite_top),
.ALUSrc(ALUSrc_top), .RegWrite(RegWrite_top));

//ALU Control
ALU_Control ALU_Control(.ALUOp(ALUOp_top), .fun7(instruction_
top[30]), .fun3(instruction_top[14:12]), .Control_
out(control_top));

//ALU
ALU_unit ALU(.A(Rd1_top), .B(mux1_top), .Control_in(control_
top), .ALU_Result(address_top), .zero(zero_top));

//ALU Mux
Mux1 ALU_mux(.sel1(ALUSrc_top), .A1(Rd2_top), .B1(ImmExt_top),
.Mux1_out(mux1_top));
```

```
//Adder
Adder Adder(.in_1(PC_top), .in_2(ImmExt_top), .Sum_out(Sum_
out_top));

// AND Gate
AND_logic AND(.branch(branch_top), .zero(zero_top), .and_
out(sel2_top));

//Adder Mux
Mux2 Adder_mux(.sel2(sel2_top), .A2(NextoPC_top), .B2(Sum_out_
top), .Mux2_out(PCin_top));

// Data Memory
Data_Memory Data_mem(.clk(clk), .reset(reset),
.MemWrite(MemWrite_top), .MemRead(MemRead_top), .read_
address(address_top), .Write_data(Rd2_top), .MemData_
out(Memdata_top));

//Mux
Mux3 Memory(.sel3(MemtoReg_top), .A3(address_top), .B3(Memdata_
top), .Mux3_out(WiteBack_top));
endmodule

/*
// testbench
module tb_top;

reg clk, reset;

top uut(.clk(clk), .reset(reset));

initial begin
clk = 0;
reset = 1;
#10;
```

```
reset = 0;
#400;
end

always begin
#5 clk = ~clk;
End
endmodule
*/
```

Figure 9-2 shows the formats of the four instruction classes, which are arithmetic, load, store, and conditional branch instructions.

Name (Bit position)	Fields					
	31:25	24:20	19:15	14:12	11:7	6:0
(a) R-type	funct7	rs2	rs1	funct3	rd	opcode
(b) I-type	immediate[11:0]		rs1	funct3	rd	opcode
(c) S-type	immed[11:5]	rs2	rs1	funct3	immed[4:0]	opcode
(d) SB-type	immed[12,10:5]	rs2	rs1	funct3	immed[4:1,11]	opcode

Figure 9-2. *The formats of the four instruction classes*

Figure 9-3 defines the logic in the control unit as one large truth table that combines all the outputs and that uses the opcode 7 bits as inputs.

Input or output	Signal name	R-format	lw	sw	beq
Inputs	I[6]	0	0	0	1
	I[5]	1	0	1	1
	I[4]	1	0	0	0
	I[3]	0	0	0	0
	I[2]	0	0	0	0
	I[1]	1	1	1	1
	I[0]	1	1	1	1
Outputs	ALUSrc	0	1	1	0
	MemtoReg	0	1	X	X
	RegWrite	1	1	0	0
	MemRead	0	1	0	0
	MemWrite	0	0	1	0
	Branch	0	0	0	1
	ALUOp1	1	0	0	0
	ALUOp0	0	0	0	1

Figure 9-3. *The logic in the control unit*

The ALU control lines and their respective functions are depicted in Figure 9-4.

ALU control lines	Function
0000	AND
0001	OR
0010	add
0110	subtract

Figure 9-4. *The ALU control lines and their respective functions*

The truth table for the four ALU control bits, which is called operation, is illustrated in Figure 9-5.

| ALUOp | | Funct7 field | | | | | | | Funct3 field | | | |
ALUOp1	ALUOp0	I[31]	I[30]	I[29]	I[28]	I[27]	I[26]	I[25]	I[14]	I[13]	I[12]	Operation
0	0	X	X	X	X	X	X	X	X	X	X	0010
X	1	X	X	X	X	X	X	X	X	X	X	0110
1	X	0	0	0	0	0	0	0	0	0	0	0010
1	X	0	1	0	0	0	0	0	0	0	0	0110
1	X	0	0	0	0	0	0	0	1	1	1	0000
1	X	0	0	0	0	0	0	0	1	1	0	0001

Figure 9-5. *The truth table for the four ALU control bits (operation)*

Simulation of the Designed RISC-V Processor

We select Flow ➤ Run Simulation ➤ Run Behavioral Simulation from
the menu toolbar to view the waveforms on the wave window. So, in the
opened simulation window, we click the Restart button, and then we right-
click the signal "clk" and set the force clock period to 10ns as illustrated in
Figure 9-6.

Figure 9-6. *Setting the force clock parameters for signal "clk"*

We also right-click the signal "reset" and set the force constant value of it to 1 as shown in Figure 9-7.

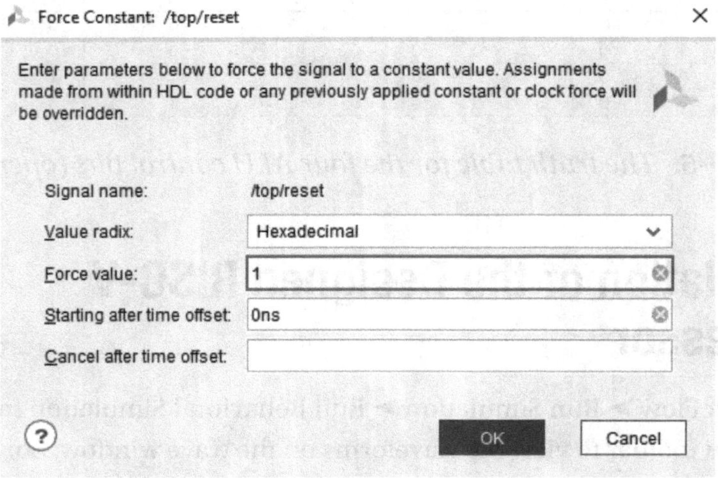

Figure 9-7. *Setting the force constant value of signal "reset" to 1*

Now, we run the simulation for 20ns, and then we right-click the signal "reset" and set the force constant value of it to 0 as shown in Figure 9-8.

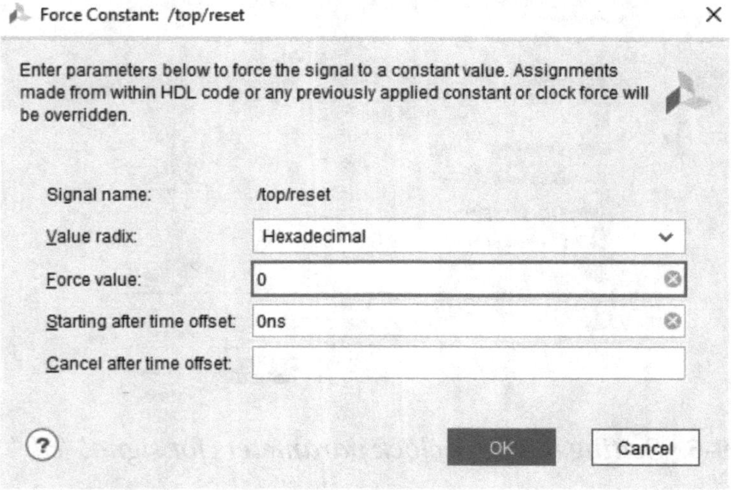

Figure 9-8. *Setting the force constant value of signal "reset" to 0*

Now, we run the simulation for another 80ns, and then we click the Zoom Fit button to view the simulated waveforms on the wave window as illustrated in Figure 9-9.

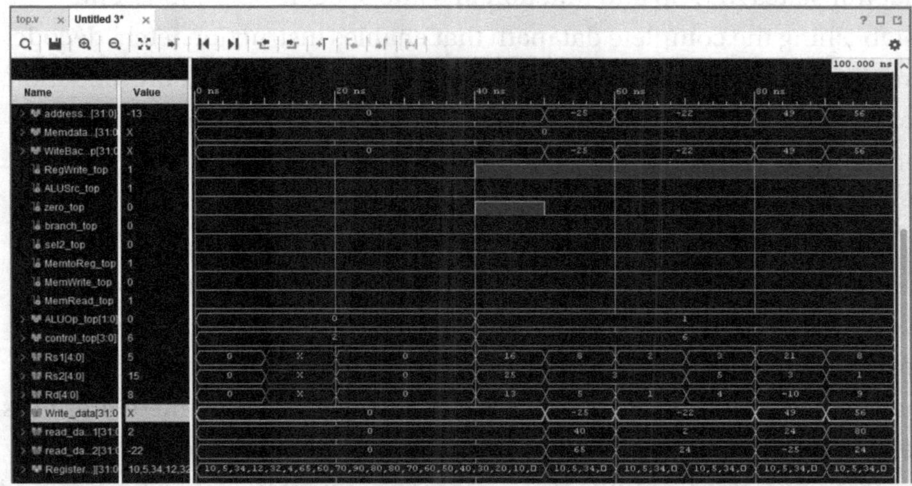

Figure 9-9. *The simulated waveforms on the wave window*

Summary and Key Takeaways

In this final chapter, we reached the pinnacle of digital design by implementing a complete RISC-V processor, demonstrating how fundamental digital logic concepts culminate in a functional computing system. We began with the architectural overview of a simple RISC-V implementation scheme, examining the datapath components and their interconnections. The comprehensive Verilog implementation covered all essential processor elements: program counter, instruction memory, register file, control unit, ALU, and data memory, along with the necessary multiplexers and supporting logic for proper data flow.

Key technical achievements included implementing the instruction decoding mechanism, designing the control unit that generates appropriate signals based on opcodes, creating the ALU control logic that translates ALUOp and function bits into specific operations, and establishing the complete datapath that enables instruction fetch, decode, execute, memory access, and write-back stages. The simulation validation confirmed correct processor functionality across various instruction types including R-type arithmetic operations, I-type immediate instructions, load/store operations, and conditional branching.

This chapter successfully bridged the gap between theoretical computer architecture and practical hardware implementation, showing how software instructions physically execute in hardware. The modular design approach emphasized throughout the book proved essential in managing the complexity of processor design, with well-defined interfaces between components enabling systematic development and testing.

By completing this RISC-V processor implementation, you have gained the comprehensive skills needed to understand, design, and implement complex digital systems, from basic logic gates to complete processors, preparing you for advanced work in computer architecture, FPGA-based system design, and custom computing applications.

Index

X, Y, Z